Quicknotes

christian history

GUIDEBOOK

CAROL SMITH AND RODDY SMITH

BARBOUR
PUBLISHING

Developed and produced by The Livingstone Corporation. Project staff included Christopher Hudson and Carol Smith. Special thanks to Christopher Morthland for his work on the sidebar material.

Published by Barbour Publishing, Inc., P.O. Box 719, Uhrichsville, Ohio 44683, www.barbourbooks.com

Our mission is to publish and distribute inspirational products offering exceptional value and biblical encouragement to the masses.

 Member of the
Evangelical Christian
Publishers Association

contents

Dedication

This work and the effort that went into it are dedicated to...

...the Christian communities that have nurtured the history and the future of faith in my life: Orange Hill, Hickory Grove, First Dayton, First Joshua, Glen Ellyn Bible, Green Memorial, Mecklenburg Community, and Belmont. Thanks.
Carol Smith

...my father, Ralph Smith, who showed me with his love of history that God is the God of all ages and places. As he read and studied, he showed me that there is real joy in discovering God's hand upon the wondrous mosaic of history as He fulfills His plan of love and salvation for mankind.
Roddy Smith

Special thanks to Christopher Morthland who added more than a spoonful of wit and humor to this book. Because of his efforts, the history included here not only informs but at times even delights.

introduction

World history is the story of people in the past trying to make sense of the life that they had been handed. These people existed within cultures that they influenced and were influenced by. World history is politics and nations, alliances and affiliations, tribal societies on a global scale. It is people and events and the ramifications of all of them.

World history is happening now. The experiences of this current generation around the world are being recorded as fodder for future scrutiny. Someday someone will write a book evaluating what we are bringing to the global table right now.

Christian history is a twofold story line in the midst of the history of the world. It is a record of God's hand reaching into the lives of people through the incarnation of Jesus Christ and then the indwelling of His Holy Spirit. Christian history is also a record of what people of faith have done with the knowledge and experience of God's work. There are a lot of mysteries involved. We don't always know in the moment what God is doing. We don't always know if people are working on behalf of God's plan or in spite of it. Whether we understand or not, whether we agree or not, the events and actions that have happened in the name of Christ (whether He ordained them or not) have become a part of the Christian history of our world.

The history of the Church of Christ has much to offer us. It gives us the time to sort through what has happened and how we, as individuals and cultures, have been affected by it. Once we understand that, it leaves us with choices to make.

What have we learned from our accomplishments and mistakes?

From a faith perspective, how will we interact with our culture?

How will we influence and interact with governments?

How will we treat our political enemies in light of the message of Christ?

How will we deal with the weak in our world?

How will we affect the world, both individually and as a global body united by faith?

 QUOTABLES

"The kind of events that once took place will by reason of human nature take place again."
*Thucydides,
Greek Historian*

"History is a set of lies agreed upon."
*Napoleon Bonaparte,
French General and
Emperor*

"The history of the world is but the biography of great men."
*Thomas Carlyle,
English Historian*

"History is more or less bunk. It's tradition. We don't want tradition. We want to live in the present and the only history that is worth [anything] is the history we make today."
*Henry Ford,
American Industrialist*

WHERE DO WE START?

The first thing we know about Christian history is Genesis 1:1. "In the beginning God created. . . ." God gave us this world. The Bible teaches that Christ was present even then. Then God inhabited the world through the historical God-man Jesus to redeem us spiritually, to connect with us eternally, to claim us as His own.

Through the Old Testament we can trace God's hand through the people that accomplished His work: Adam, Noah, Abraham, Isaac, Jacob, Joseph, David, Solomon, Elijah, Elisha, the prophets—all pointing the way to Christ's life and redemptive work.

Through the New Testament we trace God's hand through the work of the Spirit and the people that He energized: the original disciples (now referred to as apostles), including Paul, early-church leaders, and missionaries like Silas, Barnabas, Timothy, Titus, Priscilla and Aquilla, James.

By the end of the first century A.D., the documents which would eventually comprise the Bible had been written. The eye-witnesses to the phenomenon that was "the life of Christ" were all but gone. The world was left with two legacies:

1. A burgeoning organization called the catholic (universal) church, and

2. A written record of the earliest church organization made up of biographical accounts, theological documents, and letters written by church leaders. We call this the New Testament.

With these two legacies, the church moved forward claiming the power and presence of the Holy Spirit. Individuals took and were granted leadership and authority. The structure of the church took a more firm shape. The church functions as the *body of Christ*. That means for all practical purposes the church operates as the physical representation of Jesus in the world. There are times as we look back through the history of the church that we may wish that weren't so, but it is.

HOW IS THE INFORMATION ORGANIZED?
Each chapter of this book explores a period of history. For each of those time periods these key questions are addressed:

What was the basic culture of the time?

What were the most significant historical events of that time period?

What were the events and who were the people who most influenced the cause of Christ and the development of the church?

How did the church influence its culture, and how was the church influenced by its culture?

The intent of this writing is not to be a catalogue of all of world history. Instead, the intent of this writing is to trace a thread throughout the tapestry of world history. God has always been about something in our world. Through Christ He blasted through time and space and connected with humanity in a new way. Since then the church has been about representing God in the world through the power of the Holy Spirit. It's been a bumpy ride, to say the least.

WHAT ARE THE BASIC ISSUES?

One thing has stayed the same throughout the history of the church: The church has been from the beginning a group of people trying to live in relationship with God and figure out how to communicate that relationship to their culture. The earliest variety of churches asked themselves these kinds of questions:

How much should we stand apart from our culture, and how much should we integrate into it?

How do we best communicate the message of Christ?

What kind of structure should we take on as an organization?

What kind of authority should we give our leaders?

How do we stay true to the kind of holiness that God requires, yet remain accessible to a culture that holds different standards?

In many ways the church today faces the same challenges that the first churches at Jerusalem, Antioch, Rome, and Constantinople did. Looking at how they answered these questions, where they succeeded, and where they failed may very well help us do a better job at this church thing. We stand on their shoulders, seeing farther behind and ahead.

Let's learn well.

A walk through the centuries

BEFORE THE TIME OF CHRIST

Civilizations of all kinds were developing in the world before Christ walked the earth. Lands were being conquered. Rulers were rising and falling in power. By 3000 B.C., writing was developing, and so histories were recorded. The world seems to have begun its population around Mesopotamia (where Abraham, father of the Jews, made his home) and from there spread out. All around the shores of the Mediterranean different cultures developed: the Greeks, the Macedonians, the Romans. These early civilizations still affect our everyday lives and even patterns of thinking in the most basic of ways.

THE LIFE OF CHRIST

The life of Christ is such a small amount of time compared to the years of the world. Thirty-three years. And only three or fewer of those years spent in public ministry. Yet, the life of Christ changed the course of history. It is on His years of teaching and work that the early church based its choices about how to formalize this movement first called "the Way" and later called Christianity.

SET THE STAGE!

The invention of pottery was a major step forward for ancient civilization. Before that, people used bark or animal skins to hold water. Imagine the difficulty of heating water in those days. Stones had to be heated in the fire and then dropped in the water until it was hot enough to boil. With the advent of pottery, water pots could be placed directly over the fire. This changed *everything* about cooking and cleaning.

Pottery also allowed protective storage in a way that was not previously possible. Think of pottery as the first bakeware and Tupperware, without the home parties and silly games.

About the same time pottery was invented, wild dogs were being domesticated in the Americas, and the people of Jericho were building the first wall around the town (which would be rebuilt many times before Joshua brought it down thousands of years later).

Jesus' life functioned on two levels in the history of Christianity. On one level, He was God's punch through time and space to redeem His world. On another level, Jesus' human life and work was the founding of a world religion. To take one without the other is to not fully understand the impact of Jesus' life on earth. To understand Jesus' role as the guru of Christianity without understanding His deity is an empty faith. To recognize His deity without understanding the impact Jesus' life made on the course of history, whether He was believed or not, leaves us unaware of the world we live in and the general understanding of the Christian faith.

THE EARLY CHURCH (FROM PENTECOST TO A.D. 300)

The decisions made by the church during this time were revolutionary. It was as if they had been given a new world with no rules and no established roles, then left with the responsibility to define how it all should work. Building a house leaves people with an overwhelming amount of decisions. Building a faith movement must have been that times ten.

It was like leaving a baby on a busy street corner to figure out its way home. The baby has to first understand its own body and how to function as a person. Then the baby has to figure out where it's going and how to get there and whom to ask for help along the way. That was the task ahead of the early church, just as confusing and precarious at times.

At first the infant church was governed by those who had worked directly with Jesus. As they passed away, their writings became the rule of thumb collected into what we know as the New Testament. From there the church leaders had to make the best educated choice they could make. The role of the bishops was established, a form of authority, government, and communication. These people did what any people do. They looked around them to see what kinds of organizational structures were working, and they tried to implement some of those structures. If they hadn't, in human terms, the Christian faith could have split into many permutations very early on.

The early church established a baseline: the person of Christ. They fought to nail down that the Christian faith was, at the

 SET THE STAGE!

Humans throughout the ages have catalogued their experiences through whatever means were available to them, even cave walls.

In the Western world, the Greek Herodotus is often considered the "father of history." He lived in the 400s B.C. His *Histories* was written after he traveled throughout the Near East in an attempt to catalogue the hostile history between the Persian and Greek empires.

Thucydides was also a Greek historian. His *History of the Peloponnesian War* recorded much of the Greek cultures of Athens and Sparta.

When Greece became part of the Roman Empire, historians such as Polybius followed suit recording the rise of the Roman Empire. Later Julius Caesar himself recorded his victories in Gaul in *Commentaries on the Gallic War*. Other Roman historians included Sallust (Crispus), Livy, and Tacitus.

Historians continued their work throughout the Middle Ages and into the Renaissance, but it was not until the 1800s that history actually became a discipline all its own in the universities. Since then historians have continued to perfect their craft of documentation and reflection.

bottom line, God in Jesus, sacrificing Himself to be in relationship with humanity. Believing that Christ was God was essential to the faith. Protecting that truth in purity was where much of the energy of the early church was spent.

THE ROMAN EMPIRE (A.D. 300 TO A.D. 590)

There are two sides to every coin. Constantine, the emperor of the Roman Empire, converted to the Christian faith. In fact, he made it the state religion. Yea!

Yea?

It *is* yea, right?

This one event propelled Christianity to the forefront of the bulk of the world. It made the church safe to grow. In the sense that the message of Christ's sacrifice would freely spread, this was the best of news. It was wonderful that the church didn't have to fear persecution. This very safety factor made the church vulnerable to other enemies, though. The corruption of power. The dilution of the truth. The enemies within. Heresy.

Without a doubt the heresy that typified the era of the Roman Empire was the heresy of Arianism. This was the belief that Jesus was not equal to God, but was the next best thing. Arianism touched on the most significant point of agreement— the person of Jesus Christ. Orthodox Christianity held firm its stance that Jesus was both parts in one, God and man. The fight between orthodox Christianity and Arian beliefs was as strong as any modern religious prejudice or conflict.

The church formalized its structure with a hierarchy of bishops that resembled the emperor hierarchy of the Roman Empire. The end of this age is marked by the fall of the western half of the empire (modern Spain, France, and Italy).

THE MIDDLE AGES (A.D. 590 TO A.D. 1517)

The first part of the Middle Ages is a mystery in many ways. With the fall of the Western Roman Empire to invading barbarians, the progress of mankind took a few steps back. The world as they knew it went into a period of chaos and disarray.

In what had been the Western Roman Empire, the church

was actually the unifying factor of this time period. While rulers came and went, the bishops continued in their spiritual authority. It is the church that actually kept communication open and some kind of organizational structure in place, first through monastics and then through the popes (the powerful bishops of Rome).

By the end of the Middle Ages, the papacy (system of popes) had declined and what was left of the Eastern Roman Empire (the Byzantine Empire, which was a primarily Greek culture) was gone. The church was badly in need of reform (as was the general culture), but there was disagreement on where to start. Did they need to start all over with a new system? Did they need to do more education? Did they need to reject the church altogether?

THE REFORMATION (A.D. 1517 TO A.D. 1648)

It was during this period of history that America was discovered and that what we now call the "Protestant Reformation" occurred.

Movements to reform the Christian church began before Martin Luther, but it was his famous demonstration posting ninety-five theses to the Wittenberg door that still stands as the marker of the Protestant Reformation. Several other reformations took place as well: Ulrich Zwingli, John Calvin (Reformed and Presbyterian churches), the Anabaptists, and then the Mennonites, the Anglicans and Episcopals (the British movements affected by Calvin's teaching). There was also a counter-reformation that happened within the Roman Catholic Church at the same time that these new movements were coming into their own.

THE ENLIGHTENMENT (A.D. 1648 TO A.D. 1789)

The seventeenth and eighteenth centuries were typified by closing minds as well as opening minds.

In the church, orthodoxy was battening down the hatches. The movements of the Reformation and the denominations that sprang from them became more and more fixed in the beliefs and practices that had become their distinctives. It's an easy thing to understand. These denominations had formed out of a desperation to do the right thing. It would make sense that they would hold tightly to their attempt. Unfortunately, the church of Christ lost some unity, and blood was shed in the process.

At the same time, the general culture of the world was opening its mind to resemble more of the philosophical and moral culture that we recognize as "modern." The celebration of humanity (humanism) took the form of a renaissance in the arts: literature, painting, sculpture, philosophy. What we now call "humanities" in the college forum found its birth right here. The crafts of thought and creativity were alive and well.

Before this time the Christian church had faced some competition, such as Islam, but the competition was outside of the church walls. This new way of thinking, this humanism, this rationalism, this individualism, this philosophy was something that could integrate into the church. The church had something new to reckon with, a new understanding of humanity and each person's role within that.

 QUOTABLES

"The twentieth century has proven to be a terrible disappointment."
Winston Churchill, 1922 (before the Great Depression, World War II, and the Cold War)

NINETEENTH CENTURY: REVIVALS AND REVOLUTIONS

The 1800s were full of change. Political upheavals such as the American Revolution, the French Revolution, and the independence of Latin America put a face on the journey toward autonomy that had been the struggle of societies since the Roman Empire and Middle Ages. Liberalism (a religious counterpoint to orthodoxy) and modernism were on the rise in Protestant circles, while in the Catholic world there was a return to the ancient. (It was during this century that the Catholic Church declared the pope infallible.) The Industrial Revolution changed the way people worked and lived.

The nineteenth century was full of missionary expansion throughout the world: Asia, the Pacific, Africa, Latin America, and the world of Islam.

TWENTIETH CENTURY

During the course of world history, civilization seemed to be working on the assumption that life could get better and better. Invention, industrialization, technology all forged ahead. But humans, with their need for power and freedom, stayed the same. In the twentieth century, the population faced the realization that for all our best efforts, societies were still flawed, the earth was still being abused, there were still cruel rulers in power. The dream of any kind of utopian society seemed clearly a myth.

Christianity in the twentieth century existed mainly in three forms: Protestantism, Roman Catholicism, and Eastern Orthodox. The church in all three of these branches found a parallel experience to the general culture. The time was typified by "anti-colonialism," which means in lay-terms, "nobody wanted to belong to anybody else." Churches didn't want to be forced to adhere to a denomination. Races of people didn't want to remain unheard. Countries wanted to establish their own governments.

The Catholic Church opened its mind to modern ideas. The Protestant Church began to address a need to evaluate its practices in light of a world that had changed around it. The Eastern Orthodox Church faced the ramifications of the Soviet revolution on the whole of Europe.

In the end, everything became more decentralized, and yet with the increased technology the world grew smaller.

TWENTY-FIRST CENTURY

And now what?

CHAPTER ONE

The Roots of the Christian church

Civilizations began around the Mediterranean Sea and spread out from there. Jesus lived in Israel to the east of the Mediterranean. Christianity spread out from that area, as well. Because of that, most of this book focuses on the eastern European and Middle East parts of the world. Here's a look at what was happening around the world during the events described in this chapter.

For the discussions in this book, the world can be divided into six major areas:

1—The Middle East: *The area to the east of the Mediterranean. Includes Palestine.*

2—Europe: *The area to the north of the Mediterranean*

3—Africa: *The continent to the south of the Mediterranean*

4—Asia and the Far East: *The areas east of Europe and the Near East. Includes Russia, China, India.*

5—The Americas: *Canada, North, Central, and South America*

6—Australia and the Pacific Islands: *The islands off the coast of the Far East*

UNDERSTANDING THE TIMES

Early humans invented in order to survive...at least at first. They harnessed fire to keep warm. They invented spears to protect themselves and to help them in the never-ending quest for food.

But as soon as they had the basics of survival covered, they invented for the same reasons we do, to increase convenience and enhance performance. From the earliest days, humans have looked for a better life. They invented the wheel, not because they couldn't move, but because they couldn't move as much or as fast without it. They invented writing, not because their survival depended on it, but because communication, commerce, and leaving a legacy did. One of the first "machines" invented was the spear thrower. It was simply a stick that hooked onto a spear. By using this tool instead of just an arm, a person could throw a spear with much more power. Spears were pretty useful before the thrower was invented, but they became even *more* useful when used with a complementary tool.

It's important to understand this about people who lived in a time few of us would want to endure (point the way to the inside plumbing and air-conditioning, thank you very much). Even though they were at a different place on the timeline, they were still like us in that they were building relationships and trying to find ways to make life a little easier.

Ancient civilizations also invented for the sake of creating. They carved sculptures from stone and antlers. Because they needed statues to live? No. Because they were created beings,

 DID YOU KNOW?

The elaborate white marble tomb constructed for Mausolus, a provincial ruler in fourth-century B.C. Persia, was one of the Seven Wonders of the Ancient World. Since that time, many such edifices have been referred to by the same name as the crypt that holds the remains of Mausolus, the *Mausoleum.* So, really, if your name were Bob it would actually be a Bob-o-leum, and maybe if your name were Peter it would be a Petroleum and if your name were Lynn...

made in the image of the Creator so, naturally, they created. That's this author's guess anyway. Necessity may be the mother of invention, but creativity is an aunt who loves to babysit.

The earliest people learned to make fire. This gave them the freedom to live in colder climates without having to pack up and move when the seasons changed. But they moved on from there to use fire to cook, to mold metal, to provide light, and for countless other not-necessarily-essential uses.

Infant civilizations may have been "roughing it" compared to us, but they wasted no time climbing their way up the ladder to a better life. In fact, that's what the early years of the world were all about.

WRITE IT DOWN

A major dividing line in history is the invention of writing. It happened around 3000 B.C. It seems that no sooner was writing invented than there were bookworms, historians, and librarians. (Does that say something about the nature of humans? Maybe that we've always had the desire not only to live out our days, but to record them for posterity, as well.) Once writing was developed, people could keep track of information and events for others to learn about.

 SET THE STAGE!

At about the same time people started writing things down, wheeled vehicles began to be used. Also around this time the Mesopotamians were beginning to work with iron, and the Sumerians began building harps and flutes.

For our purposes here we'll refer to the era before writing as "prehistory" and the time from the development of writing through the emergence of the Roman Empire culture as "ancient."

Some of the first writing was made up of pictures. These pictures probably functioned as bookkeeping aids for Sumerian merchants and traders. Later, the Sumerians used chopped-off reeds to make wedge-shaped patterns in clay. This kind of writing was called cuneiform. The important difference was that it represented sounds, not just objects as picture-based writing did. It was like "Hooked On Ye Olde Fonnixs."

While the Sumerians developed the first phonetic alphabet we know of, writing developed concurrently along several varied paths in different cultures.

Egypt: Hieroglyphs, pictures usually written on sheets of papyrus

Sumer: Cuneiform, wedge symbols for sounds or syllables

China: Characters that stood for objects rather than sounds

 SET THE STAGE!

Where there was writing, there were authors (okay, scribes). Where there were authors, there were books (okay, clay tablets). Where there were books, there were libraries (okay...wait, there really *were* libraries). A collection of over 30,000 clay tablets has been discovered in the Sumerian city Nippur.

The Assyrian king Sennacherib formed a library in his palace somewhere around 700 B.C. His grandson, Ashurbanipal, formed an even larger collection of ancient records. Write on!

MOBILITY

In the ancient world, civilizations were often mobile. Whole cultures, such as the Hebrews, moved from place to place. Sometimes moves came because of weather changes, other times because of unfriendly new neighbors. ("Beholde! Yon neighborhood goeth to the dogges!") When permanent, stationary communities finally did form, they usually did so by a river or body of water that provided trade, travel, escape, and fertile land.

As people learned to grow crops and to make lasting structures to keep warm in cold weather, they started staying put. Villages, then towns, then cities, then city-states were formed.

GOVERNMENT

Today we think of government as white marble buildings and elected officials. From the earliest tribes, though, there was some form of government and, with it, politics.

Before 3500 B.C., most government happened when tribes enlisted some members to care for supplies or defense. Government was as much a function of survival as power. As civilization developed from prehistoric to ancient, tribes turned into villages and towns. By 400 B.C., the Greek culture had established a democracy of city-states, self-ruled, but aligned with each other. In the 200s B.C., the Roman government took things a step further. They left local authority in place but placed the local authorities under a central authority that we would categorize today as federal government.

 DID YOU KNOW?

Built-in appliances aren't only modern conveniences: Ancient houses have been discovered with ovens built into their walls.

Wealthy Romans lived in houses with enclosed gardens and atriums. Many lower- and middle-class city dwellers lived in apartment buildings, some of which were five stories tall. This was long before the invention of the elevator, so grocery day must have been a real workout. Most farmers lived in mud-brick huts.

TECHNOLOGY

When we talk about stages of development in the past, we often refer to them in terms of the technology and materials people used. You will hear terms like:

The Stone Age: When most tools and weapons were made of stone.

The Bronze Age: While people may have used metal before 3000 B.C., it was around then that bronze was invented in the Middle East and began to replace stone as the standard for tools and weapons. Bronze began as a combination of copper and arsenic. The arsenic was eventually replaced with tin. The initial use of bronze coincided with the development of writing, which accelerated progress in every area of human life.

The Iron Age: Even before 1500 B.C., craftsmen had begun the practice of smelting iron ore to obtain iron for tools. It was not until around 1500 B.C. that iron came into wide use. The great

THE MORE THINGS CHANGE...

(Death, Taxes, and Other Immutables)

Ever since the invention of money, governments have been finding ways to collect taxes. In A.D. 61, Queen Boudicca of East Anglia (in what is now England) led a revolt against taxes levied by the Roman government. Her words on the subject could have just as easily been spoken during the American Revolution or any number of wars fought over taxation: "How much better to have been slain and to have perished than to go about with a tax on our heads! Yet why do I mention death? For even dying is not free of cost with them: Nay, you know what fees we pay even for our dead. Among the rest of mankind death frees even those who are in slavery to others; only in the case of the Romans do the very dead remain alive for their profit." Boudicca *was* eventually killed by the I.R.S. (Imperial Roman Soldiers, that is), but not before leading her troops in the sacking and burning of several Roman cities in the British colony, including a town we now know as London.

thing about iron was the price. It made strong metal available to even the village carpenters and masons. Because of iron, coins came into wider use, as well as much stronger farming equipment.

These "ages" don't represent fixed time periods. Different civilizations went through them at different times as they learned to use fire and metal to create different kinds of tools and weapons. For the sake of clarity, cultural development is often identified by these categories.

TRADE

Trade means simply "buying and selling." Think of all the places around you that you can walk in, pay money, and carry something out. That's trade.

In the ancient world, trade started as literally *trading* one thing for another. A farmer had extra wheat that he would trade to someone for some of *his* extra corn. Trade had to do with getting what you needed by supplying what you had.

Eventually, as civilization developed, trade became a profession of its own. Babylonians were the earliest merchants that we know of. There were also Phoenician merchants, who were known for trading by sea in the ancient world. (And don't forget the ancient pirates who came along about the same time. That part of trade is called "the black market.")

Merchants became middlemen. They didn't just barter product for product. Instead they became dealers: They traded their goods for *money* rather than just for other goods, as was done in earlier times. The earliest pieces of money were, in fact, actual weights that could be placed on one side of the scale to measure out how much grain (for instance) was in the other side of the scale. Still later, money came to represent not actual merchandise, but actual gold sitting in a vault somewhere.

Trade had a lot to do with where cities were built. Often, construction happened next to a body of water so that imports and exports could arrive and depart easily and safely by boat.

 SET THE STAGE!

While historians have looked back through the ages and labeled different eras such as the Bronze Age and the Iron Age, it's important to keep in mind that all developments were in flux. While bronze was first in use around 3000 B.C., it was in use only for the wealthiest. The poor were still using stone tools until possibly even past the beginning of what we call the Iron Age.

Look at it this way: Right now, there are amazing new discoveries on the market. Wireless communications abound. But we still have people using rotary phones rather than touch-tone, much less wireless. Technology happens in waves. Speaking of waves, microwaves are a good example. Microwave ovens were introduced in the 1950s, but it wasn't until the 1970s that they were used widely in homes, and it was even later that they became standard appliances in new apartment buildings. CDs are the same way. History books already list that CDs were first introduced in 1982, yet who doesn't know of somebody's aunt or granddad that doesn't have a compact disc player yet?

Don't forget when you read through history that the lines are blurry, and many times new ideas (like, say...fire) took a while to catch and spread.

LIKE US?

Even though technology was much simpler in the ancient world without the use of electricity, there were many similarities

SET THE STAGE!

Weights weren't the only unusual forms of currency in ancient times. Shells and beads were often used as money. Some money was directly representational: In China, early coins were miniature hoes and spades, which carried the value of those very items. In early Sumerian transactions, the clay tokens used as money could be redeemed *only* for the items represented on them. Specific denominations represented rams, ewes, and units of various grains.

Technology hoarding played a role in what could be used as money. For three thousand years, China jealously guarded the secret of silk making. Silk was so valuable that it was used as currency for centuries. On a smaller scale, the Hittites did the same with iron. The first *fixed-value* coins we know of came from the region of Anatolia, Turkey, and were made about 700 B.C. out of electrum, an alloy made with gold and silver. The really great thing about money was that it didn't die or spoil as farm animals or crops might and that it was usually smaller and easier to transport than the goods for which it could be traded. For these reasons, money became a more universal medium of exchange: It could be traded for *anything*. Depending on the market and his own needs, a particular person might not want to trade for a sheep, but most people would gladly trade for a small, portable token worth one sheep. Because of all the different denominations that developed, money also greatly simplified the trading and haggling process. Imagine what it must have been like before money.

Boy: Paper, mister?

Man: How much?

Boy: One sheaf of wheat.

Man: Um...do you have change for a goat? I left my wheatfold in my other tunic.

between the ancient people and modern cultures.

Once people owned land, there was a distinct difference between the lifestyles of the rich and poor. Since the rich could afford more education and luxuries, we know more about their end of the cultural spectrum when we look back through history.

There were toys and games. Yes, life was hard, yet there was time to play (and no TV to distract). Children in ancient Egypt had balls and rolling toys. Adults had board games similar to checkers or chess.

TIMELINE OVERVIEW

In the midst of world history...

Christian history unfolds...

Beginning of time: God creates the world

3800 B.C. Sumer: The Sumerians settled in Mesopotamia. The Sumerians established arithmetic based on ten (because of the ten fingers they could count on), and they divided a circle into sixty subsections, which later became the minutes and seconds that we use today. They also made great gains in the development of writing. Some say they invented it.

3760 B.C. Start of Hebrew calendar

3372 B.C. The start of Mayan calendar

2700 B.C. Construction of Stonehenge begins in England.

c. 2600 B.C. Egypt: Construction of the pyramids has begun. (Egyptians discovered papyrus and ink for writing. They built the first libraries.)

c. 2000 B.C. Greek culture begins to develop.

c. 2000 B.C. Abraham, Father of the Jewish nation, moved from Ur (Sumeria) to settle his family in Canaan, the land that was Jesus' eventual birthplace. Abraham's son was Isaac.

1800 B.C. Joseph (Isaac's grandson) was sold as a slave into Egypt. Eventually Joseph's whole family moved there to survive a famine. The descendants of Joseph and his brothers grew into the nation known as the Jews (or Hebrews). They were a nation of slaves.

1500 B.C. The Canaanites invented the first alphabet.

Egypt: Sundials were in use.

1400 B.C. God used Moses to lead the enslaved Hebrew people out of Egypt. This was called the Exodus. The people began their journey back to Canaan, the land Abraham had claimed. Their journey would require military force because the land had been resettled in the meantime.

1000 B.C. Israel splits into Israel (to the north) and Judah (to the south).

950 B.C. Celts invade Britain. Assyrians invent inflatable skins (life rafts) for soldiers to cross bodies of water.

800 B.C. Greece: Homer writes the *Illiad* and the *Odyssey*. (This is the traditional date. A more popular date is often 700 B.C.)

Europe: Ice skating becomes a popular sport.

770 B.C. The first Olympic Games were held (untelevised, of course).

c. 750 B.C. Rome became a city. False teeth were invented in Italy shortly after.

750 B.C. Assyria assimilates Israel into its jurisdiction.

600 B.C. Japan had just been established as a nation.

599 B.C. Greece: During this century philosophy began to develop.

c. 550 B.C. India: Prince Siddhartha Gautama, founder of Buddhism, was born.

Greece: Aesop just wrote his fables.

China: Confucius was born.

The lock and key and carpenter's square were invented.

c. 600 B.C. The people of Judah were taken captive into Babylon, once again losing the land promised to them since their forefather Abraham.

500 B.C. Greece: Pythagoras, a mathematician, discovers that the square of the hypotenuse of a right-angled triangle is equal to the sum of the squares of the other two sides. (Remember the Pythagorean Theorem in geometry?)

Halloween originates in a Celtic festival.

India: A surgeon performs the first known cataract operation.

500 B.C. The first Hebrew exiles returned to Jerusalem from Babylon and began, once again, to rebuild.

447 B.C. Greece: The Parthenon is built in Athens.

430 B.C. Greece: Hippocrates founds the science of medicine, becoming the "Father of Medicine" (thus the Hippocratic oath). Hippocrates wrote the oldest medical books that still exist. He taught the world that sickness comes from physical causes rather than superstitions or evil.

Continued

TIMELINE OVERVIEW (CONTINUED)

In the midst of world history...

427 B.C. Greece: Plato is born.

399 B.C. Greece: Socrates, one of the great Greek philosophers, dies.

384 B.C. Greece: Aristotle is born. During his lifetime (until 322 B.C.) he pioneered a rational approach to science based on observation. You could call him the Father of the Scientific Method.

359 B.C. Philip becomes king of Macedonia, establishing the strongest army in the world and conquering Greece. A year later his son, Alexander, is born. Philip hires Aristotle to tutor his son.

338 B.C. At the age of twenty, Alexander (who became Alexander the Great), son of Philip, becomes king of the Macedonians and begins to increase his kingdom. He conquers the Persian Empire as well as Egypt. He claims Babylon as his capital, but dies at the age of thirty-two.

312 B.C. Construction begins on the Appian Way, the first Roman road (all of which lead to Rome, you know).

300 B.C. Alexander the Great establishes his empire. Aristarchos states that the earth rotates on an axis and is *not* the center of the universe.

250 B.C. Erastitratos discovers that the brain, instead of the heart, is the center of nerve activity.

100 B.C. Rome: Marcus Vitruvius, an architect, wrote a book on city planning including clocks, hydraulics, and military engines.

Greece: the first steam engine was being envisioned.

Phoenicia: glassblowing was invented.

50 B.C. Egypt: Cleopatra VII and her brother Ptolemy XIII become joint rulers.

44 B.C. Julius Caesar is assassinated by a group of Romans led by Brutus and Cassius (you too, Brutus?).

37 B.C. Mark Antony (Roman) marries Cleopatra VII (Egyptian), building a powerful alliance.

30 B.C. Cleopatra VII and Mark Antony commit suicide.

Japan: Sumo wrestling was about to rise to the forefront.

27 B.C. Augustus Caesar (emperor formerly known as Octavian) becomes the new Roman ruler (he is the official who ordered the census that caused Joseph and very pregnant Mary to travel to Bethlehem where Jesus was born).

Christian history unfolds...

400 B.C. The last book of the Old Testament, Malachi, is written. This book closed with the arrival of John the Baptist, Jesus' cousin, which is the event that opens the New Testament.

320 B.C. Ptolemy of Egypt captures Jerusalem.

250 B.C. The Septuagint (a Greek translation of the Old Testament) is written. Greek was the common language of that time so this was a BIG deal. It made the Bible accessible to the common folk, an ongoing struggle throughout history, even to today. Jesus and His disciples probably used this translation. (Remember, there was no mass production at this point, so copies were not as abundant as they are today.)

198 B.C. Judea is now under Seleucid ruler Antiochus.

167 B.C. Antiochus begins persecuting the Jews. He dedicates the Jewish temple to the worship of the Greek god Zeus. The prophet Daniel and the gospel writers refer to this as the Abomination of Desolation. Copies of the Jewish law were destroyed. Jews were forbidden to practice their faith, punishable by death.

c. 166 B.C. Judas Maccabeus and his brothers lead a revolt against Antiochus. About 165 B.C. Judas rededicates the temple. He leads the Jewish nation into a time of prosperity and independence.

37 B.C. Judea falls under Roman occupation. Herod the Great is appointed as king (he rebuilt the temple at Jerusalem). As a part of Rome, the Hebrews settled throughout the Roman empire, though Judea was still considered their homeland.

26 B.C. Pontius Pilate becomes governor of Judea at a time of great political unrest. Factions among the Jews exist, as well as factions between the Jews and their non-Jewish neighbors.

5 B.C. Jesus was probably born, though traditionally His birth is thought of as five years later.

4 B.C. Herod the Great dies. His kingdom is split between his sons.

People were concerned with their appearance. From the earliest records we find references to cosmetics, jewelry, and "fashion" accessories.

There were musical instruments and singing. When people didn't have instruments, they made them.

Once people had their necessities taken care of, they started trading for conveniences. People

? DID YOU KNOW?

The boomerang was originally developed as a hunting weapon and has been around for over 5,000 years?

That people have been skiing for over 3,000 years?

That sculpture has been around even longer?

didn't trade just necessities. They traded crafts such as baskets or pottery. Next time you go to a craft fair or flea market, you're reinventing the ancient marketplace.

Prehistoric and ancient people lived in a time when medicine was mystery. Often people died from accidents or diseases before their thirtieth birthday. Yet, they were people making a living, streamlining their lives and asking, "How could I make this easier or better?" In these ways, they were very much like us.

THE STORY OF THE TIMES

Where does Christian history begin?

In the beginning the Word already existed. He was with God, and he was God. He was in the beginning with God. He created everything there is. Nothing exists that he didn't make. Life itself was in him, and this life gives light to everyone. The light shines through the darkness, and the darkness can never extinguish it.

JOHN 1:1–5 NLT

Christ is the visible image of the invisible God. He existed before God made anything at all and is supreme over all creation. Christ is the one through whom God created everything in

19

heaven and earth. He made the things we can see and the things we can't see—kings, kingdoms, rulers, and authorities. Everything has been created through him and for him. He existed before everything else began, and he holds all creation together.

COLOSSIANS 1:15–17 NLT

By definition, Christian history is the history of Christ and His followers, Christians. The earliest record we have of Jesus Christ is creation. Most of the rest of the Old Testament, in fact, points ahead to the coming of Christ. The Hebrew people based their hopes and dreams on it. They lived their lives in the faith that one day God's deliverer would come. The prophets spent their lifetimes preaching about the Messiah to come. The word

SET THE STAGE!

Prophets in the Old Testament, such as Isaiah, foretold the coming of the Messiah and the sacrifice He would make.

He was oppressed and afflicted, yet he did not open his mouth; he was led like a lamb to the slaughter, and as a sheep before her shearers is silent, so he did not open his mouth.

By oppression and judgment he was taken away. And who can speak of his descendants?

For he was cut off from the land of the living; for the transgression of my people he was stricken.

He was assigned a grave with the wicked, and with the rich in his death, though he had done no violence, nor was any deceit in his mouth.

Yet it was the Lord's will to crush him and cause him to suffer, and though the Lord makes his life a guilt offering, he will see his offspring and prolong his days, and the will of the Lord will prosper in his hand.

ISAIAH 53:7–10 NIV

"Christ" is a Greek word for the Hebrew word "Messiah," which means the anointed one, the liberator.

We often think of Christian history as starting with the incarnation of Jesus (when God became human and took on a body), or even the foundation of the church at Pentecost. The first roots of Christian history lie in creation, though, and those roots grew as civilizations found their way from infancy to organized societies.

HOW DO WE KNOW WHAT HAPPENED?

Obviously, the earliest histories of the world are fuzzy at best. There was no formal writing process. All we have are artifacts, research, and best guesses.

We can't document beyond a doubt how many years passed before writing was invented. We do know, though, that even the earliest of cultures wanted to leave a message of some kind. We know that before there were even letters of the alphabet, there were pictures on cave walls.

 DID YOU KNOW?

Umbrellas have been in use for thousands of years; however, they were originally used to shield the user from the sun or from the gaze of jealous gods. Only in fairly recent times did people begin using them to keep dry in the rain.

Besides cave drawings, history was also passed down through generations by stories, or "oral tradition." In our world today oral tradition is still very much in place. It's why Southerners in the U.S. sometimes still get emotional about the Civil War. It's why the same ghost stories have been told for generations around campfires. It's why people often say, "My granddaddy always said…"

Since around 3000 B.C. we've had the advantage of the written word. So while oral traditions are still a part of our culture, we now have verifiable records of historical events. As soon as writing was invented, the ancient history buff grabbed his reed and started taking notes.

The importance of written language in our world cannot be underestimated. Can you imagine not having writing? For us today it would mean no e-mail, no letters, no street signs, no legal contracts, no notes on the fridge, not to mention no menus, and no sign to let you know which restroom is out of order. It also

SET THE STAGE!

It's often funny, or just plain weird, how languages develop and how certain things get their names.

The ancient Phoenicians got their name from the Greek word *phoinos*, which means red. The Phoenicians were famous for a reddish dye that they traded all over the known world. Speaking of trade, the Greeks got a fair trade for naming the Phoenicians: Phoenicia gave them a very important word in return. The Phoenician port of Byblos was a big trading center for many things, including books. So much so that Byblos came to mean book in Greek. The Greek word *byblos* is the one from which we get our word *Bible*.

would mean no books, which means no Bible. For the ancient world, it meant that there was no way to keep track of anything or to let anyone know something without talking to them. The world was much more fragmented. Foreigners would have seemed much more foreign. We talk today about the world getting smaller and smaller as communication becomes more effortless. Before writing, the world must have seemed endlessly flat with no way to ever get to the other end.

EARLIEST CIVILIZATIONS

The first civilizations began close to rivers in temperate climates where water and plants were readily available. Eventually farming began when, rather than hunting for wild plants and berries to eat and *hoping* there would be enough, farmers began to cultivate their choice of food plants. They settled in fertile areas and traded with their crops when they grew more than their families needed. They raised herds of animals and domesticated dogs to help with those herds. They invented irrigation to water their land. All of these developments allowed civilization to spread because survival was not dependent on being by a river or in a place with a year-round berry-hunting climate.

Homes developed as society developed. The first constructed dwellings were made of mud and grasses, sometimes with supports of wood or bone. Homes were also made of animal skin tents. Eventually mud bricks were invented and later even covered with plaster. Gradually, homes were clustered together to form villages and then towns.

THE SUMERIANS

The Sumerians were the first people to settle in Meso-potamia. Mesopotamia was the fertile area just north-east of present-day Palestine. Sumer was made up of city-states or cities that functioned as independent nations. Each had public buildings, a water supply, a royal palace, and a temple called a ziggurat (sounds like a large, crooked rodent). The public buildings were the center of the communities. The houses of the citizens were built around the perimeter, much like a town square with outlying neighborhoods. Beyond the houses were the farmlands.

 IMAGINE THAT!

April Fool's Day may have biblical roots. Many histori-ans believe that the original April Fool's trick, that of send-ing people on false errands, symbolized Noah's sending out of a dove too early after the flood, which he did on the first day of the Hebrew month that corresponds to our month of April.

While some kind of writing or alphabet was being developed concurrently in several civilizations, the Sumerians were known as the first society to develop an alphabet and a form of writing, and they invented the base-ten number system we all use today. They divided a circle into sixty parts, which eventually became the seconds and minutes that we use today. From around 3000 B.C., the Sumerians wrote on clay tablets, many of which still exist.

 SET THE STAGE!

Sumerians had statues of themselves made and left them in the temples to "pray" when they couldn't be there in person. (This does not work with the *real* God.)

One of the Sumerian city-states was Ur (now in Iraq). It was from Ur that Abraham came.

ABRAHAM

It is significant that the father of the Jews, the many times great-grandfather of Jesus, came from the very place in which one of

SET THE STAGE!

About the time that Abraham left Sumer, the Greek civilization was just beginning to develop. Greeks called their land Hellas and called themselves Hellenes. They referred to all non-Greeks as barbarians. Greek culture developed as a group of fiercely independent and patriotic city-states, the best known being Athens and Sparta. The city-states never united formally into a nation but shared a common language, religion, and culture. The most advanced city-states were the earliest democracies.

the earliest forms of writing originated. The Bible tells us that God called Abraham to leave his home in Ur, a city-state of Sumer, and travel to Canaan, which later became Israel. Abraham's move happened around 2000 B.C.

Abraham is a key player in Christian history for several reasons: He was the father of the Jews. He was a righteous man with whom God *personally* made a pact, or covenant. God promised Abraham a large family of descendants that became the nation of Hebrews, later called Israelites (after Abraham's grandson Israel) and still later called the Jews. It was from Abraham's bloodline that the Messiah, the Christ, would come.

From the point of God's covenant with Abraham, the survival of Abraham's tribe became a crux point in Christian history. If deliverance was to come through a descendant of Abraham, then the survival of that family line was imperative to God's plan.

ABRAHAM'S LEGACY

You can trace the path of the Messiah's coming through the branches of Abraham's family tree. Abraham had a son named Isaac. Isaac had twin sons who fought over the family leadership. Jacob (later called Israel) won out and ended up with twelve sons. The descendants of these sons were known as the twelve tribes of Israel. The prophets foretold that the Messiah would come through the tribe of Judah, one of Jacob's sons.

One of Israel's most famous kings, David, was also from Judah's bloodline. David descended from the specific family line of Ruth. At the end of the book of Ruth, she bears a child, Obed, who is David's grandfather. It was through David's specific branch of the family tree that Jesus descended.

Another reason that Abraham is so important to Christian history has to do with land. Some of the earliest records that we have of God's interaction with Abraham revolve around God asking Abraham to move to a new land, a land that God promised Abraham would belong to him and his descendants. That land was the land called, at that time, Canaan. (You might have heard some old hymns refer to "Canaan Land" or the "Promised Land." These references have to do with God's call to Abraham to travel to a new home.)

SINNERS AND SAINTS
ABRAHAM

You've heard George Washington referred to as the father of our country, right? Well, Abraham was literally the father of the nation of Israel, the direct progenitor of the *entire* Hebrew race. His name was originally Abram, which means "exalted father," until God changed it to Abraham, which means "father of a multitude."

Abraham was what you might call a "late bloomer": He was circumcised at age ninety-nine, and the next year he and his wife had a son. When God told the one-hundred-year-old man that he and his ninety-year-old wife would conceive a child, Abraham literally *fell on his face laughing*, which would have been understandable if anyone but God were making such a prediction. Years later, after he had learned to take the Lord *much* more seriously, Abraham was ready to sacrifice his son to please God. The "joke" was on Abraham this time, however, as God was just testing his faith. He passed with flying colors and lived to the ripe old age of 175.

This piece of land known first as Canaan, then as Israel, and later Palestine, has been a significant issue in Christian history since that time. The Jews repeatedly lost the land and then tried to reclaim the land. The Crusades during the Middle Ages were about reclaiming that land. The land of Canaan has been an ongoing source of ownership disputes. Throughout history this land has been a concern of the church.

THE EGYPTIANS

At the same time that the Sumerian culture was developing, the Egyptians were becoming a society. The Egyptian civilization grew up around the Nile River. The Nile flooded every year. The flood deposited rich soil (called silt) along the banks, which was ideal for farming wheat and barley (for food and drink) and flax (for clothlike linen).

The Egyptians developed the custom of embalming as a part of the process of preparing a body for the afterlife. They also built the pyramids as elaborate tombs.

 DID YOU KNOW?

Ancient people in the Egyptian city of Alexandria sometimes ate meals in underground graveyards to include dead family members in daily activities.

Ancient Egyptian rulers wore fake beards...even the women!!

Egypt played a significant role in the preservation of the nation of Hebrews, who descended from Abraham. Abraham's grandson Jacob had twelve sons. Ten of those sons cruelly sold their half-brother Joseph into slavery. His journey led him to Egypt, where he rose in position until he was second in command to the king. While this is a miraculous story, it became even more miraculous when a famine hit Canaan. Jacob's same ten sons traveled to Egypt to buy food and eventually discovered they were facing the same brother they left for dead years earlier. In the end, through Joseph's integrity and mercy, the entire family moved to Egypt and was saved from a famine.

In Egypt the group of seventy extended family members grew into a nation of slaves. They functioned in the Egyptian culture, yet maintained their separate identity. The Egyptians used the Hebrew slaves to build the cities of Pithom and Ramses as supply centers for the king (Exodus 1:11). Through the leadership of Moses, the Hebrews eventually left Egypt to reinhabit Canaan, an event we now refer to as the Exodus, yet another miraculous way that God preserved the bloodline of the Messiah to come.

THE GREEKS

The Greek culture developed on the north side of the Mediterranean Sea. Greek, or Hellenist, culture eventually influenced the church as well as the world in so many ways they are difficult to number. The Greeks were pioneers in philosophy, medicine, and mathematics. The Greeks were conquered first by the Macedonians, then the Romans. Rather than alter Greek thought, each of these powerful cultures assimilated Hellenist thought into their own. This is why Jesus probably read and studied Greek translations of scripture. It's why the New Testament was written in Greek. It is why Jewish writers often referred to non-Jews as Greeks.

The Greek philosophers were the first to say, "Hey, there *has* to be a reason for the stuff that happens in life!" They laid a foundation for the reasoning that affects the way

 SET THE STAGE!

During the 500s B.C., the Greeks developed philosophy, which means the "love of wisdom." Socrates, Plato, and Aristotle were some of the most famous Greek philosophers. Aristotle tutored Alexander the Great. The logical thought processes and ways of approaching problems developed by Greek philosophers still influence the way we approach everything from belief systems to science, medicine, and law. In fact, the Hippocratic Oath doctors take is named for Hippocrates, a Greek "lover of wisdom."

Sparta and Athens were the two most famous Greek cities. There was a distinct difference between the women of Sparta and the women of Athens. Athenian girls were taught to be housewives. Spartan girls were trained in sports, so as to be better mothers for warriors.

SET THE STAGE!

After the Hebrew nation divided, Israel was the name of the Northern Kingdom. The people of Israel were infiltrated, exiled, and assimilated by Assyria, a cruel and barbaric nation to the east. Many Assyrians moved into Israel and intermarried with them. The resulting nation came to be known as Samaria and its people as Samaritans. Hebrews to the south (Judah) developed a fierce bigotry toward the Samaritans.

By the time Jesus walked the earth, the hatred between His people and the Samaritans was so great that His disciples were amazed that He would even walk through Samaria. Not only did Jesus disregard the racism of His people, He evangelized Samaria through a less than upstanding Samaritan woman (John 4).

It is the understanding of this cultural prejudice that gives even more power to Jesus' parable of the Good Samaritan who showed neighborly love in a way that the religious Jews of the story did not (Luke 10).

we think about life, do research, and solve problems even today. Many of the scientific discoveries made by Greeks are still standards. It was a Greek who first envisioned the atom, though he had no technology for verifying the existence of one.

EXODUS TO EXILE

Around 1400 B.C., the Hebrews were freed from slavery in Egypt and began their trek back to the land God had promised Abraham. After forty years of wandering they arrived, but of course the land had been inhabited in the meantime. In order to reclaim their property, they would have to go to war. Many battles later, each of the tribes descended from Jacob's sons had claimed their land (except for the tribe of Levi, who worked to maintain the tabernacle rather than maintain their own land).

The Hebrews established a monarchy with some success at first. King Saul was the first king, followed by King David and then the famous King Solomon. Eventually civil distress divided the kingdom into the northern kingdom of Israel and the southern kingdom of Judah. Both kingdoms went through a succession of good and bad kings. With each evil king the nation would succumb to idolatry and weaken politically and spiritually. Then the cycle would reverse with reforms led by a king faithful to Jehovah (the Hebrews' name for God).

Through these cycles, the nation weakened over time. Israel was eventually defeated and assimilated into exile in Assyria. Judah held out longer, but around 600 B.C. Judah was defeated and taken to Babylon. The books of Daniel and Esther in the Old Testament were set during this time.

FOUNDING OF ROME

Around the time that the people of Judah were taken to Babylon, the foundation for the Roman Empire was being laid. The existence of Rome was central to the history of Christianity. But where did Rome come from? By around 700 B.C., the boot-shaped peninsula that we now know as Italy had been settled by several different peoples. The Etruscans inhabited the northern portion. The Latins controlled the central mountainous territory. The Greeks held colonies in the south.

Tradition has it that the city of Rome (located about halfway down on the western

 SET THE STAGE!

Babylon was the capital of the region called Babylonia. The Babylonian empire lasted from around 3500 B.C. until around 200 B.C. At various times it was controlled by several different kingdoms, including Persia and Macedonia (under Alexander the Great).

Babylon experienced two high points as a kingdom. The first was from the nineteenth to the seventeenth centuries B.C. under several rulers, starting with Hammurabi. The second was around 540 B.C. under the rule of Nebuchadnezzar II. It was under Nebuchadnezzar that the people of Judah, including the prophet Daniel, were taken into exile. During this time Babylon was under the rule of Persia. It was because of this relocation that Esther, an exiled Hebrew, was able to become a Persian queen.

Eventually Babylon became a part of the Persian Empire. Under the rule of King Cyrus of Persia, the Jews were given the opportunity to leave Babylon and return to Jerusalem. (Archaeologists have uncovered Cyrus's actual decree that allowed the people to return.)

SINNERS AND SAINTS
CLEOPATRA VII

Sometimes history seems more like an episode of a modern "trash-talk" show than a dignified record of solemn events. Take, for instance, the complicated romantic tangle surrounding Cleopatra VII:

Pharaoh Ptolemy XII, Cleopatra's first husband (who was also her *brother*), drowned while fleeing the army of his sister-wife's boyfriend, Julius Caesar. Pharaoh Ptolemy XIII, Cleopatra's *other* brother Ptolemy (who was also her second husband), was murdered by order of his wife/sister so that her son by Caesar, Caesarion (who later changed his name to Ptolemy XIV), could rule Egypt. That same year Caesar was assassinated, and his power split between his grandnephew Octavian (who, for some reason, changed his name to Augustus instead of Ptolemy like everyone else), his close friend Marcus Antonius, and some guy named Lepidus. Cleopatra, having presumably run out of brothers, married Marcus Antonius, even though he was already married to Octavian's sister (Cleo's ex-lover's great-niece). Octavian, after having Caesar's assassins killed, went to war against Marcus (his brother-in-law) and, upon defeating him, ordered him to commit suicide, which (like an idiot) he did. Distraught over her third husband's death (even though he wasn't related) and fearful of his brother-in-law (who was her ex-boyfriend's great-nephew), Cleopatra also killed herself. Octavian then had Caesarion/Ptolemy, Cleopatra and Caesar's son (who was his cousin *and* sort of a nephew by marriage), killed.

Makes you feel a lot better about your own family, huh?

coast or the shinbone part of the boot) was founded by the Etruscans. The city was built on the tops of seven hills and was inhabited by both Latins and Etruscans. The first kings of Rome were Etruscan, but by 500 B.C. Rome was under its own rule.

RESETTLEMENT AND REVOLT

Around 500 B.C., some of the Jews were freed from their exile in Babylon. They returned to Jerusalem and the surrounding areas and began to rebuild, first their homes, then the temple. The books of Ezra and Nehemiah in the Old Testament describe this resettlement. Within 150 years, though, Jerusalem fell again under the rule of Egypt.

ALEXANDER THE GREAT

In the middle of the fourth century B.C., Philip became the king of Macedonia. He conquered Greece, assimilating the rich Hellenist culture into his own. In fact, Philip hired the Greek philosopher Aristotle to tutor his son Alexander. In 338 B.C., Alexander succeeded his father to the throne. Alexander enlarged the borders of the kingdom by conquering the Persian Empire, as well as Egypt. Through these conquests, Alexander spread elements of Greek, or Hellenist, culture, including the

 DID YOU KNOW?

In pagan Rome, priests were employees of the government and were appointed or elected to office. It was their job to intercede with the gods to try to obtain favor on behalf of the imperial government.

Mice were considered a great delicacy in ancient Rome. Popular potables (drinks) of the time included a beverage made from salted, rotten fish guts.... *Mmmm.*

The average age for marriage of well-off children in the Roman Empire was between fifteen and eighteen years for boys and thirteen to fourteen for girls. Parents arranged most marriages, with matches being made for social, political, or economic benefit to the families of the bride and groom. Children had little, if any, choice in the matter.

Ancient Rome had a fire department, complete with officials, investigators, and large squads of firefighters, who wore battle gear as they "fought" the flames.

Greek language, over most of the known world. This provided a common linguistic denominator for a wide array of people, which later facilitated the spread of the gospel.

Alexander died twelve years later after claiming Babylon as his capital. His kingdom was divided among three of his generals. The Antigonids ruled Macedonia. Ptolemy took control of Egypt and ruled there until 30 B.C. The family of Seleucus ruled the land from the Mediterranean spreading west. It was in this turn of events that the Jews came under Seleucid rule under a man named Antiochus.

THE MACCABEAN REVOLT

Antiochus persecuted the Jews under his rule. He even went so far as to dedicate the temple in Jerusalem to the worship of the Greek god Zeus. In response, the Jews revolted under the leadership of Judas Maccabeus and his brothers. The temple was rededicated the next year (165 B.C.), and the Jews entered a time of prosperity and independence under the Maccabees.

BACK TO ROME

By around 275 B.C., Rome had become Italy's leading power. By A.D. 100, its empire covered half of Europe, most of the Middle East, and the north coast of Africa.

In 37 B.C., Judah came under Roman rule. Herod the Great was appointed king of Judah by the Roman government. This laid the foundation for Jesus living at a time when His homeland was occupied by Roman rule. The Roman government played some role in many of the events covered in the Gospels. The disciple Matthew was a tax collector for the Roman government. It was Roman soldiers who stood guard at the tomb. After Jesus had ascended into heaven, it was Roman roads that the apostles traveled to carry the gospel. It was Roman law that, for a time, protected them as they went. It was in Rome that severe persecution and torture of Christians took place. It was in Rome that the Catholic Church grew and formalized. It was from Rome that the inquisitions were established. It was from Rome that the Crusades were launched.

SINNERS AND SAINTS
VERGIL

Vergil (70–19 B.C., also spelled *Virgil*) is considered to be the premier poet of ancient Rome and one of the greatest writers in the history of the world. Some even say he foretold the birth of Christ.

Vergil studied rhetoric and philosophy with plans to be a lawyer but proved too shy for the job and decided to instead try his hand at poetry. His first serious poems were good enough to garner him a wealthy patron, who gave him a house. His masterwork, the *Aenid*, was the official Epic of Rome. The *Aenid* was unfinished when Vergil died, and the poet, thinking the work not yet polished enough, left orders for its destruction. Many Christians in the 300s through the Middle Ages considered Vergil to be a prophet, pointing to a section of the fourth book of his *Ecologues* wherein he predicts the coming of a new age to be brought forth by a marvelous child. From the time of his death, Vergil's influence continued to grow. His works were used as textbooks in Roman schools, by early Christian writers who found parallels between his beliefs and their own, and even by fortune-tellers and superstitious people who would open up a book at random and interpret a verse as prophecy. Perhaps Vergil's greatest sphere of influence was within the ranks of poets and authors who came after him. Dante, Petrarch, Milton, Wordsworth, Tennyson, and T. S. Eliot are but a few of the famous literary figures who acknowledge a great debt to the works of Vergil.

ULTIMATE IMPACT OF AND ON CHRISTIANITY

You can look at Christian history as a tree with too many branches to count. The trunk of the tree represents the life, work, and teaching of Jesus Christ. The branches represent the people to whom He entrusted His continuing ministry in the world. But if you could cut a cross section, you'd see an elaborate section of roots.

CREATION

God has revealed through His Word that Jesus Christ was a part of creation. It is with this holy act that God began inviting us into a relationship with Him. It was through the story of creation that the stage was set for just how far God would go to connect with us. He would sacrifice Himself. That is the deepest root of Christian history.

JUDAISM

It was through a people, in fact a family, that God planted the genealogical seed for our redemption. Looking back, we see a nation of people persecuted throughout the years; a nation that started as one childless couple who revealed themselves to be both faithless and faithful. In many ways, there could not be a more contemporary example. Abraham and Sarah laughed at God's proposition. Then they gave themselves to His promise. Then they took it back and tried to work it out in their own strength. Then they depended on God to clean up the mess they had made. Then they left the consequences for future generations to deal with. They are not so far from us in shortcomings or in hopes. It is comforting that the earthly lineage of Christ, God's promised deliverer, came from people who made mistakes and had human failings much like we do.

From Abraham to Isaac to Jacob to Jacob's sons and on until the birth of Jesus, God worked through a personal connection with individuals. He has never been a mass marketer. It all comes down to one kind of question, "Will you take Me at My word?

Will you put your trust in Me?"

MIRACLES

We look back now at the roots bulging beneath the soil, and it seems obvious the miracles that God used to preserve the bloodline according to His promise:

Joseph's sad trail to Egypt and his rise to power (Genesis 37–39)

The protection of Jacob's family as they grew in Egypt (Genesis 47)

The Exodus (Exodus 1–15)

The story of Ruth and Naomi (Ruth)

It's interesting to note the twists and turns that the path took:

Abraham and Sarah's mistake with Hagar and her son Ishmael (Genesis 16–21)

Abraham's near sacrifice of Isaac (Genesis 22)

Jacob and Esau's battle over the family birthright (Genesis 25–27)

Joseph's preservation in Egypt through slavery and then jail (Genesis 39)

The famine in Canaan around 1800 B.C. (Genesis 43)

The exiles of the Hebrews to Assyria and Babylon (2 Kings 24)

What is really amazing about this period is that the Hebrews survived at all: a nomadic group of people who, from a political standpoint, seldom held a clear title to their land; a people often given to civil unrest and hostile relationships with neighbors; a people that lost every treasure they held, except God's promise that He made with one man who took God at His word.

THE PROPHETS

The prophets were men who lived through all parts of the roots of Christian history. They were the commentators, the town criers, the poet laureates, the national evangelists. They spoke of the survival of their people. They spoke of the Christian history to come. Their writings were among those that Christ Himself studied and taught. Their words were words that He recited to stake claim to His deity.

"Do not think that I have come to abolish the Law or the Prophets; I have not come to abolish them but to fulfill them."
MATTHEW 5:17 NIV

"He said to him, 'If they do not listen to Moses and the Prophets, they will not be convinced even if someone rises from the dead.'"
LUKE 16:31 NIV

He said to them, "This is what I told you while I was still with you: Everything must be fulfilled that is written about me in the Law of Moses, the Prophets and the Psalms."
LUKE 24:44 NIV

Within this period of history the roots were formed. The societal mores were established into which Jesus entered as a person. The empire of Rome was established, which affected Jesus' ministry and death but also facilitated the coming evangelism of the Good News.

CHAPTER TWO

The Life of Christ

But although the world was made through him, the world didn't recognize him when he came. Even in his own land and among his own people, he was not accepted. But to all who believed him and accepted him, he gave the right to become children of God. They are reborn! This is not a physical birth resulting from human passion or plan—this rebirth comes from God.

So the Word became human and lived here on earth among us. He was full of unfailing love and faithfulness. And we have seen his glory, the glory of the only Son of the Father.

John pointed him out to the people. He shouted to the crowds, "This is the one I was talking about when I said, 'Someone is coming who is far greater than I am, for he existed long before I did.'"

We have all benefited from the rich blessings he brought to us—one gracious blessing after another. For the law was given through Moses; God's unfailing love and faithfulness came through Jesus Christ. No one has ever seen God. But his only Son, who is himself God, is near to the Father's heart; he has told us about him.

JOHN 1:10–18 NLT

👁 UNDERSTANDING THE TIMES

The world at the time of Christ was not that much different from the world before or the world immediately after. The time of Christ was thirty-three years, with the bulk of Christ's ministry happening in the last two to three years. It was God ripping through the time-space continuum and touching humanity.

Jesus was born in a Middle Eastern kind of culture that was occupied by the sophisticated Roman/Greek culture. That means there was a lot of diversity. Within a day's walk, you could see a primitive shepherd's hutch as well as a multilevel Greek bath that would put some modern spas to shame.

There was a sense of well-being in that a large portion of the world was controlled by the Romans who were inventive, cultured, and achievement oriented. And yet, among Jesus' people, the Jews, there was unrest. There were foreign soldiers on their village streets. They were ordered to pay taxes to a king that had nothing to do with them. Jesus was born into a nation that had been oppressed and exiled over and over again. Now they were in their homeland, but with intruders in control.

JESUS AND THE CHURCH OF HIS DAY

The Jewish religious community of Jesus' day was an ordered one. The rules were set. The powerful people were protected. There was a comfort in the status quo. During Jesus' three or so years of public ministry, He did as much to unsettle the typical way of doing things as the Roman occupation did.

Jesus' extended family, friends, coworkers, and acquaintances dealt with His culture as differently as your own do. Some were probably amazed at the imports available to them because of the many foreigners in the land. Others were probably reclusive, antigovernment-control thinkers who retreated more naturally than they joined. People have always been people with opinions to act on and to share. It was no different in Jesus' day.

There were plenty of fears to go around, as well. This question of control was always at the forefront. Could the Roman officials make changes in the temple worship? Did the Jews have to alter their worship or way of life because a foreign government said to? Would they lose their land again? Would they be persecuted?

THE STORY OF THE TIMES

400 YEARS OF SILENCE
Four hundred years passed between the writing of the last prophet, Malachi, and the life of Christ. During that time a *lot* happened in the world. For instance…

Aristotle lived and died, leaving us with the scientific method (without which not only would science be different, but junior high science teachers would be at a total loss).

Alexander the Great conquered most of the civilized world before he was thirty-two years old.

A Greek translation of the Old Testament was written (probably the translation Jesus used).

The earth was discovered *not* to be the center of the universe, and the heart was discovered not to be the center of the nervous system.

Jerusalem fell under the control of Ptolemy of Egypt, then Seleucid ruler Antiochus. The Jews revolted under the leadership of the Maccabeus brothers, winning the Jews a time of autonomy until 37 B.C.

The Roman Empire lost its status as a republic when Octavian declared himself the emperor and his power was confirmed by the Roman Senate. He changed his name to Augustus Caesar and appointed Pontius Pilate as the governor of Judea.

AUGUSTUS CAESAR
The first caesar was Julius Caesar. But Caesar was a family name rather than a title. He was a shrewd military and political leader who did much to elevate the Roman Empire. He was not so shrewd as to avoid assassination in 44 B.C. (an event memorialized by William Shakespeare in the the sixteenth century).

After Julius Caesar was assassinated, the empire was governed by the triumvirate of Mark Antony, who aligned himself with

TIMELINE OVERVIEW

In the midst of world history...	Christian history unfolds...
37 B.C. Herod the Great rules Palestine as the King of Judea.	
27 B.C. Octavian becomes the first Roman Emperor, Augustus Caesar.	**c. 4 or 5 B.C.** The birth of Christ and John the Baptist
4 A.D. Herod the Great dies.	After Herod's death, Jesus' family settles in Galilee.
	c. 7 A.D. Twelve-year-old Jesus' parents accidentally leave him behind in the temple after the Passover.
14 Rome: Augustus Caesar is succeeded by Tiberius Caesar.	
23 Rome: birth of Pliny, Roman historian and writer	
26 Judea: Pontius Pilate becomes procurator.	**27** Jesus is baptized by John the Baptist and begins his public ministry.
	28 John the Baptist is executed by Herod Antipas, ruler over Galilee and Perea.
37 Herod Agrippa becomes king of Northern Palestine. Caligula Caesar becomes Emperor of Rome.	**30** Jesus' crucifixion, resurrection, and ascension
41 Caligula is assassinated.	
50 Rome becomes the largest city in the world, one million inhabitants.	

Cleopatra of Egypt, Marcus Lepidus, and Octavian, Julius's nephew and heir. By 27 B.C., Octavian had forced Lepidus into retirement and defeated Mark Antony in battle. Octavian then declared himself the Roman emperor with the consent of the Roman Senate. Octavian took on the family name, Caesar, from Julius. He claimed the name Augustus, which means "exalted."

Political might and intrigue paid off for the newly named Augustus Caesar. He became the emperor of the most powerful empire on earth at that time, which had functioned as a republic until his reign. Augustus accomplished many things, including sound currency, a functioning postal system, good harbors, and refined highway systems.

Augustus was known for keeping the peace. He was so loved by the Roman people that they declared him a god after his death. This becomes even more meaningful when you understand that of the four emperors following Augustus Caesar, including the notorious Nero, not one died a natural death.

It was this Augustus Caesar who ordered the census around 5 B.C. that brought Mary and Joseph to Bethlehem where Jesus was born.

In those days Caesar Augustus issued a decree that a census should be taken of the entire Roman world.
LUKE 2:1 NIV

JESUS IN THE TEMPLE

The only account that we have from the Christian New Testament of Jesus' childhood is the account of His trip to the tabernacle when He was twelve. Jesus' parents traveled to Jerusalem every year to celebrate the Passover feast. This feast commemorated the Hebrews' exodus from slavery in Egypt under the leadership of Moses. The feast was combined with a weeklong festival of unleavened bread. Jesus' family probably traveled with many others. It was like a yearly vacation to Jerusalem with holy implications.

When Jesus was twelve, He engaged the teachers at the temple in conversation, evidently amazing everyone there. When Joseph and Mary found Jesus, Mary lightly scolded Him and then took Him home.

Beyond this reference we know virtually nothing about Jesus' growing up or the fate of His father who is not mentioned in the accounts of Jesus' public ministry. What this one reference does tell us, though, is that Jesus went through childhood as a human. It also tells us that Jesus was a natural enough kid that His parents were sometimes confused when His deity slipped through.

Later in the historical picture, whole nations would divide over the nature of Jesus' deity. Was He all human? Was He all God? Was one part subjugated to the other? In this story we see both sides revealing themselves at the same time.

More than in this one instance did significant events happen in Jesus' life around the Passover. John lists one of Jesus' first public appearances as around the Passover. The meal Jesus shared with His disciples before His death was a Passover meal. The custom by which a prisoner was released, the people requesting Barabbas, was a Passover custom.

At Jesus' death, He indeed did become the Passover lamb, once for all giving His life to save His people's souls.

THE PALESTINE OF JESUS' DAY

When Jesus was born, His homeland, Palestine, was under Roman rule. In fact, Jesus was born in a time described as *Pax*

❓ DID YOU KNOW?

Cleopatra's Needles are the two obelisks (large stone pillars dedicated to the worship of the Egyptian sun god, Re) that stood for a time at the entrance to the temple of the cult of the Roman emperors, at which the Roman leaders were worshiped as gods. Construction of the temple was originally begun under the reign of Cleopatra VII, her intent being to build a temple to her husband, Mark Antony (Marcus Antonius). Roman emperor Augustus (who defeated Mark Antony in battle and ordered his suicide, which led in turn to Cleopatra's taking of her own life) completed the unfinished temple and dedicated it to worship of the Roman emperors. No one is sure why the obelisks are called Cleopatra's Needles: It was Augustus, not Cleopatra, who had the obelisks moved to the site of the temple *after* her death.

Construction of the temple was completed within a few years before the birth of Christ. The origin of the needles, however, appears to be from the reign of Thutmose III 1400 years earlier. Ramses II, whom most historians believe to be the same one from which Moses won freedom for God's people, added marks of his own to Cleopatra's Needles well over a thousand years before she was born. In the late 1800s, Egypt made a gift of Cleopatra's Needles, giving one to the United States and one to England. The two obelisks currently reside in New York City's Central Park and along the Thames River in London, respectively. Each pillar is nearly 70 feet tall and weighs close to 200 tons.

Romana, or the Roman Peace. Because of the rule of Rome, there were many advantages culturally. Still, those advantages didn't camouflage the fact that Jesus' homeland was occupied by foreigners or that the occupation was enforced militarily. It was this Roman occupation that provided a backdrop for each event in the life of Christ.

The religious climate of Jesus' day was certainly affected by the occupation. To the Jews, faith wasn't an issue relevant only to the Sabbath or the temple; it was their cultural identity. To have their very lives infiltrated by the Hellenistic (Greek) philosophies and thoughts of the day was repugnant. It countered the very foundation of their understanding of themselves. The Jews had a rich legacy passed down from God's covenant with Abraham through many years of scratching and clawing their way to survival as a people. They were involved in repeated land disputes. They fought to keep their bloodline pure in order to keep their worship just as pure.

Throughout the Old Testament the Hebrews, later known as the Jews, had struggled among themselves as to how much to blend in with the cultures around them. The kingdom divided into two regions: the southern, Judah, and the northern, Israel. The whole northern region had been assimilated by Assyria, a cruel and powerful culture to the east. By Jesus' day that region was known as Samaria. The prejudice of the Jews against the Samaritans was only a token of the power of their cultural pride.

 DID YOU KNOW?

According to tradition, the Septuagint, a Greek translation of the Old Testament Scriptures and probably the version studied by Jesus, was translated by the order of the pharaoh of Egypt (one of the Ptolemy line, who were Greek speakers of Macedonian descent) for his library in the mid 200s B.C.

COPING WITH THE OCCUPATION

The Jews of Jesus' day divided into several factions in response to the Roman occupation.

1. The **Zealots** were the guerrilla warriors of Jesus' day. They were the terrorists, the bands of fighting men that hid along the road and revealed their resistance through violence.

2. The **Essenes** were the escapists. They retreated to a monastic-like existence in the wilderness. They prepared themselves for God's kingdom but left everyday life in order to do it.

3. The **Sadducees** were the conformists. If you can't beat 'em, after all... The Sadducees controlled the highest Jewish governing council called the *Sanhedrin*. Their influence was not as much among the common people as among the sophisticated elite. They represented the part of Jesus' culture that embraced the Greek influence and any privileges that went along with it.

4. The **Pharisees** were the dyed-in-the-wool Jews. They were zealous, but not in a military way. They embraced the Jewish laws and rituals to the point of using them as armor. Jesus

butted heads with most of the leadership of his day, but especially with the Pharisees.

 SET THE STAGE!

The Roman occupation of Palestine was in no way more obvious than through the presence of the Roman army which numbered over 300,000 men as early as 20 B.C.

In the early days of the Roman Empire, most of the Roman army was made up of farmers. Because of this, most military campaigns were waged during the summer, between spring planting and harvesttime.

At the time of Christ, the Roman military was a professional troop. The men could come from anywhere and any class or status. When they joined the army, they received wages and Roman citizenship. In essence, the military were government employees.

The military were responsible for guarding borders and fighting enemies, but also for constructing roads, aqueducts, bridges, and tunnels, not to mention city walls.

The army was organized into *legions*. Each legion was made up of 6,000 men, including cavalry and construction crews. Each legion also included foot soldiers called *legionaries*. Each legionary served under an officer called a *centurion*. It was a centurion who asked Jesus to "just say the word" to heal his sick servant (Matthew 8:8). It was also a centurion who watched the crucifixion, then praised God and claimed, "Surely, this was a righteous man" (Luke 23:47).

JESUS AND JOHN THE BAPTIST

John the Baptist was a member of Jesus' extended family. We are first introduced to their relationship through their mothers, Mary and Elizabeth. Mary traveled to see Elizabeth while both ladies were pregnant. When Mary greeted Elizabeth, John "leapt" inside of Elizabeth at the recognition of Jesus' presence. Elizabeth then prophesied through the power of the Holy Spirit.

Elizabeth gave a glad cry and exclaimed to Mary, "You are blessed by God above all other women, and your child is blessed. What an honor this is, that the mother of my Lord should visit me! When you came in and greeted me, my baby jumped for joy the instant I heard your voice! You are blessed,

because you believed that the Lord would do what he said."
LUKE 1:42–45 NLT

What a comfort Elizabeth's prophecy must have been to Mary, a young woman in a position unlike any other has ever been. Mary stayed with Elizabeth for three months before returning to Galilee. The next time the Bible gives a record of Jesus and John is when Jesus traveled from Galilee to be baptized by John. Both men were adults.

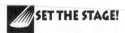

SET THE STAGE!

The Sadducees and Pharisees tested Jesus throughout His ministry. He was the new teacher on the block, and as His ministry progressed, His claims became more outlandish and heretical in the ears of the religious order.

> *That same day the Sadducees, who say there is no resurrection, came to him with a question. "Teacher," they said, "Moses told us that if a man dies without having children, his brother must marry the widow and have children for him. Now there were seven brothers among us. The first one married and died, and since he had no children, he left his wife to his brother. The same thing happened to the second and third brother, right on down to the seventh. Finally, the woman died. Now then, at the resurrection, whose wife will she be of the seven, since all of them were married to her?"*
>
> *Jesus replied, "You are in error because you do not know the Scriptures or the power of God. At the resurrection people will neither marry nor be given in marriage; they will be like the angels in heaven. But about the resurrection of the dead—have you not read what God said to you, 'I am the God of Abraham, the God of Isaac, and the God of Jacob'? He is not the God of the dead but of the living."*
>
> *When the crowds heard this, they were astonished at his teaching.*
>
> *Hearing that Jesus had silenced the Sadducees, the Pharisees got together. One of them, an expert in the law, tested him with this question: "Teacher, which is the greatest commandment in the Law?"*
>
> MATTHEW 22:23–36 NIV

SINNERS AND SAINTS
POLYCARP

Did you know that Jesus' disciples had disciples of their own? Polycarp was a Christian leader and was later made a saint. He was a disciple of John, who was a disciple of Jesus. As the church organized, Polycarp became the bishop of Smyrna (Smyrna was a city in what we know today as Turkey). Polycarp lived in the time when the church transitioned from a group led by the apostles to what we call the Early Church. In the middle of the second century, Polycarp was martyred for his faith.

John the Baptist took seriously his role as the "front man" for Jesus. He was the one who prepared the way. John had a public ministry before Jesus did. He also gathered disciples before Jesus did and willingly lost his disciples to Jesus.

John was not a man to play political games. He took a stand against the king who was living in adultery with the queen. At the first opportunity, John's death was requested by the queen. Some historical sources also suggest that the king was only too willing to dispense with John because of the king's jealousy over John's influence. Whatever the reason, John was beheaded after seven months in prison.

Jesus had the utmost respect for John. When John sent a message from prison asking Jesus to confirm that He was the Messiah, Jesus told His disciples, "I assure you, of all who have ever lived, none is greater than John the Baptist" (MATTHEW 11:11 NLT).

JEWISH WORSHIP IN THE TEMPLE

Jesus was probably raised going to church in two different places, the temple and the synagogue. The temple was in Jerusalem. It was where his family traveled to celebrate Passover.

The temple that Jesus worshiped at in Jerusalem was built (or rebuilt) by Herod the Great. The construction was begun around 20 B.C. The actual temple was built in a year and a half out of white marble and gold. The outbuildings were still under construction throughout Jesus' life. In this respect, there was always a building program going on. The buildings were not considered complete until A.D. 64 (eighty-four years!). Once Jesus, describing His own death, referred to rebuilding the temple in three days. In their response, the Jews said the temple had been under construction for forty-six years.

As Jesus entered the temple, He would have faced four walled courtyards. The first was called the Court of the Gentiles. Anyone could enter there. Buying and selling happened there, including animals for sacrifices. It was this area that Jesus would have cleared when He cleansed the temple of the merchants (John 2).

Within the Court of the Gentiles was the temple and the other courts. Non-Jews were not to enter these areas. The Inner Court was next, with a small area cordoned off called the Women's Court. Both men and women could enter this area to give their offerings. It was probably here that the widow offered her two coins, acting as an object lesson for Jesus' disciples (Mark 12). The other part of the Inner Court held an area for Jewish men only and the Priests' Court. The actual temple resided in the center of all these somewhat concentric courts.

There was a porch at the entrance to the temple. Inside was the Holy Place, where only the officiating priest could enter to trim the lamps, bring the incense, and replace the ceremonial bread. Inside the Holy Place was the Most Holy Place separated by curtains, or veils. The Most Holy Place was seen as the place where God's presence dwelled. Only the high priest entered this room and only once a year.

SET THE STAGE!

The Tabernacle was the precursor to the temple. It was a portable tentlike structure. Moses received the plans from God and oversaw the construction while the Jews were traveling from Egypt back to Canaan.

Solomon's Temple was the first permanent temple structure built by the Jews in Jerusalem. The plans and preparation were made by King David. The actual construction was under King Solomon's care. This temple was destroyed when Jerusalem fell to the Babylonians.

Zerubbabel's Temple was built, or rebuilt, when the Jews returned home to Jerusalem from Babylon. It was probably built to many of the same specs as Solomon's temple, but was not nearly so grand (the senior citizens who had seen the original temple actually wept at the disparity between the two). This temple was not completely destroyed but was plundered and damaged when Pompey captured Jerusalem in 63 B.C.

Herod's Temple was a political and religious feat. He probably hoped this would win him some loyalty from the religious Jews. He also rebuilt temples for other gods.

THE SYNAGOGUE

The synagogue was a mainstay of Jewish religious instruction. Rather than existing in one place like the temple, synagogues were anywhere that there were Jews to gather. Some say the synagogue originated with Moses. Others say that during the exile of the Jews into Babylon the people started meeting together on the Sabbath, which grew into the traditional synagogue.

However they began, by the time Jesus walked through the Capernaum dust, synagogues were probably as much a part of His life as Sunday school is to a Baptist deacon's kid. The synagogues were the main vehicle for the influence of the Pharisees. Because Jesus spoke at the synagogue in whatever town He visited, He had ample opportunities to interact with (and even irritate) the Pharisees.

Typically, there were at least two leaders at every synagogue. One was elected by the people. He cared for the property and the general order of the service. He was called the "Ruler of the Synagogue." In a sense, he was like a committee head at a church who kept everything running smoothly. (Jairus, who asked Jesus to heal his daughter, was the ruler of the local synagogue. Luke 8:41) There was also a paid minister who often lived at the synagogue and cared for the furniture, the scrolls (which were premium in a land before printing presses), and carried a lot of ceremonial responsibilities.

A SERVICE AT THE SYNAGOGUE

When the people met together at the synagogue, the men sat on one side and the women sat on the other. The service involved prayers and blessings that were memorized much as many Christian churches today pray the Lord's Prayer or recite the Apostles' Creed. Each service included scripture lessons or readings that could be read by any member, including the children. First there was a reading from the Pentateuch (Genesis–Deuteronomy), then from the prophets.

A sermon followed the reading from the prophets. The sermons were not given by the same person each week. The ruler of the synagogue invited visitors or members to give the "message of encourage-ment." It was this custom that enabled Jesus, and later Paul, to take part in so many synagogue services. Often today when a minister visits a church, he or she will be asked to share in the service in some way. That's how it was in the synagogues in the early part of the first century. It was in this very scenario that Jesus proclaimed His role as Messiah:

 SET THE STAGE!

Each synagogue service began by the people reciting Deuteronomy 6:4–5, called the Great Shema.

Hear, O Israel: The LORD our God, the LORD is one. Love the LORD your God with all your heart and with all your soul and with all your strength.
DEUTERONOMY 6:4–5 NIV

The scroll of the prophet Isaiah was handed to [Jesus]. Unrolling it, he found the place where it is written:

"The Spirit of the Lord is on me, because he has anointed me to preach good news to the poor. He has sent me to proclaim freedom for the prisoners and recovery of sight for the blind, to release the oppressed, to proclaim the year of the Lord's favor."

Then he rolled up the scroll, gave it back to the attendant and sat down. The eyes of everyone in the synagogue were fastened on him, and he began by saying to them, "Today this scripture is fulfilled in your hearing."

LUKE 4:17–21 NIV

JESUS' MINISTRY

While Jesus worked within the synagogue structure, His typical form of ministry followed John's example much more so than that of the traditional Hebrew worship. Like John, Jesus preached out among the people. When He sent His disciples out, He encouraged them to do the same. Jesus' ministry involved healings and exorcisms and miracles, as well as teaching. These signs showed God's power and supported Jesus' claim to be sent directly from God the Father.

Jesus' public ministry was actually a very short time, just two to three years as estimated from the Gospel accounts of His life. In that time Jesus established a prominent role in the community (today we would say He got a good buzz going about Himself). He also accomplished loads of miracles and sermons. He established a following of disciples, zeroing in on twelve that He invested Himself in completely.

The first part of Jesus' ministry was much more public than the rest. As the end of His life neared, He spent more time with the twelve disciples, training them to carry on His work.

JESUS' DISCIPLES

A significant part of Jesus' ministry was investing in the people who followed Him. There were twelve disciples that seemed to be a core group for Jesus. Three of those seemed to be the closest yet (Peter, John, James). Jesus had many more disciples than that, though. Luke 10 describes a scenario in which Jesus sends out seventy-two disciples.

There were women in Jesus' core group as well as men. These women provided financial support for Jesus' work and life. They were a part of His community.

Not long afterward Jesus began a tour of the nearby cities and villages to announce the Good News concerning the Kingdom of God. He took his twelve disciples with him, along with some women he had healed and from whom he had cast out evil spirits. Among them were Mary Magdalene, from whom he had cast out seven demons; Joanna, the wife of Chuza, Herod's business manager; Susanna; and many others who were contributing from their own resources to support Jesus and his disciples.
LUKE 8:1–3 NLT

Jesus' disciples watched His deity revealed on a daily basis. It was the disciples who heard not only the parables but the private explanations of the parables. It was the disciples who had to deal with the worship, the reverence, the surprise, and the awe of following a man who claimed to be God, yet didn't conquer the world —at least not the way the general culture expected.

It was the disciples who were left alone in a locked room in that dark few days between Jesus' death and resurrection. It was the disciples who had to wonder why they didn't realize there was a traitor among them. It was the disciples who were left standing, looking up when Jesus took His final leave.

 SET THE STAGE!

One of those days Jesus went out to a mountainside to pray, and spent the night praying to God. When morning came, he called his disciples to him and chose twelve of them, whom he also designated apostles: Simon (whom he named Peter), his brother Andrew, James, John, Philip, Bartholomew, Matthew, Thomas, James son of Alphaeus, Simon who was called the Zealot, Judas son of James, and Judas Iscariot, who became a traitor.
LUKE 6:12–16 NIV

And it was the disciples who were praying together in the upper room when the Holy Spirit invaded and the Christian church as we have come to know it experienced its inauguration at Pentecost.

 **SET THE STAGE!**

Here are the instructions Jesus gave His disciples before sending them out.

Calling the Twelve to him, he sent them out two by two and gave them authority over evil spirits.

These were his instructions: "Take nothing for the journey except a staff—no bread, no bag, no money in your belts. Wear sandals but not an extra tunic. Whenever you enter a house, stay there until you leave that town. And if any place will not welcome you or listen to you, shake the dust off your feet when you leave, as a testimony against them."

They went out and preached that people should repent. They drove out many demons and anointed many sick people with oil and healed them.
MARK 6:7–13 NIV

JESUS' TEACHING

Jesus taught frequently. He was the master of the teachable moment. He taught through regular discourse, like sermons...

Now when he saw the crowds, he went up on a mountainside and sat down. His disciples came to him, and he began to teach them, saying: "Blessed are the poor in spirit, for theirs is the kingdom of heaven. Blessed are those who mourn, for they will be comforted."
MATTHEW 5:1–4 NIV

. . .and He taught through parables or stories.

Jesus told them another parable: "The kingdom of heaven is like a man who sowed good seed in his field."
MATTHEW 13:24 NIV

He taught of God's love...

"For God so loved the world that he gave his one and only

Son, that whoever believes in him shall not perish but have eternal life."

JOHN 3:16 NIV

…and of the kind of love that God's children should show.

"By this all men will know that you are my disciples, if you love one another."

JOHN 13:35 NIV

He taught about how to approach God…

People were bringing little children to Jesus to have him touch them, but the disciples rebuked them. When Jesus saw this, he was indignant. He said to them, "Let the little children come to me, and do not hinder them, for the kingdom of God belongs to such as these. I tell you the truth, anyone who will not receive the kingdom of God like a little child will never enter it."

MARK 10:13–15 NIV

…and how to pray.

"But when you pray, go into your room, close the door and pray to your Father, who is unseen. Then your Father, who sees what is done in secret, will reward you. And when you pray, do not keep on babbling like pagans, for they think they will be heard because of their many words. Do not be like them, for your Father knows what you need before you ask him. This, then, is how you should pray: 'Our Father in heaven, hallowed be your name…'"

MATTHEW 6:6–9 NIV

Jesus taught difficult truths…

"Whoever eats my flesh and drinks my blood remains in me, and I in him. Just as the living Father sent me and I live because

of the Father, so the one who feeds on me will live because of me. This is the bread that came down from heaven. Your forefathers ate manna and died, but he who feeds on this bread will live forever." He said this while teaching in the synagogue in Capernaum. On hearing it, many of his disciples said, "This is a hard teaching. Who can accept it?"

JOHN 6:56–60 NIV

...and had difficult confrontations.

"Do not judge, or you too will be judged."
MATTHEW 7:1 NIV

"Why do you look at the speck of sawdust in your brother's eye and pay no attention to the plank in your own eye?"
MATTHEW 7:3 NIV

"Woe to you, teachers of the law and Pharisees, you hypocrites! You are like whitewashed tombs, which look beautiful on the outside but on the inside are full of dead men's bones and everything unclean."
MATTHEW 23:27 NIV

Jesus taught about money and love. He taught about loving God and being fair to the people around you. He taught about radical living that claims forgiveness first and revenge never. Jesus' teaching stirred up the people around Him. It certainly stirred up the religious leadership of the day. His was a call to a new kind of living that didn't take the place of the law of the Old Testament. Instead, He took the law one step further...

"You have heard that it was said to the people long ago, 'Do not murder, and anyone who murders will be subject to judgment.' But I tell you that anyone who is angry with his brother will be subject to judgment."
MATTHEW 5:21–22 NIV

*"You have heard that it was said, 'Do not commit adultery.'
But I tell you that anyone who looks at a woman lustfully has
already committed adultery with her in his heart."*
MATTHEW 5:27–28 NIV

*"You have heard that it was said, 'Eye for eye, and tooth for
tooth.' But I tell you, Do not resist an evil person. If someone
strikes you on the right cheek, turn to him the other also."*
MATTHEW 5:38–39 NIV

THE HOLY SURPRISE

To understand the impact of Christ, you have to be able to put
yourself in the shoes of the people around Him. They were nego-
tiating what was, by nature, an impossibility. That God would live
among them in the form of a boy then a man who grew up just
like they did? We have no reason to believe that Jesus bypassed
the learning curve we all experience as we mature. We learn
appropriate and inappropriate behavior even when right and
wrong are not involved. Jesus grew up like we all did, yet differently. As friends and neighbors watched, the Gospels give us
glimpses of their surprise....

*Coming to his hometown, he began teaching the people in
their synagogue, and they were amazed. "Where did this man
get this wisdom and these miraculous powers?" they asked.
"Isn't this the carpenter's son? Isn't his mother's name Mary,
and aren't his brothers James, Joseph, Simon and Judas?
Aren't all his sisters with us? Where then did this man get all
these things?" And they took offense at him. But Jesus said
to them, "Only in his hometown and in his own house is a
prophet without honor."*
MATTHEW 13:54–57 NIV

*Without warning, a furious storm came up on the lake, so
that the waves swept over the boat. But Jesus was sleeping.
The disciples went and woke him, saying, "Lord, save us! We're
going to drown!" He replied, "You of little faith, why are you*

*so afraid?" Then he got up and rebuked the winds and the
waves, and it was completely calm. The men were amazed
and asked, "What kind of man is this? Even the winds and the
waves obey him!"*
MATTHEW 8:24–27 NIV

*On hearing his words, some of the people said, "Surely this
man is the Prophet." Others said, "He is the Christ." Still others
asked, "How can the Christ come from Galilee? Does not the
scripture say that the Christ will come from David's family
and from Bethlehem, the town where David lived?" Thus the
people were divided because of Jesus. Some wanted to seize
him, but no one laid a hand on him.*
JOHN 7:40–44 NIV

Jesus' contemporaries had to negotiate face-to-face what the
Christian church has struggled with ever since: "How did God
become a man and still be God?" His neighbors, the everyday
citizens who crossed paths with Jesus, must have struggled with
His claims to deity when they also experienced Him as a regular
guy. The struggle of the everyday citizens was small, though,
compared to the struggle of the religious leaders of the day.

THE POLITICAL PROBLEM

Why exactly weren't the religious and governmental leaders of
Jesus' day thrilled with His message of the kingdom of God?

From God's perspective, Jesus Christ died on the cross as a
substitute for us. He took the
punishment for the sin that is
born in our hearts and sepa-
rates us from God. He died so
that we could live forever connected to God.

From the perspective of the
religious leaders of the day,
Jesus died for an entirely different set of reasons. They did

DID YOU KNOW?

While the Books of the
Old Testament recount
the events of a period of
thousands of years, those of
the New Testament mostly
remain within a time frame
of about 125 years.

not believe that Jesus was who He said He was. And even if He was, He wasn't helping their cause. They claimed He was a blasphemer. After all, who was He to claim to be God? There was no God but Jehovah. Who was He to claim to be king? There was no king but Caesar.

They didn't get it.

But what they did get was that suddenly this grassroots Messiah was stirring something in the hearts of people. He was confronting the status quo. He was putting at risk the power that belonged to the ruling bodies.

> Many of the people who were with Mary believed in Jesus when they saw this happen. But some went to the Pharisees and told them what Jesus had done. Then the leading priests and Pharisees called the high council together to discuss the situation. "What are we going to do?" they asked each other. "This man certainly performs many miraculous signs. If we leave him alone, the whole nation will follow him, and then the Roman army will come and destroy both our Temple and our nation."
>
> And one of them, Caiaphas, who was high priest that year, said, "How can you be so stupid? Why should the whole nation be destroyed? Let this one man die for the people."
>
> This prophecy that Jesus should die for the entire nation came from Caiaphas in his position as high priest. He didn't think of it himself; he was inspired to say it. It was a prediction that Jesus' death would be not for Israel only, but for the gathering together of all the children of God scattered around the world.
>
> So from that time on the Jewish leaders began to plot Jesus' death. As a result, Jesus stopped his public ministry among the people and left Jerusalem. He went to a place near the wilderness, to the village of Ephraim, and stayed there with his disciples.
>
> JOHN 11:45–54 NLT

The fear that the religious leaders had was that Jesus would upset the Roman government, who would then destroy the temple and disperse the people as had been done many times previously. They felt a competition with Jesus that seemed to them a fight to the death. When Jesus entered Jerusalem and the people cheered, the Pharisees were downhearted.

> *Those in the crowd who had seen Jesus call Lazarus back to life were telling others all about it. That was the main reason so many went out to meet him—because they had heard about this mighty miracle. Then the Pharisees said to each other, "We've lost. Look, the whole world has gone after him!"*
> JOHN 12:17–19 NLT

When it comes to not getting it, though, the people as a whole didn't get it, either. They wanted not only spiritual freedom, but political freedom. They wanted God to step down as the Old Testament prophets promised and knock the socks off their enemies. They weren't particularly thrilled with a man who could be assassinated so easily.

Politically, the cards were stacked against Jesus. Spiritually, He was God giving up His life to establish a connection with the likes of us. Politically, He was a down-and-outer with a price on His head and a contract about to be taken out on His life.

JESUS' FINAL WEEK

Jesus last week is referred to as the Passion Week. You've probably heard of "Passion Plays." They are reenactments of the events of Jesus' last week.

The Passion Week begins with Jesus' entry into Jerusalem. This is often called "The Triumphal Entry." Jesus fulfilled a prophecy by riding into the city. The people cheered Him on, shouting their support and throwing their coats down in His path as an act of deference. Jesus then proceeded to the temple where He pitched a holy fit and ran the merchants right out of the temple court.

It was during this final week that Judas made his agreement with the priests.

Then one of the Twelve—the one called Judas Iscariot—went to the chief priests and asked, "What are you willing to give me if I hand him over to you?" So they counted out for him thirty silver coins. From then on Judas watched for an opportunity to hand him over.

MATTHEW 26:14–16 NIV

The Passion week ended with Jesus' celebrating the Passover meal with the disciples. We now refer to that as the Last Supper. It was the perfect picture of what Jesus came to do. If the group of men followed Jewish tradition, they ate foods that commemorated the foods that the Jews could make quickly and eat on the run the night before their escape from slavery in Egypt. Their meal would have included roasted lamb, bitter herbs, and bread without yeast.

During the Seder, or Passover meal, Jesus instituted a new tradition. He gave His disciples bread, describing it as His body. He gave them wine, describing it as His blood. To this day the Christian church recreates this act of Communion in memory of Jesus' sacrifice. It is a spiritual souvenir of sorts that He Himself passed down to us.

JESUS' ARREST

After the meal, Jesus went to the garden to pray, evidently a place He and the disciples frequented (John 18:2). He prayed for His disciples and then for all His followers to come. Then Judas found Him and pointed Him out with a kiss.

Judas came to Jesus with a crowd including chief priests, soldiers, officers of the temple, and elders (Luke 22:52; John 18:2). This crowd came to Jesus after dark with weapons including swords and clubs, all to arrest a man who didn't resist, who even provided healing for one of the mob.

Jesus requested that His disciples be released and proceeded into the events ahead. From Jesus' prayer in the garden we know that He was aware of what was to come. He even prayed that God would release Him from this fate if that was possible. But, in the end, He obeyed.

JESUS' TRIAL

Jesus' trial happened in several stages. He was first questioned by Annas. Annas had been appointed high priest in A.D. 6 by Quirinius, governor of Syria. By A.D. 15, Annas had been deposed, and his five sons became high priests as well as his son-in-law Caiaphas. Jesus was probably led to Annas first because he was the head of the family.

During this questioning the Sanhedrin were gathering with Caiaphas, the current high priest. Annas sent Jesus to them as a prisoner. Jesus remained silent as the Sanhedrin produced false witnesses who perjured themselves ineffectively in contradictory testimony.

At that point Caiaphas played his trump card. "Are you the Christ?" In the eyes of the Sanhedrin Jesus incriminated Himself by answering "yes." In essence, Jesus confirmed His identity as God, which was blasphemy in the eyes of these men. But while the Sanhedrin considered blasphemy as punishable by death, they were a religious body, not a governmental body. They could not sentence Jesus to death. For that they had to find a reason to take Jesus to a Roman court.

PLAN B

The closest government official who could grant the request of the Sanhedrin was Pontius Pilate, the procurator (administrator) of imperial Rome in Palestine. Pilate was in town because of the Passover feast (in case he needed to maintain order). The whole lot of the arresting mob evidently walked to the home of Pontius Pilate. There they claimed that Jesus was being accused of three things:

1. We have found this man subverting our nation. (He's raising a lot of damaging ruckus.)

2. He opposes payment of taxes to Caesar (not exactly true), and

3. He "claims to be Christ, a king" (Luke 23:2 NIV).

The only complaint that seemed of national interest to Pilate was Jesus' claim to be king. That could be treason. Yet, when Pilate questioned Jesus, it was clear that national security was not at risk. Pilate basically acquitted Jesus. Jesus' accusers continued to raise objections until Pilate, wanting to be done with

SINNERS AND SAINTS
A PLAGUE OF HERODS

The Herods were a politically important Jewish family who served the Romans as government functionaries (regional kings, governors, etc.) in areas of the empire with large Jewish populations.

Herod II

With some exceptions, they were generally known as a nasty, greedy, ambitious bunch and were not well liked by their own people. Many times an historical record refers to someone simply as "Herod," leading to confusion and the feeling that "This guy was *everywhere*—all the time—for at least a couple of hundred years." Here's a listing of some important, and not so important, Herods:

Herod the Great: who rebuilt the Temple of Jerusalem (Yea!) but then had all the babies of Bethlehem slaughtered (Boo!) trying to prevent a certain Lord and Savior from reaching adulthood.

Herod Antipas: before whom Christ appeared during the trial. He also ordered the beheading of John the Baptist.

Herod Agrippa II: last of the Herods. The apostle Paul appeared before him.

Herod Agrippa I: Guess whose dad he was? Go on…guess. He was also a friend of the Roman emperor Claudius.

Herod Archelaus: Kind of sounds like some sort of foot parasite.

Herod of Chalcis: who was the brother of Herod Agrippa I. Guess whose uncle he was?

No, really, guess…

Herod Phillip: The only Herod without a dorky name.

Herod DeDaugge: A false saint rumored to cure supplicants of headaches. (We made this up. Can you figure it out? Say it out loud. . . .)

? DID YOU KNOW?

Names are often one of the most confusing parts of history. In some cultures the family name comes first, followed by the given name (as in Caesar Augustus and Pontius Pilate). Sometimes a person's job title became part of his name: The names Butcher, Gardener, and Shoemaker have obvious roots. The names Smith, Cooper, and Collier come from the words meaning blacksmith, barrel maker, and coal carrier. Pilate was the name of the governmental position held by Pontius Pilate. Sometimes the reverse happened and someone's name came to represent the position he held. Caesar started out as a family name but eventually came to mean "emperor."

People often changed their names to signify a change of position: Octavian took the name Gaius Julius Caesar Octavianus in 44 B.C., after his great-uncle Julius Caesar's murder when he inherited partial rule of the empire. Upon becoming emperor, he again changed his name, this time to Caesar Augustus.

Most popes and many kings took different names upon taking office. Often they would choose the name of a great king or pope before them to honor the name and/or lend a sense that they carried some of the same attributes of a famous former ruler. Some felt that a new, and perhaps more dignified, name would help them to better fit a new role and help people who were already familiar with them adjust to their new status. Besides, when it comes right down to it, "King Biff" and "Pope Lefty" just don't quite have the right feel to them.

the whole thing, decided to send Jesus to Herod Antipas, the regional king.

Jesus was from Galilee, which was part of Herod's jurisdiction. Herod was pleased to see this Jesus that he had heard so much about. He unsuccessfully tried to chide Jesus into doing something miraculous, but was unimpressed with either Jesus' guilt or innocence. So he sent Him back to Pilate. The Bible notes that previous to this day Pilate and Herod had been enemies, but with this exchange they became friends (Luke 23:12).

A FRUSTRATED JUDGE

Pilate was caught between a very solid rock and the hardest of places. The Sanhedrin were forcing his hand to convict an innocent man. His very own wife was warning him about dreams she had had and Jesus' innocence. Pilate talked to the accusers multiple times, trying to talk them out of executing Jesus, but the mob ruled. He tried to get the people to choose Jesus over another prisoner (and over the heads of the Sanhedrin), but they asked for Barabbas's life to be spared (a custom of releasing one

SINNERS AND SAINTS
PILATE

Pontius Pilate was the Roman representative in Palestine when Jesus lived there. Pontius was a family name. Pontius Pilate was his official title. He governed from A.D. 26–36. He is the one Roman official listed in the Apostles' Creed: "[Jesus] suffered under Pontius Pilate." Pilate is now notorious for washing his hands of Jesus' blood in an effort to rid himself of the guilt of condemning an innocent man.

Because the Jews of Judea had a reputation for being difficult, the procurator of Judea answered directly to the emperor. This gave Pilate great authority, which he often used foolishly.

In his day Pilate was notorious for his hostility toward the Jews. He baited them time and again with acts such as placing symbols for Roman deities in the temple and appropriating temple taxes for civic improvements. Pilate's rule in Judea was an ongoing feud with the Jewish leadership.

In the trial of Jesus, Pilate lost to the wit of the religious leaders. They outsmarted him on his own turf, by taunting him with jabs at his own loyalty to Caesar. "If you let this man go, you are no friend of Caesar" (John 19:12 NIV).

Pilate is lost to most history books after he was sent to Rome six years after Jesus' trial. Some ancient historians claim that Pilate took his own life, but the traditions contradict each other. One legend even says he jumped from a cliff.

SINNERS AND SAINTS
TIBERIUS

Tiberius was the second emperor of Rome, succeeding Augustus. Both of Rome's first two emperors held power during part of the life of Christ: Augustus at the time of His birth and childhood and Tiberius during the ministry, death, and resurrection of Jesus.

Tiberius was a well-liked and successful military commander under Augustus. Seeing his capabilities, Augustus decided that Tiberius would make a good addition to the royal family and commanded him to divorce his wife and marry the emperor's own daughter Julia. Tiberius followed orders, but his marriage to Julia was not a happy one, and he went off to live by himself. Eventually, Augustus recalled Tiberius to Rome and made him heir to the Empire. He is remembered as an emperor with good administration skills who kept a balanced budget and upheld good relations with countries friendly to the Empire.

prisoner at Passover) and Jesus to be crucified.

Pilate got the creeps before it was over with. He even begged Jesus to help. When the religious leaders began to use the name of Caesar, Pilate finally threw in the towel (literally in some ways). The leaders questioned Pilate's loyalty to Caesar if he allowed someone else to claim to be any kind of king. This was a veiled threat to make Pilate look disloyal before the emperor. At this point Pilate made his grand exit, literally washing his hands of the responsibility. With that he released Jesus to the crowd.

JESUS' EXECUTION

Jesus was killed by hanging on a cross. It was a torturous death that usually resulted in asphyxiation much like a hanging by rope. The execution was a public display. Jesus was one of three that were crucified at the same time. The other two were thieves.

Jesus' death seemed to be the end of a dream and the futility of those who believed in Him. At least four Roman soldiers were present. They divided Jesus' clothes among themselves. Jesus' mother, Mary, was present, as was John, His disciple.

While death by crucifixion is a slow process, it was typically hurried along when the soldiers broke the legs of the people being executed. This took away their last ability to hold themselves up in order to breathe. Jesus was dead before the soldiers came to break His legs. This fulfilled a specific prophecy that His bones would not be broken.

Jesus was buried in a tomb on loan from Joseph of Arimathea. The threatened religious leaders had gotten what they wanted, but can you believe that they were still scheming?

> The next day, the one after Preparation Day, the chief priests and the Pharisees went to Pilate. "Sir," they said, "we remember that while he was still alive that deceiver said, 'After three days I will rise again.' So give the order for the tomb to be made secure until the third day. Otherwise, his disciples may come and steal the body and tell the people that he has been raised from the dead. This last deception will be worse than the first."
>
> "Take a guard," Pilate answered. "Go, make the tomb as secure as you know how." So they went and made the tomb secure by putting a seal on the stone and posting the guard.
> MATTHEW 27:62–66 NIV

So finally Jesus' grave was posted with Roman protection so that the power of the Christ from Nazareth wouldn't leak out of even a sepulcher.

JESUS' RESURRECTION

It is Jesus' resurrection that sets Christianity apart. Jesus was not the first to claim He was the Messiah. He was not even the first to be executed for those claims. He was the first, though, to give His life and then be given His life back by God. Many world religions still hold sacred the graves of their founders. Christianity holds sacred an empty grave. The power of Jesus' resurrection can not be overestimated in the history of Christianity or in the individual lives of believers.

The typical tombs or graves of Jesus' day were usually either caves or holes dug into stone cliffs. Caskets were probably not involved. Instead the bodies were wrapped in "grave clothes." While embalming had been invented in Egypt before the time of Christ, the Hebrews were not known for embalming their dead. Remember when Jesus asked for Lazarus's tomb to be opened? Martha pointed out that decomposition would be too far along to open the tomb (John 11:39).

Stones were used to block the entrance to the tombs. Such a door to an ancient grave could weigh one to three tons. This is significant in light of the theory that Jesus didn't really die on the cross, He just fainted. As the theory goes, after being buried, Jesus woke up and made His own way out of the grave, pushing aside the stone. Granted, Jesus could have moved a stone if needed. But would He have fainted? There are inconsistencies in that theory.

No eyewitness accounts of Jesus' actual resurrection have been recorded. While there were guards at the tomb, Matthew writes that when the angel appeared and the earth shook, the guards fainted. The records we have are of witnesses to the empty grave and to Jesus' appearances after the resurrection.

THE RESURRECTED JESUS
The Gospels record a number of times that Jesus appeared after His resurrection. He appeared to the women who went to visit His grave and found an angel. He appeared to two believers on their way to Emmaus. He entered a room through locked doors to greet the disciples and confront Thomas's doubts. He cooked breakfast on the beach for the disciples. He commissioned His followers to carry on the work. Finally, He allowed the disciples to see Him ascend back to heaven.

THE EVENTS OF JESUS' LIFE AS RECORDED IN THE GOSPELS

The Gospels (Matthew, Mark, Luke, John) tell about Jesus' life from four different perspectives. They don't all list the same events or in the same order. The table below shows the events of Jesus' life and where those events are listed in the Gospels.

	MATTHEW	MARK	LUKE	JOHN
Jesus' deity				1:1–18
Jesus' family tree	1:1–17		3:23–38	
Jesus is announced			1:5–56	
John the Baptist, cousin and coworker to Jesus, is born			1:57–80	
Joseph hears about Jesus' birth	1:18–25			
Jesus' birth			2:1–20	
Baby Jesus goes to the temple			2:21–40	
The wise men visit	2:1–12			
Jesus' family escapes to Egypt	2:13–23			
Jesus grows up			2:41–52	
Jesus' baptism	3:13–17	1:9–11	3:21–22	1:29–34
Jesus is tempted three times	4:1–11	1:12–13	4:1–13	
Jesus calls His first disciples	4:18–22	1:16–20	5:1–11	1:35–51
Jesus' inaugural miracle				2:1–11
Jesus' stand in the temple				2:12–25
Jesus and Nicodemus				3:1–21
John the Baptist teaches about Jesus				3:22–36
Jesus and the Samaritan woman				4:1–42
Jesus teaches in Galilee	4:12	1:14–15	4:14–15	4:43–45
Jesus heals a royal official's son				4:46–54
Jesus teaches in Capernaum	4:13–17		4:31–32	
Jesus begins a ministry of healing and teaching	4:23–25; 8:1–4, 14–17; 9:1–8	1:21–2:12	4:33–44; 5:12–26	
Jesus eats at Matthew's house	9:9–13	2:13–17	5:27–32	
Jesus talks about fasting and introduces a new way of thinking	9:14–17	2:18–22	5:33–39	

	MATTHEW	MARK	LUKE	JOHN
Jesus heals on the Sabbath (creating a conflict with the religious leaders)	12:1–21	2:23–3:12	6:1–11	5:1–47
The twelve disciples are confirmed	10:2–4	3:13–19	6:12–16	
The Beatitudes (Blessed are the...)	5:1–12		6:17–26	
Jesus discusses the law	5:17–48		6:27–36	
Jesus discusses giving and prayer	6:1–8, 14–7:12		6:37–38	
Jesus teaches about heaven	7:13–29		6:43–49	
Jesus responds to a Roman centurion	8:5–13		7:1–10	
Jesus heals a widow's son			7:11–17	
Jesus responds to the doubts of John the Baptist	11:1–30		7:18–35	
Religious leaders express their doubts	12:22–45	3:20–30		
Jesus defines His true family	12:46–50	3:31–35	8:19–21	
Jesus teaches a series of kingdom parables	13:1–52	4:1–34	8:4–18	
Jesus stills a storm	8:23–27	4:35–41	8:22–25	
Jesus casts out legions of demons	8:28–34	5:1–20	8:26–39	
Jesus heals people of disease and death	9:18–34	5:21–43	8:40–56	
Jesus is rejected in His hometown: Nazareth	13:53–58	6:1–6	4:16–30	
Jesus commissions the ministry of the twelve disciples	9:35–10:42	6:7–13	9:1–6	
John the Baptist is beheaded	14:1–12	6:14–29	9:7–9	
Jesus feeds over 5,000 people by multiplying bread and fish	14:13–21	6:30–44	9:10–17	6:1–15
Jesus walks on water	14:22–36	6:45–56		6:16–21
Jesus claims to be the Bread of Life				6:22–71
Jesus explains true purity	15:1–20	7:1–23		7:1
Jesus casts out a demon	15:21–28	7:24–30		
Jesus miraculously multiplies fish and bread	15:29–39	8:1–10		
Religious leaders ask for a sign and the tension mounts	16:1–12	8:11–21		

	MATTHEW	MARK	LUKE	JOHN
Jesus heals a blind man		8:22–26		9:1–41
Peter confesses that Jesus is the Messiah	16:13–20	8:27–30	9:18–20	
Jesus predicts His death for the first time	16:21–28	8:31–9:1	9:21–27	
Jesus' transfiguration	17:1–13	9:2–13	9:28–36	
Jesus casts out a demon	17:14–21	9:14–29	9:37–43	
Jesus predicts His death a second time	17:22–23; 20:17–19	9:30–32	9:44–45	
Peter finds a coin in the fish's mouth and uses it to pay a temple tax	17:24–27			
Jesus warns against temptation	18:1–35	9:42–50	9:46–50	
Jesus and the cost of being a disciple	8:18–22; 19:1–2		9:51–62; 14:25–35	
Jesus teaches with authority at the temple and the controversy surrounding Him becomes heated				7:10–53
Jesus forgives a woman caught in adultery				8:1–11
Jesus speaks openly about Himself as deity and is almost stoned				8:12–59
Jesus explains Himself as the Good Shepherd				10:1–21
Jesus commissions seventy-two disciples			10:1–24	
Jesus tells the story of the Good Samaritan			10:25–37	
Jesus visits Mary and Martha			10:38–42	
Jesus teaches about prayer	6:9–13		11:1–13	
Jesus confronts religious leaders			11:14–54	
Jesus teaches some difficult and sobering parables			12:1–13:21	
Religious leaders threaten to stone Jesus				10:22–42
Jesus spends time healing and teaching			13:22–14:24	
Jesus tells parables about a lost coin, a lost sheep, and a lost son			15:1–32	

	MATTHEW	MARK	LUKE	JOHN
Jesus teaches His disciples within hearing distance of the Pharisees			16:1–17:10	
Jesus raises Lazarus, His friend, from the dead				11:1–44
Jesus heals ten lepers, but only one says thanks			17:11–19	
Jesus talks about the unexpected coming of the kingdom			17:20–37	
Jesus tells two parables about prayer			18:1–14	
Jesus teaches about marriage	19:3–12	10:2–12		
Jesus welcomes, honors, and blesses little children	19:13–15	10:13–16	18:15–17	
Jesus' conversation with the rich young man	19:16–20:16	10:17–31	18:18–30	
Jesus teaches about having a servant's heart	20:20–28	10:32–45	18:31–34	
Jesus heals the blind	20:29–34	10:46–52	18:35–43	
Zaccheus follows Jesus in faith			19:1–10	
The parable of the servants who invested the king's money			19:11–27	
Religious leaders begin to plan Jesus' assassination				11:45–57; 12:9–11
Jesus rides into Jerusalem to a cheering crowd	21:1–11, 14–17	11:1–11	19:28–44	12:12–19
Jesus curses a fig tree, and it quickly dies	21:18–19	11:12–14		
Jesus takes a stand in the temple again	21:12–13	11:15–19	19:45–48	
Jesus clarifies His mission even more boldly				12:20–50
Jesus talks about the power of prayer	21:20–22	11:20–26		
Jesus stumps the religious leaders	21:23–27	11:27–33	20:1–8	
Jesus tells more parables about the kingdom of God	21:28–22:14	12:1–12	20:9–19	
Jesus fields significant questions	22:15–40	12:13–34	20:20–40	

	MATTHEW	MARK	LUKE	JOHN
Jesus stumps the religious leaders again	22:41–46	12:35–37	20:41–44	
Jesus openly warns against the religious leaders	23:1–39	12:38–40	20:45–47	
A widow gives all she has, and Jesus teaches from her example		12:41–44	21:1–4	
Jesus talks with His disciples more about being ready for the events to come	24:1–25:1–51	13:1–37	21:5–38	
Religious leaders agree on the strategy for Jesus' arrest	26:1–5	14:1–2	22:1–2	
A woman anoints Jesus with expensive perfume	26:6–13	14:3–9	7:36–8:3	12:1–8
Judas makes the deal to betray Jesus	26:14–16	14:10–11	22:3–6	
Jesus and the disciples prepare for the Passover meal (an important Jewish celebration)	26:17–19	14:12–16	22:7–13	
Jesus humbles His disciples by taking the role of a servant and washing the disciples' feet (a custom of the day in light of the unpaved roads)				13:1–20
Jesus acknowledges Judas's plans to betray Him	26:20–25	14:17–21	22:21–30	13:21–30
Jesus and His disciples share "the Last Supper"	26:26–28	14:22–24	22:17–20	
Before they leave their last meal together, Jesus talks with His disciples about the future	26:29–30	14:25–26		13:31–14:31
Jesus foretells Peter's denial (which Peter, of course, denies)	26:31–35	14:27–31	22:31–38	
Jesus teaches about the Holy Spirit				15:1–16:33
Jesus agonizes in prayer	26:36–46	14:32–42	22:39–46	17:1–18:1
Jesus is betrayed by Judas and arrested	26:47–56	14:43–52	22:47–53	18:2–11
Jesus goes through a religious trial before Caiaphas	26:57, 59–68; 27:1	14:53, 55–65;15:1	22:54, 63–71	18:12–14, 19–24
Peter denies knowing Jesus	26:58, 69–75	14:54, 66–72	22:54–62	18:15–18, 25–27

	MATTHEW	MARK	LUKE	JOHN
*Judas kills himself	27:3–10			
Jesus' trial	27:2, 11–31	15:1–20	23:1–25	18:28–19:16
Jesus' execution hanging on a cross	27:31–56	15:20–41	23:26–49	19:16–37
Jesus' burial	27:57–66	15:42–47	23:50–56	19:38–42
Jesus' resurrection	28:1–15	16:1–11	24:1–12	20:1–18
Jesus appears to two believers on "the road to Emmaus"		16:12–13	24:13–35	
Jesus enters a room through locked doors to be with the disciples		16:14	24:36–43	20:19–23
Jesus confronts Thomas's doubts				20:24–31
Jesus cooks breakfast on the beach for the disciples				21:1–25
Jesus gives what we now call the "Great Commission"	28:16–20	16:15–18		
Jesus appears to the disciples one last time			24:44–49	Acts 1:3–8
Jesus returns to heaven		16:19–20	24:50–53	Acts 1:9–12

*Also recorded in Acts 1:18–19

ULTIMATE IMPACT OF AND ON CHRISTIANITY

The life of Jesus *is* the ultimate impact of and on Christianity. The work He came to do, His life, His death, His resurrection were God's ultimate act of sacrifice to establish a redemptive connection to His creation.

Jesus' life connected the before and after of the span of Christianity, the roots and the branches. He answered the call of the prophets. He propelled God's spirit into the world. He was the difference between God existing in the inner room of the temple and existing in the hearts of people.

JESUS DEITY

The fact that Jesus was mysteriously both God and human is the benchmark of Christianity. It is a subject that Christian scholars have spent generations, centuries even, examining. In the years to come the Roman Empire would rip back and forth against a

 SET THE STAGE!

Luke records this during the Crucifixion:

> By this time it was noon, and darkness fell across the whole land until three o'clock. The light from the sun was gone. And suddenly, the thick veil hanging in the Temple was torn apart. Then Jesus shouted, "Father, I entrust my spirit into your hands!" And with those words he breathed his last (Luke 23:44–46 NLT).

The veil that was torn in the temple was the veil between the Holy Place and the Holy of Holies. Since the days of the first tabernacle there had been an inner chamber where God's presence was to have dwelt. Only the high priest entered, and only once a year for a specific ceremony. The priest who entered even entered with twine tied to one leg so that should he die in the face of God's holiness he could be dragged out of the chamber without anyone else having to enter.

Jesus' death on the cross accomplished a monumental thing. It destroyed the boundary between God's presence and God's people. The veil ripped. A divine act. A powerful image of what had been accomplished.

variety of views regarding Jesus' deity. Settling this issue (as the Catholic Church was established) was a huge claim for the body of Christ to stake. Jesus was the first to lay the foundation, though. It was the one sticking point for Him. "Who do people say that I am?" He asked the disciples. "Who do you say that I am?" He asked further. Jesus' claim to deity was the crux of His mission: God giving His life for the life of His creation. In order for His followers to understand the kingdom He was establishing, they had to understand who He was.

JESUS' LIFE AND WORK

Jesus' ministry is the foundation of the church. While the institution of the Christian church has often floundered and even failed in its goal to administer Christ's work, it is that work as recorded in the New Testament that the church returns to again and again to find its way home.

Jesus lived a life that was radical and yet gentle. He turned morality on its ear by appealing not only to our actions but to our intentions. He pointed humanity to God in a way that had never been done before. He remained apart from the popular religious culture of His day and yet affected it deeply enough to be considered a fatal threat.

Jesus maintained a role in His historical setting that was balanced between action and reflection, resistance and submission. He was a Renaissance man before the Renaissance even gave us the cultural subreference. He ignored the bigotry of His society in regard to gender and race. He rose above the status quo in a way that seemed to risk His very mission, by rejecting the hollowed-out religion of His people. Jesus was in no way politically correct for His day and time. While He remained sinless, He disregarded merely religious mores, calling His followers to a life of freedom that was bred from higher standards of love and purity than they had ever been held to previously.

JESUS' WORDS

Certainly not all of Jesus' words were recorded for us. Wouldn't it be wonderfully enlightening to hear His casual conversations with people along the way? But the words that were recorded in the Gospels are a mainstay of Christian history. They have been memorized, marked in red, twisted, and reclaimed over and over. We don't understand them all, but they are what we return to, seeking God's direction, as we carry on the work of His Son.

JESUS' RESURRECTION

The resurrection of Jesus Christ was an act of God. It was a victory of life over death, both physically and spiritually. It was the ultimate of victories, an expression of the power of God that reigns supreme over every other event. That God would even come into the world requires an act of faith beyond easy description. That God would deliberately reverse the effects of evil in the world, with the promise of that reversal finding an eternal existence, requires an act of faith that can only be supplied by God Himself.

One of the greatest testimonies to the truth of the resurrection is the transformation in the lives of Jesus' followers. A ragtag group hiding in a hidden room transformed into a dream team of spiritual activists, some even martyrs. Men who doubted, who denied, who ran away, who hid, found the strength to face mobs, kings, cultures, and creeds with a message of which they were so sure, they wagered their eternal existence on it.

The resurrection of Jesus laid the foundation for the coming of the Holy Spirit, God indwelling not a temple built by worshipers, but the temple within His worshipers. From that perspective Christianity made the attempt to organize and infiltrate the world. The rest of this book describes the path of God's people as they tried and failed and tried again even into this day and age.

CHAPTER THREE

The Early Church
(from Pentecost to A.D. 300)

When Jesus came to the region of Caesarea Philippi, he asked his disciples, "Who do people say that the Son of Man is?"

"Well," they replied, "some say John the Baptist, some say Elijah, and others say Jeremiah or one of the other prophets."

Then he asked them, "Who do you say I am?"

Simon Peter answered, "You are the Messiah, the Son of the living God."

Jesus replied, "You are blessed, Simon son of John, because my Father in heaven has revealed this to you. You did not learn this from any human being. Now I say to you that you are Peter, and upon this rock I will build my church, and all the powers of hell will not conquer it.

MATTHEW 16:13–18 NLT

Jesus came and told his disciples, "I have been given complete authority in heaven and on earth. Therefore, go and make disciples of all the nations, baptizing them in the name of the Father and the Son and the Holy Spirit. Teach these new disciples to obey all the commands I have given you. And be sure of this: I am with you always, even to the end of the age."

MATTHEW 28:18–20 NLT

On the day of Pentecost, seven weeks after Jesus' resurrection, the believers were meeting together in one place. Suddenly, there was a sound from heaven like the roaring of a mighty windstorm in the skies above them, and it filled the house where they were meeting. Then, what looked like flames or tongues of fire appeared and settled on each of them. And everyone present was filled with the Holy Spirit and began speaking in other languages, as the Holy Spirit gave them this ability.

Godly Jews from many nations were living in Jerusalem at that time. When they heard this sound, they came running to see what it was all about, and they were bewildered to hear their own languages being spoken by the believers.

They were beside themselves with wonder. "How can this be?" they exclaimed. "These people are all from Galilee, and yet we hear them speaking the languages of the lands where we were born! Here we are—Parthians, Medes, Elamites, people from Mesopotamia, Judea, Cappadocia, Pontus, the province of Asia, Phrygia, Pamphylia, Egypt, and the areas of Libya toward Cyrene, visitors from Rome (both Jews and converts to Judaism), Cretans, and Arabians. And we all hear these people speaking in our own languages about the wonderful things God has done!" They stood there amazed and perplexed. "What can this mean?" they asked each other....

Peter replied, "Each of you must turn from your sins and turn to God, and be baptized in the name of Jesus Christ for the forgiveness of your sins. Then you will receive the gift of the Holy Spirit. This promise is to you and to your children, and even to the Gentiles—all who have been called by the Lord our God." Then Peter continued preaching for a long time, strongly urging all his listeners, "Save yourselves from this generation that has gone astray!"

Those who believed what Peter said were baptized and added to the church—about three thousand in all. They joined with the other believers and devoted themselves to the apostles' teaching and fellowship, sharing in the Lord's Supper and in prayer.

TIMELINE OVERVIEW

In the midst of world history...

Christian history unfolds...

c. 30 Pentecost—Believers begin to organize and evangelize.

31 Stephen is martyred in view of Saul of Tarsus (who later becomes Paul, the Apostle).

32 Saul is converted.

37 Rome: Emperor Tiberius is succeeded by Caligula.
Judea: Herod Agrippa becomes king of northern Palestine.

41 Rome: Caligula is assassinated; Claudius becomes emperor.

41 James, brother of John, son of Zebedee, is murdered by order of Herod Agrippa I, king of Palestine.

48 Paul's first missionary journey begins.

54 Rome: Claudius is assassinated, and Nero succeeds him to the Roman throne.

58 Buddhism is introduced in China.

62 James, Jesus' brother, is killed by command of the Jewish high priest.

64 The great fire destroys parts of Rome.

64 Persecution begins by Nero.

c. 65 Mark's Gospel is written.

66 Jews revolt against the Romans (until 70), refusing to make sacrifices to the emperor.

67 Death of the apostle Paul

69 Year of the four emperors in Rome. Vespasian is the last.

70 Titus (Vespasian's son) destroys Jerusalem.

c. 70 Destruction of Jerusalem by the Romans
"Christian" and "Jew" become mutually exclusive terms.
Matthew's Gospel is written.
End of the Apostolic Age

c. 75 Luke's Gospel is written.

79 Rome: Mt. Vesuvius erupts, burying Pompeii and Herculaneum under ash.

81 Rome: Emperor Titus is succeeded by Domitian.

90 Greece: Birth of Ptolemy, astronomer and mapmaker

97 Rome: Trajan becomes emperor (last period of Roman expansion).

c. 95 The Gospel of John and Revelation are written.

101–117 The Roman Empire at its zenith

132 The Jews fail in rebelling against the Romans. They are dispersed from Judea in what is known as the Diaspora (135).

135 Judea: The Romans drive the Jews out of Jerusalem and rename the area Palestine (referring back to the Philistines who once lived there).

c. 150 Justin Martyr writes his *Apology*.

177 Irenaeus, Bishop of Lyons, battles Gnosticism with *Against Heresies*.

185 Origen surfaces with *Against Celsus* and *On First Principles*.

200 Tertullian writes and speaks in Latin in defense of Christianity, including his famous *Apologeticum*.

250 Rome: Emperor Decius makes emperor worship required by law.

250 Systematic persecution of Christians is started by emperor Decius.

251 Cyprian, bishop of Carthage, surfaces with *On the Unity of the Church*.

286 Emperor Diocletian divides the empire in two and rules the Eastern half, giving Maximian the Western Empire.

290 By this time most large cities of the empire had received some testimony to the gospel.

296 Persia fights with Rome, surrenders Mesopotamia.

303 Diocletian orders persecution, bans Christians from public service, destroys churches and Christian books.

303 Last of the great persecutions begun by Diocletian.

A deep sense of awe came over them all, and the apostles performed many miraculous signs and wonders. And all the believers met together constantly and shared everything they had. They sold their possessions and shared the proceeds with those in need. They worshiped together at the Temple each day, met in homes for the Lord's Supper, and shared their meals with great joy and generosity—all the while praising God and enjoying the goodwill of all the people. And each day the Lord added to their group those who were being saved.

ACTS 2:1–12; 38–47 NLT

It was there at Antioch that the believers were first called Christians.

ACTS 11:26 NLT

UNDERSTANDING THE TIMES

From the perspective of faith, these times were exciting and bewildering. You could walk down the dirt road and pass a new Christian who knew about and understood the work of Christ, who had been there at Pentecost and was totally up on what God had done in the world. By the same token, you could pass someone who had heard of Jesus but hadn't heard the news of His crucifixion or resurrection or of the coming of the Holy Spirit.

Had there been international satellites and an ancient CNN, the spread of the news would have been instantaneous. As it was, the news spread faster than imaginable, but in clusters, not waves.

This huge thing had happened, but in stages and in regions of the country. It was as if they would have had to ask each other, "Okay, how much have you heard? Have you gotten the latest?"

While Apollos was in Corinth, Paul traveled through the interior provinces. Finally, he came to Ephesus, where he found several believers. "Did you receive the Holy Spirit when you believed?" he asked them.

"No," they replied, "we don't know what you mean. We haven't even heard that there is a Holy Spirit."

"Then what baptism did you experience?" he asked.

And they replied, "The baptism of John."

Paul said, "John's baptism was to demonstrate a desire to turn from sin and turn to God. John himself told the people to believe in Jesus, the one John said would come later."

As soon as they heard this, they were baptized in the name of the Lord Jesus. Then when Paul laid his hands on them, the Holy Spirit came on them, and they spoke in other tongues and prophesied. There were about twelve men in all.

ACTS 19:1–7 NLT

 SET THE STAGE!

According to Peter, the events of Pentecost listed in Acts were the fulfillment of this prophecy:

" 'In the last days, God said, I will pour out my Spirit upon all people. Your sons and daughters will prophesy, your young men will see visions, and your old men will dream dreams. In those days I will pour out my Spirit upon all my servants, men and women alike, and they will prophesy. And I will cause wonders in the heavens above and signs on the earth below—blood and fire and clouds of smoke. The sun will be turned into darkness, and the moon will turn bloodred, before that great and glorious day of the Lord arrives. And anyone who calls on the name of the Lord will be saved.' "

ACTS 2:17–21 NLT

In twelve to sixteen months of ministry, what God accomplished through Jesus had changed the face of faith. Suddenly God's children came to Him not through a bloodline, but through faith in Christ's work. The rites and traditions of the Jewish faith were fulfilled in Christ. Besides that, the message needed to go out. There was a missionary zeal that was beyond urgent, and whose power is felt even today.

In terms of the Roman Empire, life felt much the same. Pax Romana (the Roman Peace) was still in place, which facilitated missionaries' journeys. The land of the Jews was still occupied by the Romans. There was still a strong Greek influence. But in the middle of all that, a message of truth was infiltrating the business of the world. The path of that message is what the rest of this book is all about.

THE STORY OF THE TIMES

The earliest days of the Christian church are recorded in the book of Acts.

There were seven weeks from Jesus' resurrection to the day of Pentecost. During forty days of that seven weeks, Jesus spent some time with the disciples. According to the first chapter of Acts, Jesus appeared to His disciples, teaching them about the kingdom of God. Evidently they still questioned whether He was going to bring a political victory to the Jews right then or later. Can you imagine their position? It seemed they had lost their friend, their teacher, their savior. Then He was back among them, but only sometimes popping in and out. It must have been an unusual situation. "Jesus sightings" must have been the hot topic of conversation. Since the disciples couldn't know at that time exactly how things were going to play out, they didn't know what might be coming next—an army? Another trial?

During His time with His friends, Jesus taught them not only about the kingdom of God, but also about the coming of the Holy Spirit. He also prepared the disciples, also referred to as the apostles, for their role in carrying on His ministry. He warned them specifically not to leave Jerusalem until the Holy Spirit arrived.

THE FEAST OF PENTECOST
The Day of Pentecost was the day it all happened. The word Pentecost comes from the Greek meaning "the fiftieth day." It was the Feast of Weeks, or Harvest, or Firstfruits. It always fell

SET THE STAGE!

Throughout the history of the church there has been discussion, dissension, and disillusionment about this issue of speaking in tongues. The information we are given in the text of Acts 2 is that people spoke miraculously in languages that they had no previous ability to speak, and that foreigners could hear the words spoken in their own vernacular. Since then the act of "speaking in tongues" has been portrayed in two categories. The first is most often called "glossalalia," or "ecstatic utterances." It includes not necessarily a language that any of us would recognize. Some call it a prayer language. (Some skeptics call it merely a trained response.)

Another view is the sudden miraculous ability to speak a foreign language. Some define the gift of tongues as a general skill at languages.

Paul gave instructions in regard to the use of "tongues" in church services. The rule of thumb was clarity and not confusion. In denominations that embrace tongues-speaking as a welcomed gift, often an understandable interpretation is necessary to validate the "prophecy" as from God.

Many denominations hold to the view that tongues is a gift that passed away. "Love never fails. But where there are prophecies, they will cease; where there are tongues, they will be stilled; where there is knowledge, it will pass away" (1 CORINTHIANS 13:8 NIV) Others include tongues-speaking as a valid part of their service of worship. Many settle for some middle ground such as redefining the gift as "creative communication."

on the fiftieth day after the Passover feast. Corn was the last Palestinian crop to ripen. The dedication of that crop was the focus and origin of this festival. As the years passed, it also became commemorative of God's giving of the Mosaic Law. But it was the events of the first Pentecost celebrated after Jesus' resurrection and ascension that gave the holiday a significance to the whole Christian world.

WHAT WE KNOW AS PENTECOST

Typically when modern Christians think of the day of Pentecost we don't think of corn harvests or of the Passover. We think of the Holy Spirit. On that first day of Pentecost after Jesus'

SINNERS AND SAINTS

STEPHEN

As the early church organized, they elected seven men to care for the widows of the community. Among those seven elected was Stephen, a man full of "Spirit and wisdom." Stephen was particularly gifted and knowledgeable. He was able to work "wonders."

Stephen debated with Jews as to whether Christ was the Messiah. He was very convincing. When his sparring partners could not win the argument, they instead hired people to lie about Stephen, misquoting him regarding the temple. The temple was a hot button of that day. It was a money-maker for one thing. Talking about the temple being torn down was like talking about tearing down the stadium in a town that builds most of its income on a football team. Besides that, the spiritual implication of a person talking against the temple in any less than a reverent way was overwhelming for that culture. Stephen quoted Jesus as saying, "You can tear down this temple, but in three days I'll rebuild it." Jesus, of course, was referring to Himself. The men who plotted against Stephen twisted these words to stir up the crowd.

After the false accusations, Stephen stood before the council defending his Christian beliefs. Because he stood firm in his belief that Jesus was God in the flesh, Stephen was stoned to death.

---

ascension, a group of believers, including the apostles, were gathered in a house in Jerusalem. They consistently spent time praying together. We aren't given any indication that this meeting was an unusual event. It was their regular habit.

Then suddenly a roar happened. It must have been around nine A.M. It sounded like a windstorm. It filled the house. There were visual effects as well. What looked like flames settled on each person as they were each given the ability to speak other languages.

The roar that filled the house could be heard elsewhere because other Jews in Jerusalem began to gather at the house to see what the hubbub was all about. Evidently what shocked these Jews the most was that they were hearing their native languages spoken. If you can imagine, it was like United Nations meetings where a person talks, but what each of the delegates hears in their earphones is an interpretation of what's being said into their own language. This was like that but no earphones were necessary.

It must have been a wild scene because some of the people looking on thought the believers were drunk. Peter's response was that it was way too early in the morning to be drunk (some logic stays with us). He explained the miracle as God pouring out His Spirit, just as the Old Testament prophet Joel had predicted and just as Jesus had foretold.

PETER'S STAND

At the miracle of Pentecost, Peter stepped up to the plate to explain to his world the phenomenon of Jesus' resurrection and the coming of the Holy Spirit. This is the same Peter who denied Jesus ten weeks earlier (Mark 14), then was commissioned by Jesus to take care of His sheep (John 21).

Peter stood with the other apostles. He referred to Old Testament prophecy, as well as the great King David. His hearers asked a typically human question, "If all this is true, what are we supposed to do about it?" Peter's answer was clear: "Repent [turn away from your sin] and be baptized." That day three thousand people were added to the number of Nazarenes, or Christians, that gathered in Jerusalem.

ORGANIZING FOR MINISTRY

The next step was figuring out the worship practices of this new sect, or group. Before His death Jesus had commissioned the disciples to remember Him through Communion, the ceremonial breaking of the bread and wine. He had also commissioned them to do the same kinds of things He did: miracles, wonders, healings. These early believers even entered into some kind of communal living where they shared all their belongings.

Understand that these people didn't have a concept of when Jesus would return. During the forty days after His resurrection, Jesus had popped in and out of their lives. The Holy Spirit had arrived, but they still had the promise of Jesus returning one day. Understand that these people weren't sitting down in a dry business meeting deciding what bylaws to pass on to two thousand years of worshipers. Instead, they were suddenly experiencing God's presence with them, inside of them, empowering them.

In the midst of understanding this new way of experiencing God's presence, the early church members were deciding how to continue Jesus' work until He returned from wherever He was. They started with the last things He told them. They organized into ministry teams to take care of widows and orphans, to teach the believers, and to evangelize those who hadn't heard. They did much the same things that churches do today. They were a growing religious movement, deliberately organizing to get the word out and honor God with their lives as individuals and as communities. It is from this strategy that the next crucial forty years of ministry poured out.

THE GOSPELS

The first four books of the New Testament are the Gospels credited to Matthew, Mark, Luke, and John. Luke then wrote Acts as a follow-up to his Gospel. The Gospels were not written immediately following Christ's death. They weren't the primers for these earliest Christians. These early Christians had the Old Testament law and prophets, the verbal stories of Jesus' work, and the eyewitness of the apostles who had been with Jesus. The Gospels were written between A.D. 65 and 95 while Christian history was being made. You can imagine that the writings were probably gobbled up, copied by hand, passed around.

Suddenly there were actual writings to return to, to meditate on. When the early church leaders asked themselves the question,

"What would Jesus do?" (which they certainly must have asked), they had a record to return to for answers.

SINNERS AND SAINTS
CALIGULUS CAESAR

At the point of Paul's conversion, the Roman emperor was Caligulus Caesar. Caligula, as he is commonly known, was named as successor to the throne by his uncle, Tiberius Caesar, and began his reign after the death of Tiberius in A.D. 37, during the days of the early church.

Caligula was prone to murderous rages and insane whims and was perhaps the least well liked of all Roman emperors. Within one year of assuming office, he had nearly bankrupted the once rich Roman treasury. He made his horse a Roman senator. He caused riots when he tried to have a statue of himself erected in the temple of Jerusalem. He also performed many other acts too heinous to be mentioned here. Thankfully, his rule was brief. He was assassinated in A.D. 41. His death adds an appropriately macabre footnote to an already bizarre life. It is said that he screamed out to one of his attackers: "Strike me again, for I still live."

ARE WE JEWS OR ARE WE NOT?

The early church was a religious movement that sprang out of the Jewish religion. Some referred to the followers of this new movement as the "Nazarenes." Other's referred to the movement as "the Way." The Sanhedrin had consistent problems with the movement because it gradually stepped farther and farther away from the practices of Judaism. While at first the movement was a sect of Jewish worshipers, they gradually became a group unto themselves.

You can understand why the Sanhedrin was unsupportive when you remember that it was the Sanhedrin that put Jesus on trial and saw Him executed. It would have been maddening that even after Jesus' death His following grew. Worse even that Jesus' followers might depart from Jewish tradition.

For a time the Jewish leadership worked to incorporate the new believers into their faith. They asked them to be circumcised (now there's a test of commitment) and to adhere to Jewish religious laws. The problem was this: The good news of Jesus was that our connection with God was won through our faith in His sacrifice, not through our hard work. This was a hot button issue of the day and continued to be for quite some time.

SAUL OF TARSUS, THEN PAUL THE APOSTLE

One of the most influential members of the New Testament church was Paul. Paul was considered an apostle even though he did not become a disciple of Christ until after Pentecost.

SINNERS AND SAINTS
CLAUDIUS

Claudius reigned as emperor of Rome when Paul left for his first missionary journey. He ruled from A.D. 41 to 54. His family, ashamed that he stuttered and had a partially disabled leg, kept him hidden from the public in his younger years. Claudius used the time to study and became a well-educated man. He ordered the Roman army to conquer Britain and made Thrace (now the Balkan peninsula) a Roman state in A.D. 46. Under Claudius, many great public works and building projects were accomplished. He was known as having a weakness for women, having been married several times and having given much political power to his "secretaries" (most of whom were former slaves of his). It is believed that his last wife poisoned him.

BREAKING NEWS

THE LYSTRA TRIBUNAL WEEKLY

PAUL GETS STONED

It was a grisly scene here in Lystra last week as a crowd of stone-toting heathens viciously attacked a visiting missionary of the Christian movement (also called "the Way") and left him for dead outside the city.

Ironically, the missionary, Paul Saulus, had once been an enemy of the same movement for which he nearly gave his life last week, at one point having earned the nickname "Saul the Persecutor" for his harsh treatment of Christians. After the death and miraculous resurrection of Jesus of Nazareth, the renegade rabbi who founded the new church, Saul became one of the movement's biggest champions and, from a home base in Jerusalem, set out on the road to spread the word.

Reportedly he hit his first bump in that road when he and his associate Barnabas entered Lystra. The pagans there began to offer sacrifices to the missionaries, which, while a touching display of good intent, ran drastically counter to Paul's reason for being there.

As Paul was trying to stop the sacrifices and get his point across, a group of Jews from Antioch and Iconium (a notoriously anti-Christian bunch) took advantage of the misunderstanding to stir up the crowd against the missionaries. The mob then stoned Paul and dumped his seemingly lifeless body outside the city limits.

Incredibly, Paul survived to walk back into the city and leave the next day for Derbe.

Time will tell whether or not the Christian movement lasts, but this reporter, at least, can't help but be impressed by their chutzpah and "love thy neighbor" attitude.

Emmanuel Khan

Paul (who previously was known as Saul of Tarsus, persecutor of Christians) was confronted by Christ on a road. Christ asked, "Why are you persecuting Me?"

This was a turning point in Paul's life from which he never recovered. Previous to this moment Paul had been an avid persecutor of Christians. He was present at the stoning of Stephen; in fact, Stephen's clothes were laid at Paul's feet. When Paul faced Christ's accusations, he was struck blind until a man named Ananias came to minister to him.

Because Paul had been such a ringleader in the oppression of the Christian faith, the early church leaders were hesitant to take him into their confidence. What if he was faking his conversion in order to go "under cover" to find more Christians to imprison and kill? But in Jerusalem a man named Barnabas (who later traveled with Paul in the missionary journeys) helped Paul find his way into the trust of the apostles and the early church.

The church was amazed at Paul. First they knew him as a man who would do anything to suppress the heresy he considered Christianity to be. Then he became a man who took it upon himself to convince everyone that Jesus was the Christ. Goes to show what a personal encounter with the God of the universe will accomplish in a stubborn human heart.

PETER'S MINISTRY

Some of you are saying, "I am a follower of Paul." Others are saying, "I follow Apollos," or "I follow Peter," or "I follow only Christ." Can Christ be divided into pieces?
1 CORINTHIANS 1:12–13 NLT

Peter and Paul were both leaders in the early church. Peter's role is spoken of less as Paul ascends to the role of front man for the message of the gospel, but not before Peter plays a huge role in the foundation of the church.

After Peter took his stand on the day of Pentecost, he remained in leadership with the other apostles. He and John healed the lame man (Acts 3:7). Peter facilitated the exposure of Ananias

SINNERS AND SAINTS
BARNABAS

Barnabas's name meant, loosely, "encourager." It fit him well.

The New Testament gives us several snapshots of Barnabas. When Paul first came to faith, the early Christians were afraid of him and understandably so! Weeks earlier, Paul had been on a rampage against the faith. Now suddenly he was on board? It was Barnabas who represented Paul to those first believers and asked them to give him a chance.

Barnabas then became a coworker with Paul. At first the Bible talks about "Barnabas and Paul," but soon Paul rose in leadership and they were referred to as "Paul and Barnabas." From what we know about Barnabas, he was the generous kind of man who could put his ego aside and put ministry first on the priority list when someone else might have been more petty about it.

Before the second missionary journey, Paul and Barnabas had a conflict so intense that they stopped traveling together. The conflict centered around Barnabas's desire to give John Mark a second chance (Mark had deserted them in their first journey) and take him along. Paul partnered with Silas instead and left Barnabas to deal with John Mark. Evidently Barnabas made a good investment. In Paul's later writings he refers to John Mark as his associate.

Paul's letter to the Galatians reveals one more snapshot of Barnabas. Paul complained that Peter had been inconsistent in his commitment that the Gentile converts to Christianity didn't need to adhere to Jewish laws. In Galatians 2 he writes that "even Barnabas" had been affected by Peter's mistake. What a compliment, in an odd sort of way. "Even Barnabas." As if Barnabas was the *last* person that Paul would have expected to make a mistake.

SET THE STAGE!

By the end of the first century A.D., many Romans had grown tired of the highly codified paganism of the empire, which was mostly based on ritual and bribery to obtain favorable treatment from a large pantheon of gods. The Roman gods were generally seen as aloof or indifferent toward people. This helped to open the way for Christianity, which stressed an emotional relationship with one God who was not aloof but instead loved believers as His children and offered eternal life in exchange for faith-based obedience.

and Sapphira, who lied to the fellowship about some land they had sold (Acts 5). He represented the apostles at their arraignment before the Sanhedrin (Acts 5). Peter traveled to Samaria with John and there confronted Simon (Acts 8). He also toured Judea, raising Dorcas from the dead (Acts 9).

A major turning point in Peter's ministry came through a vision he experienced while he was in Joppa. In this vision, God released him from the Jewish requirements in regards to clean and unclean foods and commissioned him to minister to Gentiles (Acts 10). This was a major shift for Peter traditionally and caused him a great deal of conflict with the traditional Jewish leaders (Acts 11).

Paul mentioned Peter twice in his letters. In the letter to the Galatians, Paul describes a confrontation he had with Peter because Peter had allegedly backed down from his stance in support of the Gentile believers. Paul also mentioned Peter in his first letter to the Corinthians in a reference to the early church leaders including their wives in their ministry travels.

PETER'S ENDURANCE

Peter miraculously escaped prison during the persecution by Agrippa I in A.D. 44 (Acts 12). After that he began to recede from the forefront in the story of the early church as recorded in Acts. Peter is last mentioned in the account of the Council of Jerusalem where he spoke as a champion for the freedom of the Gentile believers.

Peter's final presence in the New Testament is found in the

two letters he wrote from Rome to the believers in Asia Minor (what is now Turkey). Tradition holds that Peter went to Rome shortly after Paul's first imprisonment there and eventually died a martyr at the hand of Nero. (See John 21:18–19.)

SINNERS AND SAINTS
SILAS

Silas was a prominent player in the early church movement. He traveled with Paul and Barnabas to deliver the official statement of the Jerusalem Council regarding the lifestyle practices of Gentile believers. Silas later traveled with Paul on the second missionary journey. In their journeys, Silas shared in beatings and imprisonments with Paul, as well as in church leadership. While Paul is the upfront guy, Silas was a big part of the early church movement.

THE ACTS OF THE MISSIONARIES
Over the last half of the book, Acts concentrates primarily on the missionary efforts fronted by Paul and a few other early church leaders, including Luke, the writer of Acts. Jesus had commissioned the apostles to spread the good news:

> But when the Holy Spirit has come upon you, you will receive power and will tell people about me everywhere—in Jerusalem, throughout Judea, in Samaria, and to the ends of the earth."
>
> ACTS 1:8 NLT

The first part of Acts records the spread of the gospel through Judea and Samaria to the Jewish and near-Jewish constituency. This last portion of Acts reveals the fulfillment of the "ends of the earth." The Word traveled to the world outside of Judaism: the Gentiles.

The church at Antioch was a large church. It was also the first

Gentile church. In Acts 13 the church at Antioch commissioned Barnabas and Saul as missionaries to the Gentiles, sending them off on their first journey.

THE MISSIONARY TEAM #1

Paul's first trek was to the island of Cyprus and the main cities of Galatia. Previous to this journey, Paul had been referred to only as Saul. At the beginning of this trip, though, Paul confronted a sorcerer named Elymas. From the point of this confrontation, the name Paul was used rather than Saul. It was also from this point on that Paul was considered the leader of the journey.

Paul and Barnabas left for this trip with a young man named Mark. Mark left the troupe mid-task evidently against Paul's wishes. The rest of the journey was spent in the cities of Galatia. In Pisidian Antioch, missionary efforts started as a synagogue sermon, Paul's first sermon recorded in Acts. Quickly the impact was felt more in the Gentile believing community, which made the Jewish subculture very uncomfortable and eventually led to the Jerusalem Council.

THE COUNCIL AT JERUSALEM

Before the Christian church had separated out from the Jewish religion, there was quite a pull and tug regarding what traditions mattered to this new way of looking at faith. Acts 15 describes what we now refer to as the Jerusalem Council.

In Antioch some men were teaching that circumcision was necessary for salvation. This was (obviously) at a time when circumcision was not the standard practice for all baby boys. In fact, circumcision was one of the things that set the Jews apart from other cultures. (It was one of the identifying practices that God established with Abraham when the Jewish nation was only a fading gleam in Abraham's aged eye.) Paul and Barnabas debated these men in Antioch, then took it one step further—Jerusalem.

This issue, basically whether becoming a Christian meant converting to Judaism, had to be settled. It was key to the spread of the good news of Jesus' work. In Jerusalem, Paul and Barnabas met with the apostles and elders. Their opposition was the

Pharisees whose political power depended on new believers adhering to their decisions. After much deliberation, Peter took the stand that God had granted the Holy Spirit to both Jews and Gentiles. If God didn't have a problem with Gentiles having faith without becoming Jews, who were the Jews to argue?

The Council wrote a letter to the new Gentile believers. The letter suggested these lifestyle requirements:

1. Abstain from food sacrificed to idols.

2. Abstain from blood.

3. Abstain from the meat of strangled animals.

4. Abstain from sexual immorality.

◄─────────────────────────────────●

BREAKING NEWS

THE OLDE TIMES

MISSIONARY JAILBIRDS

Paul, the famed Christian missionary, and his traveling companion, Silas, were imprisoned this week in the Roman colony Philippi. According to reports from various sources, the men were thrown in jail for a form of disturbing the peace. They were then beaten and placed in the high security ward, but they were not held against their will for long.

A mysterious earthquake shook the prison doors loose but, unbelievable as it may seem, the prisoners remained in their cells. The next morning the jailer was left to his duties as if nothing had happened.

Avis Libertus

●─────────────────────────────────►

Paul, Barnabas, and some others delivered the letter to Antioch, and the Christians there were grateful. Not a winning blow for the Pharisees.

CHANGING SALVATION

Understand the phenomenal change that had taken place. Until the work of Christ, being a child of God had mostly to do with Jewish lineage. Jews were raised to be God's children. That didn't mean that faith had no place. God counted Abraham as righteous because of his faith (Genesis 15:6). It didn't mean that obedience was unimportant. If the Old Testament stressed anything it was obedience—not just ceremonial obedience, but heartfelt obedience.

Nevertheless, don't underestimate the change that was being made here or the leap that these people were having to take. Suddenly God was saying a new thing. He was saying, "My children are born through faith. I've paid the price for their adoption and everyone willing is welcome."

This would have been unsettling to a people whose whole social, religious, and political structure was based on a certain pattern of relationship based on an obedience evidenced by ritual. It took the wonders and the signs that the apostles witnessed to enable them to embrace this new way of thinking.

MISSIONARY TEAM #2 BECOMES TWO TEAMS

When Paul and Barnabas prepared for their next journey, the one team separated into two. Remember John Mark, who abandoned the first trip? Barnabas, true to his encouraging nature, wanted to take John Mark again. Paul disagreed. Because of that, what would have been one trip doubled. Barnabas and John Mark traveled back to Cyprus. Paul joined efforts with Silas and revisited the congregation already founded in Galatia. Paul then added one more member, Timothy, and traveled into Europe to Philippi in Macedonia. Paul may have actually added another member at this point because Luke's narrative in Acts changes to a first person "we" rather than a third person "they."

From Macedonia, Paul and the troupe traveled to Thessalonica where Paul left Timothy and Silas behind to minister while he traveled on to Athens. After a disappointing time in Athens, Paul made a final leg to Corinth. It was there that he first met his two good friends Aquila and Priscilla. It was also there that

SINNERS AND SAINTS

NERO

Nero is remembered today as a cruel and crazy ruler. In fact, many authorities believe that Petronius wrote the first Roman literary novel, the *Satyricon,* as a spoof on Nero's later outlandish behavior. The first years of Nero's rule were quite peaceful, though. He became the emperor in A.D. 54. It was during this early portion of his reign that Paul was brought to him the first time and released.

Nero was born Lucius Domitius Ahenobarbus (think he got teased in school?) and was also called Nero Claudius Caesar Drusus Germanicus (by those with sufficient lung capacity). The great-great-grandson of Augustus, Nero was the last descendant of the house of Caesar to rule as emperor of Rome. Nero's father died when he was young. His mother (Agrippina the Younger, sister of Caligula) married her uncle Claudius, who was emperor at the time. Claudius adopted Nero as his eldest son (and, thus, heir), and Nero married Claudius's daughter Octavia, who was his stepsister as well as his cousin.

Within a year of Nero's being named successor to the throne, Claudius died mysteriously, which made the teenaged Nero the most powerful man in the world. (Many believed Nero's mother had poisoned Claudius so that her son could become emperor.) Nero, who had been having an affair with his mother, had Agrippina murdered in A.D. 59 after several unsuccessful previous attempts. A suspicious and paranoid man, Nero trusted no one and killed almost anyone he believed was less than completely loyal. In 62, he lost his two political advisors, one to death and the other to retirement. Then he ordered his tutor, the well-known author Seneca, to commit suicide. He divorced Octavia, had her killed, and then married Poppea Sabina. When his second wife, pregnant and tired after a day at the

Continued

SINNERS AND SAINTS (CONTINUED)

races, complained a bit too much, he kicked her to death. He ordered the execution of Roman senators who questioned his actions.

Many blamed him for the fire that destroyed much of Rome in A.D. 64. A coup attempt by powerful aristocrats failed, which led to more executions in A.D. 65. Nero protested his innocence, blaming Christians for the fire, and began a relentless persecution of members of the early church. He ordered the death and torture of many Christians and had some of them fed to wild animals for public entertainment. Thus began a cruel period of persecution. Tacitus, a secular historian, writes, "Their death was made a matter of sport; they were covered in wild beasts' skins and torn to pieces by dogs or were fastened to crosses and set on fire in order to serve as torches. . . ." The apostles Peter and Paul were martyrs during Nero's persecution.

In A.D. 68, military commanders from many Roman provinces, fed up with Nero's paranoid behavior and fearful of his cruelty and unpredictability, revolted. Nero committed suicide in A.D. 68 after some of his enemies falsely convinced him he had been sentenced to die. He was just thirty-one years old.

Despite being a homicidal maniac (which, considering his upbringing and family history, came as no surprise to some), Nero was a great appreciator of the arts. He was a poet, an actor, and an accomplished musician. Legend portrays him as having played the fiddle as Rome burned (his instrument of choice was actually more like a harp). His last words are purported to have been: "Alas, what an artist is dying in me."

Silas and Timothy caught up to him with news of the church at Thessalonica. Within a few months, Paul had written the two letters that we know as 1 and 2 Thessalonians to straighten out some misunderstanding among that church about the second coming of Christ. Paul may have written his letter to the Galatians during his stay there.

After a journey back home through Ephesus and Jerusalem, Paul landed once again in Antioch.

MISSIONARY TEAM #3

When Paul left Antioch for what we refer to as the third missionary journey, it was for an extended stay. Paul returned to Ephesus and stayed over two years growing the church there. At first Paul ministered through the synagogue. Soon he established a more independent kind of ministry teaching at the school of Tyrannus for about two years. Ephesus was a trade center, so the teaching and ministry of Paul could spread from there to the far reaches of the empire.

While Paul was in Ephesus, he received disturbing news from the church in Corinth. In response, he wrote a letter to the church there that is now lost, as well as the letters we know as 1 and 2 Corinthians. Paul then finished out his return trip by spending time first in Macedonia and then in Corinth. From Corinth he wrote a letter to the Roman Christians, laying a foundation of teaching preparing them for his visit. We know that letter as the book of Romans in the New Testament.

PAUL IN JERUSALEM

After his time in Ephesus, Paul returned to Jerusalem on his way to Rome in spite of warnings that his welcome there might not be warm. Consider the conflict between him and the Jewish leaders. Paul's rearing had been steeped in religious rituals and obedience to the Mosaic law of the Old Testament. His zeal was so great that he spent a part of his adult life trying to crush what he considered a blasphemous heresy—the Christian faith. Then, upon his conversion, he turned that same zeal toward spreading the faith. It would be fair to describe Paul as a man who went to extremes.

In the transition to his ministry to the Gentiles, Paul wholeheartedly supported faith in Christ apart from Jewish tradition.

While he didn't condemn his Jewish brothers for maintaining their cultural traditions and heritage, he did not in any way connect those traditions or that heritage to this new thing God was doing. This was a step too far for traditional Jewish leadership. They bucked against Paul's leadership in much the same way that they had against Jesus—schemes and harassment.

SINNERS AND SAINTS
VESPASIAN

After the death of Nero, Rome went through three emperors (Galba, Otho, and Vitellius) before the fourth, Vespasian, finally proved to be capable of holding the job. Vespasian (whose full name was Titus Flavius Vespasianus) was a war hero. He led soldiers in the Roman conquest of Britain and led the imperial forces in crushing a Jewish rebellion in Judea. He was also a statesman, having been a successful Roman senator. Statesmanship, however, did not get him the position of emperor: He took Rome by force  with legions of the army under command. Despite a violent beginning, his reign is noted for its stability and for building projects such as the famed Colosseum and the Temple of Peace. He also endorsed education, founding several professorships during his tenure. During the time of Vespasian, the senate passed the first known statement of the powers of the emperor. Vespasian named his son Titus to succeed him.

DID YOU KNOW?

With all the versions of the Bible that were made, haven't you ever wondered if typos slipped through unnoticed? Well, typos were there, but hardly unnoticed. In fact, whole versions were named after the typos found in them. Here are just a few....

The Camel's Bible, which stated, "And Rebekah arose, and her camels" (oops, shoulda' been "damsels").

The Ears to Ear Bible, in which Matthew 13:43 was rendered, "Who hath ears to ear, let him hear."

The Fool Bible, printed during the reign of Charles I, in which Psalm 14:1 is rendered, "The fool hath said in his heart there is a God." (Big no-no. The fool has said there is *no* God.)

The Judas Bible, in which "Judas" is substituted for "Jesus" in Matthew 26:36.

The Placemaker's Bible, in which "placemakers" is substituted for "peacemakers."

The Wicked Bible, in which the "not" was omitted from the seventh commandment. It read, "Thou shalt commit adultery." (The fine charged for this mistake helped ruin the printer, Barker and Lucas.)

There were versions also nicknamed for certain idiosyncrasies:

The Bear Bible, for the Spanish Protestant version with a bear on the title page.

The Breeches Bible, for the Geneva Bible that stated, "And they sowed figge-tree leaves together, and made themselves breeches."

The Bug Bible, for the Coverdale's Bible that rendered, "Thou shalt not nede to be afrayed for eny bugges by night." (bugges=terror)

The Complutensian Polyglot, a six-volume set that contained the Hebrew and Greek texts, as well as the Septuagint, the Vulgate, and the Chaldee paraphrase of the Pentateuch, among other study helps.

The next morning a group of Jews got together and bound themselves with an oath to neither eat nor drink until they had killed Paul. There were more than forty of them. They went to the leading priests and other leaders and told them what they had done. "We have bound ourselves under oath to neither eat nor drink until we have killed Paul. You and the high council should tell the commander to bring Paul back to the council again," they requested. "Pretend you want to examine his case more fully. We will kill him on the way."

ACTS 23:12–15 NLT

PAUL'S TRIAL

At the temple in Jerusalem, Paul was falsely accused of defiling the temple. Because he was a Roman citizen, he was not beaten during the arrest and questioning by the Sanhedrin. Paul was then sent to Caesarea to avoid an assassination plot against him.

In Caesarea Paul appeared before Felix, the governor, and proclaimed his faith. Felix kept Paul an unsentenced prisoner for two years. When the new governor, Festus, came into office, the Jewish leadership approached Paul's condemnation again. Paul appealed his case to Caesar, which was his right as a Roman citizen.

PAUL'S ROMAN IMPRISONMENTS

After meeting with Herod Agrippa II (who unofficially declared Paul innocent), Paul was sent to Rome accompanied by Luke. In Rome Paul remained under a loose house arrest, but continued his ministry. During that imprisonment, he wrote the letters we know as Colossians, Philemon, Ephesians, and Philippians.

After this Roman imprisonment, the details get a little disjointed. Piecing together historical fact and details from the pastoral letters that Paul wrote (1 and 2 Timothy and Titus), it looks like Paul was released from this imprisonment after two years. We think he revisited Ephesus, stationing Timothy as pastor there. He probably visited Macedonia and left Titus behind on Crete to minister. He may have even visited Spain. By the autumn of 64, at the outbreak of Nero's persecution of Christians, Paul was imprisoned in Rome again on a much tighter leash. He was executed in Rome in late 66 or early 67. Tradition holds that he was beheaded.

THE FALL OF JERUSALEM

By A.D. 66, the Christians and Jews had separated out into their own subcultures. The Palestinian Jews were still under Roman rule and still resented it. In A.D. 66 the Jews revolted. The result was a four-year bloody war. The Jews did keep the Romans out of their land, but they never achieved peace and lost many lives.

In A.D. 70, a soldier named Titus led the forces of Emperor Vespasian, broke through the walls of Jerusalem, and totally

THE DELPHI ORACLE YEARBOOK

TOP STORIES OF A.D. 79

The Roman community of Pompeii fell this year to the power of Vesuvius. The volcano erupted suddenly and powerfully, spewing forth a mushroom cloud of doom that darkened the skies for many miles in every direction and rained down ash on surrounding communities. A burning river of lava flowed through the town of Herculaneum, leaving nothing but desolation in its wake. Pompeii was destroyed not by lava, but by the ashes and gases that traveled through the air covering the city, encrusting it like a tomb. At least two thousand people lost their lives, including Pliny the Elder, who left the relative safety of his home some miles away to attempt a rescue mission by boat. In a journal found near his body and now in the possession of his nephew, Pliny the Younger, the elder Pliny tells how choppy seas caused by the eruption prevented the departure of his boat.

In the last entry, Pliny had grown tired, possibly from lack of breathable air, and had lain down to rest. His body was found unscathed near the home of a friend whom he had been attempting to evacuate.

At first, some survivors returned home to dig up belongings, but Pompeii is now being forgotten by all but a few tunneling treasure hunters. The Delphi Oracle staff would like to give a proud salute in remembrance of the Roman citizens (and slaves) who lost their lives during the destruction of this once popular resort town.

Igneous Magmus

DID YOU KNOW?

The Bible is considered by many literary critics to be one of the finest literary achievements *ever* and is renowned not only for the quality of its writing, but also its breadth of scope. The Bible contains fine examples of *numerous* literary styles, including love poems, philosophical treatises, letters, parables, heroic epics, a census, laws, prayers, historical accounts, songs, and lamentations.

destroyed the city and its temple. Every synagogue in Palestine was burned to the ground. The Wailing Wall in Jerusalem is all that remains of the temple that was destroyed in this conflict.

While the fall of Jerusalem was a Jewish event, it functioned as a dividing line. While some of the apostles, such as John, lived beyond this date, it really is the end of what could be called the Apostolic Age. The Good News had spread. The Christian church was now separate from the Jewish faith. The girth of the church was wider than the apostles could reach, so leadership became more and more decentralized. From this point on, the organization of the church became an important topic, since the original leadership was gone.

A DARKNESS

From the fall of Jerusalem, an informational darkness falls on the history of the early church. That darkness lasts from around A.D. 70 until dawn starts breaking about 110. During this time the church was formulating in three ways:

The Canon of the New Testament scripture

Creeds of stated beliefs of the church

Church structure and organization (from Jewish tradition to a bishop-led church structure)

These three elements began to take shape and form as the church left the familiar territory of Judaism and apostolic leadership. Peter and Paul were no longer available for comment. The Jewish community had withdrawn completely. It was time for the church leaders to make decisions and to decide on what basis those decisions would be made. The first answer to that question came in the canon of the New Testament.

MARCION

Sometimes it takes a troublemaker to motivate a decision. Marcion was the troublemaker that motivated the early church leaders to organize the New Testament and consider it finished. (The finished list is called a canon.)

Marcion was the first person to put out an official list of the biblical canon, at least the way he thought it should be. Marcion's idea was that the God of the New Testament was in opposition to the God of the Old Testament. Because of that, Marcion didn't include the Old Testament in his list of "real" scriptures. Of course it would follow that he wouldn't include any recent writings that included parts of the Old Testament. So his list included:

 SET THE STAGE!

The Christian church did include the Old Testament in their Bible (which Marcion did not), but even today there are different versions. The Apocrypha is a collection of twelve to fifteen books (depending on how you cluster them). The Roman Catholic Church includes the Apocrypha in their list of the Old Testament canon. Typically Protestant churches do not.

- His own edit of the Gospel of Luke (deleting, if there was such a concept then, any reference to the Old Testament)
- Ten letters of Paul (who, according to Marcion, understood that grace beats out law in a spiritual version of Rock, Paper, Scissors)

By the time Marcion made his list public, the New Testament books that we know today already had function in the church. Even though there was no official table of contents, the power of these books caused them to be gathered and shared among churches. So when Marcion established his subjective cut-and-paste play list, the church leaders heard it as heresy and began to organize a response.

THE CANON

By A.D. 90, churches were already circulating Paul's letters. By A.D. 100, the gospels were circulated as a collection. By A.D. 120, Paul's letters were gathered into a collection so they could be more easily circulated.

The Bible began to stand on its own before any council was formed to declare it as a finished work. The power of the writings was not easily disputed. But it became a wise move for the church to make an official list. The most important criterion they used was apostleship. Could the writing be traced back to an apostle as the writer or a main source?

Understand that the people making these huge decisions were people like us. They were caught up in their world, in their generation, and were doing the best they could. They were transitioning out of a period of time when the leaders, the authorities, the representatives of Jesus' life and ministry were slowly leaving the scene. How could they best crystallize the leadership of these men in preparation for the time that the men themselves would be unavailable? How? By gathering the writings of these men and turning to those writings when a decision needed to be made.

If there were no such writings to appeal to, it would be difficult to have any unity among believers, no standard to come back to. The task ahead was too broad-reaching and too urgent to spend time on disorganization and basic befuddledness. The church was at a place where they needed a foundation to build on. The New Testament Canon, based on the teachings and writings of the apostles who shared in Jesus' ministry, was the best place to start.

THE SHORT LIST

One of the first suggested lists of the New Testament Canon was compiled around A.D. 190. It's called the Muratorian Canon because it was discovered by L. A. Muratori (so the early church didn't call it the Muratorian Canon, understand?).

The canon of the New Testament wasn't officially finalized until around A.D. 400, but the list was very similar throughout the years from Marcion's excommunication in A.D. 144 to the Council of

DID YOU KNOW?

The final list we know as the New Testament was a process.

200 Muratorian Canon
Four Gospels
Acts
Paul's letters to the
Romans
Corinthians
Galatians
Ephesians
Philippians
Colossians
Thessalonians
Paul's pastoral letters to
Timothy
Titus
Philemon
James
1 & 2 John
Jude
Revelation

The Apocalypse of Peter
Wisdom of Solomon

250 List Used by Origen
Four Gospels
Acts
Paul's letters to the
Romans
Corinthians
Galatians
Ephesians
Philippians
Colossians
Thessalonians
Paul's pastoral letters to
Timothy
Titus
Philemon
1 Peter
1 John
Revelation

300 List Used by Eusebius
Four Gospels
Acts

Paul's letters to the
Romans
Corinthians
Galatians
Ephesians
Philippians
Colossians
Thessalonians
Paul's pastoral letters to
Timothy
Titus
Philemon
1 Peter
1 John
Revelation (with some doubt
of authorship)

Not *really* on the list, but well known
James
2 Peter
2 & 3 John
Jude

400 Final List from the Council of Carthage
Four Gospels
Acts
Paul's letters to the
Romans
Corinthians
Galatians
Ephesians
Philippians
Colossians
Thessalonians
Paul's pastoral letters to
Timothy
Titus
Philemon
Hebrews
James
1 & 2 Peter
1, 2, & 3 John
Jude
Revelation

Adapted from Church History in Plain Language, *Bruce Shelley, Word Publishing, 1995.*

Carthage. The writings of the apostles rose to the top with their power and authority to lead the churches in the way of Christ.

CREEDS

The importance of scripture to the early church can never be overestimated. Here was a new faith rising up among people of every nationality and religious background. There had to be unifying factors in order for it to be the same faith. The most central unifying factor, of course, was the person of Christ.

In order for people to understand what they were putting their faith in when they put their faith in Christ, there were the scriptures to teach and explain who Jesus was.

Also, there were creeds based on the truths of the faith. These creeds could be recited at assemblies to affirm this new thing that God was doing first through His Son and continuing on through His Spirit. Creeds helped distinguish between heresy and truth by delineating the core truths of Christianity. They were a kind of catechism that functioned as a part of the worship services and, in some denominations, still do today.

CHURCH STRUCTURE AND ORGANIZATION

While the Christian faith was still functioning as an offshoot of Judaism, the form took a similar shape to Jewish worship. The annual feasts provided calendar markers. The synagogues provided a place for teaching. The apostles provided leadership. With the destruction of Jerusalem, the separation of Christianity from Judaism, and the martyrdom of many of the apostles, there was a sudden vacuum of structure and leadership.

The early church eventually filled in that vacuum with bishops. As Paul planted churches around Europe and the Near East, he left behind leadership: bishops, or elders and deacons. The deacons were a service body as they were just after Pentecost. The bishops were more similar to the synagogue leaders, who presided over the assembly. The duties of the bishops were honed as the years passed. Their role became more and more powerful. As early as A.D. 112, Ignatius encouraged the church to follow the bishop as they would follow Jesus. Bishops were responsible for passing on ceremonial traditions, as well as having the authority to teach and interpret the Bible.

While the power of the bishops proved dangerous in the years to come, their organizational layer provided cohesiveness to the early church. The church is the body of Christ, an organism and an organization. The bishops were the regional directors of the organization and the central nervous system of the organism.

As the years progressed, the role of bishop became multi-

SINNERS AND SAINTS
IGNATIUS

Ignatius was the bishop of the first Gentile church, the church of Antioch in the early part of the first century. Ignatius wrote letters to various churches much as the apostle Paul did. While the letters of Ignatius did not become part of the Bible, they were influential in how the church was structured, particularly in the practice of having one main pastor (bishop) in charge of each church. Ignatius was martyred in Rome and later made a saint by the Catholic Church.

layered, much as the role of pastor can be today. A pastor of a small church often fills several roles. A pastor of a large church specializes more and has staff to fill specific leadership roles. Pastors today sometimes fill roles such as denominational chairpersons. The bishops of the early church may have been over one congregation or over a region of congregations. As the centuries progressed, a hierarchy developed amidst the different levels of leadership.

THE AGE OF CATHOLIC CHRISTIANITY
By the end of the second century, the term "catholic church" connoted that the church was universal (not just local congregations) and that it was orthodox (not heretical). Remember that there

SET THE STAGE!

"On the day called the Day of the Sun all who live in cities or in the country gather together to one place, and the memoirs of the apostles or the writings of the prophets are read, as long as time permits; then, when the reader has ceased, the president verbally instructs, and exhorts to the imitation of these good things. Then we all rise together and pray." (Justin Martyr, an adult, circa A.D. 150)

"On Sundays we go to church. Brother Jim reads out of the Bible, usually a story about Jesus. Then Pastor Williams talks for a while about how we can live like Jesus. At the end we sing a song and pray, and usually somebody gives me a big hug before I leave." (Justin Owens, a third grader, A.D. 2001)

was not a meaning attached yet to "catholic" or "protestant." The Christian church was the worldwide body of believers; that's what "catholic" meant. It wasn't until the time of the Reformation when the protesters broke off from the Christian church that the real delineation between Catholic and Protestant took on a meaning similar to a modern understanding.

JUSTIN MARTYR

During the early church period, there were Christian leaders rising to prominence, besides the bishops. These leaders were Christian thinkers and writers who influenced their culture for the sake of Christ.

One such man was named Justin. Justin was a seeker of truth. He, like seekers today, explored all the schools of thought available to him: Stoics, Platonists, Aristotelians, Pythagoreans, etc. His heart began to bend toward Christianity, though, when he began to explore the Jewish prophets. Through his study of the scriptures Justin became a Christian. (His conversion is described in his writings called *Dialogue with Trypho.*) Then he began to explain his faith to the world at large. Today we call Justin an apologist, not a person who apologizes for his faith, but a person who defends or explains his faith. His most famous work, in fact, is *Apology*, a statement of the moral principles in Christianity.

SINNERS AND SAINTS
MONTANUS

Montanus's role regarding the early church was similar to the New Age movement's role regarding the church today.

Around the middle of the second century, Montanus came on the scene. His primary message was a good one: a life of holiness and separation from the world. He worked with two prophetesses, Prisca and Maximilla. Montanus and his prophetesses spoke not as preachers but more as people channeling the Holy Spirit. They slipped into an ecstatic, dreamlike state. They claimed to be receiving revelation directly from God in a new age of the Spirit.

This was a little too far for the church to follow. Was there any way to verify if Montanus's words came directly from God? Montanus did gain followers who maintained that anyone who didn't listen and follow Montanus's leading was a blasphemer (spitting in the face of God, so to speak).

In a sense, Montanus taught that the Old Testament way of understanding God worked for a time. Then Jesus' revelation of God worked for a time. But all that was past. A new day had dawned in which the Spirit was the way of revelation. While the truth of God's Spirit indwelling each believer was a powerful new thing to negotiate, the early church couldn't say that Jesus' revelation and the apostles' carrying out of that revelation was anything in the past. Instead, to the church the Old Testament was the preparation for what Christ did. The New Testament church was then the continuing work of Christ.

In the end, Montanus was an important presence in pushing the church to clarify God's revelation and to establish the New Testament scriptures.

Around A.D. 150, Justin lived in Rome teaching Christian philosophy. It was there he was be-headed for his faith. Today he is often referred to as Justin Martyr.

Justin represented a new way of thinking. He was the first to use Greek philosophy to explain Christian doctrine. Other thinkers of his day, such as Tertullian, considered this inappropriate. Instead they chose to keep separate the "secular" philosophers and Christian theologians. This same tension can be felt in the modern world today. It is related to the issue of how the church best accomplishes the task of being "in" the world, but not "of" the world. Both Justin and Tertullian accomplished great things for the kingdom.

Other apologists of the early church were Tatian (a student of Justin), Irenaeus (also influenced by Justin), Theophilus, and Augustine.

IRENAEUS

Irenaeus lived around the middle of the second century. He became a bishop, but along the way was a writer, a theologian, and one of the most significant thinkers of the early Catholic Church. He was famous for being a peacekeeper in church conflicts and for taking a stand against Gnosticism. His most important work was *Against Heresies,* written specifically to attack Gnosticism.

TERTULLIAN

Tertullian was born in Carthage, Africa, about A.D. 150. Once he converted to Christianity, he began writing books promoting the Christian faith. He wrote in both Greek and Latin. Perhaps his most famous work was *Apologeticum.*

Tertullian has been referred to as the "Father of Latin Theology." Now that doesn't mean Latin as in "Latin music," referring to South America. It means Latin as in "Ancient Latin." He was also the first person to use the Latin word for Trinity. He was a powerful and influential writer.

GNOSTICISM

Gnosticism was really a variety of movements. Their main

similarity was that they were led by a guru or philosopher who professed to have a special knowledge (gnosis). There was a huge conflict between early Christians and the Gnostics, much as there may be between conservative Christians today and a leader in the New Age movement. The Christians saw the Gnostics as enemies of the truth.

Normally the Gnostics accepted the idea of salvation and of a supreme God and of a heavenly realm in action. They were accused by the Christians of dualism, which meant instead of seeing body and spirit as a united thing, they separated out the material understanding of the world from the spiritual understanding. For a Gnostic to claim Jesus was fully human was highly

 SET THE STAGE!

Most of the creeds of the early church were created to battle heresies. The Apostles' Creed, still recited in many churches today, was written to stand against the heresy of Gnosticism. While it was finalized in the 700s, some forms of it existed as early as the 200s. This is a precursor to the Apostles' Creed called the Old Roman Creed.

I believe in God Almighty
And in Christ Jesus, His only Son, our Lord
Who was born of the Holy Spirit and the Virgin Mary
Who was crucified under Pontius Pilate and was buried
And the third day rose from the dead
Who ascended into heaven
And sits on the right hand of the Father
Whence He comes to judge the living and the dead.
And in the Holy Ghost
The holy church
The remission of sins
The resurrection of the flesh
The life everlasting.

undesirable. Their distaste for anything merely human was huge. To believe Jesus was born of a virgin was no problem for a Gnostic. The miraculous, the spiritual, the mysterious was acceptable to them. To believe Jesus was "born" at all was a big problem.

The Gnostics tended to see people in three spiritual planes. The upper class lived by a special knowledge. The lower class lived by faith. The spiritually disadvantaged were just not capable of "getting it." It's obvious then in what class the Gnostics would place anyone who didn't agree with their assessment.

THE PERSON OF CHRIST

The early church drew a simple line in the sand doctrinally. It was the person of Christ. Any belief that took away from either the humanity of Christ or the deity of Christ was considered heresy. Christianity, after all, was about accepting God's sacrifice and extended hand through Jesus. While the churches of this period had different personalities and challenges (and eventually different worship practices), they were unified by this one truth, that Jesus Christ was God's presence in the world, unique from anything before or after. Embedded in that truth was the understanding that the work of Christ accomplished something in terms of God's connection to His creation, namely, us.

The heresies that plagued the early church were permutations of this understanding of the person of Christ:

The **Ebionites** were a Jewish-Christian sect that taught Jesus was merely a very obedient man who became the Messiah.

Docetism (from the Greek verb "to seem") granted that Christ was not really a man, but only *seemed* to be a man and *seemed* to suffer and die.

Arianism (which appeared in the next centuries) stated that Christ was of God, but not equal to God.

Gnosticism believed to possess a special knowledge of the spiritual and a disdain for the material world. Why would a Messiah have a *body*, of all things?

THE SPREAD OF CHRISTIANITY

Throughout the Roman empire, the population of Jews has been estimated at 7 percent in any one place. That meant that not all Jews lived in Palestine in a rather closed community. "Hellenists" is a term that applies to Greeks. There were Hellenistic Jews who were Jewish by descent, but they had grown up in more of a Greek culture than a Jewish one. These Jews were more open-minded to new traditions because they had been exposed to more. They also were quicker to accept a new way of thinking. As this new way of thinking about faith spread across the kingdom, it found a welcome among many of the Hellenistic Jews. There was enough heritage to be recognizable, yet a better way of relating to God than merely through rituals and sacrifices.

Another element of the Roman culture played a role. The Greeks and Romans were rarely averse to taking on any new god that came along as they gobbled up lands and peoples around them. As Christianity was spreading across the empire, the Roman culture as a whole had entered a time of apathy and disinterest in the current religious climate. Any new news was welcome.

Once Jerusalem was destroyed, Christianity found several centers for growth. When you study the people and movements of the time, you'll hear city names like Rome, Antioch (Syria), Carthage

 SET THE STAGE!

Long after Greece had ceased to be a dominant military power, Hellenistic (Greek) thought and culture continued to shape the world. Roman views on philosophy, art, architecture, music, science, medicine, and law were heavily influenced by Greece. Before the rise of Christianity, the Romans had even come to adopt most of the elements of Greek religion as their own. Athens was an important cultural center for both the Macedonian and Roman Empires. For centuries after the Romans conquered the Greeks, well-off Romans finished their higher education not in Rome but in Athens. Athenian schools carried the same sense of prestige that might today be attached to British universities such as Cambridge and Oxford. Athens continued to be a key player through the end of the Roman Empire in 476. The Byzantine emperor Justinian closed the schools of philosophy in Athens in A.D. 529, and Athens lost its position as a leading cultural center of the old world. By that time, however, it had already earned a place in history and in the teachings of most advanced societies.

(Africa), and Alexandria (Egypt). Often the bishops of these more frontline cities became influential across the empire. And, of course, the bishop of Rome was eventually known as the pope.

CHRISTIANS IN THEIR CULTURE

In many ways the early church had a glowing testimony. Tertullian quoted his countrymen as saying, "See how these Christians love one another." That didn't change the fact that Christianity was actually atheism within the Roman culture. Do you get that? Atheism is the denial of God's existence. In the Roman Empire there were many gods, including the emperor. Christianity denied the existence of all those gods, including the deity of the emperor. The Christian faith that seems so standard today, so embedded in our society, was actually countercultural at this time.

In the first century, most of the persecution toward Christianity actually came from within Judaism. In fact, the Romans often had to quell riots or mobs that arose against the first Christians. As the second century dawned, that changed.

The Christian's creed was that Jesus was Lord, the one and only to be worshiped. That was a dangerous moral for the Romans. The continuity of their entire sprawling kingdom was the emperor to whom the people paid daily homage. Christians were hard-pressed to take part. Not only did they stand against worshiping the emperor, they were always trying to add to their numbers, constantly evangelizing.

In essence, the Roman Empire had an ever-growing faction of its society that refused to play along with the unifying code. That didn't set well in an age where an empire had to keep tight reins of control in order to even exist. The Christians were referred to by a Greek word that meant "different ones." They were different in their obstinate refusal to take part in idol worship. They also were known for a moral purity at a time when cultures were hedonistic to the point of self-annihilation.

Christians of the Roman Empire actually faced many of the same issues that Christians today face. What do we do with a holiday that actually has to do with very non-Christian themes (such as modern Halloween)? Do we say, "Oh, it's harmless"? Do we take part or create a similar alternative? Do we instead appear as prudes and have no part? These questions of cultural involvement have been with the church from the beginning.

POLICIES AND PERSECUTIONS

The first-century Christians were often persecuted by the Jewish leadership and sometimes rescued by the officers of the Roman occupation who squelched any kind of uprising. The second-century Christians experienced persecution differently. The policy during the reign of Trajan was that *if* Christians were brought in, the authorities demanded that they recant their faith. This sometimes resulted in persecution and even martyrdom (Ignatius, Polycarp, Justin, etc.), but it wasn't an all-out search for Christians to torture and kill. Persecution was a little haphazard in those days.

MEANWHILE, BACK AT THE RANCH...

While Christianity was spreading at the peak of Roman civilization, the dominant culture in the Americas was that of the Maya. The Mayan states were a loose confederation of related peoples who shared a common language but, since they had no centralized form of government, cannot truly be referred to as an empire. Mayan civilization was at its high point from about A.D. 250–900. Like the Egyptians half a world away and many centuries removed, the Maya had an advanced form of hieroglyphic writing and buried their rulers in huge pyramids. The range of the Mayan culture covered about 120,000 square miles and included parts of present-day Mexico, Guatemala, El Salvador, Honduras, and Belize. Mayan farmers used terracing, drainage systems, and irrigation to better their crops. Scholars of the Maya studied math (they were one of the first people to have a symbol for zero), astronomy, and architecture. Strangely, the Maya never used the wheel or animals for transportation, relying instead on canoes and walking to get themselves and their goods where they needed to be. They had dogs as pets and possessed an accurate calendar. Today their descendants still live in Mexico and Central America, where there are about twenty different languages based on the Mayan tongue.

In the third century, there were periods of calm and periods of severe persecution. Under one emperor, Severus, the death penalty was prescribed for anyone who converted to an exclusive religion (one that required the believer to worship one deity and one deity only). That put Christianity in the category of "punishable by death." Some famous martyrs during this rule were Perpetua and Felicitas.

Then, mid-third century, Decius took the throne. He governed with a policy ordering citizens to sacrifice before the gods, and not only that, but to receive certificates ("libelli") stating that their sacrifices had been made. That meant Christians were faced with a few difficult choices for their survival:

Refuse to worship, walk around without a certificate, constantly looking over your shoulder in danger of arrest.

Go and worship saying to yourself, "What does it matter? I don't mean it anyway. God knows that."

Find a way to get one of those certificates so the government *thinks* I've worshiped, but (joke's on them) I never did.

In light of these bleak choices, Christians did the best they could. Some died as martyrs, including the bishops of Rome, Antioch, and Jerusalem. Others found officials that could be bribed into giving false libelli. Others gave in to the false worship.

When you look through the eyes of Decius, as unappetizing as it sounds, persecution had to be severe if it was to be effective. If he allowed Christians to die noble deaths, then he would merely add fuel to the fervor. So instead he tortured Christians in an attempt to cause them to give in before they actually died. That made their death seem meaningless. It discouraged Christians from trying. "I'll probably give in anyway eventually. If they got to *him*, they can probably break me."

AFTER THE STORM

In the aftermath of the persecution, the church had to establish some kind of policy for healing the assembly. A group of Christians could gather, and among them would be family members who had lost their loved ones to persecution. Just down the row could be another family who carried the shame of their loved one's surrender under torture. Still down another row could be a couple who had enough money to play it safe with bribed certificates. Today Western churches maintain a standing joke about congregations fighting over the color of the carpet (which has happened). Can you imagine the intensity of the emotional baggage after going through the kind of persecution that the mid-third-century Christians did?

The persecution raised questions for the church such as…

After someone has worshiped the Roman gods, are they allowed to worship as Christians again, or is this grounds for excommunication?

If someone dies denying Christ, do they die outside of faith's safe harbor?

How should the process of readmission work once someone denies or betrays their faith in order to survive?

PENANCE

It was specifically that last question of readmission that began a process with worldwide implications. The general reasoning was that in order for people who had denied the faith to come back into the assembly, some kind of reconciliation had to occur.

 SET THE STAGE!

Catacombs

During the time of the early church, before Christianity became the state religion, Christians used underground passages called catacombs in a variety of ways. Caves were hewn out of the side of the tunnels to use for graves. The walls were painted with murals. Funeral services were held there. Sometimes the Christians hid there for protection during persecution.

Cyprian, bishop of Carthage, suggested a hierarchy of sins, a kind of system that established the degrees of sin. For instance, a person who sacrificed to the Roman gods after hours of torture wouldn't be considered as liable as a person who easily and readily gave in. As you can imagine, this way of thinking quickly became cumbersome, but it did one thing—it gave the church the power of forgiveness. Penance. The sacrament of penance involved a ceremony in which the fallen one would express his or her penitent spirit and the bishop would grant penance.

SINNERS AND SAINTS
THE WRITERS PLINY

Pliny the Elder and Pliny the Younger (uncle and nephew) were Roman writers.

Pliny the Elder (a lawyer as well as a writer) is famous for his thirty-seven-volume *Natural History*, which functions now to show the state of scientific knowledge in Rome at the time. This Pliny died helping the refugees of the eruption of Mt. Vesuvius in A.D. 79.

Pliny the Younger (a governor as well as a writer) is most famous for his *Letters*, which is a ten-volume set of a variety of letters about the life of a Roman gentleman. One of those letters describes in detail the eruption of Vesuvius and the death of his uncle. Another letter to the emperor ponders the issue of what to do with Christians in an age when Christianity is outlawed. Pliny writes, "I do not know just what to do with the Christians, for I have never been present at one of their trials. Is just being a Christian enough to punish, or must something bad actually have been done? What I have done, in the case of those who admitted they were Christians, was to order them sent to Rome, if citizens; if not, to have them killed. I was sure they deserved to be punished because they were so stubborn."

As the church grappled with this new concept, opposing leaders rose and fell taking up the argument. A man named Novatian held the banner opposing the church's ability to forgive. He held the view that there were sins that were simply unforgivable. Adherents to Novatian's perspective saw the church as a group of saints, people who had accomplished righteousness and didn't mess it up too much.

On the other hand, men like Cornelius claimed that the bishop *could* forgive sins, even ones that seemed unforgivable. His view was that the church was not made up of perfect people. It was a church of sinners. As you can imagine, Cornelius's perspective was much more popular with the common folk.

Sometimes the most significant changes happen when everyone is distracted with something else. That little shift, the church's being able to forgive sins, was a drastic move. If a council had gathered with that agenda item, "Number one, can the church grant forgiveness?" the outcome might have been much different. But because the decision was made in such an uproar with some urgent problems to solve, a huge decision was made, one with permanent ramifications. While penance has taken many forms through the years, it was born in the aftermath of this persecution and eventually led to its own kind of bondage within the church.

TARGET MARKETING

Celsus, a well-known critic of the Christian movement, said, "Far from us, say the Christians, be any man possessed of any culture or wisdom or judgment; their aim is to convince only worthless and contemptible people, idiots, slaves, poor women, and children....These are the only ones whom they manage to turn into believers."

While Celsus's words were sharp, they revealed something about his day. They revealed a distinction between what the modern world calls "blue collar" and "white collar" or "upper" and "lower" class. In a sense, Celsus was correct. Most of the evangelism in the early church was to the common people. Most early Roman Christians spoke Greek, rather than the Latin of the upper crust.

Celsus's words also revealed a knowledge that where a person comes from affects how he or she comes to faith. The Hellenistic Jews were familiar with the message of the Messiah, so there was an accessible bridge between their current beliefs and the gospel. By the third century, the church was organized enough to begin to ask questions about the way they publicized this good news. The questions before them covered not only whom they were reaching with the truth, but how they were presenting the truth. True to form, there were plenty of opinions on all sides.

SET THE STAGE!

In A.D. 404, after more than a thousand years of gory entertainment, the Roman gladiatorial games were finally banned. The games usually featured armed combat between slaves and/or soldiers. For some slaves, fighting in the games was a way to freedom. Some soldiers saw gladiatorial combat as a chance for quick advancement. Winners became instant celebrities. One gladiator is reputed to have won a hundred battles. At other times people, both armed and unarmed, were forced to fight wild animals or armed gladiators for the amusement of the crowd. It was at the gladiatorial games that Christians were fed to the lions. At times naval battles were staged as part of the games, with the floor of the arena being flooded and the participants fighting from small boats.

By the way, did you know that some Roman gladiators were women?

On one end of the spectrum was Tertullian, a prominent writer and scholar. He was opposed to any mixture of "modern" Greek thought with things of the Christian faith. He would have been disgusted with any resort to make the message of Christ palatable to the Greek mind.

On the other end of the spectrum were men like Clement. Clement, dubbed the first Christian scholar, set out on a mission to get the message of the gospel to the Hellenistic intellectuals of his world. His thinking was that if the schooled of his world did not come to faith, then the faith would die out simply because there would be no one to record the faith and pass it down. Clement was like the equivalent of the Starbucks evangelist, the yuppie philosopher who lived by the truth that faith was not an enemy of reason.

Both men were intentional about God's truth, but their methods diverged greatly. Those methods diverge even today.

PERSECUTION BY DIOCLETIAN (303)

At the beginning of the fourth century, the early church became the state church under Emperor Constantine. Before

Constantine's changes, though, the church had to survive through the rule of Emperor Diocletian.

Diocletian did amazing things for the Roman Empire. He established a sense of order that had run amuck. But just before his reign ended, Diocletian, a committed and practicing pagan, turned his attention to the Christian subset of his kingdom (and not in a good way). Basically Diocletian set out to exterminate Christianity. What he did provided a preamble to the establishment of Christianity as the national religion.

ULTIMATE IMPACT OF AND ON CHRISTIANITY

The period of the early church ranks only second to the life of Christ in terms of the impact on the church today. It was during this period that almost every "given" of our modern Christian culture was established.

CHRIST'S DEITY
The line in the sand that the early church drew in regard to heresy stands firm today. Christ's unique position as God and man is the kingpin of the faith. When we step into the Christian faith, it is through the portal of Jesus' teachings and work, including His death and resurrection. If we don't step through that portal, in essence, it's not the Christian faith.

THE HOLY SPIRIT
The God of the tabernacle traveled with His people. Jesus Christ sat among the world. The Holy Spirit welcomed by that first church ushered God's presence into our very beings. How could the church ever be the same after that? One of the names for Jesus was Emmanuel, which meant "God with us." That is exactly what God did, not only through Jesus' presence, but through blowing into the world in a way that we can take Him in and live according to His power. Because of that we walk with God, not to God. Because of that we each experience Him all the time, not just when a church leader presides over our encounter.

THE CANON OF THE SCRIPTURE

Closing the canon of scripture was a huge responsibility. Trusting that God worked through the teachings of the apostles was essential. Had the church not laid its claim to the works of the apostles, the Christian faith could not have sustained itself cohesively. From this time period forward, even to this past Wednesday night, congregations have made decisions based on the same information that the early church did, the words of the men who actually walked with Jesus. That preservation of truth is phenomenal! We have access to eyewitnesses to the work of Christ. Seeing a Bible sit on the shelf for years can tame that fact, but the truth is we hold ancient documents that reach back to the hands of Jesus, His disciples, the apostle Paul. Our faith is grounded there because of the canon of scripture.

LEADERSHIP STRUCTURE

We sit today in churches and second-guess whether the problems we face are with the leadership structure itself or the abuses of that structure. While some factions of the Christian world consider the method of church leadership as immutable as the church itself, many more experiment with the grouping of leadership. One elder and a board of deacons? A body of elders and a body of deacons? A teaching elder, leader among peers? However a church establishes its leadership, there is some form of the same structure of those first believers in Jerusalem piecing together the whirlwind of experience they had just walked through.

MISSIONARY ZEAL

To the ancient Jew, their responsibility was to live a life before God and separate from the world, to be a light on a hill. With the work of Christ a new urgency was born. Carry the light. Spread the news. There came a prime directive that throughout history has motivated explorers as well as theologians. The by-products of missionary zeal are as much a part of world history as the zeal itself. To this day Christians follow in the steps of Paul, Silas, Barnabas, and Timothy. Church planters continue the exact same work, carrying the news to places that haven't heard.

UNANSWERED QUESTIONS

Just as the early church left a legacy of "givens," foundations for faith, it also left questions unanswered that are still unanswered today. Questions such as...

Do we best influence our culture by accentuating our differences or by imbedding ourselves within it?

When we try to be a part of our culture, how do we set our boundaries of behavior?

What kind of choices do we need to make in communicating the Christian message to our culture?

Do we tailor that message to our hearers, or is there a pure essence that must be maintained?

MISTAKES

The early church laid a foundation for mistakes to come, as well. Some of these mistakes (such as indulgences) caused schisms that tore the church apart, yet purified it at the same time. We live today with a legacy of content, information, structure, and flaws that equips us to say, "And now, God, in this generation teach us to be Your church."

The Roman Empire:
The Church of the Empire
(a.d. 300 to a.d. 590)

 UNDERSTANDING THE TIMES

If you could intercept mail from young pen pals who lived in the Roman Empire, you might read something like this through the generations. . . .

A.D. MARCH 13, 350

Dear Peter,

You asked me what it's like to live in Rome. I'll tell you—the streets are *always* busy. Rome must be the final destination for *everything!* There is nothing, no matter how exotic, that you can't buy for some price. There are stalls selling exotic, beautiful cloth from the East. There are foods and spices from all over the world.

Almost everybody's home here just opens into the street. When you walk by you can hear the sound of families talking and eating. You have to be careful where you walk and stay out of the gutters, if you know what I mean. I have heard that in some people's houses there are bathrooms. They have water piped in and even toilets. I hope we get one of those some day.

Our days are pretty much the same. In the mornings I play with my little brothers while Mother fixes breakfast at the hearth in our house. Most days she bakes bread. Some days she sends us to the vendor down the street with some coins to buy some fresh meat or vegetables. There is a picture of the emperor on some of the coins. We almost always have enough money for olives and sometimes even enough for an orange. Some days father comes home with an amphora. Do you have those where you live? It's a two-handled jar with a skinny neck. When father brings one home it's usually full of wine or newly pressed olive oil. In just a few days, the wine will turn to vinegar and the oil will spoil, so we have a few days of good eating so that nothing spoils. We relax beside a low table and have the best time on those days.

Usually, we keep the windows open and the shutters pulled back to let the breeze blow in. I don't know about Constantinople, but it sure gets hot here in the summer. There are public baths all over. I love going to a bath.

I think Rome is really a safe place to live. I would rather live here than anywhere else in the whole empire. It's hard to understand all the laws, but all Roman citizens like me know that they have rights. The truth is, not all that many people who I know could even read the law well, but

SET THE STAGE!

Roman fashion was simple, but elegant for its time. The main item of apparel for men and women was the tunic, a long, shirtlike garment that fell to the knee or below. Over the tunic they draped a secondary piece of clothing called a toga (for men) or a palla (for women). Togas and pallas were kind of like sheets and were wrapped around the wearer in different ways to achieve varying styles. Tunics did double duty as pajamas at night (which makes you wonder if togas and pallas did double duty as sheets and blankets). Most Roman clothing was made from wool or linen. Women's clothes were dyed in many colors, but men nearly always wore white, one notable exception being that upper-class Roman men had purple borders on their togas as a sign of their position.

most of us could recognize enough words to stay out of trouble. I have some friends who can read an inscription on one of the hundreds of monuments around the city.

Rome is a big city, and sometimes people do get robbed, but that does not happen that often. There do seem to be a lot of new people moving here, though. A lot of them seem to be coming from the Near East, Greece, and the Balkans. There are a lot of Christians coming here. Rome is getting quite a colony of them.

Father tells me that wasn't true when Diocletian was emperor. He tried hard to run them out of his capital and to make them give up their faith. Under Licinius it was suddenly fine to be a Christian. In fact, there seemed to be Christians coming out of the woodwork. They were probably Christians all along, and just then felt safe to admit it.

It seems strange to think that you and I live in the same empire, but our cities are so far apart. Father says he doesn't like it that Constantinople is so far away and yet someone there is making decisions that will impact the whole empire. He wishes they were making decisions from Rome.

Your friend,

Linus

A.D. MARCH 13, 400

Dear Leo,

Living in Constantinople is like living in an art museum. Back in the old days, Constantine brought monuments and antiques here from all over the old empire. There is an Egyptian obelisk here, a statue from Athens there. Though they tell me it is an old city, it feels new. Most of the big buildings are less than a hundred years old, and they are really beautiful. The city is full of beautiful pictures done in mosaic, thousands and thousands of pieces of colored tile. The houses are pretty good, too. Most of them were built after Constantine named the city his capital and laid out the walls himself. The streets are narrow, and the people crowd into them, rushing every direction. There are people who work for the government, a lot of them. There are priests and bishops always hurrying somewhere with a frown on their faces. Everyone is selling something. The bookseller who has a shop near the cathedral of St. Sophia has hundreds of handwritten books to sell. Mostly he has old stuff: copies of the old philosophers like Aristotle and playwrights like Sophocles, but there is plenty of new stuff, too. He always has some new writing from the rabble-rousers who think the emperor is running the church wrong.

There are always unusual people around. Last week there was a procession down the boulevard for the Persian king. It seems like he is our enemy, but we showed him just how nice we are by letting him visit our city. Word has it that the Persians are persecuting Christians—real Christians that is, not those Arians. That reminds me: A while back there was a big military parade. The army had crushed somebody and had come home to get rewarded by the emperor. Even though they were our army, they looked scary, all big German men who never smiled but looked straight ahead ignoring the crowd. There is plenty of food now, and the old people say that no army could ever get through our walls and hurt us. So, life is good.

Your friend,
Linus II

SET THE STAGE!

The Romans were anything but a barbarian culture. They had city planners who laid out plans for new towns and the rebuilding of older cities. Among the things they considered were water supplies, sewer systems, and the placement of important buildings.

A.D. MARCH 13, 480

Dear Carpus,

I'm sad to tell you that Daddy must be gone for good. Momma cried when she got the letter today. She said that the army was marching north again trying to recapture some town that King Odoacer and his men have captured. I think it is the same town where they had a fight last year. I remember that because I think it is where Daddy got stabbed. He was home for a while and that was great, except there was still not enough to eat. It doesn't make much sense to me. Momma is a Roman, but Daddy is

TIMELINE OVERVIEW

In the midst of world history...

286 Diocletian divides the Roman Empire between himself in the East and Maximian in the West.

303 Under Diocletian, the Great Persecution of Christians begins.

305 Diocletian and Maximian abdicate their thrones.

312 Constantine defeats Maxentius at the battle of Milvian Bridge to become emperor of all the Roman Empire.

313 Constantine proclaims the Edict of Toleration (Milan), allowing Christianity in the empire. He constructs the first Christian basilica in Rome.

324 Constantine reunites the Roman Empire.

330 Constantine founds Constantinople (modern-day Istanbul) as capital.

337 Constantine is baptized on his deathbed. The empire is divided among his three sons: Constantius, Constantine II, and Constans I.

351 Constantius becomes sole ruler of the Roman Empire.

361 Julian becomes emperor of the Roman Empire.

363 Jovian is proclaimed Julian's successor.

364 Valens becomes emperor of the East as his brother Valentinian becomes emperor of the West.

378 Goths attack Valens of Constantinople.

379 Theodosius becomes emperor of the Eastern Roman Empire. Constantinople is the center of power.

394 Theodosius briefly reunites the empire. He forbids the Olympic games.

395 At the death of Theodosius, brothers Honorius and Arcadius rule the Western and Eastern Roman Empires.

Christian history unfolds...

312 Constantine converts to Christianity on his way to the battle of Milvian bridge.

313 Edict of Milan: Constantine and Eastern ruler Licinius decree religious freedom for Christians.

318 The rise of Arianism (heresy which stated Jesus was inferior to God).

325 Council of Nicaea deals with the Arian heresy and the role of leaders in the church. The Nicene Creed is adopted.

330 May 11, 330, Constantine founds Constantinople, which becomes a bastion of Christianity until 1453.

330–340 Ulfilas the Visigoth becomes Christian and goes on to translate Bible into Gothic.

339 Death of Eusebius, a leading Christian thinker, writer, and the bishop of Caesarea

350 Africa: Christianity reaches Ethiopia.

361 Julian tries to reintroduce paganism to replace Christianity.

366–500 The development of the papal office

    Damasas (pope) (366–84)

    Innocent I (401–17)

    Leo I (440–61)

    Gelasius I (492–96)

370 Basil the Great becomes bishop of Caesarea, succeeding Eusebius.

374 Ambrose becomes bishop of Milan.

380 Theodosius re-recognizes Christianity as the official religion of the empire.

381 Council of Constantinople is called by Theodosius.

387 Conversion of Augustine

396 St. Augustine becomes bishop of Hippo.

401 Pope Innocent I claims leadership over the Roman church.

405 Jerome completes the Vulgate.

409 Spain: Vandals convert to Christianity.

    Persia: Christians are allowed to worship freely.

410 The beginning of the end of the empire—Alaric sacks Rome.

430 Death of St. Augustine

432 Patrick returns to Ireland as a missionary, bringing freedom to a nation that once enslaved him.

440 Leo the Great becomes pope.

Continued

TIMELINE OVERVIEW (CONTINUED)

In the midst of world history...

Christian history unfolds...

451 The Council of Chalcedon supports full recognition of Jesus' humanity, condemning Monophysitism.

452 Attila the Hun invades Gaul and Italy.

475 End of the Western Roman Empire (the East survives another 1000 years).

483 Armenia: Christians are granted the right again to practice their faith.

484 Split between the Christian churches of Rome and Constantinople. The pope refuses to recognize the emperor Zeno's authority to change Christian doctrine and excommunicates him.

488 Emperor Zeno pays Theodoric, king of the Ostrogoths, to attack Italy.

493 Theodoric becomes king of Italy.

498 Clovis, king of the Franks, converts to Christianity.

507 Clovis makes Paris his capital and introduces the Salic Law, which, among other things, kept women from inheriting land.

511 Clovis dies and his empire is divided among his four sons.

c. 524 Boethius writes *Consolation of Philosophy* while awaiting his execution.

525 Byzantine Empire (formerly the Eastern Roman Empire): Theodora, former actress, marries Prince Justinian, heir to the empire.

527 Justinian becomes ruler. During his rule, Theodora pushes through laws giving women rights of property, inheritance, and divorce.

529 Byzantine: Justinian begins to codify Roman laws. His empire has its own form of Christianity, which exists today as the Eastern Orthodox Church.

529 Italy: Monastery of Monte Cassino founded by St. Benedict. The monks there were Benedictines.

533 The "Eternal Peace" treaty is signed between the Byzantine Empire and Persia. It lasts seven years.

535 Byzantine armies start to reclaim Italy from the Ostrogoths.

550 Wales: St. David brings Christianity, becomes the first abbot of Menevia. At his death he becomes the patron saint of Wales.

563 St. Columba, an Irish monk, founds a monastery off the coast of Scotland and begins to convert the Picts to Christianity.

587 Spain: The Visigoths become a Christian people.

590 Gregory becomes Pope—this begins a transition between the ancient world dominated by imperial Rome and the Middle Ages united by the Roman Catholic Church.

597 Pope Gregory sends missionaries to England. King Ethelbert is converted and eventually appoints Augustine as archbishop of the Church of England.

out there fighting for Rome against his own people. What is so great about Rome that he would do that? They say that in the old days it was an honor to fight for the Roman Empire, but to me it would be better to just stop the war, let Odoacer be king if he wants to, and try to help everybody have food and be safe. Daddy says that we have to hold on a little longer, that the emperor in the East, wherever that is, will come sweeping down from the north and save Rome. I just don't know what will be left to save.

Good-bye, my friend,

Linus III

THE STORY OF THE TIMES

ROME AND THE PERSECUTIONS

To the Christians of the late third century, the Roman Empire must have seemed a terrible, awesome enemy. While the church struggled through persecutions, the empire flourished. While Christians sent out their missionaries, the empire expanded and unimaginable wealth poured into the capital of Rome. The spoils of war filled the city, and with that flood of wealth came the flood of conquered peoples trying to make their way in the empire.

The empire had become so big and powerful that the emperor Diocletian decided it could be run best by two emperors. He decided to divide the empire, east and west, and have both an emperor and vice-emperor (caesar) for each. The plan was for the emperor to rule for twenty years and then turn the rule over to the caesar. In 286 Diocletian appointed Maximian as emperor of the West, and he himself continued to be emperor in the East. He named Constantius Chlorus to be caesar in the West and Galerius in the East.

In 303, what is often referred to as *the Great Persecution* of Christians began. Christians were thrown out of the army and civil service. Churches and scriptures were destroyed. This was all part of Diocletian's grand plan: If the empire was united politically by the emperors and culturally by Roman culture, then it should have only one religion. According to Diocletian and Galerius, that religion was good old Roman paganism, not some revolutionary religion from that desolate colony of Palestine.

The persecution got even worse after the two emperors, Diocletian and Maximian, resigned (according to the plan) in 305. The empire cracked down on Christians. Much bloodshed followed. When Maximian's successor, Constantius Chlorus, died, his son Constantine was named emperor. By this time,

Diocletian's grand plan was falling apart, and Maximian decided to come out of retirement and put forth a challenge for the "emperorship" of the West. That meant war between Constantine and Maximian. It got even more complicated when Maximian's son Maxentius decided he wanted to be emperor and forced his own father back into retirement. To throw yet even more fuel on the fire, the Eastern emperor, Galerius, named one of his favorite generals, Licinius, as the Western emperor.

 SET THE STAGE!

Romans loved art. They valued sculpture, painting, music, and poetry. They were also some of the first people to give serious thought to interior decorating. Inside the house of a wealthy Roman, you might find the walls decorated with tapestries or frescoes (vividly colored paintings done while the wall plaster is still wet). Set in the floor you might find an elaborate mosaic, a picture made up of many colored tiles. Romans also dabbled in faux finishes, painting pillars and walls to look like marble, and other exotic building materials. In one house, which archaeologists believe may have belonged to Emperor Augustus, the walls of one room were painted as if they were part of the garden that the room opened onto.

THE CONVERSION OF CONSTANTINE

It was October A.D. 312.

Constantine was marching toward Rome to face Maxentius to determine who was to rule the West. As Eusebius told the story many years later, Constantine looked up into the sky and saw a cross of light. On that cross he read, "In this conquer." As a superstitious man, Constantine saw this sign as at least an omen and possibly much more. Then, according to Constantine, Christ appeared to him in a dream. Christ was bearing the same sign: a cross with the top bent over forming the Greek letters *chi* and *rho*, the first two letters of the Greek spelling of *Christos*.

In the dream, Constantine was instructed to paint these symbols on his soldiers' shields. He did so, and on October 28 he fought the battle of Milvian Bridge and defeated Maxentius.

On October 29, Constantine entered Rome with the two symbols of Christ, *chi* and *rho*, painted on his helmet. It was a huge symbol. In a matter of hours Christianity went from being an irritating cult to a faith acknowledged by the emperor himself. Of course the legitimacy of Constantine's miraculous conversion was then, and still is, discussed and debated. Constantine himself was not baptized until he was on his deathbed in 337. Nevertheless, with his conversion everything changed for the church.

FREEDOM OF RELIGION

The two victorious emperors at the battle near Milvian Bridge proceeded to each

 SET THE STAGE!

For those of you keeping a scorecard, the lineup for this fight goes like this:

Maxentius, son of **Maximian** (not a crowd favorite but decent bloodlines)

versus

Constantine, son of **Constantius** (popular but does he have what it takes?)

In Constantine's corner, by way of an alliance, is Licinius who has no bloodline claim to the throne but has powerful military friends.

The battle itself took place at Milvian Bridge. Later, Constantine would tell his biographer, Eusebius of Caesarea, the story of the battle and how it changed history.

take half an empire. Constantine took the West and Licinius the East. Great arrangement, right? In 313 they met in Milan and issued a joint decree that has become known as the Edict of Milan. Though the original Latin version of this document has been lost, Eusebius of Caesarea provided a Greek translation. The opening of that version translates to English as:

From now on every one of those who have a common wish to observe the Christian worship may freely and unconditionally endeavor to observe the same without any annoyance or disquiet.

For fourth century Christians this was revolutionary stuff.

SET THE STAGE!

In Constantine's Roman Empire, breakfast was generally a light meal, consisting mainly of bread and cheese. Lunch had a bit more variety, with fruits, olives, or (mostly for the wealthy) fish and meats added to the mix. For supper, the main meal of the day, the Roman diet varied greatly between different social classes. Well-to-do Romans had suppers made up of several courses including a first course of appetizers like eggs, vegetables, and shellfish, an entrée course of meat, fish, or poultry, and a dessert course of various fruits with honeycakes. For the less well-off, supper might be porridge, bread and cheese with some olives, or a piece of fruit. There were no drive-through restaurants and no pizza-delivery places. Spices were expensive and sometimes hard to find. Burgers, fries, chips, soda pop, and ice cream weren't yet invented. For the most part, the poorest among us today have access to a broader range of delicacies than the richest Romans in the days of the empire.

It was the fulfillment of hundreds of years of prayers. With this edict, Christians could meet freely to worship throughout the empire. To say that the edict placed Christianity on the same plane as Roman paganism would not be entirely accurate. The edict simply decriminalized being a Christian. Old Roman paganism would never go away completely, but the Edict of Milan went a long way to open the floodgates of Christian fervor within the empire.

THE RISE OF ARIANISM

With the emperor on their side, the Christians of the fourth century must have felt pretty good. After all, the years of persecution, especially under the emperors Decius and Diocletian, were over and believers could get serious about spreading the gospel even further throughout the empire. Most Christians did not realize that the next great challenge to the survival of the church would not come from the Romans or the barbarians that lurked on the empire's borders. The threat would come from within.

Around 318, Arius, who was a senior official in the church of Alexandria, Egypt, challenged the very substance of the relationship between God and Jesus. According to Arius, Jesus and God were not one and the same. Jesus was an inferior being to God, not having the inherent divinity, purity, wisdom, and goodness that God possessed. Arius preached this belief and began to gather converts to his cause. It is not surprising that this message would catch on. Among nonbelievers, the divinity of Jesus was a sticking point. It was easy enough for the people of the time to accept the divinity of the God the early Christians described. There were lots of gods around for the people to follow. What's one more? All in all, the Romans had simply adopted the Greek pantheon of gods, renamed them, and absorbed them into their religion. Adding another god to that list, even one whose followers claimed was the only true god, was not a tremendous adjustment.

THE DEITY OF CHRIST

The divinity of Christ was another matter. Though the Romans pictured their gods in human form, and even the emperors were declared gods at times, the Romans knew the difference between a god and a man. Jesus was troubling for that reason. To make the case even stickier, the Christians

MEANWHILE, BACK AT THE RANCH...

Shortly after the conversion of Constantine, the Gupta dynasty came to power in present-day Bangladesh and Northern India. Gupta rule of the region began when Chandragupta I gained control of the small kingdom of Magadha and expanded to other areas through war and marriage into other royal lines. The Gupta line of kings reigned from about A.D. 320 to 500. This was a time period of cultural growth for the region: Many of the classical forms of Indian dance, music, literature, and sculpture developed under Gupta rule. Gupta mathematicians were among the best in the world and, among other things, developed the Hindu-Arabic numerals we use today and invented the decimal system. Students of many countries and religions came to study at the Buddhist monastery at Nalanda, which was well known for its libraries. Like the Romans, the Gupta had long-standing problems with the Huns. Between about A.D. 500 and 550, Hunnish invaders took over most of the Gupta region.

SET THE STAGE!

When we look back at whole nations converting just because a national leader did, our modern sense of autonomy stands on its ear. Authority was a much stronger concept in ancient days, though. In the Roman Empire, the undisputed head of the household was the paterfamilias, which means *father of the family*. The paterfamilias had absolute control over all matters. He could sell his children into slavery or kill them if he wished, and nothing would be done about it. While the paterfamilias lived, all family possessions belonged to him. Even adult sons could not own property or have legal authority over their own children until the paterfamilias died. And you thought *your* dad was rough.

preached that God and Jesus were essentially the same, two parts of the same Godhead, which was completed by the Holy Spirit. The concept of the Trinity remains difficult for many people to understand even after two thousand years of scholarship; imagine how it must have been in A.D. 318!

So Arius began to gather followers. In fact, they started to increase so quickly that Bishop Alexander of Alexandria was forced to try some discipline. He called a council of Egyptian and Libyan bishops who excommunicated Arius and some of his followers. Unfortunately, Arius had enlisted some powerful followers who rose to his defense.

The conflict escalated as powerful bishops argued and formed alliances. One powerful supporter was Eusebius of Nicomedia. Nicomedia was the political capital of the East. The church there was one of the most powerful as well. What had started as a small doctrinal conflict in North Africa was becoming a national issue that was eventually laid on the table of the emperor. Constantine had hoped that Christianity would be a unifying force in the empire. He had seen it as something that Roman citizens could rally around regardless of their geographic or ethnic background. With the growing argument over what was now called Arianism, quite the opposite was becoming true.

To make matters more urgent, Constantine was now the emperor of both the Eastern and Western empires. Whereas he had hoped that one faith would help reconcile the differences between the Roman West and the essentially Greek East, Arianism threatened to tear the two empires apart.

In the end, Arianism never gained a toehold in the West. Orthodox Christianity was powerful there. In the West, Arianism gained popularity only among the barbarian tribes. Arianism caught on quickly in the East, however.

THE COUNCIL OF NICAEA AND DOCTRINE
To try to stifle the conflict, Constantine sent the Spanish bishop Ossius to attempt to reconcile Arius and Alexander. When that effort failed, Constantine called for a meeting of bishops at the place that is now Ankara. Later that year, however, he changed the location to the city of Nicaea where he had an imperial palace. The council was held in 325. Though Constantine had hoped that the council would have universal attendance so its rulings would have widespread power, only 120 bishops attended, and only a few of those had come from the West. Bishop Sylvester of Rome did not come, but he did send two presbyters.

At the council, Constantine put his support with the opponents of Arianism. After all, the beliefs that Arius was preaching were causing trouble in his empire: There had even been riots in Alexandria. Arius proclaimed that the Son of God was a created being who, though he was very much like God, was not present with God in eternity past. Constantine proposed the concept of "homoousios," which meant "of the same substance." Jesus and God were not only similar, as Arius believed, they were made of the same essence. Though the two beings were different, their basic substance was the same. The council sided with the emperor. Whatever they believed, they were not foolish enough to oppose him. To make things clear, they even created a creed of belief that comes down to us today as the Nicene Creed.

THE COUNCIL OF NICAEA AND CHURCH ORGANIZATION
Since the 120 bishops were already together at the Council of Nicaea, they decided to work on some other issues of importance to the church. The faith was still growing rapidly, and the old

SET THE STAGE!
THE NICENE CREED

The Nicene Creed has been modified many times since it was compiled by the Council of Nicaea, but in its original form it appeared this way:

We believe in one God, the Father Almighty, maker of all things, both visible and invisible; and in one Lord, Jesus Christ, the Son of God, only begotten of the Father, that is to say, of the substance of the Father, God of God and Light of Light, very God of very God, begotten, not made, being of one substance with the Father, by whom all things were made, both things in heaven and things on earth; who, for us men and for our salvation, came down and was made flesh, was made man, suffered, and rose again on the third day, went up into the heavens, and is to come again to judge both the quick and the dead; and in the Holy Ghost.

systems of organization were becoming obsolete. Since the early days, the church hierarchy had evolved around its strong leaders. By the fourth century, these strong leaders were bishops with many churches under their authority. Often, the priests who led local churches simply reported to the parent church that had sent them on their missionary work and supported them. Through the years there arose powerful bishops in these home churches and a wide range of procedural and organizational policies. The Council of Nicaea attempted to make some rules that would create uniformity among the churches. Once again, the church leaders and the emperor felt that the church of an empire should be well run, like an empire. The Council of Nicaea issued twenty canons dealing with church organization and policy. These canons ranged from instructions for admitting people to the church to rules governing the behavior of deacons and clergy.

Most people in the churches of the empire would not have cared one way or the other about most of these rules. However, the council did one thing that caused some friction down the line. The council strengthened the organization of the church.

The power of the bishops was increased, and not only that, but specifically the bishops of Rome, Alexandria, Antioch, Caesarea, and Jerusalem were given greater power. As you will notice, only one of those cities would have naturally fallen under the power of the West, and that was Rome itself. Since the large majority of the bishops at the council were from the East, they naturally placed more power in their own region.

 SET THE STAGE!

The people of the Roman Empire were divided into several distinct social classes. The most important distinction was between slaves and citizens. Citizens of the empire had certain legal rights, whereas slaves had virtually none. Some slaves were able to buy or earn citizenship, and others were given their freedom as a reward for good service. One guaranteed route to citizenship was via military service in the imperial army. For this reason, people in conquered lands often volunteered for military service rather than be carted off as slaves. For centuries, this practice helped keep the Roman army strong.

Within the ranks of citizenry, there were other more exclusive subgroups, including:

Equites (EHK wuh teez), the middle class made up of merchants, prosperous landowners, government workers, and civil servants;

Roman senators and their families, who were the upper class;

The Roman emperor and the imperial family. Emperors were, at some times during the Roman empire, worshiped as gods. This definitely put them at a different social level.

Priests and other clergy enjoyed varying degrees of status during different eras of the empire. At some points, Christian clergymen were imprisoned or executed. At other times, the pope exercised more power than the emperor.

CONSTANTINOPLE

It was an uneasy alliance between Constantine and Licinius that had assured Constantine's victory over his rival Maxentius. In fact, it was such an uneasy alliance that by 324 Constantine had ousted Licinius and become emperor of both the East and West. The entire empire was his from England in the West to

Africa in the South to India in the East. He spent the next several years consolidating his power; then on May 11, 330, he dedicated Constantinople as his new capital. It was not a totally unexpected move. According to Suetonius, emperors all the way back as far as Julius Caesar had considered moving the capital away from Rome. Rome had been the capital of the Roman republic, and there would always be the memory of that era in the city. Whenever hard times arose, so would the rumblings about the republic whispered in the streets of Rome.

There was no such history at the new capital. Constantinople was founded on the site of the old city of Byzantium. It is said that Constantine himself laid out the boundaries of the new city. He chose wisely in the location of the city. Byzantium sat on the peninsula of the Bosporus. Not only was the city in an ideal position as a port, but it was also nearly invulnerable to attacks from both sea and land. From the city, the navy could easily control all the shipping between the Black Sea, the Aegean, and the Mediterranean. Economically, then, Constantine put his new capital right in the center of activity. With this new location, he

 IMAGINE THAT!

Early Christians' hymns often affirmed doctrines. The Arian Christians had their own hymns as well.

> The uncreated God has made the Son
> A beginning of things created,
> And by adoption has God made the Son
> Into an advancement of himself.
> Yet the Son's substance is
> Removed from the substance of the Father:
> The Son is not equal to the Father,
> Nor does he share the same substance.
> God is the all-wise Father,
> And the Son is the teacher of His mysteries.
> The members of the Holy Trinity
> Share unequal glories.

(from *The Holy Fire: The Story of the Fathers of the Eastern Church*, Robert Payne, St. Vladimir's Seminary Press, 1980) could control all the trade between East and West.

While many of Constantine's grand schemes did not survive many generations after his death, his choice of Constantinople would endure for centuries. In fact, the city would endure the collapse of the Western empire, the fall of Rome, the ascendance of powerful barbarians, and the Middle Ages before it would fall to the Ottoman Turks in 1453. It was, for over eleven hundred years, a bastion of stability in an ever-changing world. It was a refuge from the encroaching "dark ages" and a place where Christianity could endure, uninterrupted. The city and the faith it protected became a bridge between the ancient world and our own.

CONSTANTINE AND THE CHURCH

Constantine may have been baptized only on his deathbed, but he was a great friend to Christians from the time of his conversion. He did more than just give Christians the right to worship. He also granted the Christian clergy the same rights as the established state clergy of Rome. The clergy were exempted from having to pay taxes. Any man could bequeath property to the church, which would then have the rights of further inheritance. From a legal point of view, the church was given actual status. In fact, the church courts (episcopal courts) were given power to decide civil suits.

Constantine was also a church builder. As emperor, he poured great amounts of money into building churches throughout the empire. Both the basilica of Saint Peter and the basilica of the Lateran in Rome are ascribed to him. He wanted to preserve relics (religious artifacts) and the historical story of Jesus. To do this, he sent scholars to Palestine and founded the Church of the Holy Sepulcher at the place of Christ's burial, the Church of the Ascension on the Mount of Olives, and the Church of the Nativity in Bethlehem. When he died in 337, Emperor Constantine left a legacy of good rule politically and as a supporter of Christianity.

Throughout his rule, Constantine took an active part in the religious conflicts that occurred during his reign. During the conflict over Arianism, he called the Council of Nicaea. Constantine was forced to act similarly in the church conflict associated with Donatism.

IMAGINE THAT!

According to some sources, St. Nick may have attended the Council of Nicaea!

Santa Claus was a bishop in the early days of the church. The name "Santa Claus" comes from the Dutch "Sinterklaas," which means "Saint Nicholas." Nicholas was the bishop of a place called Myra in the kingdom of Lycia in Asia minor. Legend says that Nicholas was among those imprisoned by the emperor Diocletian, was released by Constantine, and attended the Council of Nicaea. Nicholas is credited with many miracles and is considered to be the patron saint of sailors, travelers, merchants, bakers, and (of course) children. Santa's red outfit may have evolved from the robes commonly worn by bishops. Another legend says that Nicholas gave a gift of gold to three girls who could not get married because they had no dowries. Many historians think that this particular legend may have evolved into the gift-giving associated with Santa Claus. Many countries still observe a separate holiday for St. Nicholas in early December.

DONATISM

Donatism was a heretical Christian movement during the fourth and fifth centuries. The followers of the movement claimed that the validity of the sacraments depended on the moral character of the minister. The movement had its roots in the consecration of a bishop of Carthage in 311. One of the three consecrating bishops was believed to be a *traditor:* clergy who handed over their copies of the Bible to the persecutors sent by the Roman emperor Diocletian. Because this one bishop was not squeaky clean in their eyes, a group of seventy bishops opposed his consecration and formed a synod at Carthage. They believed that the church must exclude from its membership people who have committed serious sin, and because of that no sacrament could rightly be performed by a *traditor*. The synod excommunicated the Carthaginian bishop when he refused to appear before it. Four years later when the new bishop died, the theologian Donatus the Great became bishop of Carthage, and the movement took its name from him.

Constantine wanted badly to settle this dispute. The issue was submitted to various ecclesiastical bodies and in 316 to the emperor himself. In each case the consecration of the bishop elected originally, in 311, was upheld. At first the emperor attempted to curb the Donatist movement by force, but in 321 he adopted a policy of tolerance. This approach did not make the movement go away, so it required the attention of other emperors as well. The policy of tolerance was reversed by Constantine's youngest son, Constans I, who persecuted Donatists. In 411, a debate between the Donatist and Catholic bishops was held at Carthage to settle the dispute. The outcome once again went against the Donatists. Consequently, they were deprived of all civil rights in 414, and in the following year, their assemblies were banned under penalty of death. The movement then began to decline, but it survived another three hundred years or so before it disappeared.

 SET THE STAGE!

When Greeks first used the word "barbarians" (or a similar form), it implied any person that spoke a language that a Greek wouldn't understand. During the time of Alexander the Great, the term had become one of condescension. It implied any group that did not absorb the Greek culture.

By the time Constantine ruled, the term "barbarian" was used for the Goths, Vandals, and Huns. It implied a lesser people in sophistication who lived outside of the Roman Empire.

MEANWHILE, BACK AT THE RANCH...ER...PALACE

After Constantine died, the empire was divided among his three sons, Constantius, Constantine II, and Constans. It was not long before an empire-sized family feud broke out, and there was a real struggle for power. In the competition, Constantine II was killed in 340 and Constans in 350. That left only Constantius. His competition dead, he ruled the empire alone until 361. He had no children to follow him as emperor, so he toyed with the idea of one of his two (living) cousins, Gallus or Julian, succeeding him. He originally named Gallus his caesar and heir, but changed his mind and had him killed instead in 354. As the remaining cousin, Julian was named Caesar in 355 and went on to rule as emperor in 361–63. He tried to reinstate paganism as the state religion. The remaining pagans were thrilled as Julian paid for temples to be constructed. By that point there were no pagan temples at all in Constantinople. Julian held pagan festivals and even made educational reforms designed to promote paganism and discourage Christianity.

When Julian was killed in battle in 363, the head of his court guards, Jovian, was proclaimed emperor by the army. Jovian was a devout Christian who followed the Nicene Creed. Once again, Christianity was elevated.

When Jovian died suddenly in 364, his brother Valens became the emperor of the Eastern empire. As an Arian, Valens reminded the empire that the official Christianity was still that which had been declared by the former emperor Constantius. In fact, he made life miserable for those who opposed Arianism, though his persecution was not systematic. The Christians of the time found that sometimes a Christian emperor could cause them as much fear and anxiety as the pagan Julian.

At Jovian's death, his other brother, Valentinian I became emperor of the Western empire. Unlike Valens, Valentinian believed in the Nicene Creed—the creed that had stood against Arianism at the Council of Nicaea. He was not an intolerant emperor, however, and made religious toleration, even of paganism and Arianism, the rule for his kingdom.

BACK IN ROME

Although the majority of the political action moved from Rome to Constantinople for many years after Constantine, the political growth of the church was certainly led by the bishop of Rome, the pope. The popes kept their eyes and ears open, watching the emperors and how they wielded power. They learned a lot. Under Constantine, the church had gained a new political power, and the popes began to use it. Eusebius had shown the model. If the church is a reflection of the kingdom of heaven, it is only right, the bishops reasoned, to rule the church as a king would.

As a result, starting with Damasas (366–84), the popes began to increase their power within the church and extend that power into the political arena. It was Damasas who asserted the theory that the bishop of Rome is the direct descendent of the disciple Peter. He made that theory part of the papal doctrine. If his assertion were true, then the bishop of Rome would have a legitimate claim to a direct line of power flowing from the disciples to him. By this argument, Damasas asserted that the bishop of Rome had primacy over all other bishops.

Pope Innocent I, who served from 401–417, took it even further. He declared that nothing done in the provinces of the Roman Empire (since the church *was* the church of the empire) was finished unless it had come to his knowledge. In that way he asserted that his decisions affected "all the churches of the world," not just those churches under the local jurisdiction of the Roman church.

BASIL THE GREAT

The church was in a mess in 370 when Basil the Great succeeded his equally famous predecessor, Eusebius, as bishop of Caesarea. The conflict between orthodox Christians and Arians was more complicated every day. The emperor Valens had added to the fray. Basil's role was to get things back on track.

SET THE STAGE!

The Roman day began at sunrise. Lamp oil was expensive, and oil lamps gave off scant light, so daylight was valuable and not to be wasted.

Basil had been born into a wealthy Christian family in about 330. The family lived in Caesarea, in Cappadocia, north of Antioch. He had all the advantages of his family's wealth and a good education at Constantinople and Athens. He chose to reject the easy life to become an ascetic living on his family's estate. Unlike many of his more "worldly" Christians, Basil focused his life's work on biblical study. He took the discipline and academic skills of his classical education and put them to work on understanding and promoting his faith.

BASIL'S WORK AND WRITINGS

In 364, Basil was ordained as a presbyter. By 370, he was ordained as bishop. He was much more than a political appointee, though. From the beginning, he opposed the form of Arianism that was presently the state religion. As if that were not enough to make powerful enemies, he opposed Damasas's (the bishop of Rome) assertion that the pope was the supreme judge of the church. Basil *was* diplomatic enough to agree with Damasas on the pope's authority in the area of doctrine.

Basil made major contributions to the church in two areas: the doctrine of the Trinity and the monastic life. No one before Basil had laid out the real issues of community and love in living the monastic life. In his day, monks were often merely hermits who chose to separate themselves from the world. Basil taught that there is a community of people that make up the monastics and that love is at the core of their faith and actions.

His writings on the Trinity were attempts to sift through all the conflicting doctrines that swirled around the church at the time. In addition to the Arians, there were the Pneumatomachians (say *that* three times fast), who denied that the Holy Spirit was divine. Basil opposed them in his work *On the Holy Spirit*. He was the first to really solidify the accepted formula for the Trinity: one substance (*ousia*), and three persons (*hypostaseis*). He and two fellow Capadocians, Gregory of Nyssa and Gregory of Nazianus, finally convinced many of the Eastern church leaders in this concept of the Trinity.

MEANWHILE, BACK AT THE PALACE AGAIN...

The emperor brothers, Valens and Valentinian I, had more troubles than just religious doctrine squabbles. After hundreds of years of conflict, the Goths once again became thorns in the brothers' sides. The Goths were an important group of ancient German people. They were a prototype of the barbarian tribe. Though their original home is clouded in prehistory, we know that up until the early part of the third century they lived along the Southern coast of the Baltic. For reasons that are basically unknown, they migrated southward by the fourth century and

SINNERS AND SAINTS
EUSEBIUS

Eusebius of Caesarea was a bishop and a historian. In fact, he is sometimes called the Father of Church History. He was involved in the Arian controversy and the Council of Nicaea. Some historians even describe Eusebius as having a trace of Arianism in his theology. Nevertheless, this bishop voted against Arius at the council of Nicaea and continued on to become one of the church's leading thinkers and writers. He, in fact, became the emperor's biographer. The stories we have today about Constantine's conversion come largely through the writings of Eusebius.

Eusebius's *Ecclesiastical History* was an account of the church up until 324. In this work and in another, *Life of Constantine,* most likely written by Eusebius, the writer not only tells the story of the church, he paints a portrait of it in light of the politics of his day. The church was portrayed in this work in terms of a Christian emperor and a Christian empire. Both the empire and church were earthly images of the kingdom of heaven. God had used both the empire and the church to save humanity. First, the empire brought order to the world and was a reflection of how God ruled the universe as a sole monarch. Then the church brought further order to the world by replacing polytheism with monotheism. Constantine himself was portrayed as an earthly image of the *logos,* the force that brought order to the world. It is much the same way Christ Himself was portrayed in the first chapter of John's Gospel. To Eusebius, the Christian emperor was the image of the all-powerful one God.

Eusebius liked to tread in deep water theologically. He died in 339, but the influence of his writings was tremendous and long lasting. In fact, much of the theology

Continued

SINNERS AND SAINTS (CONTINUED)

of the Middle Ages, hundreds of years in the future, can be traced back to Eusebius. He believed in the power of a good ruler to fight back the forces of darkness. To him, the empire he lived in was a good, clear reflection of God's plan for the universe. There were dark days ahead, but from Eusebius's writings you wouldn't have known it.

settled in the area of the Black Sea. In that region they became a large tribe, practiced piracy, and began to harass the Roman Empire.

During the reigns of Valens and Valentinian, the Goths were building in power and influence along the borders of the empire, and as the legions dwindled, they moved ever closer. Valentinian died in 375 and was succeeded in the West by his sons Gratian and the child Valentinian II. When Valens died while campaigning against the Goths in 378, Gratian named Theodosius as the Augustus of the East. Valentinian II was really just a child, and though he officially ruled for seventeen years, he played no important role at all in the empire. Things were quite different for Gratian and Theodosius, however.

Like Valentinian, the two men believed in the Nicene Creed and opposed Arianism. Unlike their predecessor, they saw no room for religious toleration. In that regard, there was a certain bishop who may very well have influenced that policy.

AMBROSE, BISHOP OF MILAN

Ambrose became the bishop of Milan in 374. To put it mildly, he was an unlikely choice. He was the son of a high-ranking official in the emperor Constantine's government. He had been educated and groomed to assume a similar position in government. When he finished his studies in the law, he was appointed governor of the area surrounding Milan. Presumably his journey up through the ranks of government had just begun. Then, in 374, the bishop of Milan, who was an Arian, died. A riot actually broke out as the church tried to name his successor. Surprisingly, the people began to call for Ambrose, their governor, to be named bishop. There was only one problem: Though Ambrose was a Christian, he had never been baptized. Not one to miss this opportunity, Ambrose was baptized and eight days later was a bishop.

Ambrose took his new job seriously and applied both his intellect and his political skill to the position. He began to preach and to study the scripture. He also began to wield power in a new way. He worked to influence imperial policy at the highest level. In those days, Milan was the seat of imperial power in the West, and Rome was the center of power for both the pagan Senate and the Western church. Ambrose worked to convince Emperor Gratian to eliminate paganism and discontinue the policy of tolerance which Valentinian I had instituted. He actually convinced the emperor to give up his religious title, *pontifex maximus*. In effect, this action removed the head of the state, pagan religion.

AMBROSE VS. POLITICS

In 385, Ambrose found himself in direct conflict with the mother of the emperor Valentinian II. Justina was an Arian and wanted to take over the cathedral of Milan for Arian worship. She not only had the power of the young emperor behind her, she also had a small army of Arian, German mercenaries to use for muscle. In 385, she had her mercenaries besiege the cathedral with Ambrose in it. The stage was set for a terrible scene of violence, but it never happened. For some reason the troops withdrew. Perhaps Justina was bluffing, or it could be that the Germans feared reprisals for the anti-Arian emperor Theodosius in the East. Regardless, Ambrose had made his point: The church would not back down to the throne.

Ambrose was also not afraid to take on the Eastern emperor Theodosius. Much of Theodosius's sizable army consisted of German mercenaries. To be ready to fight, they were garrisoned throughout the empire. One group was headquartered in the rich, prosperous city of Thessalonica. Unfortunately, the leader of these soldiers was either incompetent or lax, and the soldiers virtually ran amok committing crimes and behaving badly as garrisoned troops always have. The people of the city got fed up with their actions and revolted against the army, killing officers and many regular soldiers.

This infuriated Theodosius, who ordered the massacre of many of the city's citizens. For this action, Ambrose excommunicated the emperor and demanded public acknowledgment of his guilt. In spite of his power, the emperor was forced to obey Ambrose's instructions for this confession and penance. Amazingly, Ambrose forced the emperor to not wear his imperial garments and finery during the time of penance.

To be sure, Ambrose of Milan placed the church in a different role in the power structure of the Roman Empire. It was a change that would continue to evolve for a thousand years.

 SET THE STAGE!

Pope is a word that comes from the Greek word "pappas." It's the name a child called his father, like "daddy." The Roman Catholic Church considers Peter the first pope. Early in the church's history, all bishops (regional pastors) were called popes. In the early 500s, the name came to be used only for the bishop of Rome and continued that way. (Popes were also called "pontiffs.")

Up until the year 873, popes were allowed to get married and have children.

"Papacy" is a term that refers to the system of bishops and popes. "See" refers to the jurisdiction of a bishop. "Cardinals" are bishops with high-ranking positions in church structure.

Most popes have been Italian, but not all. During his leadership, a pope today lives in the Vatican, which is a country unto itself within Rome. (The Vatican is 109 acres and has its own stamps, flag, and communication system.)

IMAGINE THAT!

Asceticism is the practice of denying or punishing yourself in order to accomplish something spiritually. It could involve giving up something, like when a person fasts or remains celibate. It could involve discomfort, like when someone wears uncomfortable clothing, sleeps on the floor, or even hurts himself. In the story of Elijah's challenge to the prophets of Baal, you see asceticism at work in idol worship. In order to get their god to respond, the false prophets cut themselves, perhaps to show the vehemence of their requests (1 Kings 18:20–29).

Many Christian ascetics flogged themselves or each other with whips in gruesome public displays. On the other hand, some regarded public suffering as ostentatious and overzealous. Because of this, many ascetics began to keep their suffering a private matter between themselves and God. One such man was Thomas Becket the archbishop of Canterbury in the 1100s, who was later made a saint. A common ascetic practice was the wearing of "hair shirts," very uncomfortable garments made of the coarse hairs of camel or goat. The shirts pricked the skin and caused the wearer to itch profusely. Becket managed to completely hide the fact that he wore a hair shirt until, after his death, one was discovered under his other garments.

Whatever the form of self-inflicted suffering, the ascetics saw it as a means of spiritual growth or accomplishment. There were many Christian ascetics, including Basil. To deny the body seemed to them to be a way to strengthen or clarify the soul.

A CHRISTIAN EMPIRE—THEODOSIUS THE GREAT

Constantine had decriminalized being a Christian. He had made religious toleration the law of the land. For a radically new religion trying to grow in an old, ordered empire with an established state religion, that was a huge gift. The succeeding emperors had dealt with the Christian church in each his own way, some persecuting Christians, others persecuting the enemies of the church. There was no going backwards, however, to the time before Constantine. Because of his policies the church itself had grown in power and influence to the point that being an enemy of the church had serious consequences.

That didn't mean that the empire itself was Christian. It was still a very mixed bag of old paganism, Arianism, various sects of

Christianity, and plenty of localized sects. That lack of unity was another product of religious toleration. But, as the church grew in power, bishops such as Ambrose of Milan were able to influence the emperor to take the empire in a new direction.

In 379, Theodosius became emperor of the Eastern Roman Empire. He came to power the old-fashioned way. He was the son of a famous father, also named Theodosius, who had been a very successful general in the army under Emperor Valentinian I. Before his appointment as Augustus in 378, Theodosius had shown little interest in the Christian faith, but he was baptized that year in Thessalonica by the bishop of the city, who was a follower of the Nicene Creed. The fact that Theodosius chose the Nicene rather than the Arian faith was to have a huge impact for many years.

THEODOSIUS AND ARIANISM

It was not the best of times to be the emperor of the East. Theodosius was faced with two huge problems. First, the religious bickering that was a constant element in Eastern politics was threatening to tear the empire apart. (Constantine had faced much the same situation when he called the Council of Nicaea.) Second, the Goths, who had been around the borders of the Eastern empire for hundreds of years, had become a truly serious threat to the empire. If that problem was not handled, there might not even be an Eastern empire.

 SET THE STAGE!

Possibly the first monk was a 4th-century Egyptian hermit named Anthony of Thebes. Anthony, like many people of that time, did not want to be exposed to the corruption and temptations of society, so he became a solitary hermit (as opposed to the rare "social hermit"). This must have proved a little too lonely because eventually he formed a community with several other hermits (at which point one must assume they were officially monks, because they certainly weren't hermits anymore). Anyway, the idea caught on with the help of men like Basil the Great.

During the rule of Valens in the East, Arianism had taken the leading role in Eastern religion, but there were constant squabbles and debates with the rival Nicaeans. It is hard for us in the twenty-first century to picture the social unrest that these religious conflicts caused. Perhaps the closest parallel in recent history was the unrest over the war in Vietnam in the sixties. The populace was polarized, and each side had very strong feelings about their opinions. The streets of Constantinople, the capital, were the sites of numerous fights, arguments, and protests over even minor religious ideas. Theodosius somehow had to restore order.

Upon his arrival in the capital as the emperor, Theodosius asked the bishop of Constantinople, an Arian, to renounce his Arianism and join the followers of the Nicene Creed. The bishop refused and, bowing to the power of the emperor, moved his meetings outside the gates of the city where he continued to have Arian meetings. With the city's churches now empty, all of them were taken over by Nicaean believers. By 380, the emperor was ready to make an astounding policy statement in this area. He decreed that only those who believed in the Trinity of Father, Son, and Holy Ghost were members of the catholic (universal) church. All the others were "mad and insane people" who were not part of the church and had no right to even assemble. Since Constantine's time there

 SET THE STAGE!

Though Latin and Greek were the languages used by the Roman government and higher social strata throughout the empire, most Roman subjects still used their native languages. People in Britain, Scotland, Ireland, and Gaul (a land located where modern-day Belgium, France, and part of Germany are now) spoke Celtic. In other parts of the empire, people spoke Berber, Aramaic, or one of a host of other languages. Even though most of the lower classes in lands outside Italy never had the opportunity to learn formal Latin or Greek, many words from both languages seeped into their languages over time. A prime example in English, a Germanic tongue, is the very word *language*, which comes from the Latin word for tongue.

had been the distinction between Catholic Christians and heretics. Because of this decree, that distinction became the law.

COUNCIL OF CONSTANTINOPLE

In spite of this apparent intolerance, Theodosius was anxious to establish peace within the Christian church. Toward that goal he called a religious council in 381 at Constantinople. Only members of the Eastern church participated, and for a long time it was not even considered significant to be called an official ecumenical council. The main business of the council was to condemn the new semi-Arian heresy of Macedonius that claimed that the Holy Spirit was a created rather than an eternal being. It also declared that the Holy Spirit was of one essence with the Father and the Son.

Politically, the council tried to settle a growing problem of unity between the church in Rome and the rest of the church. The council declared that the patriarch of Constantinople ranked next to the bishop of Rome. Instead of causing greater unity, this decree caused all kinds of trouble between the church in Constantinople and the bishops of other Eastern sees (jurisdictions of the bishops) whose power was much older.

DEALING WITH THE PAGANS

Besides dealing with all these conflicts within the Christian church, Theodosius still had millions of pagans to worry about. He decided that in order to have a unified empire, there could be only one religion. That religion was to be Christianity. Through a series of decrees, the emperor outlawed all the things that the pagans did to observe their religion. They were forbidden to offer sacrifices, to read the future by observing the entrails of animals, and to even visit their temples. This, in effect, closed the temples, which were often looted and torn down soon

 DID YOU KNOW?

At its height of influence, the Roman Empire had between 50 and 70 million subjects, almost a million of whom lived in Rome. At the time, Rome was the biggest city the world had ever seen.

thereafter. His last decree against the pagans was in 392. It outlawed all pagan activities and made disobedience of these prohibitions an offense against the emperor. For all intents and purposes, that ended paganism as an established religion. Without the opportunity to practice the religion, it just died.

DEALING WITH THE GOTHS

The Goths were not a new problem for the Roman Empire of the late fourth century. They were an old nemesis. For reasons that are still not completely clear, near the beginning of the Christian era, the Goths moved southward from their original home on the southern shore of the Baltic Sea. They migrated as far south as the Black Sea and settled there. The Dniester River divided the Goths living in that area into the eastern Goths (Ostrogoths) and the western Goths (Visigoths). The Black Sea area had been colonized by Greeks, whose cultural level was high. The Goths benefited from contact with these Greeks and attained a level of cultural development higher than any of the other barbarian tribes that were to invade and harass the Roman Empire.

The area of the Black Sea was a good place to live, but full of temptations. By sailing through the Bosporus, the opportunity was there to launch piratical raids as far as Greece itself, and the Goths did just that. By land, the Goths reached southwest to the banks of the Danube River—the actual border of the Roman Empire. When the empire fell into anarchy in the third century, the Goths simply crossed the Danube and attacked the empire itself. The emperor Gordian was forced to pay them tribute in the third century. The emperor Decius had been forced to march against them in 251 and was killed in the effort. In 269, Claudius had succeeded in defeating them, but by 275 the emperor Aurelian had been forced to simply give up territory to them. The Goths became part of the empire itself in that they became mercenaries for whichever Roman leader could afford their services. Constantine had used them during his conflict with Licinius.

To further complicate matters, the Goths had begun to be Christians in the late third century. The first were probably converted by Christian prisoners captured in Asia Minor on one of their sea raids. The Gothic Christians were even represented at the Council of Nicaea by their bishop, Theophilus. Christianity had truly spread among the Goths during the fourth century because of the work of one man—Ulfilas.

ULFILAS

Ulfilas was a member of the Visigoth tribe, though the nationality of his birth is disputed. Some say he was the descendant of a Christian Roman prisoner. Others say he was a Greek, but born in Gothic territory. Regardless, he spent a number of years in Constantinople and was ordained there as a bishop by an Arian bishop. When he returned to the Goths, he preached Arian Christianity to them for a number of years. Since he wanted his people to have access to the Gospels, he actually invented a Gothic alphabet, based somewhat on the Greek letters, and translated the Bible into the Gothic language. Through his efforts, the Visigoths became an Arian Christian people.

THE HUNS

The peaceful relations between the Goths and the empire ended in 376. The fault did not really lie with either the Goths or the Romans; it lay with the Huns. The Huns had come sweeping out of the East. Research indicates that they were nomadic people who originated in north central Asia. Although they resemble the Mongols and Magyars in some ways, they appear not to have been related ethnically to them. The Huns were organized into ravaging military hordes riding small, rapid horses. In the third century B.C., they invaded China, where part of the Great Wall was built to repel them. By the fourth century A.D., they had turned westward and reached the area of the Black Sea where they attacked the Goths mercilessly, killing woman and children indiscriminately. They overran the Ostrogoths, who became a subject people to them. The Visigoths to the west fled to the southwest to the northern bank of the Danube. There they pleaded with the Roman officials to let them cross into the relative safety of the empire. These "barbarians" themselves offered to become farmers and supply soldiers to the army.

Though there was some opposition, the Goths were allowed to cross the Danube and live in the empire.

THE GOTHS FIGHT BACK

Before long the Goths became fed up with terrible treatment and broken promises from their Roman "landlords." In 378, they mobilized and marched toward Constantinople. The emperor Valens was at war in Persia, but when he received the news of the Goths' actions he marched to meet them. The two armies met at Hadrianople. Valens was killed, and the Roman army was completely defeated. There was no force left to stop them, so the Goths overran the Balkan peninsula as far as the walls of Constantinople.

This was the situation in which Theodosius found himself when he became emperor. His solution was simple. He put together an army, not from the ranks of traditional Roman legions, but from the Goths themselves. There were Goths still loyal to the empire, and there were, as always, some who were loyal to who paid them. With this mercenary army, Theodosius was able to defeat the invading Goths. He had not found the solution to the Gothic problem, however. In fact, he had opened the door to an era of dependence upon the Goths as his army. Militarily that worked. Socially it ushered in hundreds of years of troubles between the native populations of the empire and the Germanic people

SINNERS AND SAINTS
ATTILA THE HUN

Attila is probably the most famous of the Huns. The crest, or symbol, for Attila and his barbarians was a skull with horns. He was referred to as the "scourge of God." For all his ferocity, though, Attila did not die in battle. He failed to appear one morning after a feast. His men broke into his chambers to find that Attila had asphyxiated from a severe hemorrhage in his nose. In other words, the mighty warrior died from a nosebleed.

among them. The terrible problems that occurred at Thessalonica and caused so much trouble between Theodosius and Ambrose of Milan were just the beginning. The dependence of the army on Germanic mercenaries would, in the end, have terrible effects. The Germans learned the Roman tactics and methods of warfare and grew into a foreign army within the empire. The advantages that had allowed Rome to fight back its invaders of hundreds of years were simply lost to the enemy.

So, when Theodosius died in Milan in 395, he had not really solved the two main problems that had faced him when he first came to Constantinople. Although the Second Ecumenical Council in Constantinople in 381 had presented a united front against nonorthodox Christianity, it never provided any substantial unity of faith within the empire. Of course that disunity was aggravated by the inclusion of thousands of Arian Goths as an integral part of the empire: as soldiers who wielded tremendous power and influence.

His successes were also tremendous, however. While the empire was not united behind a single religious creed, it had become a Christian empire. Theodosius drove the final nails into the coffin of paganism. And though there were pagans for hundreds of years to come, they were powerless to convert the empire back to its old Greco-Roman self.

AUGUSTINE

It is unusual for a man to be able to influence an entire generation. Augustine was able to influence the Christian religion for nearly sixteen hundred years. It was not something he set out to do. Augustine once prayed, "Lord, make me chaste, but not yet." He was a man who lived and loved passionately and wrote about it in his autobiographical *Confessions.* He was a man who did not come to be a Christian lightly and easily. For Augustine, it was a journey through all the possible answers until he found the truth.

Augustine was born in the land that is now Algeria in 354. His mother was a devout Christian and Augustine was, from the start, reared in the faith. Though he attended the required catechism classes as a child, he was not baptized until 387. His path to that baptism is the subject of his *Confessions*. He had the good fortune as did many children of his age to study the literature and philosophy of Greece and Rome. In 373, he had happened to read a work by Cicero that convinced him he should love divine wisdom. When he looked at the Bible however, he did not see that wisdom but barbarity. He became a follower of Manicheism, which taught that truth was found in reason and encouraged an ascetic lifestyle, but not one devoted to Christ. That lasted about nine years; then he began to distrust that reason was necessarily the way to wisdom.

AUGUSTINE TRIES SOMETHING NEW

Disillusioned, Augustine moved to Rome and even dabbled in Epicurianism, that taught that happiness is the highest good. Though it led him to the world of pleasure, it did not satisfy his desire for truth. Then, in 384, he gained an appointment as an imperial rhetorician in Milan. There he fell under the influence of Bishop Ambrose. It was from Ambrose that Augustine learned that even a brilliant man could have Christian faith. Ambrose shared with him the Neoplatonist idea that God was a perfect spiritual being, and that understanding God came through insight and vision. Insight and vision were the products of contemplation.

Finally, in 387, as Augustine sat in a garden in Milan, he heard a child's singsong voice say, "Take it and read; take it and read." Augustine picked up Paul's letter to the Romans that he had with him and read 13:13–14: "Let us behave decently, as in the daytime, not in orgies and drunkenness, not in sexual immorality and debauchery, not in dissension and jealousy. Rather, clothe yourselves with the Lord Jesus Christ, and do not think about how to gratify the desires of the sinful nature."

He would later write that at that instant the "light of faith" had come to him, and he was converted. He was soon baptized, and in 388 he founded a monastic community in North Africa. By 391, his brilliance evident to almost everyone, he was pressured into becoming the bishop of the North African city of Hippo. He quickly became the "go-to guy" to ask about every possible heresy that was making inroads into the Christian community.

AUGUSTINE VS. HERESIES

Like the emperor Constantine, Augustine opposed the heresy of Donatism. There were thousands of Donatists in his see (or jurisdiction), and they threatened to leave the faith and form a rival church. They believed that the clergy which had turned over scriptures to Emperor Diocletian under persecution were not fit to lead the church or administer sacraments. Augustine agreed that there were some in the church who were not holy, but the church was. The sacraments, he argued, were not holy and effective because of the priest's righteousness, but because God operates through them.

His opposition to the Pelagians was equally brilliant. Pelagius had taught that God's grace played a role in man's salvation, but that man's work was at the core. He did not go quite so far as to say man could save himself, but he did go so far as to deny that sin was inherited from Adam and Eve. Augustine's answer to that teaching was simply that man could not even choose to be truly good unless God led him to it. In fact, God had already chosen those who would be redeemed—the elect. The challenges of these heresies forced Augustine to delve deeper and deeper into the really "sticky" issues of the faith, such as original sin, the roles of grace and free will in turning to God, and the doctrine of predestination.

Augustine was also witness to the collapse of the Western Roman Empire. The Vandals, an Arian Germanic tribe, were

 SET THE STAGE!

Just as men such as Augustine found spiritual growth in monasteries, women turned to convents. In a time when most women had to live lives of total obedience, first to their fathers, then to their husbands, joining a convent was actually one way of gaining power over their own lives. Nuns could learn to read and write and do many other things usually "off limits" to women. Some of the higher-ranking female clergy, like abbesses, wielded considerable political power.

History shows us over and over that sometimes what appears to be a cage is indeed a throne, and vice versa.

besieging Hippo when he died in 430. Rome had been sacked in 411. This collapse had prompted his most famous work, *The City of God*. Some people blamed the Christians for the empire's collapse. In *The City of God*, Augustine argued that since Cain and Abel there have been two cities: the City of God (the faithful) and the City of Man (pagan society). Though the pagan society has flourished in the past, it is God's plan that His City of God will endure forever.

ALARIC AND THE VISIGOTHS' INVASION

Alaric, king of the Visigoths, was primed for trouble, and the Roman Empire was virtually a sitting duck, waiting to be plundered. Alaric was born around 370. In 395, he attacked Greece and plundered its cities. In 397, he met the Western Roman army, led by the great general Stilcho, and was defeated. After his two-year campaign of pillaging against Greece, he was driven out of the country. That was far from the end of the troubles he would cause Rome, however. In 408, he attacked Italy itself, and after having success, he exacted a tribute from the emperor of three thousand pounds of pepper. The spice was considered a fitting tribute because it supposedly had medicinal value, and it could be used to hide the taste of the spoiled meat the Visigoth army often had to eat.

The pepper must not have been enough because in 409, Alaric once again attacked Italy.

THE END OF ALARIC

The Visigothic king had no real plan for taking over the empire. Sacking the capital was enough. Soon after he plundered Rome he retreated out of the city to the south and soon died. The actual damage to the empire of Alaric's success was small. The emotional impact was immeasurable. The "eternal city" was proven vulnerable. Some of the blame can be placed on the emperor Honorius, who had his best general Stilcho murdered in 408 as a result of the first Visigothic siege of the city. Somehow, the empire had just lost its ability to sustain its armies.

Though Alaric died, the fact that he had conquered the

unconquerable city would become part of the Roman psyche. It was a bad omen for the things that were to come.

MEANWHILE...ON THE FRINGES OF THE EMPIRE
Within the bounds of the Western Roman Empire, things seemed to fall apart in the fifth century. Rome had been conquered. The Vandals were becoming a grave threat to the empire. They had swept westward out of Germany, across the Rhine in 406, and had pillaged much of what is now France. Then they had turned their attention southward, and in 409 they crossed the Pyrenees into Spain. Though they lost this Spanish territory to the Visigoths who overran them in 415, they were able to cross to North Africa and actually capture Rome's nemesis from centuries past, Carthage. By 439, they had established a grain industry that made much of North Africa

---

SINNERS AND SAINTS
JEROME

When you think of biblical scholars today, whom do you think of? If you had lived around A.D. 400, you may have thought of the name Jerome. Jerome was born in modern-day Croatia. He spent part of his life as a monk in the desert. Then he was ordained as a priest and landed a position as secretary to Pope Damasus I. After the pope died, Jerome spent his energies founding monasteries for men and women.

In the midst of all this, Jerome was a writer and a scholar. His most important work was the Vulgate, a Latin translation of the Bible. He also wrote *Against Jovinian*, defending the monastic life, and *Famous Men,* highlighting 135 Christian authors and their works.

Jerome was a mover and a shaker in his day. If there had been a local Christian bookstore, his name would have been on the best-seller and new release shelves.

dependent on them. Their power base grew, and as the century approached its midpoint they were poised to attack the Italian peninsula itself.

In the North, there was increasing instability in the British Isles. There was a brief ray of sunshine in that gloom, however. That ray was an ex-slave who would take the Christian message to Ireland.

ST. PATRICK

Around 390, Patrick was born in Roman Britain. He was the son of Christian parents, though he did not take his faith too seriously as a child or teenager. When he was sixteen, he was captured and taken into slavery in Ireland. He eventually escaped and walked two hundred miles to the coast. There, he was able to gain passage on a ship carrying hounds by taking a job as a dog tender. His journey took him first to France and finally to a monastery.

Whenever he dreamed of going home to the British Isles, he would think of the Irish children begging him to share the Gospels with them. He felt compelled to return to them, but he felt that he was just not prepared. So he returned to France and entered a monastery to study and prepare.

In 432, he returned to Ireland and began to preach. Drawing from his experience as a slave in that country, Patrick used the world around him to explain Christianity to the Irish. While scholars continued to debate and argue about the Trinity, Patrick simply explained it in terms of the shamrock, a symbol every Irishman could understand. Three leaves and yet one plant.

In the end, Patrick was able to overcome conflicts with the Druids, who were still pagans, and spread the word of Christianity. After thirty years of ministry, he had founded around three hundred churches and baptized around 120,000 believers.

Patrick's contributions to the church were far greater than mere numbers, however. Patrick organized Christianity in Ireland around monasteries. These monasteries, hidden away from the terrible events of the next five hundred years, became the

BREAKING NEWS

DATELINE: AUGUST 25, 410

ROME—THE IMPERIAL CITY

There has been increasing unease here in the capital. For some time, reports have circulated of Visigoths approaching the city*. These rumors were initially dismissed as an urban myth related to the Visigoth siege of Rome two years ago until recently, when proof surfaced that a large body of armed Visigoths was nearing Rome. At a press conference yesterday, sources close to Emperor Honorius assured the media that the Roman legions were allowing Alaric's forces to advance as part of an elaborate trap. The barbarians were to be surrounded by our superior army and crushed. The emperor was in Ravenna and unavailable for comment.

Tensions have steadily mounted in this ongoing conflict since Visigoth troops first invaded near the Alps in 401. At that time it was believed that a minor police action would be sufficient to quash the barbarian incursion on imperial borders, but in recent years the fighting has escalated. The barbarians seemed to keep coming back with fresh supplies. It has long been known that the Visigoths were receiving military aid from the rebel factions in Constantinople. Some of the invading horde have undoubtedly been trained in the army of the false empire. It seems probable that Constantinople's military intelligence services have been feeding information to Alaric's army. The Visigoths always appeared to be one step ahead. Yesterday, it proved to be a fatal step for Rome.

Last night, Alaric led Visigothic forces in an all-out assault on the city walls. They invaded the jewel of civilization and pillaged it as casually as they might some backwoods outpost in Britain or northern Gaul. They set fires. They did all the things invading hordes do: They attacked women and children; looted and plundered; they went through the town like a typhoon, leaving a wake of mayhem and destruction.

Today a veil of smoke hangs over Rome like a funereal shroud. Outside my room I hear guttural voices speak a language I do not know. How long before they find me? And what then? It's the end of an era, maybe the end of time. Rome, after standing for eight hundred years, has fallen. The city that conquered the world has in turn been conquered.

For empire news, this is Janus Paulus.

*Initial rumors of a unit of "stealth" barbarians, or "Invisigoths," *did* prove to be untrue.

repositories of ancient Christian texts. As the darkness of the barbarians descended on Europe, eventually engulfing even Rome, these Irish monasteries were the keepers of the flame of early Christian scholarship and knowledge.

Ireland would not officially become a Catholic country until the 1100s when the pope gave Henry II, the king of England (that was of course still Catholic), sovereignty over Ireland. The Irish had been Christians for a long time before and had preserved the faith while the world outside their country had been shaken to the core. That was a fitting tribute to Patrick, the man who had chosen to minister to those who had enslaved him.

MEANWHILE...BACK IN ROME

In 440, Leo became the bishop of Rome. He was born in Tuscany and rose through the bureaucracy of the church to its highest position. Like Damasas and Innocent I, Leo advanced the idea that the bishop of Rome has primacy within the church. He also managed to get backing from Emperor Valentinian II for the status of the bishop of Rome. Of course, by that time the edicts of the emperor carried much less weight than they had in the past. Barbarians were making inroads at all points of the compass against Rome, and an edict from the emperor was nothing to them.

Like the other great church leaders of the fourth and fifth centuries, Leo was drawn into the religious controversies of the day. When a whole element of the church wanted to reject Christ's humanity, to make him a nonhuman deity, Leo argued against that point of view vehemently. His view was rejected at the Council of Ephesus in 449; in fact, his *Tome*, written for the occasion, was not even allowed a hearing. However, that work was one of the major sources for the decrees of the Council of Chalcedon in 451. In his *Tome* he argued that Christ was fully divine and fully human, and yet he was not a split personality.

Leo was willing to take on real-life political issues as well. He understood the power the barbarians held. In 452, he was able to convince Attila the Hun to turn back from Rome, and in 455 he was able to minimize the damage to Rome when it was captured by Gaiseric the Vandal. In his hands, the office of the pope began to act like a civil ruler as well as the head of the church. The keys to the empire were being passed from the emperor to the pope.

THE COUNCIL OF CHALCEDON

In the fifth century, religious controversies were also political powder kegs. The power of the Western Empire was slipping so badly that it would need only a small shove to collapse. The Eastern Empire was always at the heart of controversy because it encompassed such an incredibly diverse population. In addition, as the power of the church grew, the problems of the church grew in significance to the empire. One way this phenomenon showed itself was that the strong religious centers grew more and more powerful politically. The Western cities of Rome and Alexandria tended to bond together to oppose the Eastern cities of Antioch and Constantinople. Coupled with the natural competition between the two halves of the empire, the situation could become really volatile.

One of the flash points in the East-West conflict was, once again, the nature of Jesus Christ. The Alexandrian position, expressed best by Apollinarus, focused on Christ as the incarnation of the divine Word (*Logos*). Eventually, Apollinarus went so far as to say that at the Incarnation, the Word replaced Jesus' human soul, so His humanness was simply that He walked around in human form. That idea went a little too far, and in 381 the second ecumenical council in Constantinople had condemned his teachings.

In contrast, the point of view from Antioch emphasized the humanness of Jesus. To the Antiochenes, Jesus' humanity was complete and normal. The differences of opinion turned into a long-distance shouting match between Cyril, patriarch of Alexandria, and Nestorius, patriarch of Constantinople, when Cyril accused Nestorius of saying that Jesus was two separate beings, or "natures," in one body. To settle the issue, a third ecumenical council was called in Ephesus in 431. Cyril, revealing a truly scheming nature, arranged to have his opponent, Nestorius, thrown out of the council before he or his supporters had even arrived. Somehow he also pressured the emperor Theodosius II into condemning and exiling Nestorius. Without the opposition present, the council went Cyril's way, but nothing was really settled and the hard feelings between the two sides got even harder.

 IMAGINE THAT!

Legendary tales have been passed down about St. Patrick. The most notorious is that he charmed the snakes of Ireland into the sea to drown, and thus there are no snakes in Ireland. Some say that the shamrock became the traditional symbol of Ireland because he used it in his sermons.

In Ireland, St. Patrick's Day is a national holiday and primarily a religious one. It is honored with religious services and family and community gatherings. Oh, and lots of people wearing shamrocks.

AND IT GETS WORSE...

Then, as if to throw fuel on an already dangerous fire, an old monk living in Constantinople named Eutyches claimed that although Jesus was both human and divine, his humanness was swallowed up by the divine "like a drop of wine falling in the ocean." (This is referred to as the Monophysite point of view.) He was condemned for heresy by the patriarch of Constantinople, but of course the patriarch of Alexandria supported his view. So, in 449, Theodosius called another council in Ephesus. In Rome, Pope Leo thought he had a solution and sent it to the council (which never even let it be read). This council agreed with Eutyches. Infuriated, Pope Leo called the council the "robber synod" and petitioned the emperor for another council on the subject.

In 450, the emperor Theodosius died after falling off a horse. That was good fortune for Leo and those who opposed the Monophysite point of view that Eutyches proclaimed. The emperor's sister Pulcheria, along with her husband, Marcian, supported Leo's views and called another council to be held at Chalcedon, just across the Bosporus from Constantinople. This council, held in 451, reversed the previous two councils. The position it expressed was clearly more influenced by the "humanness" point of view from Antioch.

SOME REALLY BAD BARBARIANS

The Huns were an irresistible force. They had overrun everything in their path, including the other barbarian tribes that lived around the northern borders of the Roman Empire. As early as 410 they had attacked the empire itself, exacting tribute from an empire that could not deal with them any other way. By 425, they had even advanced on Constantinople and were stopped not by a military loss, but by a plague that decimated their ranks. In 433, the Huns turned up the pressure on everyone else around them when Attila became their king. By 440, he had overrun and pillaged most of the small barbarian kingdoms and begun to turn his attention toward Rome. By 450, he had become a serious threat to Rome. Under his leadership, the Huns had triumphed over the Alans, Heruls, Ostrogoths, and Visigoths. They had overwhelmed most of Italy. In 451, Attila was finally defeated at the Battle of Chalons by a Roman army led by Flavius Aetius with substantial help from the Visigoths.

This defeat slowed down the Hunnic onslaught, and in 452 the pope Leo I was able to convince Attila to spare Rome. The Hun king died in 453, and with his death so died the threat from the Huns. The damage had been done, however, and the stage had been set for even more disaster.

 SET THE STAGE!

Before the fall of the Roman Empire, Latin was the most common language. Knowing that, you can understand why the *Vulgate* was such a big deal.

The name "vulgate" actually means "popular." The *Vulgate* is a Latin translation of the Bible. It was translated by St. Jerome at the request of Pope Damasus I. Jerome finished the translation in A.D. 405.

In A.D. 405, the only Bibles available were the original Greek and Hebrew manuscripts, some Aramaic versions of the Old Testament called Targums, and a Greek version of the Old Testament called the Septuagint. The problem was that most people spoke Latin. What did they have to read? So while we think of Latin as a formal language practically in disuse, to those people it was a fresh, current kind of thing. It was hip. It was helpful. It was the opportunity to hear from God without going through someone who speaks a whole different language. It was the same as you going to the Christian bookstore and finding a Bible written in plain old, understandable English…for the first time…ever.

This was a huge event. The Vulgate became the official Roman Catholic translation in 1546. You will hear it referred to as the Douay-Rheims or the Douay Bible. This is because the Old Testament was first published in Douay, France, and the New Testament was first published in Rheims, France. This version of the Bible breaks down the chapters and verses a little differently than the Protestant Bible, and it includes some books that the Protestant Bible doesn't.

The *Vulgate* has been revised several times through the years. Right now it's not the only approved Catholic Bible. But it was the first. The *Vulgate* is a good example of how we can look at something as archaic or foreign or stuffy, but if we put it in its historical context, it was the coolest news on the block.

SCORECARD

In the Red corner:

Jesus was of one nature—divine *and* human at the same time.

And in the blue corner:

Jesus was of two natures—divine and human, but the two do not intermix.

Round 1—381 Second Ecumenical Council

The winner: the blue corner

Round 2—431 Third Ecumenical Council

The winner: the red corner

Round 3—449 The "Robber Synod"

The winner: the red corner

Round 4—451 The Council of Chalcedon

The winner: the blue corner

As usual, the council did not settle the problems but, in fact, may have given them greater momentum. Since the empress had "run" the council, its decrees had the power of imperial law. That upset many of the Eastern churches because they followed the position which Cyril had proposed that Jesus was of one primarily divine nature. The conflict continued to escalate and finally came to a head under the emperor Zeno, causing a split between the Eastern and Western churches.

MEANWHILE...BACK TO THE VANDALS, OR "HOW THE WEST WAS LOST"

When we last saw the Vandals in 439, they had conquered Carthage and established themselves as an economic power in North Africa. By 455, they had also established themselves as a sea power and decided to take on the empire itself. They attacked Rome and found the city without leadership and totally unprepared for attack. The Italian peninsula had been under almost constant attack for nearly fifty years. There was no will to fight back and no real Roman army to do the fighting. The Vandals, led by Gaiseric, conquered the city and then plundered it for fourteen days. Their pillaging was so complete that the name "Vandal" remains, to this day, a word for a person who destroys without reason. Significantly, it was the pope, Leo, who probably saved the city at all by begging Gaiseric to control his troops and end the fourteen-day sack of Rome. There was no governmental power that could exercise any influence. But the power of the church throughout the lands of the old Roman Empire was great enough to exert a small bit of pressure, even on a conquering Vandal. It should also be pointed out that the Vandals were Arian Christians, having been converted as early as 409 in Spain.

The fall of Rome really was the end of the Western Empire, though its final demise was not until 476. In the interim, there was almost constant war against the Vandals. The barbarians set up puppet emperors, only to have them deposed by other barbarians. There was no true Roman army at all. The army that represented the empire was simply another army of barbarians. The process of turning the army from Roman legions to a Germanic army had started eons before and was accelerated by Theodosius. There was no Roman army to defend Rome, only a foreign army to help divide the spoils.

Finally, in 476, the barbarian Roman army revolted and named one of the barbarian officers, Odoacer, as emperor. Soon afterward, Odoacer deposed the last "proper" emperor Romulus Augustulus. He then sent the official symbols of the emperor to the Eastern emperor, Zeno, and asked to be recognized as the ruler of the West.

MEANWHILE...IN CONSTANTINOPLE

Zeno had his own problems to worry about. He had not expected to become emperor. When Emperor Leo I died, his grandson Leo II, then a six-year-old boy, had taken the throne. Leo II died as a young boy, but as he was dying, he appointed his father, Zeno, as his successor. At this time, of course, the final collapse of the West was imminent. When Zeno received Odoacer's request to be named ruler of the West, he had little recourse but to grant it. After all, with Romulus Augustulus out of the way, he was technically the emperor of both East and West.

It was not long, however, before Odoacer made it clear that his act of supposed faithfulness to Zeno was just a sham. Having no real means to strike back at Odoacer, Zeno decided to use the

Ostrogoths. Zeno had learned a lesson or two from the mistakes of Emperor Leo I. In 467, Leo had his general Anthesius named emperor of the West and had mounted an attack on the Vandal kingdom in North Africa. Though he assembled a huge fleet of over one thousand ships and an army of 100,000 men, the expedition was a disaster. Zeno would not take that kind of risk.

ZENO'S PLAN

The Ostrogoths had been subjects of the Huns until Attila's death in 453. After the collapse of Hunnic power, the Ostrogoths had stayed where they were, just on the edge of the empire, and had begun harassing and pillaging towns in the empire itself. Under the leadership of Theodoric, they had carried out raids on the Balkan Peninsula and even threatened Constantinople itself.

Zeno's plan was simple: He could get rid of his troublesome Ostrogoth neighbors in the north and settle the score with Odoacer at one time. Emperor Zeno was able to point out to Theodoric that there were quite rich provinces in Italy to the east ready for the taking. These provinces would be much easier to conquer than any battle with the powerful Eastern Roman Empire. Theodoric must have agreed, because in 488 he turned his attention to Italy. By 490, his Ostrogoths had laid siege to Odoacer's principal city of Ravenna. Though the siege lasted three years, in March 493, Odoacer finally surrendered to Theodoric. The king of the Ostrogoths invited his conquered foe to dinner and had him murdered. Thus began the Ostrogoths' reign over Italy that lasted until 554.

FROM POLITICS TO RELIGION

So Zeno was able to solve his major political problem. Unfortunately for him, that was not the only problem he faced. He also faced the continual religious bickering in his empire concerning the nature of Jesus. The Council of Chalcedon had alienated most of the Eastern Christians who were Monophysites (believed that Jesus' humanity was swallowed up in His divinity). Once again an emperor was faced with his empire being torn apart by religious conflict. Zeno's answer

SINNERS AND SAINTS
ODOACER

Odoacer was the barbarian chieftain who overthrew the Western Roman Empire in A.D. 476. It was an inside job: Odoacer was trained in the Roman army and led Germanic troops from his homeland in the service of the empire. When Rome refused to give his legions land in return for their faithful service, Odoacer took control of the entire Western portion of the empire. For many years an uneasy truce existed between Odoacer and Zeno (the emperor of the Eastern Roman Empire), with Odoacer feigning subservience to the East and Zeno not officially recognizing the German king's authority in the Western empire. In 488, Zeno sent the Ostrogoth king Theodoric (another barbarian leader who, unlike Odoacer, had remained loyal to the empire) to Rome with an army. Odoacer fled to Ravenna, finally surrendering in 493, and was executed. Historians regard Odoacer's conquest of Rome as the official end of the Roman Empire in the West.

was to issue the Act of Union (*Henoticon*). In this document, Zeno tried to be just vague enough about the nature of Jesus to provide some common ground between the two sides of the argument. He actually condemned both Eutyches and Nestorius, whom he saw as the two extremists on each side of the argument. Though the *Henoticon* seemed to calm things down for a while, it actually caused Zeno even more trouble. Christians started fighting over whether or not they were obliged to follow religious doctrine issued by the government instead of the church. (Imagine American Christians adopting a religious belief just because it was issued by the president!)

Pope Leo in Rome had exactly the same problem with the

Henoticon. So, in 484, he excommunicated both Zeno and Acacius, the patriarch of Constantinople. In response, Acacius quit mentioning the pope in his prayers (he showed them!). Despite the excommunication, the *Henoticon* remained the official imperial policy until 518, although most Christians simply paid it no attention and continued to believe as they had before. Instead, the fifth century ended with a barbarian ruler in Rome and religious discord among Christians rampant in the rest of the old empire.

MEANWHILE...ON THE FRINGES OF THE EMPIRE

The spread of Arianism (the belief that Jesus was an inferior being to God) had been so extensive since Alaric's conversion that there was actually only one barbarian tribe that attacked and entered the Roman Empire as true pagans and not Arian Christians. That tribe was the Franks. The Franks were a group of Germanic tribes that had settled along the Rhine between present-day France and Germany by the third century. The Salian Franks, led by their first great ruler, Clovis I, moved into Gaul (presently France) and overran the Romans in 486.

CLOVIS

Then, in the last years of the fifth century, Clovis married a Catholic Christian princess, Clotild, from the tribe of the Burgundians. As Frankish history tells the story, Clovis then agreed to become a Christian if the Christian God would give him a victory in battle over a rival tribe. Not long afterward, Clovis defeated the Alemanni at a battle near present-day Strasbourg. Afterwards, he and three thousand of his soldiers were baptized. The Franks became a Christian tribe.

Clovis and the Franks showed a great devotion to the Catholic church and to the pope. That does not mean that they deserted their barbarian lifestyle or molded their royal policy around Christian doctrine. Clovis founded the Merovingian dynasty of Frankish rulers, which was characterized by brutality and harsh living conditions. However, as the Middle Ages began, the Franks would play a crucial role in the conversion of other tribes.

SINNERS AND SAINTS
BOETHIUS

The end of the fifth and beginning of the sixth centuries were turbulent times. In the field of philosophy, however, the era produced a true giant. Boethius (whose full name was Anicius Manlius Severinus Boethius) is considered one of the founders of the Middle Ages because his ideas and approach had tremendous influence on medieval education and thought. He was educated in Athens and Alexandria and served under the Ostrogothic king Theodoric as he ruled Italy. It is notable that he was the last of the Western scholars to be completely familiar with the Greek texts of Aristotle's work. After the collapse of the West, it was impossible to get access to those works that were lost to Western scholars until the twelfth century.

Boethius's plan was to translate the works of Plato and Aristotle into Latin. Unfortunately, he was only able to complete Aristotle's works on logic. He also wrote five works in which he defended orthodox theology. In one of these he used Aristotle's methods of logic to analyze Christian belief. For that work he has been called the father of "scholasticism," a religious movement that applied classical logic to interpreting Christian writings and beliefs.

In his last years, Boethius was accused of treason against Theodoric. He was imprisoned, and while he awaited execution, he wrote his most famous work, *The Consolation of Philosophy*. In this work, the writer has a dialogue with a character called "Philosophy," who shows him how to triumph over his desperate situation and find contentment. It was a message that found its true niche in the dark days of conflict and plague in the Middle Ages, and has great relevance today.

THE MORE THINGS CHANGE...

(Death, Taxes, and Other Immutables)

After Gaul invaded Rome, Romans held yearly crucifixions of dogs to punish them for failing to warn Rome of the approaching invasion. Only in recent times have people started to remember that animals can't think like we (some of us anyway) do. Here's a look down through the ages at idiots who thought of capital punishment as an effective tool for animal training.

1500s Lions were crucified outside of many North African towns in an attempt to let other lions know they weren't welcome. At the same time, marauding wolves were often hanged in German woodlands and left as examples to other wolves.

1547 A sow and her baby piglets were convicted of beating a child in France. The sow was sentenced to die at the gallows. Her six offspring, being minors, were let off with a stern warning.

1981 Kenya: A tortoise was accused of killing six persons by means of witchcraft. Elders of the accusing tribe ordered the animal executed, but the tribesmen were too frightened of the creature. The tortoise was freed (on bond?) while the Kenyan government investigated the case.

It's all pretty weird, huh? At least there's no record of lions ever having been fed to the Christians.

The Frankish conversion laid the groundwork for a new kind of alliance that would continue into the Middle Ages. Clovis's conversion to Catholic Christianity forged an alliance between the barbarian leader and the pope. Whereas an Arian tribe might threaten the pope, the Franks were, to some extent, an ally of the pope. Similarly, whereas the pope might oppose an Arian tribe, he would probably be an ally with the Franks. These alliances, which crossed the borders of politics and religion, became the norm in European culture. That norm began with Clovis and continued almost to the current day.

HEY! THIS COULD BE A MOVIE!

If someone were to tell you that in the sixth century the Eastern empire would be dominated by a guy who

1. inherits the throne from his uncle

2. marries the most beautiful woman in the empire, and

3. recaptures the lands that had been lost to his empire

…what would you say? It sounds like a movie script, right? The fact is, however, it all happened in the life of Justinian I.

The setting was Constantinople. There was a young actress, Theodora by name, who was beautiful, clever, probably promiscuous, and quite a character "around town." Following a bad time in her life when her behavior had become the scandal of the city, she disappeared and moved to Africa. Some years later she returned a very different person altogether. She was certainly still beautiful, but gone was her desire to be an actress and to live the wild lifestyle. Instead, she spent her time spinning wool and pondering the religious issues of the day.

One day the heir to the imperial throne, Justinian, saw her and was captured by her beauty. He took her to court, gave her high social rank, and soon married her. When he ascended the throne soon afterward, she became the empress of the Byzantine Empire. Thus began one of the great partnerships of history.

 **SET THE STAGE!**

The conversion of the Franks illustrates the general pattern of how barbarian tribes were Christianized. They were usually approached by missionaries and were not the objects of an organized conversion effort. Typically, the leader of the tribe would be converted, and his people would follow. In most cases, it was the influence of Catholic wives and princesses that would bring about the conversion.

EMPEROR JUSTINIAN

Justinian became emperor in 527. He came to the throne with the ideals of not only an emperor but a Christian, as well. He saw himself as a descendant of the Roman caesars, and saw it his duty to restore the empire to the size and glory of the first and second centuries. As the lawful successor to the caesars, he had a lawful right to the territory now held by the barbarians in the West. The restoration of the empire was a Christian goal, as well. Justinian felt he must free the orthodox Christians from the oppression of the Arian Germans who ruled over them. In his opinion, the Germanic

SET THE STAGE!

After the fall of the Western Roman Empire, the Eastern Roman Empire was referred to as the Byzantine Empire. Its capital, Constantinople (which is now Istanbul), was built on the site of the ancient city Byzantium.

kings were merely vassals to the Byzantine emperor who had given them the permission to rule in the West. The emperor Anastasius had given Clovis the rank of consul and had officially recognized the right to rule of the Ostrogothic king Theodoric.

As a Christian emperor, Justinian felt he had the responsibility of propagating the true faith within his empire, whether that was to pagans or heretics. As a result, Justinian, the Christian emperor, became an emperor of war. He had three major enemies to conquer: the Vandals in North Africa, the Ostrogoths in Italy, and the Visigoths in Spain.

VANDALS, OSTROGOTHS, AND VISIGOTHS

Justinian attacked the Vandals in 533. The emperor's armies, led by the brilliant general Belisarius, quickly recaptured the entire Vandal kingdom. Justinian was overjoyed and called his general back home. Just after the army left, though, the Moors rebelled and a terrible struggle began. It was fifteen years before the territory was actually secured for the empire.

Still worse was the war against the Ostrogoths. In 535, the emperor attacked the Ostrogoths in Dacia (present-day Romania) and in Sicily. The attack in Sicily was led by Belisarius, who was just home from his (short-lived) victory in North Africa. Once again, the general proved his worth by capturing Sicily without much difficulty and recapturing Rome not long after that. Soon after that, the Ostrogothic capital, Ravenna, opened its gates to Belisarius. Italy seemed to be recaptured for the empire, and Belisarius returned to Constantinople with the captured Ostrogothic king.

As in North Africa, however, the war was not over. A new Ostrogothic king emerged in Italy. His name was Totila, and he was a gifted leader and warrior. He counterattacked the emperor's armies so successfully that Belasarius was recalled from another war in Persia to deal with the problem. Even the great general could not stop the Ostrogoths, and eventually they had recaptured their territory in Italy. Justinian then replaced Belasarius with another gifted general, Narses. Finally, in 552, Totila's army was defeated at the battle of Busta Gallorum, and the war with the Ostrogoths was over.

JUSTINIAN AND THE VISIGOTHS

This twenty-one-year war had devastated Italy. It prevented the development of industry and emptied the fields of farmers. Rome had been captured and recaptured so many times it lay largely in ruins. It had descended from the seat of power of the great empire to become a second-rate city of no importance, except that the pope chose it as his refuge.

Justinian's last military offensive was against the Visigoths. The Visigoths had once held southern France and Spain, but in 507, while being attacked by Alaric II, they lost their land north of the Pyrenees to the Franks led by Clovis. In 550, Justinian sent a small naval force to attack the Visigoths in the southeast corner of the peninsula. The attack had remarkable success, and an imperial province in southern Spain was reestablished.

The result of all these offensive wars was that Justinian doubled the size of his empire. The empire stretched from western Spain to the Euphrates River. The emperor's hopes were not all fulfilled, however. He had not recaptured western North Africa or most of Spain. The entire province of Gaul (France) was not only still out of his control, but he had been forced to cede Provence over to the Franks. All in all, however, his military accomplishments were astounding. The empire had to pay the price for them, though. Justinian had "inherited" a huge government surplus from his preceding emperors. Procopius, who was a contemporary of Justinian and wrote about the emperor (and not very flatteringly), estimated that Justinian took over a reserve of 320,000 pounds of gold worth between 65 and 70 million dollars. At the end of Justinian's reign the surplus was gone.

SET THE STAGE!

Justinian built the Church of Holy Wisdom, or St. Sophia, during his reign. Construction required over 10,000 workers. The building is still standing as a museum today in Istanbul.

THE JUSTINIAN CODE

Justinian left his most enduring legacy in the field of law. He believed that it was the emperor's duty to lead the people in war, but also to create a strong legal basis for governing them in times of peace. He believed that it was God who gave the emperor the right to create laws and to interpret them. In many ways, the emperor was then a lawgiver with the authority to do so from God Himself.

Roman law, perhaps once the greatest institution of the ancient world, had declined steadily over several hundred years. Justinian set about codifying and collecting it. It was a mammoth task that was begun in 528. Amazingly, by April 529, the *Justinian Code* was published. It was divided into ten books and contained the imperial law from the reign of Emperor Hadrian to the time of Justinian. In the year 530, Justinian instructed his assistant, Tribonian, to put together a commission that would read, edit, and summarize the writing on the law by all the important jurists of Roman law: about two thousand books in total. The results were published in 533 in fifty books entitled the *Digest*.

These great works, and others commissioned by Justinian, preserved the Roman law that provided the basis for the laws governing society up to the present. In the twelfth century, when Europe would "rediscover" Roman law, it was through these documents commissioned by Justinian. In many places, the *Code* simply became the law of the land with very little change.

FAMILIAR RELIGIOUS ISSUES

On the religious front, there was trouble as always for the emperor in Constantinople. The conflict between the Orthodox Church and the Monophysites raged. The emperor himself held to the belief that Christ was of a divided nature in one being. His wife, Theodora, was of the opposite, or Monophysite, view that

Jesus was of one nature—simultaneously divine and human. The Monophysites in the empire were furious about the Council of Chalcedon and therefore opposed the emperor on this religious question. Justinian had the good sense to listen to his wife about this and tried to appease the Monophysites. He let some of their exiled bishops go home, and even invited Monophysite bishops to participate in conferences and religious events in Constantinople.

This position got the emperor in trouble with the Orthodox Church, however. One pope, Agapetus, even threatened to excommunicate the emperor if he did not condemn the Monophysites. The emperor did enough in that regard to satisfy the pope. As Justinian grew older, he turned more and more to his wife's point of view. Though he worked many years to unify the church over the issue of the nature of Jesus, he, like so many others, failed.

BENEDICT AND HIS MONASTIC ORDER

It would be a mistake to look at the sixth century and think that it was solely a time of war and imperial maneuvering. There were, as there had been since the beginning, devoted Christians who wanted no part of the world around them. The

SINNERS AND SAINTS
THEODORA

Empress Theodora, wife of Justinian, former actress, was an activist for human rights. She acted as an advisor to her husband and changed laws to improve the lives of her people, particularly women and the poor. Some of the laws she influenced gave women the rights to receive inheritances, own property, and file for divorce if necessary. She also established homes dedicated to the care of impoverished girls.

political chaos, the religious turmoil, and the fragility of life drove some Christians further and further from the world they saw around them. Some of these Christians, such as the hermit Anthony, tried to escape the world through acts of incredible self-denial. Others desired to escape the world but desired the community of Christians like themselves. One of the first of these was Pachomius, who as early as 320 had begun to practice communal monasticism. He had focused on keeping life simple and self-denying, but not extreme asceticism. As we have seen before, both Basil the Great and the Irish Christians converted by Patrick practiced a simple monastic lifestyle.

However, the real father of European monasticism was Benedict of Nursia. He was born into a wealthy Italian family and went to study in Rome. Though Rome was supposed to be a Christian city, Benedict found it immoral and left to become a hermit. Even as he lived alone he gained a reputation as a spiritual man, and soon families were sending their sons to him for training in the Christian faith. These students became a small monastic group. He might have stayed there for years, but one of his students, upset with Benedict over some issue of discipline, tried to poison the teacher. Afraid for his life, Benedict left the area. In 529, he moved to Monte Cassino where he destroyed a pagan temple that stood there and built a monastery.

BENEDICT'S MONASTIC GOVERNMENT

More important than this single monastery is the rule that Benedict wrote to govern life there. He saw the monastery as a self-sufficient entity: Any contact with the outside could be hazardous. The monks had to grow the food, make their clothes, construct their own buildings, and produce the furnishings. He had seen with his young students before that a youthful commitment was not always the final decision in a man's life. So he allowed for the first year of a would-be monk to be a trial period, after which the monk or the abbot could decide the boy's future. It was only after that first year that the novitiate would have to take the three vows: poverty, chastity, and obedience. Then he was required to surrender all his goods to the community, to avoid all sexual relations, and to always obey the monastery's rules.

A big part of the rules would govern worship. The Benedictine order of monks had seven services each day, including a vigil service at about 2:00 A.M. In addition, the monks were required to practice individual devotions each day: reading the Bible, praying, and meditating.

It was, and is, a disciplined life for those in the Benedictine order. As the ancient age turned into the Middle Ages, the role of the monastic life evolved greatly. Monastic orders were to become incredibly important as part of the religious and social fabric of Europe. Though the different orders would each be unique, they owed their basic framework to the groundwork laid by Benedict.

CELTIC MISSIONARIES

Out on the fringes of the old, now defunct Roman Empire, the church had some growing pains in the mid-to-late sixth century. Around 563, a missionary named David took Christianity to Wales, where he founded a monastery. At his death he became the patron saint of Wales.

 SET THE STAGE!

Monks fulfilled a number of important roles in Western culture. In many places, they were the primary healthcare providers (back then, HMO would have stood for Holy Monastic Organization) and grew healing herbs with which to minister to the sick. They were also often the only literate members of the community and thus were the chroniclers, historians, and tutors of the nobility and of society as a whole. Monks were responsible for the preservation and survival of much ancient art, literature, and knowledge. Since they were the only ones who could read and write, they were also the book publishers. This was a big job: Before the invention of the printing press, books were made one at a time *by hand*. Since every monastery was supposed to be as self-sufficient as possible, each monk might also have a regular "job" (i.e., farmer, blacksmith, carpenter) that he performed at the monastery. Add all that in with plenty of time set aside for prayer, and it makes you wonder if these guys ever *slept*.

IMAGINE THAT!

Part of the role of monks such as Benedict and Patrick was that of scribe or translator. They often re-created manuscripts by hand. Along with real gold and silver and rare inks in many colors, a type of red lead was used to color elaborately drawn capitals in what were called illuminated manuscripts. The initial letter of a passage in these books was often so ornately embellished that it was a small work of art. The red lead was called minium, and the capitals on which it was used came to be called miniatures. Eventually, the word miniature was used for any small artwork and later still to describe anything diminutive. Today we often use "mini" as a prefix meaning small. Think about that the next time you have "Frosted Red Lead Wheats" for breakfast or see someone wearing a "red lead skirt."

Then in 563, an Irish monk named Columba, who had founded several monasteries in his native land, left for Scotland with twelve companions. They landed on a western Scottish island, built some crude houses and a church. From there they set about converting the Picts, the neighboring Scottish tribe that lived nearby. Though they met with opposition from both the leaders of the Scottish tribe and the Druids, in just a few years the twelve men had evangelized all of Scotland and northern England. Even while he was evangelizing, Columba founded a large monastery on the island of Iona. After his death, the monastery continued and became the center of Celtic Christianity, sending out missionaries and founding other monasteries. Before it was torn down during the Reformation, the monastery was the burial site of forty-six Scottish kings and the Irish monk who started it all.

MEANWHILE...BACK IN ROME

Rome was not what it had been. It was not the capital of an empire. It was not the center of culture for the known world. It was not even the home of law and scholarship it had been. The city still had some prestige, however, to Christians. After all, it was the city where both the apostles Peter and Paul had brought Christianity. It was also the home of the bishop of Rome, the pope. The power of the pope had increased even as the power of the Western Empire had been destroyed. Even under the Ostrogoths the papacy had survived. Popes such as Leo I and Dioscorus had played major theological roles in shaping Christian doctrine, often in opposition to an emperor.

The pope who would do the most to increase papal authority was Gregory I. Gregory was born in 540 to a noble Roman family. He followed his family's tradition and went into public service, becoming the prefect of Rome, the city's highest civil office. He was unhappy in the job, however, and quit it. Soon afterward he joined a monastery, hoping for a quiet life of study and piety. However, after a few years his administrative skills had risen to the surface, and he was named abbot. Then, when the pope died in 590, Gregory was unanimously asked to become pope. Gregory refused, but the public prevailed, and he became the bishop of Rome, the pope.

 DID YOU KNOW?

The Picts were a tribe that lived on what is now Scotland *long before* the Scots did. The word "Pict" means "painted" in Latin and comes from the same root as our word "picture." They were called "Picts" by the Romans because they tattooed and painted their skins. The Picts disappeared around A.D. 900.

Even as the pope, Gregory held to many of the monastic Benedictine ideals he had adopted in his life as a monk. He was, however, very adept at managing affairs of the world. When the Lombards threatened to attack Rome, Gregory asked the Eastern emperor for help. When none came, he organized the armies, mustered the troops, and established treaties in order to establish peace. He also dealt extensively with the Franks, who held great power in present-day France and Germany. He tried very hard to reform life under the Merovingian kings. These kings appointed bishops as they pleased and even sold church appointments. Unfortunately, his reforms had little effect.

BRITISH MISSIONARIES

Gregory's relations with the Merovingians did have one long-term effect, however: missionary efforts to England. In 597, he sent a team of forty monks to England, led by Augustine, a leader of the pope's own monastery. They were accompanied by Frankish interpreters. The first attempts were made in the area of Kent where the local king, Ethelbert, was married to a Catholic Frankish princess. The king accepted Christianity, and so his kingdoms and three other areas he governed became Christian, as well.

In 597, Ethelbert appointed Augustine as archbishop of the church in England. The newly converted Ethelbert gave Augustine a palace in Canterbury that became the first seat of the church in England. Unfortunately for Augustine, he was not a very good evangelist. His successes with the Anglo-Saxons were slow, and he failed in his attempt to bring the Celtic Christians into the fold of the Catholic Church. Nevertheless, he did manage to give the Catholic Church a foothold in England.

 DID YOU KNOW?

The Romans constructed forts and walls across Britain's northern border to protect the colony from fierce invaders from Scotland (called Picts) and Ireland (called Scots). The Scots eventually moved from Ireland to what is now called Scotland. While the Western Roman Empire weakened and fell, Germanic tribes, first the Jutes and then Angles and Saxons, invaded Britain and pushed the Britons north into Scotland. The name "England" is Anglo-Saxon in origin and translates as "land of the Angles."

GREGORY'S INFLUENCE

Since the Visigoths in Spain had become Christian in 587, the church in Rome now had influence over some major political players in southern and middle Europe: the Visigoths in Spain, the Franks in Gaul and Germany, and the Anglo-Saxons in Britain. No other political leader in the world, including the Eastern emperor, could say as much.

Gregory had a significant impact on theology as the epoch passed from the ancient time to the Middle Ages. It was his beliefs on purgatory that would shape Middle Ages thought on the subject. It was his writings that would bring angels to the forefront of Christian theology. It was his writing on the saints' lives that would frame Christian literature for the next eight hundred years. It was his writing on saints and relics that would convert dead religious figures into icons and turn their remains into holy talismans. Finally, it was Gregory who finally confirmed the power and the authority of the papacy. As the world in Western Europe sank further and further into chaos and despair, it would be the church, led by the pope, who would be there to help pick up the pieces.

ULTIMATE IMPACT OF AND ON CHRISTIANITY

The real significance of this short era of history on the church today is that it not only survived, it flourished. No fortune-teller could have predicted that would happen under the terror attacks of Nero or the systematic persecution under Diocletian. It is indeed amazing that Christians went from criminals to emperors in such a short time. This was the era that gave the modern church much of its structure. Though we live in a post-Reformation era where there is tremendous diversity in denominations and sects, the basic organization within a church and among churches of similar beliefs still reflects the one established in this time period. A diocese is still a diocese; a synod is still a synod; there are still bishops over groups of churches; there are still councils (conventions these days) that establish orthodoxy.

Of course there are, as there were then, churches that do not fit these established patterns. Perhaps this era even established the right for churches to be different. It is no accident that both John Calvin and Martin Luther, two of the architects of the church for the past five hundred years, went back to Augustine for inspiration. The spiritual diversity of the world we live in now was certainly matched in this era. We will see in the next part of this book what happened to that diversity in the Middle Ages.

CONSTANTINE

The significance to the modern Christian of the emperor Constantine cannot be overstated. Through his conversion he converted Christianity. Before Constantine, the Roman Empire seemed like a huge growling enemy of the church. The persecutions were only a part of that adversarial relationship. Just as pervasive was the basic conflict between the two value systems: the Greco-Roman worldview and the Judeo-Christian worldview. It is not surprising that the early church had success in the Near East and Greece, where new ideas were often applauded and accepted. The actual growth of the church of Rome is another matter.

An outsider of the Roman Empire wanted inside. He wanted Roman citizenship. He wanted in the circle of commerce and power that ruled most of the world of that day. People all over the empire began to worship Roman gods, even if they still worshiped their own. To be truly powerful in the Roman world you had to know Greek, possess the fashion and culture and learning of Greece, and be a Roman. The apostles even had to remind their followers not to fall into Greco-Roman ways but to hold fast to their faith as the measure of their wealth and success.

 DID YOU KNOW?

People think of the Celts as being Scottish or Irish in origin, but Celtic tribes once roamed large parts of the world. The oldest known historical evidence of the Celts comes from graves found in Austria and dates from around 700 B.C. Other evidence shows that the Celts also lived in France, Switzerland, Portugal, Spain, Bulgaria, and Greece, among other places. Most of the Celtic peoples outside of Ireland, the U.K., and Brittany (an area in France) were wiped out or assimilated by the Romans.

With Constantine's conversion all that changed. Suddenly it became not only all right to be a Christian, it became the "Roman thing to do." Suddenly, instead of small groups of Christians banding together, it was "hip" to be Christian. We should face the fact that when the emperor became a Christian, a lot of people just followed him. When he built churches all over the empire, people went to them. Surely some people went merely because the emperor had sent a representative to establish the church. Certainly some people went out of curiosity to see the beautiful decorations. Some people went because they really were Christian. Regardless of their reasons, the important fact is that they went. They went to the new churches, heard the gospel, and became new Christians in great numbers. As we say here in modern times, the emperor got them in the door, and the Word kept them coming back.

The significance of Constantine is that he used the tool of the empire to promote the Christian faith. He started the process of a truly organized church run on the model of an empire. Whether you agree with that development or not, it spread the faith and laid the groundwork for the church to take the leadership role over Europe in the Middle Ages.

THE MORE THINGS CHANGE...
(Death, Taxes, and Other Immutables)

Since the early days of Christianity, there have been people whom others called saints. The definition had changed quite a bit over the centuries, and different denominations have developed differing criteria for what makes a saint a saint. Some of the earliest writings of Christendom refer to *all* believers as saints. In the 200s, the term was reserved only for martyrs. In the 300s, the term "saint" was used in specific reference to bishops. In the early days of the church, saints were declared by popular acclaim, and many were venerated only on a local or regional level. Eventually the church took control, developing a stringent set of qualifications for sainthood and reserving the power to canonize (add someone to the list of saints) for the pope. During the Middle Ages, many people got so carried away with adoring the saints that they prayed more to them than they did to God. During the Reformation, both the Protestant and Catholic churches sought to curb this practice and focus people's attention back where it belonged, on God! Some of the newer denominations, including the Mormons (who also call themselves "Latter Day Saints"), have revived the original practice of calling all believers saints.

ARIANISM

The Arian controversy seems very removed from the modern time. Today, most Christians would say that since the Arians did not believe in the divinity of Jesus, since they believed that Jesus was inferior to God, they could not even be called Christians. Case closed. It was not that simple then, as the failure of the Council of Nicaea to kill the movement shows, and it is not that simple now. Arianism caught on and spread like wildfire, especially among the barbarian tribes, because it was easy to believe. It was easy to believe that a man was born, albeit a truly wonderful man, and that man lived an earthly life as Jesus. The wisdom of Jesus comes through His words. His devotion to His ideals comes through His willingness to die heroically for them. He was a great man.

That's the trap of Arianism in a nutshell. It is still a familiar trap today as Christians describe their Jesus to a modern world. Sometimes it is just a little easier if we soft-sell the divinity part and become a little Arian for awhile. The orthodox church leaders of this era knew that, too. It would have been easier to grow new churches, to claim new tribes as converts, and to become the preeminent religion by being an Arian. Many Christians of this period took that path and flourished for a while even after they were declared heretics. As the era comes to a close however, it is orthodoxy that is on the rise and Arianism that is disappearing. The conversion of the Franks to Catholic Christianity, instead of Arianism, is a true turning point of history. Orthodoxy, in the form of the church, will endure and continue to grow, while Arianism will simply fade away. For the modern Christian, that should encourage us to hold to the truth even when it might be easier to fudge a little. In the end, the truth wins.

BASIL THE GREAT

Basil is not a household name these days like some of his contemporaries. He was a household name in his day, though. He gave the church the first really wonderful definition of the Trinity. We take the Trinity for granted as a theological rock of Christian faith. If the history of the church in the Roman Empire teaches one big lesson, it is that the nature of Jesus, and His relationship with God and the Holy Spirit, was not a settled issue until after the Roman period. As the history shows, there were church leaders and even emperors who made the clarification of Jesus' nature their life's work. In this conflict, Basil gave the church the simple definition of the Trinity: Jesus, God, and the Holy Spirit are all of the same substance but are three persons. That, in short, is the definition we still use today.

SIGNIFICANCE OF AUGUSTINE

Augustine was never an emperor. He did become a powerful bishop who led the way for the orthodox church as it faced the challenges of several heresies. His influence was perhaps the greatest of any figure of the period, however.

Augustine shaped the thought of the Christian world. While others made efforts to reconcile the Greco-Roman philosophies, especially Stoicism, and Christian faith, Augustine was able to synthesize philosophy and faith into one convincing, credible, and appealing set of beliefs. He was able to make the distinction clear between the imperfection of the clergy and the perfection of God, and then make the distinction irrelevant to the sanctity of the sacraments. He was able to define the roles of faith, grace, and works in a way that made sense. Martin Luther would come along a millennium later and revisit those roles in the light of what Augustine had to say. He tackled the issue of predestination so well that he was a major source for John Calvin's teachings.

Augustine *was* the source of wisdom in the Middle Ages. He was at the core of the development of the Age of Faith. In his own personal struggles he had tried everything and found nothing. He had followed the rules he had learned as a student, then a teacher: Understanding leads to wisdom. In his conversion, however, he had changed his mind. He would write, "Believe in order to understand." It was that philosophy that the people of the Middle Ages would embrace and follow for hundreds of years.

SET THE STAGE!
MONASTIC ORDERS

A monastic order is a group of monks (sometimes thousands, in many different monasteries) bound by a common "rule" or set of guidelines. Most orders are named after their founders (like the Benedictines after Benedict) or their place of origin (like the Cluniacs of Cluny, France). Some were known by the color of their robes. The Franciscans were called Gray Friars (though they later wore brown). Here's a little bit about just a few of the different orders:

The wealthy Cluniac order had servants do the work so they could pray full-time.

The Cistercian order had "choir monks" to pray and "lay brothers" to do the work.

The Franciscans (also called the Friars Minor, which translates as "little brothers") lived mostly *among* the people rather than in seclusion and either worked for a living or begged in the streets to get by.

Other orders include the Dominicans (Black Friars), Carmelites (White Friars), and Augustinians, just to name a few.

While each order holds slightly different beliefs and goals, most center around leading a righteous and prayerful life. Many have made significant contributions to the outside world. Much scientific research has been carried out under the auspices of a monastic order, including important early research in genetics and heredity by the Austrian monk Gregor Mendel. Many of the world's finest wines and liqueurs were actually developed and produced by monks.

BENEDICT

In the post-Reformation world we live in, the monastic orders often seem far removed from the mainstream of the church. Benedict would not have been too troubled by that. In our time, we seem to focus on the outward expression of our faith in our communities and in the world. There were, of course, missionaries such as Patrick, David, and Columba during the era 312–590, and it is certain that the church could not have grown as it did without thousands of Christians sharing the gospel in their communities. But for Benedict, that was simply not his focus. For him, the focus was inward into oneself and upward toward God.

Though most Christians do not live that way, there are two important gifts we have from Benedict. First, he gave work a moral value. According to his Rule, work was a part of the day. He showed that there was value in work, even the tedious or difficult. Second, he placed great value on both prayer and study. He brought a discipline to life by structuring the day around prayer, study, and work. Most of us today do not live a monastic lifestyle, but we do hold some of these values. Most Christians believe that hard work is an act of virtue, and we certainly place value in our prayer and study time.

The monastic life that Benedict defined will be a centerpiece of the church in the Middle Ages even until their end: Martin Luther himself was a member of a monastic order. For the most part, our modern view of the monastic life was shaped by the Reformation as the Protestants rejected so many of the old Catholic traditions and institutions. The monasticism that Benedict helped to shape may have become largely irrelevant to many of today's Christians, but the value he placed on study, prayer, moral discipline, and work still resounds in churches all across the modern spectrum.

CONCLUSION

In the end, this short period of years started the church on a path still evident today. This era turned the church, rightly or wrongly, into a powerful earthly institution. Christianity still spread house-to-house, village-to-village, and city-to-city. But beginning with this era it also grew nation-to-nation. The church became an empire within the chaos following the collapse of Rome and leading to the rise of the European states. Bishops were as powerful as princes, popes as powerful as kings. The worldwide church we see in today's world took its first giant steps between 312 and 590. Then it had the awesome task of helping to create the New World out of the ancient. That is the story to be told in the Middle Ages.

CHAPTER FIVE

The Middle Ages: church as Empire

(a.d. 590 to a.d. 1517)

 A DAY IN THE LIFE

Geoffrey Chaucer's *Canterbury Tales* is a classic of medieval literature. The unfinished poem is in Middle English, the form of English used from about 1100 to about 1485. It's the story of twenty-nine pilgrims gathered for a journey to Canterbury. The telling of their travels gives us insight into the times of the Middle Ages.

There were no children along for Chaucer's version of the trip from London to Canterbury. If there had been, and if it had been a little boy, he might have written the following:

I don't care what Mom and Dad say—it is a long walk all the way to Canterbury from London. This is my first pilgrimage and the people with us are really nice...except for that scabby-faced pardoner. He gives me the creeps, but he is a really good salesman. He has made a lot of money on this trip and hides it under his clothes. He sells little pieces of paper that guarantee forgiveness of your sins. They are signed by the pope and everything.

I like the monk, though. He isn't much like the monks who live at the monastery near my village. They are all so serious, just praying all the time. The monk traveling with us likes horses and hunting and stuff like I do, not all that religious stuff. There is a student with us from Oxford University who loves all that philosophy. He just walks along with his head in the clouds, mumbling to himself.

The knight and his squire are really grand: honest-to-goodness noble people, and I am traveling with them. The knight has been everywhere in the world, I am sure. He even fought those "infidels" somewhere. I bet he just lopped the heads off of those heathen, bloodthirsty, spawns of the devil. (That's what my dad calls them anyway!)

The stories they tell are good enough, I guess. I laughed when the miller told the story about the carpenter getting cuckolded. I don't know what that means, but everybody else laughed, too. Well, not the student—he never comes back down to the ground long enough to do that. That nice lady from Bath pretended to be embarrassed, but she laughed as hard as anybody. One of the priests who is here to take confession for the prioress had to sit down a minute before he could go on.

I hope we get to Canterbury soon. I can't wait to see where the blessed Thomas Becket stood up to the king and was stabbed to death for it. Now that's a good story. My dad tells that one sometimes. Archbishop Becket must have been a good man because all kinds of miracles can happen to you if you visit his church. Somebody told somebody else that you can see angels and fairies and stuff flying around, and that once it even rained money.

One thing bothers me, though. If he was so good, why did he make trouble for the king like the evil earls and dukes who are against our king? Wasn't the king good to the church and not make them pay taxes and stuff? I guess there is a lot I don't understand.

TIMELINE OVERVIEW

In the midst of world history...

593 China: The first printing press is invented.

610 Muhammad has a vision of the archangel Gabriel commanding him to proclaim the one true god, Allah.

622 Muhammad flees from persecution. This marks the start of the Islamic calendar.

624 China: Buddhism becomes the official religion, but other religions are allowed.

630 Muhammad captures Mecca, promotes Islam.

638 Muslims capture Jerusalem.

732 Battle of Tours

771 Pepin's son, Charles, becomes the king of Franks. He is known as Charlemagne, or Charles the Great.

772 Charlemagne conquers Saxony in Germany and converts the people to Christianity.

878 England: The Vikings are allowed to live in the Danelaw (the north) if they become Christians.

890 Nailed horseshoes are used for the first time. The shoes are cheap enough for peasants to afford.

921 Wenceslas becomes prince of Bohemia. He tries to make his people Christian but is opposed and killed by his brother in 929. He was later made a saint.

950 Europe: The padded horse-collar is introduced. Horses can pull heavier loads.

1000 China: Gunpowder is perfected.

1067 Work begins on the Tower of London.

1075 A dispute begins between the pope and the Holy Roman Emperor over who should appoint bishops.

1076 Holy Roman Empire: Synod of Worms, the bishops depose Pope Gregory. Pope Gregory then excommunicates the emperor.

Christian history unfolds...

596 Pope Gregory sends monks under Augustine to England to convert the Anglo-Saxons to Christianity.

597 Augustine arrives with thirty missionaries in England. His first convert is Ethelbert I, the ruler of Kent.

664 Synod of Whitby: King Oswy abandons the Celtic Christian church and accepts Rome's form of Christianity, Roman Catholicism. The Celtic church starts to decline.

669 Greek monk Theodore of Tarsus is sent to England as the archbishop of Canterbury to reorganize the church in England to be more like the church in the rest of Western Europe.

700 England: The Psalms are translated into Anglo-Saxon.

Islam: The Arabs capture Tunis, and Christianity all but disappears in North Africa.

731 Bede completes his history.

800 Pope Leo III crowns Charlemagne Holy Roman Emperor.

909 Monastery established at Cluny, the Cluny Abbey. The Cluniacs initiate reform of the church and build monasteries in other parts of Western Europe.

988 Russia: Vladimir of Kiev introduces the Christian Eastern Orthodox Church.

1052 England: Edward the Confessor founds Westminster Abbey, near London.

1054 Schism between East and West: the final break between the Byzantine Empire and the Roman Church. The Eastern Orthodox Church becomes completely independent.

Continued

TIMELINE OVERVIEW (CONTINUED)

In the midst of world history…

Christian history unfolds…

1077 Holy Roman Empire: The dispute between the emperor and the pope leads to civil war. Emperor Henry eventually does penance to Pope Gregory.

1083 Emperor Henry IV attacks Rome.

1088 Urban II becomes pope.

1095 Urban II launches first crusade in Council of Clermont. He appeals for volunteers to free the Christian holy places in Palestine.

1098 France: First Cistercian Monastery is founded.

The crusaders defeat the Muslims at Antioch.

1099 Palestine: The crusaders capture Jerusalem.

1106 Germany: Henry V becomes the Holy Roman Emperor.

c. 1120 China: Playing cards are invented.

1122 Concordat of Worms: Ends the dispute between the pope and the Holy Roman Emperor

1135 England: Geoffrey of Monmouth writes *History of the Kings of Britain*, including stories about King Arthur.

c. 1150 Europe: First paper made.

1152 France: Marriage of Louis VII and Eleanor of Aquitaine is annulled.

1115 Bernard establishes monastery at Clairvaux.

1150 University established in Paris.

1162 Becket is appointed archbishop of Canterbury and immediately quarrels with King Henry II.

1170 Becket returns to Canterbury but is murdered soon after.

Oxford University is founded.

1198 Innocent III—the papacy reaches its peak of power and influence.

1204 Francis of Assisi—the Franciscans

1215 England: The barons force King John to a statement of their rights called the Magna Carta.

1218 Genghis Khan conquers Persia.

1215 Fourth Lateran Council
France: St. Dominic founds the Dominican Order of friars at Toulouse.

1220 Dominicans recognized.

1228 Sixth Crusade led by Frederick II.

1233 Rome: Pope Gregory IX establishes the Inquisition.

1229 Synod of Toulouse—Dominicans can punish "heretics."

1248 Seventh crusade begins, led by Louis IX of France.

1243 Innocent IV becomes pope.

1258 Robert de Sorbon founds a religious college at Paris University, now called La Sorbonne.

1266 English philosopher and scientist Roger Bacon invents the magnifying glass.

1268 Palestine: Muslims from Egypt capture Antioch, which had been held by the Christians.

1271 Venice: Merchant Marco Polo sets out to visit Kublai Khan in north China.

1275 China: Marco Polo enters the service of Kublai Khan.

1273 Aquinas completes Summa Theologica.

c. 1290 William of Ockham born—Nominalism in philosophy, Ockham's Razor. Christ is only head of the church—the pope has *no* authority over civil matters.

1291 Palestine: Acre, the last Christian stronghold in Palestine, is captured by the Muslims. The crusades continue, but weaker and weaker.

1293 China: The first Christian missionaries arrive.

1305 Clement V named pope—stays in Avignon. For almost the entire fourteenth century no pope lived in Rome.

1312 King of France, Philip IV, persecutes whole religious order of Knights Templar to take their money and property.

1321 Dante completes *The Divine Comedy*.

TIMELINE OVERVIEW (CONTINUED)

In the midst of world history...

1337 Edward III of England declares himself king of France, starting the Hundred Years' War.

1429 Joan of Arc is appointed military commander and wins the siege of Orléans.

1430 Joan of Arc is captured and handed over to the English.

1431 Joan of Arc is burned as a witch at Rouen.

1440 Johannes Gutenberg begins printing with movable type.

1469 Ferdinand of Aragon and Isabella of Castile marry, unifying Spain.

1482 Leonardo da Vinci paints the fresco *The Last Supper*.

1484 Caxton prints *Morte d'Arthur*, the poetic collection of legends about King Arthur compiled by Sir Thomas Malory.

1492 Christopher Columbus crosses the Atlantic and arrives in the Caribbean.

1502 The first Africans arrive as slaves in the Americas.

1503 Leonardo da Vinci paints the *Mona Lisa*.

1504 The watch is invented by Peter Henlein of Nuremberg. (It had only one hand.)

1510 Sunflowers are introduced to Europe from America.

1516 Europe: Coffee is introduced.

Christian history unfolds...

1376 John Wycliffe, an Oxford University teacher, speaks out for Church reforms.

1378 The Great Schism begins—lasts 30 years. Rival popes are elected, Urban VI (pope at Rome) and Clement VII (antipope at Avignon).

1380 Wycliffe and others translate the Bible into English.

1400 Chaucer's *Canterbury Tales*—faith with trouble on the horizon.

1409 The Council of Pisa is called to resolve the Great Schism.

1415 John Hus burned at the stake.

1417 The Great Schism ends when the Council of Constance elects Martin V as the only rightful pope.

1447 Era of Renaissance popes begins.

1456 Gutenberg publishes the Bible in Latin, the first to be printed with movable type.

1473 The Sistine Chapel is built by Giovanni de Dolci.

1478 Inquisition started in Spain.

1490 West Africa: The Portuguese sail up the Congo River and convert the king of Congo to Christianity.

1498 Savonarola executed.

1508 Michelangelo starts painting the Sistine Chapel in the Vatican.

1512 Sistine Chapel completed—humanism is evident in the Renaissance.

1516 Erasmus publishes a Greek New Testament with a preface encouraging the translation of Scripture into the common vernacular of Europe. By 1559 his books were placed on the Index of Forbidden Books.

THE STORY OF THE TIMES

The Middle Ages were the time of our fantasies. They were the times of brave knights riding off to defend their land and honor. They were the times of great castles built by powerful men. They were the times when the great cathedrals rose up and towered over the land. They were the times that brought us King Arthur and Roland: heroic times when every battle was a fight between right and wrong.

But there is the darker side. They were the times of the plague when death spread over the land at an unfathomable pace. They were the times of the Crusades when men left their homes to fight the "infidel" and never returned. They were the times when barbarians and "civilized" men plundered and pillaged and transformed entire nations in their own image.

They were times when the church grew to incredible power and influence, when religious leaders held not only the reins of the church in their hands but also the entire future of the European continent. They were times when the church accomplished incredible feats and sank to incredible lows.

The Middle Ages lasted a long time. Kingdoms and peoples came and went. Great territories were lost and won and lost again. But there was one thread that tied the whole era together: The Christian church was present as a powerful unifying force that preserved order, that brought law and civilization to the wilderness, and that spread light, faith, and learning into the darkness. It was an empire.

THE BRIDGE

The Roman church played a pivotal role in the transition between the ancient and medieval worlds. It could be said that they played this role by default: There were no other western institutions to do it. The political structure of the Roman Empire had been destroyed by constant war, and the social structure had been destroyed by the repeated invasions of barbarians who brought their own "society" with them.

But the church had endured and actually become stronger, so it became the means that Roman culture was transmitted into the Middle Ages. Ever since the days of Constantine, the church had begun to reflect the structure and organization of the empire. Now, with the empire gone, the church survived as a reflection of that wonder of organizations. If they were nothing else, the Romans were great bureaucrats; the structure of their government and law was really effective and built to last. The Roman church, born into that world, adopted it. Each city was entitled to a bishop, and each province had an archbishop. Within the territory of the bishop, the hierarchy was almost identical to that of the local Roman bureaucracy.

Church law was patterned after Roman law. At first, church law had just contained the degrees of church councils. (In the Roman republic these would have been the decrees of the Senate.) Eventually, however, church law also contained the edicts of the pope much as Roman law after Julius Caesar had contained the decrees of the emperor. Just as a decree of an emperor instantly became law and policy, so did an edict of the pope.

Finally, Roman culture was passed on by the church through its adherence to the Latin language. Through this common language, the church was able to maintain a kind of unity wherever it was practiced. Almost no literature and very little learning made the transition from the ancient world to the medieval, but Latin made the transition. The literature and learning of the Middle Ages were based on the Latin models that were available. Before we jump into the Middle Ages, we should quickly look back at the legacy they inherited from the ancient times.

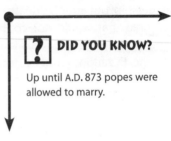

? DID YOU KNOW?

Up until A.D. 873 popes were allowed to marry.

A RECAP...

The ancient era ultimately passed because of the downfall of the Western Roman Empire. As historians will point out, *the* Roman Empire did not really fall for almost a thousand more years. The Eastern Empire survived the upheavals of the fourth, fifth, and sixth centuries and carried on, actually flourished for centuries to come. While the chaos descended on the West, the Byzantine Empire remained a stronghold of power in the East extending back to the emperor Constantine. It was also a bastion of orthodox Christianity. The previous chapter dealt extensively with the relationship between the Orthodox church centered in Constantinople and the Roman church. The Middle Ages inherit that schism between the two poles of early Christianity. Even though Justinian had restored most of the Western Empire to his imperial control, the sixth and seventh centuries were to prove disastrous for both East and West.

THE HARD TIMES ARE NOT OVER YET

The period of 565 to 610 was one of the worst in the history of the Byzantine Empire. Justinian died in 565, and with his death, the government he had set up collapsed. During this period there were three emperors: Justin II, Maurice, and Phocas. During their reigns there was almost constant war with the Persians in the East and the Slavs in the Balkan Peninsula. The Persian War went terribly under Justin II. Maurice was an excellent military leader, and the war went better under his leadership; but after his death the war turned into a protracted struggle that would not conclude for many years. The wars against the Slavs and Avars in the Balkans were simply failures for the Byzantine armies. During the reign of Phocas, every major Christian city except Thessalonica was destroyed by the Slavs and Avars. It was also during these years that the Balkans ceased to be Greek while the Slavic culture, carried in by the invaders, began to be dominant.

It was in Italy, however, where the greatest collapse of Justinian's power was felt. Italy was simply not protected well enough, and in 568 the Lombards, a group of several Arian barbarian tribes (including the Saxons who will become significant much later), entered northern Italy and conquered it. The region was later called Lombardy after the conquerors. The Byzantine ruler hid behind the walls of his capital, Ravenna, as the Lombards swept south. In a short time they had captured the entire Italian peninsula except for Ravenna and Rome.

So the West was lost again, and many of Justinian's great gains were now back in the hands of the barbarians. Justinian's policies in the West had failed to hold it for the empire. Once again, there was a great distance between the Eastern empire and the West, and that gap was ever widening.

MEANWHILE... A LITTLE TO THE NORTH

In modern-day France and Germany, the seventh century saw the power of the Franks still on the rise. Clovis had been made a consul, a position of great power and prestige in the old Roman Empire, by the emperor Anastasius (emperor 491–518), and the Franks still enjoyed their position of power as an "ally" of the empire. After the Lombard invasion of Italy, the emperor Maurice even tried to convince the Frankish king Childebert II to invade Italy on behalf of the empire and the Franks. Childebert II refused, although he did take the opportunity of Byzantine weakness to recapture some Frankish territory in extreme northern Italy.

In Britain, Christianity grew slowly, and the conflict between Roman Catholic and Celtic Christianity was unresolved. It would be the middle of the seventh century before that conflict would be settled. The Roman church maintained its presence in Britain through the archbishop of Canterbury. This church position would come into focus as a true position of power in the upcoming era as it took on the task of converting Britain into a Catholic country. It would also become the focus of conflicts that resonated across the entire European continent.

AND BACK TO ROME

In Rome, Pope Gregory dominated the interim between the ancient and medieval worlds. All through the seventh century, the Western emperors relied increasingly on the popes for support. Even Theodoric, the Ostrogoth who ruled Italy, was not altogether hostile to the church because it was an institution that could help him maintain order. Gregory strengthened the power and influence of the pope as the "boss of bosses" of the church. He also established the pope as a powerful figure in civil and political matters. When he became pope in 590, Rome was in a desperate position. The Lombards were threatening, and there was no hope of help from the Byzantine Empire's representative in Ravenna. Without the authority of the emperor, he took command of Rome, provisioned the city, and made arrangements for its defense. He commanded the generals in the field and eventually negotiated peace with the Lombards. This set the stage for the pope of the Middle Ages who would have the authority to even wage war on behalf of the church. Gregory's influence was also spiritual, however. He practically defined medieval Christianity with its interest in saints and relics, and he began the missionary effort in Britain to convert the pagans and Celtic Christians alike to Roman Christianity. In his eyes, the time was right for a religious explosion.

SINNERS AND SAINTS
ST. GREGORY I

Gregory was born to a wealthy Roman family around A.D. 540. A direct descendant of Felix III and of Agapitas I, both of whom were popes later canonized by the church, Gregory rose through the Roman political ranks to become prefect (governor) of the city-state. Shortly thereafter, he became a monk and gave away the family fortunes, in the process converting his own home and six other family estates into monasteries. In the course of his path to the papacy, Gregory served as a regional deacon and as an ambassador to the imperial Byzantine court. As pope, he almost completely reorganized the political infrastructure of the papal government and instituted management reforms affecting many of the church's holdings in Italy. He also authored a well-known book wherein he lists and details the qualities that would be found in an ideal bishop.

THE RELIGIOUS EXPLOSION COMES, BUT...
If Christianity was the religious explosion of the first six centuries A.D., the next century or two certainly belonged to Islam. Muhammad of Mecca was born around 570. In 610, he received a religious calling and began to proclaim his message of Islam. According to Islam, Muhammad had a vision of the angel Gabriel who told him to proclaim the one true God, Allah.

Muhammad's prophecy centered on the judgment that was coming to the world when reward and punishment are meted out for an individual's actions, and on the teachings of Allah, who is both teacher and judge. His message imposed five main obligations on its followers. There must be a confession of faith that Allah is the only God and that Muhammad is His prophet. The believer must pray five times a day, give charitable gifts, fast during the holy month of Ramadan, and make a pilgrimage to Mecca.

Muhammad was in Mecca when he began proclaiming the prophecy he received. His message was not well received. Arabian culture at that time was rich with different ideas and beliefs. Christianity, Jewish thought, Greek philosophy, and the religion of Zoroastrianism all contributed to the mix of religion and belief there.

ISLAM ON THE RISE

By 622, Muhammad had completely worn out his welcome in Mecca and was forced to leave. His flight from Mecca to his new home in Medina is called the Hegira. That event marks the beginning of the Muslim calendar. His prophecy found a totally different reception there. Before long he had built a large following and a strong power base. He condemned idol worship, and those who practiced it had to accept his teachings or die. Monotheists, like Jews and Christians, were tolerated and not persecuted on the condition that they pay a special tax.

In 630, Muhammad returned to Mecca and made it his city, as well. He began the conversion of the city into a Muslim city by removing all the idols. By the time he died in 632, all of

 SET THE STAGE!

Zoroastrianism was the religion of Persia. It made its first appearance around the sixth century B.C. It teaches that there are two powerful forces in the universe: one good and one evil. Those conflicting forces govern life on earth and will eventually determine the fate of the universe. The Persian rulers of the Old Testament were believers. The religion went into decline when Alexander the Great conquered Persia, but it had a resurgence in the third century A.D. It was all but destroyed when Persia fell to Islam in the seventh century. Today there are a little over 200,000 followers of Zoroastrianism. About 10,000 of these live in Iran, and around 200,000 constitute the Parsis in India.

Arabia was Muslim. His work was carried on by his father-in-law, Abu Bakr, and by his closest converts, called the "Companions." Like early Christianity, these converts had the goal of spreading their faith. Unlike Christianity, the early converts to Islam took a militant approach to spreading their faith. By 635, the Muslims had begun the conquest of Syria and Persia. By 638, they had done the unthinkable to Jew and Christian alike and captured the holy city of Jerusalem. By 669, they began their conquest of Egypt. Alexandria fell to them in 642, Mesopotamia in 646. Carthage, in North Africa, fell in 697; Tunis fell to the Muslims in 700. Soon afterward they had vanquished Christianity from North Africa altogether. The incredibly hard-fought wars of Justinian to restore Christianity to that region against the Vandals came to nothing in the end against the incredible spread of Islam. That territory remains Muslim to this day, thirteen hundred years afterward.

In the meantime, the Muslims had been spreading their faith eastward. They had entered the Punjab area of India and were threatening the capital of the Eastern Empire, Constantinople. The "empire" of Islam reached from the Atlantic Ocean to the River Indus in Pakistan. Then, in 711, the Muslims crossed the Straits of Gibraltar and attacked the Iberian Peninsula: Visigothic Spain. Within a short time they controlled that whole territory and even crossed the Pyrenees. As the eighth century approached its third decade, they were poised to attack the heartland of western Europe.

MEANWHILE...BACK IN BRITAIN

In Britain there was a smoldering religious conflict going on. Back in 563, Columba had gone to Iona, evangelized the Scots, and established a monastery that later grew into a center of missionary work. His missionary work had laid the groundwork for Celtic Christianity. Since it was established far from the influence of the Roman church, Celtic Christianity was quite different. It stressed a contemplative, monastic lifestyle and placed a large emphasis on missionary work. Celtic Christianity grew rapidly and became well established in Scotland and northern Britain.

Then, under Pope Gregory's direction, Augustine was sent to evangelize the Anglo-Saxons in southern Britain. One of his first converts was King Ethelbert I, who helped him establish a Roman church foothold in Kent in the southern part of Britain.

In 627, Paulinus of York established a Roman church in the north of Britain in Northumbria. The church was short-lived because it was destroyed when a heathen king came to power. When it was reestablished, it was Celtic, not Roman. You might think that an event like this would spark a real conflict, but in fact, it did not. In truth, there were more similarities between the Celtic and Roman Christians than differences. There were two major issues in conflict.

POINTS OF CONTENTION

The first issue was a big one: power. The Roman Christians believed that individuals were directly responsible to the chain of command that extended from the priest to the bishop, from the bishop to the archbishop, and from the archbishop to the pope. The Celtic Christians, coming from a monastic tradition, placed much greater power in the abbot.

 IMAGINE THAT!

Legend has it that Pope Gregory I, who sent Augustine as a missionary to the Anglo-Saxons, did so because he witnessed some Angles being sold as slaves. Supposedly the pope said, "They are not Angles, but angels."

The second one was simply a matter of the calendar. The two churches disagreed over the date of Easter so that the Celtic Christians were celebrating Easter while the Roman Christians were still observing Lent. Amazingly, it was this second problem that brought the conflict to a head in 664. The new king of Northumbria, Oswy, was a Celtic Christian, but his wife observed the Roman calendar. Needless to say, Easter was a confusing time at their castle. So the king called for a religious assembly at the monastery at Whitby.

SET THE STAGE!
THE DEBATE AT WHITBY—THE RUMBLE FOR THE KING

The Debate at Whitby was like a tag team match:

In the Roman corner—Wilfred the Bishop and James the Deacon.

And in the Celtic corner—Cedd the Abbot and Colman the Bishop.

This one-fall match decided the future direction of the church in England. There was just one judge at ringside: Oswy the King. This was a no holds barred match.

THE OUTCOME OF THE DEBATE

As a sort of debate, the king heard arguments from both sides. On the Roman side were Wilfred and James the Deacon. Wilfred was a Roman church bishop and missionary, and James was a successor to Paulinus, who had tried to evangelize the North for the Roman church. On the Celtic side were Cedd and Colman. Cedd was a well-respected abbot with a good track record establishing monasteries. Colman was a Celtic bishop.

They argued about Easter. The Celtic leaders went back to the father of their church, Columba, to argue their points. The Roman leaders quoted Saint Peter. That was the trump card. The king announced, despite his own personal beliefs to that point, that he would rather follow what Peter had to say because he held the keys to heaven. The Roman way won.

A NEW COOPERATION

This single incident was not the downfall of the Celtic church. For the next hundred years, however, Roman Christianity flourished and spread throughout Britain. Perhaps it was able to do so because after Whitby there was a greater sense of cooperation between the two churches. The Celtic church could benefit from being better organized and

DID YOU KNOW?

St. Columba of Ireland was the first person to record sighting the Loch Ness monster.

connected with the outside world, and the Roman church absorbed some of its rival's missionary zeal.

When Theodore of Tarsus became the archbishop of Canterbury in 669, he had the vision to appoint priests and bishops from both religious traditions. By doing so he was able to create a truly structured church in Britain, a "national" church. This spirit of organization rubbed off on some of the secular leaders, as well, and following Theodore's example, there was an upsurge in unity and organization among the many separate tribes.

Theodore also contributed to a resurgence in the development of Anglo-Saxon culture. Theodore had been well educated in Athens, and, along with several of his bishops, he founded a school at Canterbury for Mediterranean and Christian studies. Though much of this cultural development would be destroyed

SINNERS AND SAINTS
BEDE (A.D. 673?–735)

Commonly given the title The Venerable Bede, this medieval theologian also has more subtitles than a Kung Fu movie. He was, in his time, also referred to as Baeda and later as The Father of English History, St. Bede, and The Greatest Scholar of Saxon England. His compendium, *Ecclesiastical History of the English Nation,* is the primary sourcebook for English history up to A.D. 731. Speaking of "A.D.," Bede is credited with introducing the terms B.C. (before Christ) and A.D. (anno Domini, which is Latin for *in the year of our Lord)* to European literature. His works on history, theology, and science are considered by many to be the best of the era. Up to within minutes of his death from a protracted illness, Bede worked on a translation of the Gospel of St. John. When it was finished, Bede sang praises to the Lord with his last few breaths.

by the Vikings, works such as Bede's *Ecclesiastical History of the English Nation* and the incredible biblical works such as the *Lindisfarne Gospels* are prime examples of the high level of development present in Britain in the early eighth century.

THE FRANKS ON THE MOVE
The Franks did not merely sit still after their ascension as one of the top barbarian groups. Certainly Clovis had led the way with his military exploits and his political savvy. After all, he had managed to be named a consul by a Roman emperor. His claim to the lands in modern-day France, Germany, and northern Italy was legitimized (for all it was worth) by an emperor's decree. Furthermore, by becoming a Roman Christian, the Merovingian dynasty begun by Clovis became allied with the pope. Though the Merovingians were known for their brutality and not their piety, they were able to maintain that favored position with the church.

The Franks had been able to thwart every challenge to their territory. They had even ventured southward into northern Italy to recapture lands they had lost to the Lombards. In 732, however, they faced a foe unlike any they had faced before.

After the Muslims had conquered Spain and crossed the Pyrenees, they had their sights on modern-day France. They had already conquered all of North Africa and the Near East by combining military power with religious fervor. Islam not only overthrew the political powers of a country, it converted people to its beliefs or forced them to adhere to a new religious system. That method had worked so far, and that was the plan against the Franks.

The Franks were led by Charles Martel. In the Frankish tradition, he was a strong ruler who was quite happy to have the pope as an ally and to support Roman Christian missionaries to other Germanic tribes. (Remember that Gregory the Great had enlisted the help of the Franks in his efforts to evangelize the Anglo-Saxons in Britain.) He, like his predecessors, was not devout, however, and he was quick to take advantage of the church when he could. At the battle of Tours in 732, he proved a preserver of Christianity in Europe.

A MUSLIM INVASION

In 732, the Muslims moved deep into Frankish territory near the city of Tours. Tours itself had been a Roman city in Gaul and was now a Frankish stronghold. The Muslims were led by the general Abu-er-Rahman. Charles Martel (*Martel* literally means "the hammer") led his army out to meet the Muslims between Tours and Poitiers. In the battle that ensued, Martel beat the Muslims back. Furthermore, after a series of battles, he was able to drive the Muslims entirely out of Gaul and across the Pyrenees into Spain. He had halted the Muslim advance on the heart of Europe.

Of course, the Battle of Tours did not end the conflict between Christian and Muslim forces. In fact, most of the Middle Ages were punctuated with, if not dominated by, the continuing struggle between Christian rulers, secular and religious, and the Muslims. The Battle of Tours was a defining moment, however, because it preserved Europe for the Christian church. A similar defining moment had occurred in now far-away Constantinople in 718 when that city was successfully defended against the Muslims. In the century following Muhammad's death, his followers had reduced the Eastern Empire greatly in the Near East and in North Africa and had even established a powerful presence in Spain. The battles were just beginning.

MORE ON THE FRANKS...

A little more history of the Franks is in order. In the eighth century, a new group of rulers came to power in the Franks' kingdom. The Carolingians had actually run the affairs of the kingdom for a number of years as mayors of the palace under the Merovingian kings. In 751, Pepin the Short, a Carolingian, made himself king.

Although Pepin is usually overshadowed by his more famous son Charlemagne, he had a crucial role to play in the drama of the eighth century. To play his role, Pepin went back to a very old idea and a forged document.

The idea was simple: The empire and the religion should be one and the same. The idea was as old as Roman culture itself.

Constantine had adapted it, and Theodosius had finalized it. Eusebius had even written about it. There *should* be a Christian empire because the structure of the empire and the church are so similar. Rationale was that they were structured similarly because they were both structured from God's divine plan. In the chaotic aftermath of the fall of the Western Empire, the popes had tried to strengthen the papacy to assume the role of imperial power, but the times made the application of that power extremely difficult. After all, for much of that time they were practically foreigners in Rome or Ravenna as Italy was captured and recaptured. Pepin had been raised in the monastery of St. Denis near Paris, so he had a thorough understanding of the religious precedent for an imperial church. He could see the advantages of an alliance with such a powerful church, especially if he was the one to give the pope some territory of his own to rule.

SINNERS AND SAINTS
ST. BONIFACE

Boniface was born in Devon county, England, in 675. Originally named Winfrid, he became a priest at about thirty years of age and, after some years of faithful service, was given the name Boniface by the pope. Because of his tireless missionary efforts in Germany, where his efforts led to many conversions and the founding of some of the first monasteries in that country, he earned the nickname "Apostle of Germany." Boniface became a bishop and, later, archbishop of Mainz, but his most important role, historically speaking, may have been as a legate (special representative) of the pope: In this capacity, he anointed Pepin the Short, the first king of the Carolingian dynasty. Boniface was killed by pagans in the midst of a confirmation service for new converts in the Netherlands.

THE MORE THINGS CHANGE...

(Death, Taxes, and Other Immutables)

Whenever one generation looks back at another, there are a few hoots and cackles. Who hasn't looked back at their parents' or grandparents' old pictures and not laughed at outdated hair styles or clothes? Names can be the same way. Here are some popes whose names sound a little outdated these days (and what a newer generation might make of them).

Anacletus ("Suebob, meet Maryjim and Anacletus.")

Dionysius (Same name as the Greek god of wine. What's up with *that*?)

Telesphorus (successor to Radiosphorus?)

Hyginus (guaranteed to wash away sins *and* bacteria?)

Eleutherius (isn't that a type of ginseng?)

Zephyrinus (fastest of all the popes?)

Fabian (the singing pope?)

Hippolytus (the two-ton pope?)

Eutychian (sounds contagious!)

Sixtus (was he the one right after Fivus?)

Linus (imagine a pope with a security blanket)

Melchiades (who was also called Miltiades, which is *much* simpler...*not*)

Agapitus (patron saint of flatbread?)

Conon (the barbarian pope?)

Deusdedit (also called Adeodatus I; see Melchiades)

Zosimus (bless you!)

Hormisdas (did he actually *pick* that name or did he lose a bet?)

Agatho (didn't he fight Spider Man once?)

Sisinnius (you *know* he got picked on in school)

Lando (wasn't he in that space movie?)

Urban (so all those under him were sub-Urban?)

Innocent (well, I guess it's better than Pope Guilty I)

So in 754, Pepin used a forged document, the Donation of Constantine, to establish a new precedent in the relations between rulers and the pope. According to this document, the emperor Constantine had established his capital at Constantinople instead of Rome because he wanted the pope to have control of what was the Western Empire. The Donation bequeathed that part of the empire to the pope.

Pepin reasoned that if that Donation were true, he would just capture Ravenna from the Lombards and give it to its rightful owner, the pope. Pepin recovered territory in the northeast and central parts of Italy from the Lombards and gave it to Pope Stephen II. To do that, in 756 he issued the Donation of Pepin, which conferred the reclaimed territory to the pope. Most historians see this as the first stage of the Papal States, territory the pope ruled until the nineteenth century.

Pope Stephen II then placed Rome under the protection of Pepin and recognized the king and his sons as "protectors of the Romans." Even greater honors were in store for Pepin's son.

CHARLEMAGNE

Charlemagne (son of Pepin the Short, who was over six feet tall), came to the throne in 771 and almost immediately began nearly three decades of war. He took the offensive against most of his neighbors and extended his territory in almost every direction. In 774, Charlemagne was crowned king of Lombardy after invading the country and subduing the Lombards. Charlemagne then absorbed Lombardy into the Frankish Empire. Charlemagne became the first Frankish king to visit Rome, and while he was there, he confirmed the Donation of Pepin. He made it quite clear, however, that he was the king even in the papal territory. Eventually his empire stretched from the Baltic Sea in the North to the Adriatic Sea in the South. He controlled almost all of modern-day France, Italy, and Germany. For the first time in history, a large portion of Europe was actually under one ruler and under stable leadership. The time was right for political evolution in Europe.

HOLY ROMAN EMPEROR

From the pope's point of view, Charlemagne's timing could not have been better. For years, the relations between the popes and the Eastern emperors had been deteriorating. In 726, when the emperor Leo III banned the use of icons (images of Christ, the Virgin Mary, or a saint), Pope Gregory II publicly disagreed with the ban. Then he wrote the emperor a scathing letter that stated in no uncertain terms that "dogmas are not the business of emperors but of pontiffs." The pope was ready to free himself from his relationship with the Eastern emperor, a relationship as old as the divided empire itself.

Charlemagne gave him the opportunity. On Christmas Day 800, Pope Leo III crowned Charlemagne as emperor. The act was the reinstatement of the position of Western emperor created by Diocletian. The new emperor took the position seriously and began to sign all his official papers, "Charles, by the will of God, Roman Emperor."

Not wanting any more trouble with the pope, or Charlemagne, the Eastern emperor officially recognized Charlemagne's rights as Western emperor. As the Middle Ages developed, the role of the Holy Roman Emperor, as Charlemagne's successors would be called, would evolve continually, dependent on the wishes of the pope and the political climate of Germany, which became the home of the emperorship. Nevertheless, the office of Holy Roman Emperor gave the pope real political power in Europe. Kings would compete to hold the title of emperor: There would be wars fought over its succession; the church would become fabulously wealthy as kings tried to buy the job; and the office of the pope would be shaken to the core by the emerging power of the position it created. The power relationship between pope and Holy Roman Emperor would never be simple. It was not even that way under Charlemagne's rule. He was careful from the beginning to protect himself from the encroaching power of the church, while at the same time promoting Christianity throughout his realm.

 DID YOU KNOW?

The average reign of a pope is well under ten years. Pius IX holds the record for longest reign as a pope. He served the office between 1846 and 1878 for a total of 32 years.

CHARLEMAGNE AS EMPEROR

Charlemagne could read and speak Latin, but he couldn't write it. Still, he placed a very high value on education. Under his rule there was a resurgence in the value of learning that is often called the Carolingian Renaissance. The emperor sponsored a palace school at his palace in Aachen and decreed that every monastery should have a school for teaching any who had the desire and means to learn. During his rule, the monasteries in his kingdom were not only repositories for ancient writings and art, they were "factories" where these works were preserved and illuminated with beautiful drawings and calligraphy.

While much of the rest of the world swirled in confusion and cultural decay, Charlemagne gave Europe a stable beginning. He ensured that Christianity would spread as the official religion of "his" empire just as Theodosius had done in his day. Charlemagne was a ruler who truly fulfilled the position of Holy Roman Emperor. He was not a slave to the church, but he was its ally. As his power grew, so did that of the church.

ON THE OTHER HAND

Many great things happened under Charlemagne's rule. Nevertheless, there was plenty of chaos around in the ninth and tenth centuries. The Eastern empire was continuing on but was increasingly irrelevant to the West since the Frankish empire had effectively supplanted it. On the fringes of the Eastern and Frankish empires, there were dire threats to stability and culture.

IMAGINE THAT!

Until the late 700s, punctuation, spaces between words, and lowercase (small) letters were not used. These things were all introduced by scribes in the latter part of the 6th century. ITMUSTHAVBEENALOTHARDERTOREADBACKTHENHUH

Under the Bulgarian czar (originating from the word *caesar*) Malamir, who died in 852, the Bulgarians had expanded into territory that had been part of the Eastern empire. The empire had no way to throw them out.

In Persia, the Turks were growing in strength and influence. In the end they would be a threat to both East and West.

In the North, the Vikings began an era of exploring, raiding, and conquering those who stood in their way. The Vikings were Scandinavian warriors who raided the coasts of Europe and the British Isles from the ninth to eleventh centuries. They were magnificent shipbuilders and sailors, reaching as far as Greenland and North America. They expanded their influence mainly by raiding and pillaging along the coasts of western Europe. By 858, the Vikings had attacked and sacked the city of Algeciras on the Bay of Algeciras opposite Gibraltar in Spain. Though they were later run out of the country by the Muslims, the attack was an indication of how they could wage war by sea over long distances. In 862, the Norse leader Rurik made himself ruler of Novgorod, in what is now Russia. In 972, his successors moved to Kiev in what is now Ukraine. From that power base they established the dynasty that ruled Russia until 1598.

By the mid-ninth century, the Danes were attacking Britain. On New Year's Eve in 870, England's Ethelred I defeated the Danish Vikings in a skirmish in Berkshire. In 874, however, the Danes moved into Mercia, an Anglo-Saxon kingdom in central England. The Anglo-Saxon king Burgred abdicated the throne, and the Danes set up a puppet king. By 877, Exeter, in the southwest of England, had been captured by Danish forces.

ALFRED THE GREAT

Alfred the Great was the son of Ethelwulf and a man of Christian piety. His brother Ethelred took the Wessex throne in 865, and Alfred helped him in battles against the Danes. Alfred was not able to defeat the Danes decisively, so he bought peace with them with the Danegeld. (The Danegeld was a medieval land tax that was levied to pay off the Danes so they would not continue to attack. Eventually the tax was used to raise money for the military.)

In 878, however, the Danes returned, and Alfred had to flee in order to stay alive. But, in May 878, Alfred led an army that triumphed over the Danes at Edington. As a result, there was a period of relative calm. During this time, Alfred began to institute reforms. Being a devout Christian he instituted a code of laws that combined Christian doctrine with a strong, centralized monarchy.

In 885, he retook London from the Danes. Finally, in 886, he negotiated a treaty with the Danish leader, Guthrum, that divided Britain into sections which were ruled by either the Anglo-Saxons or the Danes. The Danelaw began as the term for the law that governed the Danish sections. In the end, however, it came to describe the territory that was held by the Danes.

It was under Alfred's leadership that England began to emerge as a country. He was able to unite the petty kingdoms of England against the common Danish enemy. He solidified the institution of the king as a true leader of all the Anglo-Saxons. In an act of rare vision, Alfred also recognized that, as an island nation, England needed a powerful navy and a regular standing army. He established them both.

A VERY HARD TIME

There is not a lot of history written about the time period from the middle of the ninth century to the middle of the eleventh. These were very difficult days for Western civilization. As early as Clovis in the late fifth century there had been a powerful Christian force in Europe to help hold things together. In the middle of the ninth century, the Carolingian kingship was in decline, and there was no other Christian power to replace it. The order that had seemed attainable in Charlemagne's time was becoming a fairy tale. There were continued attacks by the Muslims in the South, a new wave of attackers from central Asia, the Magyars (Hungarians), and the continual harassment by the Scandinavian barbarians in England and along the coast, extending as far eastward as the Byzantine empire itself.

This political disintegration had a similar effect on the church. Seeing this happening, the popes became more and more deeply involved in the internal politics of the fledgling European states. The situation may have been worst in Italy itself, where the pope was often the captive partisan of whatever group held power.

In the tenth century, there was an almost total collapse of order in Europe. The weakened papacy was no threat to the nobles who ruled the land in the absence of strong kings. The nobles were free to plunder the property of the church without regard for punishment. When the nobles were too weak to do this, oftentimes the land was attacked and conquered by foreign invaders who, in turn, ransacked the churches and stole their property. The nobles treated the bishops and monasteries as their own property to be sold or used as barter as they wished. Through all this, the church itself became corrupt. The offices of the church, clergy and monastic, were not respected, and many did not deserve respect. There was sexual debauchery even at the level of the pope, much less among local priests and monks. Without the support of the local secular leaders, the local church found itself unable to even police itself, much less be the standard of behavior for its parishioners.

Through all these terrible times, however, the central organization of the church somehow kept going. Then in the middle of the tenth century, the papacy got a small boost from an unexpected source.

OTTO AND THE PAPACY

During the reign of Pope John XII (955–964), a new dynasty ascended the throne of the German monarchy. Germany had been in near chaos since the collapse of Charlemagne's successors. The new dynasty began with the election of Henry I and really came to fruition under his son Otto I. Otto was a Saxon, the same tribe that had colonized England many years in the past. Otto I decided to build his power by creating close alliances with the church in Germany. He elevated the roles of bishops and abbots and gave them social privileges as nobles of the realm. He gave the church generous grants of land instead of following the typical practice of stealing land from the church. He spread his empire southward into Italy and into the area now encompassed by eastern Germany and Poland.

The job of Holy Roman Emperor had been in terrible shape since it had been inherited by Charlemagne's sons. The territory was partitioned and divided; there had even been war among brothers for the throne. At least one of the emperors (Arnulf, 899–901) had simply told the pope to crown him, and the pope, under pressure, did it. The last of the Carolingian kings, the dynasty founded by Pepin the Short, was Arnulf's son Louis, who reigned until 911 as Louis III (the Child).

Because of Otto's success, and one would hope his piety, the pope crowned him Holy Roman Emperor in February 962. That pope, John XII, would come to regret it. In 963, Otto returned to Rome and forced the Romans to promise not to elect a pope without his or his son's consent. In essence, he took over the right to name the supreme leader of the church. Even Charlemagne, as powerful as he had been, had not made that demand.

Otto's demand and the precedent it set would cause huge problems in the future over the issue of the right to appoint clergy. The church's agreement with him would cause it terrible struggles in the future, but for now it saved the papacy. The papacy attached itself to Otto's strong dynasty and survived the terrible times.

While the papacy survived, John XII didn't fare so well. In 963, Otto also convened a synod which tried Pope John XII and found him guilty of a long list of terrible crimes. He was deposed, and his successor was Leo VIII. Leo, who received all of his ecclesiastical orders in one day, was, of course, approved by the new emperor.

BACK AT THE MONASTERY

In the medieval world, in which even the pope was a political figure, the monastic life must have looked very attractive to many Christians. After all, it allowed them to separate themselves from the realities of social life and concentrate on a limited set of priorities. For those monastics who followed the Rule of Bernard, that was a very short "to do" list. Work, prayer, study, and worship constituted almost the entire experience of Bernard's adherents.

There were church leaders who were using their newfound

political power to get rich or to lead lives that were not consistent with their Christian teachings. One man who was deeply bothered by this was William the Pious, the duke of Aquitaine. His answer was to set up a monastery in 909 at the town of Cluny, which lies in modern-day, east-central France. This monastery would observe the Rule of Benedict strictly, especially the vows of poverty, chastity, and obedience. The monks of this order would be separated from the political power struggles that swirled around those in the outside world.

THE CLUNIACS

The monastery sparked a reform movement. The original monastery at Cluny became the heart of an explosion of Cluniac monasteries throughout France, Italy, and Germany, all espousing the same values as the original. In the next two hundred years, it is possible that the original monastery at Cluny may have led to the creation of over two thousand others. More important than the numbers is the fact that the reform movement worked. The Cluniac monks exemplified and promoted proper Christian behavior. As they became priests, bishops, and even popes, the influence of this move back toward simpler Christianity had a huge impact.

By the end of the eleventh century, the reform movement of the Cluniacs had run out of gas. Perhaps it was that they had been so successful they had begun to love the power. In 1098, the Cistercian order was started in the monastery of Citeaux by French ecclesiastic Robert de Molesmes and English ecclesiastic Stephen Harding. The Cistercians were a new branch of the Benedictine order, which was founded in 529 by St. Benedict at Monte Cassino. Like the Cluniacs, this new order was established to try to "clean up" the excesses the Benedictines had fallen into. Their rule, written by Harding, emphasized manual labor instead of scholarship and private rather than public, corporate prayer. The greatest of the Cistercians was Bernard. In 1115, he convinced thirty monks to follow him as he founded a new monastery at Clairvaux.

SET THE STAGE!

In medieval times monks were among the cleanest of people, since they bathed regularly *four times a year!*

BERNARD

Bernard's message was simple: He preached moral purity and personal piety. He taught that the love of earthly things must be sublimated to the love of God. To do so involved self-denial. He also taught, like Augustine had, that religious insight was the product of the heart, not the mind. Like Augustine, he was responding to the Scholastics who taught that rationality was the path to the truth. To Bernard, the goal of Bible study was to "penetrate hearts, not explain words."

Bernard became an incredibly influential man despite his early desire for the simple life. He even became active in the politics of his day to the point of deciding between rival popes. He moved on from his devotion to a simpler life, but his lessons had a huge impact on the medieval mind that sought the truth not from the facts but through inspiration.

THE DOMINICANS

The second great order of friars in the Middle Ages were the Dominicans, who were founded by the Spaniard Dominic de Guzman. He founded the order in 1215, and it was recognized in 1220. Unlike monks, who are bound to a monastery, the friar's ministry is usually outward. The Dominicans were founded when de Guzman was sent to Provence to preach. He realized that there was a huge need for an educated clergy who could communicate with the people through sermons. The Dominicans were established to teach and preach. In fact, the official name of the Dominicans was the "Order of Preachers." They soon had the nickname of the Black Friars because they wore a white habit covered by a black cloak. In contrast with the Franciscans, the Dominicans valued intellectual achievement highly. They set up schools. They established colleges and seminaries not only for their own members, but for any clergy that wanted to attend. They produced two of the leading medieval theologians, Thomas Aquinas and Albert the Great.

SINNERS AND SAINTS
ST. FRANCIS OF ASSISI

Although he lived and died humbly in the 1200s, Saint Francis of Assisi remains today one of the most well-known saints in popular culture and an influential figure in the history of Christianity. Born into a life of privilege, Francis turned his back on his family's wealth and embraced a life of poverty in emulation of Christ. He had a deep and abiding love and sense of responsibility for all of God's creation, including an affinity for animals. In *Canticle of the Sun*, he refers to the earth as a "sister" and the sun as a "brother." It was this spirit of loving stewardship that led to his being named patron saint of the environment by pope John Paul II in 1979. The Franciscans, the order of monks that bears his name, have bloomed into no less than four separate orders, including one for nuns. Franciscan monks and nuns are well known for their work with the sick and the poor. By virtue of their habits of living amongst the people rather than in a cloistered environment and of not being encumbered by material possessions or tied to one place, Franciscans were some of the most effective missionaries of the Middle Ages. For Francis, however, the failure of many Franciscan monks to totally embrace poverty led to his resigning as head of the order in the year 1220.

BUT WAIT A MINUTE...BACK IN CONSTANTINOPLE
The East and West had been drifting apart for years. Politically, the East and West had become different worlds. The capital of the Byzantine Empire, Constantinople, was safe behind its great walls, but its enemies were perched all around. There was the

ever present menace of the Muslims and periodic trouble from the Persians, the Turks, the Bulgarians, and the Slavs. As always in the East, there was political unrest because of religious doctrine. The Iconoclastic conflict had weakened (or distracted) the emperor so much he let the pope slip just a little farther out from under his power. The West was being dominated by the Holy Roman Empire, but even that was not particularly stable. Succession was always a problem as rulers jousted for the title. There were emerging powers among the kings of England and the dukes in France and Germany. The power of the pope and the Roman church was all mixed up in the political equation. The Roman church was still growing in power and influence as it spread into every community, preaching a Christian message punctuated by loyalty to Rome.

To all these differences we can add the small differences that had developed between the Eastern and Western churches. For example, the Eastern church used Greek as its language, and the Western used Latin. The Western had Jerome's *Vulgate* and almost all its scholarship in Latin, and the Eastern church had its roots in the Greek world. There were differences in the religious calendar, when Lent and Easter were to be observed. In the East, priests could marry and wear beards. In the West they could do neither. Even their theologies differed. Essentially, the differences in how the East and West viewed the nature of Jesus and the Holy Spirit had never been settled.

RIFTS IN LEADERSHIP

So, by the middle of the eleventh century, there was already tension between the pope and the patriarch of Constantinople. That tension was heightened when two stubborn men took over those positions. In 1043, Michael Cerularius became the patriarch of Constantinople, and in 1049 Leo IX became the pope. Leo wanted the patriarch of Constantinople, and so the Eastern church, to submit to the authority of the pope. In 1054, the pope sent representatives to discuss this with Michael Cerularius, but the patriarch refused to even meet with them. Feeling that the patriarch had thus offended their leader, the emissaries excommunicated Michael on behalf of Leo. The patriarch could not take that without a response, especially in his own city, so he excommunicated the pope's messengers.

By declaring each other as not "real" Christians, the two sides created a schism. Although there were many efforts through the years to heal the separation, none truly worked. The two churches, East and West, may have shared a common heritage, but there had always been differences between the two, even before the Council of Nicaea.

Pope Urban II, who would call for the first crusade less than forty years after the schism, hoped that the East and West could unite against the common enemy of the Muslims. It was a good idea, but like many other ideas of the next hundred years, it did not work out.

BACK IN ENGLAND

Anglo-Saxon kings such as Alfred the Great prevented England from becoming a Danish/Viking colony. Slowly, these kings and the powerful nobles that ruled the land pushed their Danish "neighbors" living in the Danelaw out of the country. Even during the occupation, the Anglo-Saxon clergy, led by the archbishop of Canterbury, had worked to Christianize the island.

One piece of evidence that shows that they were successful comes in an unexpected package, the Old English poem *Beowulf*. This great poem

SET THE STAGE!

1014: The ruler of Byzantium, having defeated the Bulgarian army, ordered that almost all his 15,000 vanquished foes be blinded. One in every hundred were allowed to keep one eye so that they could lead the rest home.

was probably composed by a Northumbrian poet who drew his subject matter from Scandinavian history and folk sources. It tells the story of Beowulf's struggle with the water monster Grendel and Grendel's mother; Beowulf's victory as an old king over a dragon; and his death and funeral. Though the subject matter is historical, the poem is a product of a culture that had continual contact with the Danes. While the hero is the warrior king of most Norse sagas, he also exhibits Christian traits. It would be far too presumptuous to state that Beowulf was a Christian, but his virtues are Christian, his concern for life in his old age is Christian, and the way he leads his people reflects Christian values.

IMAGINE THAT!

In addition to being a famous royal prison, a fortress, a palace, and now a museum, the Tower of London, built in the late 1000s, has been used for many purposes over the centuries, including use as a zoo. Admission to the zoo was sometimes paid in the form of a dog or cat to be fed to the lions. Everybody's heard of a dog eat dog world, but cat eat cat?

This evidence seems to show that although the Danes dominated life in and near the Danelaw, clear Christian values were still being taught and being respected. It is no surprise then that the Anglo-Saxon king Edward the Confessor founded a Benedictine abbey near London in 1052, which became Westminster Abbey.

Getting rid of the Danes was a simple matter compared to the Anglo-Saxons' next challenge. Just across the English Channel lay the region of Normandy.

THE NORMANS

The Normans were Danish and Norse adventurers and pirates who left their Scandinavian homes to attack and terrorize a huge range of territory. They attacked Britain as early as 831 and the northwest coast of France (Normandy) in 911. By 1053, they had conquered southern Italy and set up a Norman empire that would rule there for forty years. In 1066, the ruler of Normandy, William, gathered an army, crossed the English Channel, and attacked the Anglo-Saxons. The king of the Anglo-Saxons, Edward the Confessor, had died earlier in the year and had been succeeded by his brother-in-law Harold Godwineson, earl of Wessex. The Norman victory at the battle of Hastings on October 14 sealed the Norman conquest of England.

Because of the Anglo-Saxon defeat, everything changed in England. The Normans spoke French, so the official language of the government became French. The Normans had far different customs than their English subjects. Even the English language changed as a result. The Old English of Alfred the Great was gone. Replacing it was a new hybrid language, a mixture of Old English, French, and Latin. In a little more than a hundred years after the invasion, English was a very different language than it had been before. Changes that normally take centuries had happened in decades. Norman culture flowered in its new home, and Anglo-Saxon culture began to disappear.

THE PLOT THICKENS

William's invasion of England was not just another case of one tribe conquering another. The Normans were far beyond that. There was a reform movement afoot in the church. As we have seen, there was a proliferation of monastic orders during this time, many of which had the desire to reform the church and bring it back to a more holy way of life. These reforms often had political consequences, and as we will soon see, even the pope and the Holy Roman Emperor would be in conflict as a result. In 1066, there were already two sides to the argument: The pope was for reform, and many of the political leaders of the day were against it.

The issue in question was lay investiture. Lay investiture occurred when a secular leader (king, duke, mayor) formally appointed and installed someone into the clergy. (Being able to control the clergy in your territory could be a very powerful political tool in the right hands.)

The pope wanted not only to reform the church but also to make political changes so that only church leaders could "invest" the clergy. William the Conqueror was not against lay investiture, but the pope saw him as someone who would be obedient to his will. So, when William decided to invade England, the pope saw that as a great opportunity to change the leadership in England to someone on his side. The pope sanctioned the invasion, and after William's victory, one of the pope's reformers, Lefranc, was made archbishop of Canterbury. All of this worked together to change, once again, the spiritual climate in England. Along with a brand new language and culture, the Norman invasion brought the power of the papacy in England to a new high. The archbishop of Canterbury was the pope's "man in England."

THE PLOT THICKENS AGAIN...ON A BIGGER STAGE

The reform of the church led by the popes of the eleventh and twelfth centuries brought them into direct conflict with the kings, princes, and emperors that ruled Christendom. The popes were certainly right: The Church needed some reform. It was already a thousand-year-old institution that had grown into great power and influence without a great deal of policing. Of course there were corrupt clergy. Of course the church had ventured into questionable practices, such as simony (buying or selling clerical positions in the church), and should turn away from them. There needed to be reforms that would enforce existing church rules forbidding the clergy to marry and insisting on celibacy. None of these reforms would cause more than a ripple in the political pond.

But when Pope Gregory VII issued his *Dictatus Papae* in 1075, it created a firestorm. In this decree, the pope not only forbade simony and clerical marriage, he also forbade lay investiture and declared that papal power was absolute. According to the decree, *all* secular entities owed the pope submission, and he had the authority to depose kings and even emperors. Needless to say, Emperor Henry IV was not pleased to hear this. He was already a member of the antireform movement. In 1076, his opposition to the pope led to his being excommunicated by Gregory. With his empire coming in an uproar and losing support rapidly, Henry humbled himself before Gregory at Canossa in 1077 when he actually stood in the snow for three days in front of a fortress where the pope was staying in order to gain his forgiveness. But in 1080, the two again fell out. Henry was excommunicated again, so he set up Guibert of Ravenna (Clement III) as antipope. Pope Gregory appealed to the Christian world for support, but it was not enough. In 1083, after he had dealt with a civil war in Germany, Henry marched into Italy and captured Rome. Gregory was forced into retirement, and he died a year later.

The reform movement did not die with him, however. In 1183, another reformer became the archbishop of Canterbury.

ANSELM, AN ARCHBISHOP REFORMER

When William the Conqueror named Lefranc the archbishop of Canterbury, the archbishop's protégé became an abbot. In 1093, William's son, William II, made this protégé, Anselm, the new archbishop. It was a move he lived to regret. Unlike his father, William II was possessive about the power the church had, and he wanted to hold on to the royal power he had inherited. That caused him to run head-on with Anselm, who was a humble man but a real reformer at heart. The

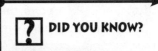

DID YOU KNOW?

Popes usually serve for life. However, Benedict IX was pope on three separate occasions, and antipope Victor IV held the office twice.

conflicts between the king and the archbishop forced Anselm into exile. When William II died, his brother Henry I became king. Soon he asked Anselm to return to his post, but before long the archbishop was back in exile after another conflict with the king. Thankfully, England's loss was posterity's gain because while Anselm was in exile he proved himself a great theologian. He wrote brilliantly on spiritual topics such as the atonement of man's sins by Christ and the path to understanding through faith. He was a Scholastic who tried to put logic at the service of faith, but faith always ended up being the cornerstone of all his intellectual explorations. Anselm resolved the "conflict" between logic and inspiration by explaining that you must have faith in order to use logic to come to understanding.

BACK TO THE HOLY ROMAN EMPEROR AND THE POPE

When we left this controversy, Emperor Henry IV had basically deposed a pope and appointed his own. Of course that situation could not last for long. In 1106, Henry V became Holy Roman Emperor. In 1122, he and pope Callistus II were able to come to an agreement on the investiture issue. It was not as simple as either side would have liked, but it did help to define the relative roles of church and temporal ruler in the Middle Ages. The investiture ceremony was not only an actual conference of authority to a member of clergy, it was also a symbolic transference of the symbols of power. In the end, the Concordat of Worms skirted around the issue of *real* authority by defining the symbolic authority. In short, the Concordat said that the king would not perform investiture with the ring and staff (which were ecclesiastical symbols). In return, the pope agreed with the emperor's right to confer the temporal rights upon the clergyman by investiture with the scepter.

Such a technical solution might not satisfy modern man, but it did seem to satisfy both sides of this controversy...at least for awhile. There was one more squabble to be settled, though.

THOMAS BECKET VERSUS THE KING

The job of archbishop of Canterbury had never been a "cushy" job. It was not that way for Augustine, who had to battle hostile Anglo-Saxons, and it was not that way for Anselm, who had to face the growing power and greed of the English kings. About seventy years after Anselm had taken the job from William II, Thomas Becket got it from Henry II. Not much had changed in the mindset of the English kings. Henry II was intent on building the power of the kingship in relation to the power of the church. To do that he had to overcome the church in three big issues: the independence of the church courts, the right of appeals to Rome, and the seizure of church property by the state.

In 1164, Henry used his *Constitutions of Clarendon,* consisting of sixteen articles of law, to assert his right to try to punish clergy who were guilty of criminal acts, and to deny their right of appeal to the church in Rome. Thomas Becket repudiated the articles, but in the resulting furor he was forced to flee to France. Finally, in 1170, a truce between him and the king was arranged, so he returned to England. Almost as soon as he arrived, he excommunicated several English bishops who had supported the king in the conflict. These bishops lashed out at Becket and on December 29, 1170, four knights, acting as a result of the king's anger, appeared in Canterbury and killed the archbishop in front of his own high altar.

As the news of the murder spread, it created a sensation all over Europe. Becket was immediately admired for his willingness to stand up to the king and die for his beliefs. The murder in the cathedral captured the imagination of the people. In 1173, only three years after his death, Becket was canonized by Pope Alexander III, and the site of his murder became one of the major shrines for Christians to visit. Faced with this public relations nightmare, the king did a public penance for his actions.

The story of Thomas Becket is also interesting because it allows us to see the people of the twelfth century as if we were looking in a mirror. Europe was a Christian place. When Becket acted as a Christian then died for his efforts, the people came to adore him. They may have feared the king or even loved him. They may have admired the pope or disagreed with him, but they loved and admired Thomas Becket the martyr.

BACK IN ROME...

Being a pope could be a tough job. In eleventh-century Europe there were constant struggles with the rulers of the political states that steadily coalesced into nations. Strong monarchies were developing in England and France though the nobles of both countries were immensely powerful. Germany was a mess of small kingdoms vying for power. The Holy Roman Emperor may have been crowned by the pope, but he was a temporal leader who brought his alliances and enemies to the throne with him. The investiture issue had been terrible and had shown how fragile the power of the pope could be if he depended on public sentiment as a part of his power. Gregory VII had defined the pope as all-powerful, but it seemed up to each pope to prove it.

 **SET THE STAGE!**

Canterbury was the religious center for the Church of England much as Rome was for the Catholic Church and Jerusalem for the Palestinian Jews.

The reform movement had enjoyed some success, but there was always the lure of the world, and some popes would soon forget that reform must be an ongoing process. Some popes in the near future would even be part of the whole problem of church corruption.

In 1088, Urban II became pope, and seven years later he began to turn the world upside down.

URBAN II AND THE CRUSADES

Almost all of Europe was "officially" Christian in the eleventh century. In most places it would have been hard to tell. When the Frenchman Urban II came to the papacy in 1088, most people thought he would simply continue the reform policies that Gregory VII had begun. This new pope was different. He did not really want to fight the constant battles with the secular leaders that the reform movement had come to exemplify. Instead, he wanted to unify the church. He even had the crazy (to many) idea to reunify the Roman church with the church of the Eastern empire led by the patriarch of Constantinople.

Early in his time as pope, an opportunity came about that he could not resist. The emperor of the Eastern empire, Alexius, asked for help against the Muslim Turks. These Seljuk Turks had defeated the Byzantine army in 1071 at the battle of Manzikert and then conquered Asia Minor. That loss depleted the area of the Byzantine Empire by more than half of its area. Truthfully, the pope had some allies in the East. The Byzantine emperor Manuel Comnenus (emperor 1143–1180) himself dreamed of uniting the Byzantine Empire with the West. He had even married his son and heir, Alexius, to the daughter of the king of France, Louis VII. To Urban, a joint effort against a common enemy was just the way to put Christendom back together in one piece. It did not seem to matter to him that the pope had actually excommunicated the patriarch of Constantinople, his counterpart in the Eastern church.

COUNCIL OF CLERMONT

In 1095, Urban called the Council of Clermont, and there he called for the cleansing of the "lands of the Christians"; in other words, running the Muslims out of any lands that were important to the church. By that definition, places such as Antioch which were not in Palestine were fair game to be retaken by Christian armies because the church at Antioch was crucial to the early development of the church. In response to his

SET THE STAGE!
CRUSADE TIMELINE

First Crusade:	1095–99
Second Crusade:	1147–49
Third Crusade:	1189–92
Fourth Crusade:	1202–04
Children's Crusade:	1212
Fifth Crusade:	1217–21
Sixth Crusade:	1228–29

call, the people responded, *"Deus vult,"* meaning "God wills it." That would become the battle cry of the thousands who responded to Urban's call and went on the First Crusade.

For months after the call at Clermont, the pope's representatives went throughout Europe recruiting leaders and soldiers to go on this quest. The recruiting worked, and many of the most powerful nobles in Europe set out for the East. These included Robert of Normandy, Robert of Flanders, Godfrey of Bouillon, Baldwin of Boulogne, Raymond of Toulouse, Bohemond of Taranto, and Stephen of Blois. Each of these powerful men brought not only knights with them but foot soldiers and servants as well. These armies would have been a chaotic affair at best. There were different languages and customs among the troops, and many of the soldiers had fought against each other in previous conflicts.

BUT WHY A CRUSADE?

Many books have been written trying to explain why the crusaders went. There were too many reasons to even try to explain. There were some who had genuine religious zeal to remove the "infidels" from the holy places of their faith. Certainly, some went with hopes of becoming rich from plunder. Still others probably went because their lives in France, Germany, England, or any other place held no hope for a better life, and the adventure of the proposed crusade could make their lives meaningful. Many were forced to go by the nobles who owned the land on which they lived. The feudal system was in high gear at this time. The person who owned the land owed protection to the people who lived on and worked it. In return, these peasants owed the landowner fealty (*fealty* was the fidelity owed by a vassal to his feudal lord. That fidelity included both a faithfulness to the feudal lord and an allegiance to him). Many went for another spiritual reason. Urban and the popes that followed him promised that those who went to fight were doing a penance that would allow them to enter heaven directly or would at least limit their time in purgatory. That could be a powerful inducement to even the impious who were looking for a way to heaven.

THE CRUSADES AND CONSTANTINOPLE

The crusaders had to pass through Constantinople on their way. It must have been a shock for the relatively refined Byzantines to see an unruly army of knights, soldiers, farmers, and servants descending on their cultured city. It was written at the time that the emperor Alexius was actually frightened at what he saw. He had thought that the pope would respond to his request by helping him recruit Western soldiers for *his* army. Instead, an army of perhaps fifty thousand men descended on his capital.

But the emperor housed and fed the soldiers well and provisioned them for the arduous trip ahead. He got the commanders to swear an oath of allegiance to him before he helped them cross the Bosporus into Asia Minor. The invasion had come at a good time. There was a power struggle going on between rival Muslim leaders in Cairo, Baghdad, and Cordoba, Spain. The crusaders were able to drive southward through Syria and capture Jerusalem in 1099. Not only was the journey terrible for a European army in the desert climate, so were the battles. Though there was some discussion between the religious and military leaders of the Crusade about the policy, in general the crusaders simply killed everyone and took no prisoners. The aftermath of their victories at Antioch and Jerusalem were almost as bad as the battles. The crusaders ran wild, killing, raping, and plundering. Those leaders who even tried were powerless to stop the carnage.

NEW TERRITORIES AND KNIGHT MONKS

The crusaders managed to conquer a strip of territory along the eastern edge of the Mediterranean. This territory was divided into the Latin Kingdom of Jerusalem, the county of Edessa, the principality of Antioch, and the county of Tripoli. When Godfrey of Bouillon was elected the ruler of the Latin Kingdom of Jerusalem, the crusaders began to think about holding their territory and began building new defensive castles. Some of these castles still exist today.

There were even two new religious orders formed to hold the Holy Land for the Christians: the Knights Templar and the Knights Hospitaler. Despite the efforts of these soldier monks, the county of Edessa fell back into Muslim hands in 1144. Though these orders could not ultimately hold the Holy Land, the organizations themselves went on for many years as powerful military organizations.

On the surface it appeared that Urban II had been utterly successful. Militarily, the First Crusade attained its goals. It did not reach its target in bringing the Christians of East and West together. In fact, the success of the First Crusade was an important element in the total alienation between East and West.

 DID YOU KNOW?

Most people think of religious orders as an exclusively Catholic tradition, but no less than three of the top religious orders are of other denominations. The Cowley Fathers and the Wantage Community are both Anglican orders, and the Monastic Brotherhood, founded in the A.D 300s, is an Eastern Orthodox order.

A SECOND CRUSADE...AND THEN OTHERS

The First Crusade was started by the pope and the Second by a monk, none other than Bernard who founded the monastery at Clairvaux. It seemed destined for success. Bernard was held in the highest regard, and so the crusade he called for was led by none other than the king of France, Louis VII, and the Holy Roman Emperor, Conrad II. They departed in 1147. Unfortunately, the crusade was one disaster after another. Those disasters finally culminated in the army's defeat at Damascus. It was there that the army was ambushed and prevented from taking the city.

After that, the army lost heart. In two years they were finished. In 1187, Jerusalem was recaptured by the Turks.

The people of Europe could simply not understand the defeat. How could a quest, called for by one of the wisest men of the age and led by two monarchs, become a failure? The pope, Innocent III, supported a new crusade. He had been carrying on negotiations with the Byzantine emperor Alexius III with the supposed goal of uniting the Eastern and Western church. Like Urban II, he believed that the only way to truly defeat the Muslims was to unite with the Byzantine Empire as a single fighting force.

THE FOURTH CRUSADE
Innocent's timing was bad. His call for a Fourth Crusade fell flat. None of the very powerful European sovereigns would or could go. Philip Augustus of France surely would not go: He had been excommunicated for divorcing his wife. John Lackland of England had just become king and was struggling to establish himself there in spite of constant conflict with his barons. In Germany, there was a struggle for the throne between Otto of Brunswick and Philip of Swabia, so neither of them could go.

The major knights of France answered the call, however. Men such as Thibault, the count of Champagne, Baldwin of Flanders, and Louis of Blois assembled their fighting men and retainers and left. The crusade went badly almost from the start. The army traveled to Venice, where they were to be transported to the East. When they could not pay the fee in full for the transport, the Venetians insisted that the army besiege a city for them, Zara, that had just pulled away from the Venetian realm. That city was supposed to supply even more crusaders. This meant that the first hostile action of the crusade was to besiege a city where crusaders lived. The pope was furious and excommunicated the crusaders and the Venetians. He later relented and raised the excommunication for the crusaders, but never raised it for the Venetians.

Many of the crusaders were still looking for a scapegoat for the disaster of the Second Crusade. So in 1204, the doge of Venice called for an attack not on the infidels, but on Constantinople itself. The siege of Zara had actually provided an excuse. During the siege and surrender of the city, there was contact between the doge of Venice and Alexius IV. Alexius was the son of a Byzantine emperor, Isaac, who had been overthrown a few years back. Alexius promised to make the empire submissive to the West if the crusaders would help restore his father to the throne. It was just the excuse the doge was looking for. When the soldiers of this crusade reached Constantinople, they besieged and captured it. They set up a Latin empire whose rulers were Baldwin I, Henry of Flanders, Robert of Courtenay, and Baldwin II.

THE LATIN EMPIRE

The Latin Empire was really the last nail in the coffin of East-West reconciliation. The First Crusade had set the stage. The lands the crusaders took were the home of many Eastern Christians. Antioch, for example, had a Greek bishop, John of Antioch, who was an ally of the patriarch of Constantinople. At one point, the emperor Alexius wanted this important city returned to his empire, but the crusaders refused. As a supporter of the Byzantine emperor, John's position became impossible, so he left Antioch and went to Constantinople. Of course, the crusaders chose another bishop, but John refused to resign. This situation occurred over and over after the First Crusade, and the hard feelings between East and West just exploded. When the crusaders attacked and captured Constantinople in 1204, any hope for unification went out the window.

The Children's Crusade was a total disaster as scores of children set out for the Holy Land only to be killed, sold into slavery, or simply die. The Fifth Crusade was aimed at capturing Egypt, but it failed. The Sixth Crusade managed to create a truce with the Muslims, but it was short-lived.

THE AFTERMATH

Christendom was not to be united, nor were the two political empires of East and West. In the end, both the Byzantines and the Western rulers realized that during the centuries of separation, the East and West had become very different. The crusaders' actions prompted more than one Byzantine writer to say that they would rather deal with the Muslim infidels than with the Christian crusaders. After the capture of Constantinople by the crusaders, there were sporadic efforts to unite East and

SET THE STAGE!

We look back at the journeys described in this chapter and call them "crusades." At the time they were called "armed pilgrimages." Members of many of the expeditions had crosses sewed onto their clothing or attached to them as accessories. From the word "crux" for "cross," the name "crusaders" came into use.

West, but none that worked.

The crusades managed to bring out the very worst in all parties involved. The crusaders were, for the most part, barely above the level of the barbarian armies of the past. When they captured a city or town, they were just as ruthless with its inhabitants as the Muslims had been. When given the chance, they would burn, pillage, and rape just as armies had done from the beginning. The holy wars of the crusades were not holy at all in their execution.

The Byzantines were not much better. They were terrible allies. They were scheming and untrustworthy. As early as the First Crusade, while the crusaders were on their way to help, the emperor had made a treaty with the Turks. Perhaps they were clever politicians, but the Byzantine emperors always played both ends against the middle. They would supply the crusaders but negotiate with the Turks. They would help provision the crusaders but not contribute very much militarily themselves.

In the end, the crusades were failures. By 1268, the Muslims had recaptured Antioch. In 1291, the final Christian stronghold of Acre in Palestine was lost. The Holy Land was back under the sole control of the Muslims, and East and West were still very far apart.

There was not much common ground between East and West to build on after the crusades. It would be two hundred years before the East would have a major impact on the West again. Until then, we head back to the West.

THE NOT-SO-WILD WEST

If a crusader could have left with the First Crusade called by Urban II and returned a hundred years later, he would have been shocked at the difference. He would have left in a time of gloom and uncertainty and returned as the Middle Ages finally started to flower. There were still some of the old problems between political rivals, but out of that chaos strong rulers kept emerging. The French and English monarchies were developing into true seats of power. The reform movement in the church continued to challenge the power of secular leaders over the church, but it did its best work in reforming itself. In the twelfth century the church had earned back a good portion of the respect it had lost. There was a real revival of sorts. It was this revival that would create some of the enduring symbols of the Middle Ages.

A MEDIEVAL BUILDING BOOM

If your little boy was really smart during the Middle Ages, and you wanted him to learn to read, you probably would have sent him to a monastery. In the twelfth century, however, a new way to educate became popular: the cathedral. These huge churches were beginning to be built throughout Europe, especially in France.

Technically, a cathedral was merely a church that was also a home for a bishop and contained a *cathedra*, or bishop's chair. There was no requirement that the church be large, except that the bishop might really like a bigger "office" than a small one. In the eleventh century alone, it is estimated that 1,587 new church buildings were built in France. In a two hundred-year period, eighty cathedrals were built in France alone, along with some five hundred other churches of considerable size. These cathedrals and churches became the center of a new innovation, the medieval town.

The crusaders who did return to their towns and villages brought home with them the experiences of completely different cultures. They had eaten new foods and spices. They had seen and worn new fabrics and clothes. As they came home, they brought some of these items with them or, more importantly, the knowledge of how to develop and sell these new items at home. Of course, all this created a business boom. Suddenly a shopkeeper in Paris might have an item from Constantinople. Suddenly a returning farmer was trying a brand-new crop that he would bring to market.

As a result, the town market became important. The economic system was still feudal and was dominated by the wealthy landowners and the nobles. But there were changes in the air as a new social class began to see the light of day: the middle class consisting of people who worked producing and selling products and services. There had always been small villages near the castles of the landowners. Now those villages began to grow and prosper economically. At the center of those towns were their churches, in more ways than one.

CATHEDRAL SCHOOLS

From the time of Charlemagne until the eleventh century, the main source of education was the monastery. In the twelfth century, the tremendous building boom of cathedrals pushed them past the monasteries in popularity. In the cathedral school, there were monks or priests who were actually licensed to teach. There were different teachers for younger and older students, and the most advanced students were taught by the chancellor, who ranked just below the bishop and the dean in cathedral hierarchy. The chancellor taught his advanced students liberal arts and theology. The students in these schools were usually destined to become clerics. Some would themselves be awarded a license to teach by the chancellor. These licenses were the predecessors of the university degree.

 SET THE STAGE!

Venice, Genoa, and Pisa (of the leaning tower fame) were cities that gained from the crusades. These cities were ports of travel so they were useful in carrying pilgrims on their journey. Also in making the travel, the merchants of these cities were able to build contacts for moving goods into other lands. The crusades changed the import/export ability of these cities.

It was the cathedral school that started the reawakening of learning in the Middle Ages. The debates were lively, and the intellectual challenges were often very difficult. The clash between students and teachers could also become quite heated.

PETER ABELARD

What do you get when you cross a strong-willed, but passionate, intellectual and the daughter of the canon of Notre Dame cathedral? Of course you get a love story that will echo through the centuries. Such was the fate of Peter Abelard. Peter was the product of a cathedral school, a brilliant student who got in trouble in school, not because he did not do his homework but because he debated his master and won. Peter's beliefs just did not fit the dogma of the day, so he was thrown out of the school and actually branded a heretic.

Not to be discouraged, he began teaching independently. One of his students was Heloise. Out of their relationship came a child, and though all sides of the issue agreed to keep things quiet, soon the word was out. Heloise ended up in a convent, and one night a group of men broke into Abelard's bedroom and castrated him. He survived the ordeal and became a Benedictine monk.

As the top thinker of his day, he pushed the boundaries of dogma constantly, was condemned for his views on the Trinity, and wrote brilliantly on the subject of the relationship between faith and reason. In other words, in one lifetime he addressed most of the religious controversies that had plagued the church for centuries. In 1142, embroiled in another religious controversy, he died in Cluny on his way to appeal to the pope.

CHANGING EDUCATION

Not everyone who wanted to learn to read and write wanted to be a monk or even attend school in a monastery or cathedral school. Some were just seeking knowledge. One of the tragedies of the first five hundred or so years of the Middle Ages is that so much knowledge from the ancient age was simply lost and forgotten. By the twelfth century, books were very, very rare and were normally locked up in the library of a monastery, well protected from the rabble of the public. Whereas knowledge was basically free in imperial Rome, and was still that way in Constantinople, in Europe knowledge had become solely the property of the church, which safeguarded it. Many, but not all, of the priests, monks, and friars that dominated the religious scene in the twelfth century could read. The general public was almost exclusively illiterate.

In the middle of the twelfth century, scholars such as Peter Abelard left their cathedral schools and began to teach publicly. These teachers were paid by their students. Abelard established his own school at St. Denis in Paris. His reputation drew students to him. There were others in Paris like Abelard, and soon there were a number of these private teachers on the left bank of the Seine.

CAN YOU SPELL U-N-I-V-E-R-S-I-T-Y?

The growing middle class of the time was highly organized labor-wise. Paris was full of labor guilds of one sort or another. Soon there was a *Universitas Societas Magistrorum et Scholarum* (Universal Society of Teachers and Students). The university was born. In 1200, the king, Philip II, officially granted the guild "university" status. Similar events took place in other cities in Europe: Bologna, Salerno, Oxford, Cambridge, Montpelier, Salamanca, Padua, and Toulouse were certainly among the first to have universities.

In a bit of early day one-upmanship, Henry II of England forbade English students from studying in Paris. A school was established in Oxford that officially became a university with a chancellor in 1215. In 1258, Robert de Sorbon, who was the chaplain and confessor to King Louis IX, founded the first college under the University of Paris. The Sorbonne was founded for indigent theological students. It opened under the name "Community of Poor Masters and Scholars" but is far better known under the name of its founder.

AN INTELLECTUAL EXPLOSION

These universities were not only the result of the changing economic times that allowed the "luxury" of education. They were a critical element of the

 **SET THE STAGE!**

The first known printed book was made in China in A.D. 868 and was called the *Diamond Sutra.* The printing press, as we know it today, had not yet been invented, so each page was painstakingly carved backwards into a block of wood, which was then inked and used to print copies. This process, called *block printing,* was later used in Europe from the 1300s until the invention of the modern printing press by Johannes Gutenberg. Block printing, while far from a perfect solution, made books affordable to some of the middle class and, along with a general rise in literacy, led to an increase in the demand for books.

intellectual reawakening in Europe that would lead eventually to the Renaissance and the Reformation. Unlike the intellectual development of the past two hundred years which was primarily scientific and technical in nature, the reawakening in the Middle Ages came from the philosophical and religious realm.

Here are two of the bright lights in this movement.

THOMAS AQUINAS

Thomas Aquinas was born to a wealthy family in Aquino, Italy. He was a fat, pious boy who first studied at the monastery at Monte Cassino. At fourteen he went to the University of Naples where he was so impressed by his Dominican teacher, he joined the order. His wealthy parents definitely had other ideas for his future, and they tried increasingly extreme means to get him to change his mind. They offered to buy him the post of archbishop of Naples, tempted him with a prostitute, and even kidnapped him. None of their efforts dissuaded Thomas from his plan for his life.

 SET THE STAGE!

Universities first began giving out degrees in the twelfth century. The word *degree* comes from the Latin word *degradus*, which means "a step on a ladder or stair." The word *grade* comes from the same root. Would that mean a grading on a curve would be a spiral staircase? Ouch…that was degrading. Ooh, stop!

Leaving Naples, he went to Paris to study. At that time Paris was the center of theological study and learning. He studied there under one of the great teachers of the day: Albert the Great. Except for short periods spent in Italy, Aquinas lived in Paris the rest of his life.

Aquinas's real love was writing and commentary. His collected writings fill eighteen large volumes. He wrote commentaries on most of the books of the Bible, analyzed

 DID YOU KNOW?

In the 1200s, some people "threw" dice by balancing them on a cat's paw and letting the cat flick the dice off. For this reason many universities banned pets.

THE MORE THINGS CHANGE...

(Death, Taxes, and Other Immutables)

Ever since people developed ways of writing things down, they have been looking for better surfaces upon which to write. Early writers chiseled or painted on stone, which was not practical or portable enough for most uses. Clay tablets proved easier in some ways but were still heavy and became brittle when they dried. Papyrus, made from reeds, was cheaper and light but was fragile and didn't age well. Parchment and vellum, made from animal skins, was light and long lasting but not cheap enough for mass production of written works. When the Chinese invented paper, it was too rough to write on and was mostly used for making clothing and as a protective wrapping for goods. Eventually, papermaking techniques were refined, and when thirteenth-century Europeans discovered that cotton and linen made a far superior paper to any previously produced, paper became the preferred medium on which to write and print.

thirteen works of Aristotle, and a large number of sermons. It was his attraction to Aristotle's theories of logic that would be a driving force behind many of his writings.

AQUINAS'S APPROACH AND WORKS

Aquinas not only appreciated the works of Aristotle, he decided to use the logical methods of the philosopher to examine Christian thought. In a nutshell, that practice *was* the method of the Scholastics. But Aquinas, like Aristotle, saw a flaw in the method. They both recognized that all human knowledge originates in the senses and that the senses cannot be trusted. That led Aquinas to a landmark idea in Christian thought: *Philosophy* is the study of information and ideas available to all men because it is the product of logic. *Theology* is not available to all men because it is the product of revelation and revelation is analyzed by logic.

His two major works reflect these distinctions. The first, *Summa Theologica*, would become a truly central work on Christian thought, although it would do so many years after Aquinas's death. It would become a summary of Christian thought on truth through revelation. The second, *Summa Contra Gentiles*, sought to support Christian belief with human reason.

Aquinas tried to reconcile the two methods he believed led to truth: revelation and reason. As we have seen, this was a conflict as old as Christian theology itself. Many of his ideas were condemned in his own time by other brilliant men and scholastics. Many years later, however, the church recognized the validity of his arguments. In fact, his works would be used by the Council of Trent (1545–1563) as the Roman Catholics sought to reform the church. Then, as a final acknowledgment, the pope declared his theology valid in 1879.

WILLIAM OF OCKHAM

Though they were barely a generation apart, William of Ockham and Thomas Aquinas came from different worlds. William was born in England, in the village of Ockham in Surrey. He entered the Franciscan order and went to study at Oxford around 1309 and completed his requirements for a master's there.

Though the details are sketchy, it appears that William was declared a heretic by the university's chancellor, and he was summoned to Avignon to see the pope in 1324. Instead of going to beg for reinstatement, William got himself in even more trouble

 SET THE STAGE!

Aristotle's works were largely lost to the West with the collapse of Rome. They entered the European intellectual scene of the Middle Ages through a circuitous path. The Muslims had a great love for learning. In fact, they had not experienced the collapse of learning in the West because of their ties back to the East. Culturally, in fact, they were far advanced over the Europeans of the seventh to twelfth centuries. They had libraries and centers for learning throughout the "dark days" of the early Middle Ages. Like the early Greek and Roman Christians, they had affection for the great Greek philosophers, so they preserved their works. Slowly, the works of Aristotle and other philosophers and poets of the Classical period seemed to "slip" their way over the Pyrenees from Muslim Spain and make their way to France.

by jumping into another argument concerning apostolic poverty. While he was at it, William called for the church to be run not by a pope but by a college of popes. His reason was clear: Christ was the only head of the church. To complete the package of beliefs offensive to the church, William said that the pope had no authority at all in secular matters, a direct contradiction of papal policy since Gregory VII. After all this, William had to leave town, so he fled to the one man who could probably protect him, the Holy Roman Emperor Louis of Bavaria, who was having his own struggles with the papacy.

Philosophically, William was a brand new creature. In a world that spoke of "universals" such as truth, beauty, justice, and the like, William argued that these "universals" did not even exist. He argued that they are just the creation of the human mind to be used for communication. Only "particular" things, things we can experience in a natural way, really exist.

His most famous principle was "Ockham's Razor." In simplest terms, the principle states that when there are several possible solutions, always look at the simplest first. As he says, "The mind should not multiply things without necessity."

Though William may sound like a true cynic to us in modern times, he was actually a man of great faith. Faith was the key to his theology. Though he constructed elaborate logical proofs for the existence of God, he recognized that they were essentially worthless in coming to *know* God. On that subject he stressed that faith was the only path to know God. In this way, he paved the way for Reformation theology still years away.

MEANWHILE...BACK IN...AVIGNON?
William of Ockham had been summoned to Avignon to see the pope. No, the pope wasn't on vacation there at the time. As the thirteenth century turned into the fourteenth, the papacy was about to enter a time of crisis. It started in 1294 when pope Celestine V was elected and then resigned. The church was not even sure if a pope *could* resign. Because of the resignation, the next pope, Boniface VIII, started his rule under a cloud of worry.

But Boniface was a very experienced canon-lawyer, so he set

about changing things. First, he issued a decree, *Clericis laicos*, that limited the power of the kings to tax the clergy. That caused some consternation as you can imagine. In response, France stopped the export of bullion (not soup, either, although the French still like a nice bouillon). That prohibition meant that the flow of money to Rome would have to find some other means. In England, Edward I threatened to remove all royal protection for the church and its properties. Eventually, the pope relented and told the kings they could disregard *Clericis laicos*, but the damage had been done. Then a bishop was arrested in France for criminal activity. The pope demanded his release, but the king refused. Then the pope reactivated the *Clericis laicos* and reasserted the pope's superiority over secular rulers.

As a result, the king of France sent an agent to get the pope and bring him back to France to settle the issue. In the meantime, the pope excommunicated the French king. The pope escaped capture by the king's agent but died soon after that in Rome.

THE STRATEGY INVOLVED

When the pope died, the French king was determined to have no more trouble with the pope. In 1305, under huge French pressure, the College of Cardinals elected the bishop of Bordeaux as the new pope. He took the name Clement V and never even went to Rome. He stayed in France partly because he loved his home and also because the French king wanted him where he could control him. One incident will provide a good example.

King Philip IV of France needed some money. The church had plenty, but he could not get at it directly. However, the religious orders such as monks and friars were vulnerable. The most vulnerable was the Order of the Knights Templar, formed during the crusades. The order had changed a lot since the cessation of the crusades. Its members had gone into the fledgling banking industry and had accumulated a great deal of wealth for the order. Philip IV prompted the pope to "discourage" this order. Soon, charges of sacrilege, sodomy, and idolatry were made against the Knights Templar. The investigators used torture to obtain confessions to these crimes. The result was the virtual destruction of the order. In some places, the property of the order went to the order of Hospitalers, also formed during the crusades. The single largest benefactor, however, was the king of France, who took the money and property of the order for his own use. All of this was done under the supervision of "his man" the pope.

POPES OF AVIGNON
There were three more popes who made their home in Avignon. John XXII (1316–1334) was an efficient but ruthless leader who worked to make the papal office more effective and to build up the papal wealth. He saw himself like the leader of a large company who has the job of maximizing profits. His spiritual contributions were few. Pope Benedict XII (1334–1342) was a Cistercian and also a Frenchman. He was more concerned with spiritual matters than his predecessor and mostly concerned with the growing problem of how the church would deal with heretics. He supported the French king in the Hundred Years' War, which began during his time as pope. His successor was Clement VI, who also supported France in the Hundred Years' War. He used the power of his office to generate money for use by the French king to wage the war. In truth, he spent money lavishly and without regard for the morality of it. His own personal life was itself immoral, and there were many who noticed. Like the previous Clement, he was in many ways a forerunner of the corrupt and lavish popes of the Renaissance who brought the papacy into terrible disrepute. It was under Clement VI that the papacy actually bought the city of Avignon.

His monetary lavishness was stopped by the next pope, Innocent VI (1352–1362). Innocent spent his time trying to reform the abuses of the church that had become so rampant under his predecessors' leadership. Also, he decided it was time for the papacy to return to Rome. The idea for the move was prompted at least a little by the roving bands of mercenaries that were the by-product of the Hundred Years' War. First he had huge walls built around Avignon, then sent an envoy to Rome to

THE MORE THINGS CHANGE. . .

(Death, Taxes, and Other Immutables)

The game of football, in one form or another, has been around for centuries.

Some versions of the game (as in the fourteenth-century poem "Sir Gawain and the Green Knight") have been played with the severed head of an enemy instead of a ball (what would you call *that* ball then?).

In 1439, at a political summit aimed at ending the One Hundred Years' War between Britain and France, the negotiators, including a French archbishop, played a game referred to as "football," probably a rugby-like game which later evolved into soccer, rugby, and American football. The archbishop got a rather nasty bruise on his leg and limped for the duration of the conference.

The game has undergone huge variations over time, one such having a field of play that was three miles long and crossed a small river.

During some time periods, women have played football with or against men. In one case, an annual game at Inverness, Scotland, a team of single women plays against a team of wives.

Multiple accounts of game-related deaths are recorded in the twelfth century alone. In Shakespeare's *King Lear*, Kent refers to Oswald as a "base football player," meaning a rude and violent man, and then (of course) knocks him down.

In 1583, Puritan writer Philip Stubbes called it "a friendlie kind of fyghte."

(It kind of makes you wonder if there was ever, somewhere during the Middle Ages, a team called the Vikings that was made up of *real* Vikings.)

reorganize control of the Papal States there. Before he could move back, however, he died. Though his successor, Urban V (1362–1370), moved back to Rome for several years, he returned to Avignon before he died. His successor, Gregory XI (1370–1378), was finally able to move the papacy back to Rome.

THE GREAT SCHISM

It would have been nice for the Roman Catholic Church if the move back to Rome had resulted in smooth transition of power and better church leadership, but it did not. The French popes had appointed a number of new cardinals during the years at Avignon. Eighty-two percent of them were from France. The resulting college of cardinals was much more independent than the ones in the past. When Pope Gregory XI died in 1387, the Romans, acting as a mob, demanded a Roman or Italian pope. The college went along and named Urban VI (1378–1389). When he became too strong, however, the cardinals got together and elected *another* pope, Clement VII.

This led to armed battles in the streets of Rome for control of the papacy. This division in the church was called the Great Schism. The rival popes settled into their own power bases, Urban VI in Rome and Clement VII in Avignon. The depth of hard feeling between the two popes made compromise impossible. The division was so divisive that the king of France actually offered to abandon the French pope. Despite all that, the conflict continued until 1417 when the greatest general council of the church in the period, the Council of Constance, was held. That council elected Martin V as the rightful pope. Under his leadership, the Great Schism was healed.

The council also made important decrees concerning two important religious leaders: John Wycliffe and John Hus. But first, a very long war.

THE HUNDRED YEARS' WAR
The history of the Hundred Years' War could fill a dozen books. It was one of the first wars in the West that encompassed all elements of the society. It was not simply a war of succession, though it was that. It was an economic war, as well.

The Hundred Years' War, 1337–1453, was a conflict between England and France to decide who would rule France. Only 271 years before, in 1066, the Normans had crossed from France to conquer England. The English king, Edward III, felt he had a hereditary right to rule in France, and in fact, the English did hold a duchy—Guienne—in that country. Edward also wanted to control the port of Flanders which was controlled by the French. The war began in 1337 when Edward, assuming the title King of France, invaded France. The early battles went well for the English. They won a sea battle at Sluis in 1340 and land battles at Crécy (1346), Calais (1347), and Poitiers (1360). At that battle the English were able to capture the French king, John II. In order to get their king back, the French agreed to the Treaty of Brétigny (1360).

This treaty awarded England Calais, Aquitaine, and a large ransom for the captured king. In return, England gave up its claim to the French crown. However, in 1369, the war resumed when nobles in Aquitaine rebelled over the issue of high taxes. By 1373 du Guesclin, the greatest French soldier of his time, had won back most of the English-held territory in France. Nothing else decisive happened until 1415, when Henry V of England defeated France's best knights at Agincourt. He then went on to reconquer Normandy and force the French to accept the Treaty of Troyes (1420). In this treaty, Charles VI of France was forced to recognize Henry as regent and heir to the throne of France, thereby disinheriting his own son, the dauphin. By 1429, the English controlled practically all of France north of the Loire River and had Orléans under siege. The future looked very bleak for France except for one shining light.

 DID YOU KNOW?

Throughout history societies have waged wars to settle national property disputes. These days we have complex deeds and surveying equipment to settle personal property disputes. Through the ages, though, people have come up with some pretty wacky ways of deciding who had rights to what land. In the 1300s, a law on the books near Zurich, Switzerland, stated that the grazing rights of a tenant farmer's chickens were to be determined by how far the man could throw a sickle from the roof of his house with his left hand. A similar law at a German estate said that chickens could roam as far as the woman of the house could throw an egg, using her veil as a sling. Suppose a German woman near the border had sailed one over the line and hit her Swiss neighbor in the head with an egg, causing him to drop the sickle which then impaled one of his chickens on the ground below? How would you rule on that one?

JOAN OF ARC

In the time of the Hundred Years' War, both the French and English armies had thrown their very best at each other. In 1429, it appeared that the French, in spite of support of the pope, were "on their last legs." Then there appeared a French schoolgirl who was hearing voices.

As a young girl, Joan of Arc began to hear the "voices" of St. Michael, St. Catherine, and St. Margaret. When she was about sixteen, the voices told her to go help the dauphin, who was being kept from the throne by the English. Joan visited the dauphin, dressed in male clothes, and she conquered his skepticism as to her divine mission. She was furnished with troops, and by May 1429 she had raised the siege of Orléans. In June, she defeated the English at Patty. Soon afterward the dauphin was crowned at Rheas, and Joan was at the pinnacle of her fortunes. Then in September 1429 she tried but failed to capture Paris. The following spring she went to relieve Camping, but she was captured by the Burgundians, who sold her to the English. They were anxious to see this young girl dead, but to avoid responsibility for such an act, the English turned her over to the church court at Rouen where she was tried for heresy and witchcraft by French clerics who supported the English. She was convicted of heresy and sentenced to life imprisonment. Afterwards she recanted her "confession." As a result, she was turned over to the secular court as a relapsed heretic and was burned at the stake on May 30, 1431, in Rouen.

BACK TO THE WAR

Joan of Arc's capture and execution did not end the string of French victories. By 1450, France had reconquered Normandy. By 1451, all of Guienne except Bordeaux was in French hands. Bordeaux fell in 1453, leaving the English only Calais (which they held until 1558). By then, England had enough troubles at home, including the War of the Roses over succession to the English throne, to let go of its foreign efforts. The Hundred Years' War caused the people of France untold misery. Their population was decimated by plague and continual warfare. An entirely new France emerged. The war had virtually destroyed the old feudal nobility. The new France would be more united under royal authority since the monarchs were able to better bypass the nobility and ally themselves with the emerging middle class. For England, it was really the end of their aspirations as a true power on the European continent. Instead, they turned back to an approach as old as Alfred the Great and worked toward being a sea power.

AN ENGLISH TROUBLEMAKER

During the years of the Hundred Years' War, there were troubles brewing in England other than just a continental war and an impending civil war. There was Wycliffe.

John Wycliffe was born in the north of England and became a leading philosopher at Oxford University. In addition, he was acquainted with one of the leading political figures of the day, John of Gaunt. John of Gaunt was caught up in the middle of the politics behind the War of the Roses in England between the Yorks and Lancasters for the right to rule as king. For awhile, John of Gaunt was actually running things, and during that time period he invited Wycliffe to come serve at the royal court. Wycliffe's beliefs were right for that role.

Unlike almost all other clergy, Wycliffe believed that the government had the right to seize the property of corrupt clergymen. This view represented a drastic reduction of the power of the church to protect itself from the government. In 1377, the pope condemned Wycliffe's views, but through his connections with powerful friends, the troublesome philosopher survived. Next, he challenged one of the central beliefs of the Catholic faith: the belief in transubstantiation. Transubstantiation taught that during the Lord's Supper the wine and bread literally became the blood and flesh of Christ. Wycliffe argued that Christ was spiritually, not physically, present in the Eucharist. To make matters worse, Wycliffe claimed that the church consisted of God's chosen people, and they did not need a priest to mediate for them with God. All of these beliefs were in total opposition to the doctrine of the church. Eventually, Wycliffe was deserted by his high friends. He had pushed too far for even them. He was forced out of Oxford along with his followers, and he went to live in the Midlands where he died in1384.

If that had been his entire life he would have been remembered as a man far ahead of his time. But, there is more. Wycliffe and his followers had the revolutionary idea that everyone should be able to read the Bible in his own language. Although there had been some "renegade" translations in much earlier times (notably into Gothic and Celtic), the church maintained that the official Bible was the Vulgate, translated by Jerome at the end of the fourth century. Beginning in 1380, Wycliffe and his followers began to translate the Bible into English. Working from a handwritten copy of the Vulgate, these scholars completed the first translation of the Bible into English. Despite church opposition, a first edition was published illegally. Then, after Wycliffe's death, a second edition appeared.

JOHN HUS

The impact of Wycliffe's teachings was not confined to England. In far away Bohemia they sparked an idea or two in a young Czech preacher and teacher named John Hus. Hus was ordained in 1401 as a priest. For much of the rest of his life, he taught at Charles University in Prague and preached at the nearby Bethlehem Chapel. The images in that chapel bothered him. In Christ he saw a humble servant, with no property and no pride. What he saw in the church officials of his day was entirely different. The church was rich. Whereas Jesus had washed the feet of his disciples, the pope had his feet kissed.

These contrasts irritated him, and he preached against them. Further, he argued that the Bible is the church authority, not the clergy. These ideas got the attention of the archbishop of Prague, who instructed him to stop preaching such heresies. Hus refused, and the archbishop excommunicated him. In fact, Hus was so popular in Prague preaching these ideas that one of the popes of the Great Schism placed Prague under interdict. In essence he excommunicated the entire city. Hus agreed to leave the city, but people followed him wherever he went and spoke.

The people were drawn to Hus's call that the church live more humbly like Christ. They were also excited about the idea that Christ alone was the head of the church. In his book *On the Church*, Hus defended the authority of the clergy but made the claim that only God can forgive sin. For Hus, the head of the church was God, and authority on earth was the Bible. No church leader, including the pope, could establish a doctrine that was contrary to the Bible.

In 1414, Hus was called before the Council of Constance, the council trying to end the Great Schism. He was condemned by the council, as was Wycliffe, for his teachings many years before. While Wycliffe was excommunicated, Hus was turned over to the secular authorities to be immediately punished. He was executed in June 1415.

The Council of Constance was trying to reestablish a church that was worthy of respect. The Great Schism had been a disaster. The church saw Wycliffe and Hus not only as heretics but also as rabble-rousers. The church was right. These two men were presenting ideas that inflamed the emotions of a church population which was becoming more and more aware of the real issues behind church doctrine. Men like Wycliffe and Hus, and many more to come, would present new ideas to the people that rang true to them. Wycliffe and Hus were not revolutionaries, nor did they trigger the Reformation. They were a spark, however, that set the hearts and minds of people aflame. They shared their knowledge, their ideas, and their convictions even though they were far from orthodox. The church was about to receive a big challenge from within its own ranks. The waves of upheaval were forming on the horizon and beginning to roll inexorably toward shore.

CONSTANTINOPLE...FOR THE LAST TIME

On a Tuesday, about one in the morning on May 28–29, 1453, the Turks attacked the city of Constantinople on three sides. The first two attacks that night were repulsed though there was great loss of life. During the third, the emperor himself, fighting as a regular soldier, was killed; the walls were breached; and the city taken. The capital of the Eastern Roman Empire, after standing against barbarians and Muslims for over a thousand years, finally fell. Many of the Greeks ran to the sanctuary of the great church of St. Sophia hoping that the Turks would spare them. It was not to be. The Turks actually rode their horses into the great church and slaughtered those who were hiding there regardless of whether they were women or children.

The Eastern bastion of Christianity had fallen. There would be no unification with the West. There would be no return to the glory days of Constantine and Justinian. Very quickly the churches became mosques, and the home of Orthodox Christianity became another Muslim city.

GEOFFREY CHAUCER AND *THE CANTERBURY TALES*

The Canterbury Tales provide an amazing portrait of the fourteenth century. It is worth the effort just to read the Prologue. (Yes, that's the section you probably had to read in school, but it has improved since you got older.) The prologue introduces all the characters and sets the scenario for the poem. The group of characters had gathered together to make a pilgrimage to one of the most holy shrines in England, the site where Thomas Becket was murdered in the cathedral at Canterbury. It was a popular pilgrimage, not a very long or hard one from London. But to pass the time on the trip, each of the characters was supposed to tell several stories. (Somewhere in the writing Chaucer changed his mind about this but did not change the prologue.) Chaucer completed some of the stories but only a small percentage. That is a real shame because often the stories are more revealing about the character who tells them than is the character's description.

In the prologue to the poem, the poet gives us a series of fifteenth-century photographs in verse. He gives us the color of a yeoman's clothes (green). He tells us how a prioress eats (daintily), and what a monk *really* loved to do. The poet's sharp eyes miss nothing, and the result is a wonderful cross-section of English life. The poem presents characters from all the social strata of medieval life. Representing the upper class or nobility is the

SET THE STAGE!

One of the most important innovations in the history of the world and the church is undoubtedly the modern printing press. Generally credited to Johannes Gutenberg, the printing press combined several other inventions to great effect. Movable type, invented by the Chinese, had been around for some time. However, the cumbersome Chinese alphabet had been a daunting factor in the development of large-scale literary printing in Asia. Likewise, paper had been around for a while, but Gutenberg used paper made of linen and cotton, which was much better than that previously known. Gutenberg combined moveable type with a wine press (for even pressure) and used paper instead of costly vellum, which greatly reduced the cost. The use of paper also enabled the use of oil-based inks, which smeared on vellum but worked well on paper. Gutenberg's own invention of the type mold contributed to the easy manufacture of the printing press. In the past, scribes had often spent *years* painstakingly copying books by hand. With the first printing press, three hundred pages could be made in a single day. Between the early experiments of Gutenberg in the mid-1400s and the turn of the century, nearly a thousand print shops sprang up, producing *millions* of books at a small fraction of the previous cost. This allowed written knowledge (including the Bible) to be accessible to a much larger segment of the population and helped pave the way for the Renaissance, the Reformation, and the Enlightenment.

knight, a man of great character and experience. He has earned our respect by fighting for his country and for his Christian faith against the "infidels." He is virtuous and brave and holds the right set of values. He has honor, he fights for his nation, and he would die for his faith. Unfortunately, the tale he tells is long and not very exciting.

THE CHARACTERS

The middle class was coming into its own in the late fourteenth century, so the poem is full of characters from this group. There is a merchant, a miller, a carpenter, all of whom are good examples of the medieval middle class that, like today's version, is very concerned with its work and the money it can make. The Miller's Tale is the most famous of this group. He is in a running

SINNERS AND SAINTS
ST. CECILIA

Cecilia is a favorite subject of painters and poets alike. She was a great lover of music and, according to legend, invented the organ. This accomplishment is even more impressive when one considers that she was blind. Tradition has it that she was martyred about A.D. 230. In addition to being the subject of numerous paintings, she can be found in Chaucer's *Canterbury Tales* and in poems by Alexander Pope and John Dryden.

Chaucer, incidentally, has another important connection to a saint. It is believed that he originated the tradition of exchanging "valentines," which are so named after St. Valentine, who was martyred on February 14.

feud with the carpenter, so he tells a rather indecent story about a carpenter. Such is life in the competitive life of the middle class, even in the Middle Ages.

The church is incredibly well represented. Almost the entire range of church clergy below the bishop is represented. Chaucer was a brave man but no fool. An insult to a bishop could mean real trouble. There are loads of monastic characters, including a monk, a friar, and a prioress. From the nonmonastic branch of the church, there are a poor country parson and three priests whose jobs are to serve the prioress. One of these priests tells another famous tale that is somewhere between a fable and a dirty story.

The summoner and the pardoner also belong to the church group. In medieval England, the summoner worked for the archdeacon, who worked for the bishop. It was the summoner's job to cite people for petty offenses that could be tried by the church court. He had the power to get someone in really deep trouble or, for the right price, to look the other way. The pardoner was in the business of salvation, literally. His job was to travel around and sell forgiveness of sins in the form of a document called an indulgence. There were indulgences printed by the church, but just as often the pardoners sold fakes.

The lower class is represented by a simple plowman. He is a simple man who simply works the land. As far as the reader can tell, he is honest and good.

The Canterbury Tales shows us what history has a hard time describing. The tales remind us that the age was filled with normal people living normal lives. Certainly, the poem illustrates that the church was a much more significant social institution then than now. But that church is not one of which even Chaucer can be proud. With several exceptions, the "church" characters are worldly and vain, concerned with money or sport or sex. The pardoner is one of the first truly distasteful characters in the literature of the English language. In fact, with several exceptions, the entire reason for the pilgrimage is not to seek spiritual rebirth but to be out in the nice spring weather for a few days. The middle class is coarse, selfish, and vulgar. The peasant class is virtually invisible.

 DID YOU KNOW?

The first book printed in English was *Recuyell of the Historyes of Troye* in 1475. William Caxton, the printer responsible for its making, also is credited with the first printing of a literary work originally written in English when he printed Chaucer's *Canterbury Tales* a few years later.

When printed books first appeared in Europe, many people, unable to understand how so many exact copies could be made so quickly, thought it to be the work of black magic.

THE POEM AND MIDDLE AGE THEOLOGY

All this has led some critics to write that the poem represents the decline of proper Middle Ages values. They see great irony in a group of pilgrims being entertained by worldly, sometimes bawdy, stories as they make a religious pilgrimage. They condemn the pilgrims as hypocrites.

All of that is a modern response to the poem. Chaucer exposed his characters' sins, but in the mind frame of the Middle Ages he did not condemn them. He withheld condemnation toward even the pardoner for whom he shows real dislike. In the theology of the later Middle Ages, each of these characters is a candidate for redemption. Enjoying a dirty story, or drinking too much, or giving in to some other human foible was certainly a sin, but forgiveness was available. The theology of guilt that held sway during the dark years of the Middle Ages was giving way to a theology of hope.

In many ways, that hope is bound up in one minor character, the clerk of Oxford. He is a truly admirable man, not for what he has done like the knight, but for what he is and what he will do. He has a deep thirst for knowledge and a desire to share it. In the age to come, men like the simple clerk will look for the truth and challenge the corruption they see in the church. They will stand in university classrooms and call for reform, for a new worldview based on personal faith and knowledge, not church doctrine. They will inspire men and kings to look for a new world.

EXPLORATION AND INQUISITION

In 1492, Christopher Columbus sailed across the Atlantic and found the Caribbean. He was not working on his own. Though he was Italian, he could not get support for his adventure from the Italians, so he went to the Spanish royal family who were believed to be risk takers. Ferdinand of Aragon and Isabella of Castile had been married in 1469. It was a marriage of enormous political consequence because it united Spain. The Muslims had been pushed out of Spain little by little since the eleventh century, but it took this royal marriage to unite the country's many regions. The era of exploration that followed Columbus's journeys would transform Spain into one of the world's superpowers. The Spanish Empire that resulted would rival any empire in history. The Spanish imported incredible amounts of natural resources, including gold and silver, from the lands of their conquests, and they exported the Christian religion.

While they sent their conquistadors to conquer and to evangelize the New World, the Spanish were dealing with their own spiritual issues at home. Theirs was a unique country in Europe. The rest had, more or less, been Christian for a very long time, from their beginnings as nations. Spain, on the other hand, had spent centuries under the control of the Muslims. In the years after the Muslims were pushed out, there developed a strong sentiment that Christianity must be protected and its enemies vanquished. So in 1478 Queen Isabella launched the Spanish Inquisition.

THE SPANISH INQUISITION

Inquisition was an old idea by this time. Inquisition was a way to "root out" heretics and get rid of them. Hopefully they could be converted to proper thinking. The first step was the "confession" in which the supposed heretic confessed his wrong. Then the church could administer the proper punishment and "treatment." As early as 1229, the Synod of Toulouse had authorized the Dominican order to punish heretics. Then, in 1233, Pope Gregory IX had established an inquisition to combat the heresy of the Albigenses. The Albigenses were Christian heretics who believed in the coexistence of good and evil. They believed that matter was evil and that Jesus only seemed to have a body. Thus, they denied the actual humanity of Christ. Once begun, the Inquisition became

 DID YOU KNOW?

Ferdinand Magellan, credited with captaining the first "around the world" sea voyage, did not finish the voyage. He sacrificed his life in battle on an island in the Philippines so that his crew could escape and finish the trip. Only one of the original fleet of five ships made the entire journey, arriving in Spain in 1522 and carrying only 18 of the 241 crew members who set out on the expedition. Although Magellan's crew did not succeed in finding a shorter trade route to the Spice Islands (which had been the purpose of the trip), they did finally prove that the earth is round.

a tool for dealing with any enemy of the church, not only heretics but Jews and Muslims as well. In 1252 Pope Innocent IV authorized torture as a means of obtaining an accused person's confession. As a further sign of the times, that same year the French king Louis IX expelled all the Jews from France.

The Spanish Inquisition was independent of the papal Inquisition. Ostensibly, it was established to punish converted Jews and Muslims who were insincere. In 1483 the Spanish Dominican monk Tomas de Torquemada took command of the Inquisition. He quickly established a reputation as a ruthless torturer to obtain the confession he wanted. Fear of the Inquisition spread throughout Spain as a result of his tactics. In 1492, the same year that Columbus crossed the Atlantic, Ferdinand and Isabella issued a decree that extended the Inquisition started fourteen years before. The decree ordered Granada's 150,000 Jews to sell everything they owned and leave the country "for the honor and glory of God." In 1499, Inquisitor General Francisco Jimenez de Cisneros introduced forced conversion to Christianity. This caused major riots among the Moors who still lived in Granada.

The Spanish Inquisition would continue in one form or another for another three hundred years.

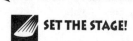 **SET THE STAGE!**

The year Tomas de Torquemada was named Inquisitor General of Spain (1483) was the same year Martin Luther was born.

THE RENAISSANCE UPON US

The Renaissance is a big enough topic for entire collections of books. It was one of the great phenomena in human history. The era was all about a rediscovery of the old Roman and Greek literature and philosophy. It was all about an explosion of artistic expression. It was all about collaboration between the church and great thinkers and artists.

Mostly, however, it was all about the rediscovery of the grandeur of humanity. Though "humanism" is a very hot topic these days, both pro and con, it was a Christian humanism that powered the Renaissance. In the rediscovery of classical

Greek writing and art, the people of the Renaissance found a hierarchy of life that made a lot of sense to them as Christians. God was certainly in heaven, and the angels were just below God. But, just below the angels the people of the Renaissance found mankind. The cosmology of the earlier Middle Ages had been dominated by the complex world of angels, saints, demons, and Satan, all of whom have control over a person's fate. It was the worldview of Pope Gregory and the grim sixth century. The world of the Renaissance was still populated by beasts and saints, and Satan was still present, but God was in control, and He had decided to save mankind. Man was still fallen as the hundreds of depictions of the Fall of Adam and Eve from the Renaissance would attest. But God, shown in beautiful, powerful human form, was there to offer His Son and raise humanity to Him.

These are the images of the Renaissance. In Leonardo da Vinci's *The Last Supper* we see a human Jesus surrounded by His human disciples. Christ's divinity is not diminished at all by this. In fact, Jesus' serenity in the light of the meal's chaos is an adequate sign of His godly nature. Michelangelo's statue of David is man at his most powerful and beautiful. In countless other works of art and literature of the era, man is shown as one of God's beautiful creations.

IMPLICATIONS

The Renaissance changed everything. It was the force that pushed Europe from the Middle Ages to the beginning of the modern age. It was a force that brought great glory to the orthodox church through the creation of beauty. Some works, such as the painting in the Sistine Chapel, still evoke awe when we see them. Most of the works were commissioned by popes or other church leaders who might not fare well if we judged them on the morality of their behavior.

POPES OF THE RENAISSANCE

The era of the Renaissance popes began with the election of Nicholas V in 1447. After the debacle of the Great Schism, the

SINNERS AND SAINTS
LEONARDO DA VINCI

During the Renaissance, forward thinking individuals were encouraged to broaden their horizons with a variety of artistic, scientific, political, and literary pursuits: The thought being that a broader range of interests and knowledge made for an individual who could better interact with the subtly rich and quickly changing world of the times. Looking back, historians dubbed such balanced and adaptable individuals *renaissance men,* and the term became popular to describe any individual possessing such diverse interests and qualities. Let's have a look at some of the accomplishments of one of the original renaissance men, Leonardo da Vinci (1452–1519).

Leonardo is regarded as one of the greatest painters in all of history. His works, including *Mona Lisa* and *The Last Supper,* are, perhaps, more popular today than they were when the already famous artist painted them. His artistic techniques and philosophy influenced many great painters of the time, including Michelangelo, Botticelli, and Raphael, and countless others through the intervening years. He was one of the first artists to make extensive use of sketches in preparation for a painting.

Leonardo designed locks for the canals of Milan and revolving stages for festivals while working as a civil engineer.

In yet another career as a military engineer, Leonardo designed artillery, fortresses, tanks, portable bridges, and primitive machine guns.

To better understand the human body and its movements for artistic as well as scientific purposes, da Vinci dissected cadavers and produced what are considered the first accurate anatomic studies of the human body.

Continued

SINNERS AND SAINTS (CONTINUED)

He detailed the form *and* function of bones and tendons and attempted to unlock the secrets of blood circulation and reproduction.

Leonardo was the first person to make a scientific study of the flight of birds. He also made designs for prototypical flying machines, including not only airplanelike devices but also a helicopter and a parachute, which influenced many later aeronautical pioneers.

He *did* have *some* failures. Leonardo tried out a new experimental painting technique while working with Michelangelo on murals for Florence's new city hall. The paint on da Vinci's mural ran, and it was never completed.

Still, his successes far outweigh his failures. He enjoyed the patronage of Pope Leo X and of King Francis I of France and made not only a good living but a lasting contribution to the world.

papacy became more and more Italian. Nicholas V set that tone from the beginning. He was very interested in making Rome beautiful and grand again, so he promoted new building and architectural adornment. The pope also had a love of things that were Greek, including the language, the literature, and even Greek humanism. He had the good fortune of being pope when Constantinople fell in 1453, and the West was flooded with refugees from the fallen capital. These refugees escaped with thousands of books and objects of art. Many of the books contained ancient works that had been lost to the West for nearly a millennium. Under his leadership, the Vatican library was reorganized.

The next pope was Alfonso Borgia of the notorious Borgia family. As Pope Calixtus III, he wanted to start a new crusade and spent fortunes of money trying to arrange it, but nothing happened. His successor was Pius II (1438–1464), who was one of the greatest humanist church leaders. He also wanted to organize a crusade against the Turks, but nothing came of that, either. Pius II was also a writer who left detailed accounts of the lavishness of the lifestyle of a pope in the Renaissance. His successor was Paul II (1464–1471), who was not at all a humanist. He was interested in throwing lavish parties and showing off the church's wealth. He was not at all interested in the office and dignity of the pope.

POPES OF THE RENAISSANCE II

Most people agree that the Renaissance papacy reached a new low under the leadership of his successor, Sixtus IV (1471–1484). This pope was an immoral man who was even implicated in an assassination plot of two members of the powerful de Medici family. He exercised nepotism in the worst way. He elevated thirty-four cardinals in his reign. Six of them were his nephews. He sold church offices and indulgences to raise money for his schemes. In spite of all this, he was the pope who built the Sistine Chapel, reorganized the Vatican library again, and condemned the excesses of the Spanish Inquisition.

The most controversial Renaissance pope, however, was Roderigo Borgia, Pope Alexander VI (1492–1503). He

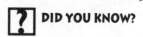 **DID YOU KNOW?**

Michelangelo's painting on the ceiling of the Sistine Chapel, done in the early 1500s, is considered to be one of the greatest works of art in the history of mankind. It is, however, an unfinished work. The artist unveiled the unfinished painting early when the pope, eager to have it done, threatened to have him "thrown down from that scaffold."

was one of Alfonso Borgia's nephews. He was the father of numerous children before his election as pope, including the infamous Lucretia Borgia. He provided for all of his children as pope—out of church revenues. Pope Alexander VI was a careful administrator, however. He was a fierce protector of the Papal States against foreigners. He even enlisted the help of the Turks to take care of problems he had with the French.

The papacy under the leadership of these men reached new highs in grandeur and new lows in moral leadership. The church had been developing and evolving as an empire with the political scene of an emerging Europe. In the era of the Renaissance, that development reached a level of decadence that paralleled that of the aging Roman Empire itself. Like the Roman Empire, the top level of leadership had lost its moral compass. It could no longer hear the voices of dissent and reform without trying to quiet them. Soon there would be voices that simply would not go away.

ULTIMATE IMPACT OF AND ON CHRISTIANITY

There is hardly an issue that faces the modern church that does not have its roots in the Middle Ages. It seems amazing that almost half of Christian history falls in this one period. While most of us would have been completely lost in the culture of the late Roman Empire, we would know our way around much better by the 1500s. In that regard, we are the inheritors of one very obvious development of that era. By and large, the layout of Europe is the product of the Middle Ages. By the late medieval period, the major powers of Europe are present. France and England are powerful countries. Germany and Italy have not become unified modern states, but they will not become so for many years to come. Spain has thrown off its Muslim conquerors and has become an empire.

ENEMIES

Each era seems to present the church with a new set of enemies. In much of the era of the "Church of the Empire," the church seemed its own worst enemy as it dealt with challenge after challenge of heresy and internal dissent. For most of the Middle Ages the church's main adversaries were the Muslims. In the simple battle for territory, the era went against the Christian church. The Holy Land was lost. North Africa was lost. For centuries even Spain was lost. Finally, even the last stronghold of Eastern Orthodoxy was lost to the Muslim Turks. The church did not lose this territory without a struggle. The crusades dragged on for years only to end in failure. The Christian church fights this same battle today. The Middle East is still a potential battleground over the same territory the crusaders won and lost almost a thousand years ago.

HEROES

This era seems to have some unexpected heroes. In many ways that is the legacy of the Franks. It was through the Franks that Roman Christianity created its first stronghold in northern Europe. While so much of the Western world was swirling toward chaos, the Franks held things together and they preserved at least a presence of Christianity against a flood of barbarism. If nothing else, modern Christianity owes the Franks a thank-you for the battle of Tours that stopped the Muslim encroachment into Europe. In retrospect, it is possible that our entire European Christian heritage hung in the balance.

The Franks were, of course, instrumental in the establishment of the Holy Roman Emperor. During the Middle Ages, this position of power seemed to work much better in theory than in practice. It did contribute, however, to the ever more complicated relationship between the church and the state. In this regard, the Middle Ages helped to demonstrate for later scholars and politicians that the church and the government could be powerful partners or serious enemies.

CONTROL ISSUES

The issues that complicate that relationship are territory and sovereignty. The lay investiture conflict was, in essence, a battle over outside, governmental control of the church. That conflict resonates in the headlines of newspapers all over the world today as the church is challenged to operate in countries with repressive government control. The other side of that issue was illustrated by the repeated influence of the church in the internal policies of European countries. We fight that battle here in the U.S. over such social issues as abortion. Many Christian leaders work extensively to influence public, governmental policy on this issue. The ability to influence government and the resistance of government to concede to religious pressure are both legacies of the Middle Ages. They are the legacies of Pope Leo III and Charlemagne, Thomas Becket and Henry II.

Theologically, there were many old battles fought. There was brilliant writing by Peter Abelard on the Trinity and on the relationship between faith and reason. There was brilliant Bible commentary from Thomas Aquinas, as well as the definitive work on finding the truth through revelation. William of Ockham would not only challenge the authority of the pope, he would challenge the entire idea that universals even existed. At times his work is frighteningly modern in its dependence on the natural world and observation.

UNITY

Through the Middle Ages there was one common thread that held the entire period together: The Christian church was present as a powerful unifying force. The Muslim challenge was great, but the church endured. The end of the first millennium A.D. was a terrible time as disorder came even to those places that had been civilized before. The church survived that, too. The fledgling nations of Europe suffered civil wars and terrible wars against each other, but the unifying force of the church repeatedly created a sense of common good, a reason to go on.

It is not that the Middle Ages came suddenly to a halt and the empire of the Catholic Church fell apart. Rather, it was more that the political, intellectual, and theological framework of the period came under increasing pressure to change. There was powerful pressure to reform the church. There was powerful pressure to redefine the relationship between the pope and the governments of Europe. There was powerful pressure to respond to thinkers like Wycliffe, William of Ockham, and John Hus. There was pressure to respond to the new technology of Roger Bacon's magnifying glass (1266) and Gutenberg's printing press (1440). There was pressure to respond to the New World being discovered and explored.

It is not that the old systems broke down, either. They were just in need of repair and maintenance. That would be the job of the Reformation.

CHAPTER SIX

The Reformation
(a.d. 1517 to a.d. 1648)

 A DAY IN THE LIFE

Old habits die hard, and old habits dying was a lot of what the Reformation was all about. The Holy Catholic Church had been the mainstay of Christianity, though its customs had become cumbersome like the Pharisees' of Jesus' day. Imagine trying to change over from those familiar traditions to a whole new way of working out faith.

A young man accustomed most of his life to confession would find it hard to stop.

We all went to church today. It still feels so strange to hear the service in my language. I always figured that the priest was talking to God, not to me. At first I didn't even understand why I needed to understand what he said. Elder Brown explained to me that he is interpreting God's Word for me and that if I don't understand the sermon, the service will have been for nothing. Does that mean that all those years my family was Catholic the sermons meant nothing?

I sorta miss confession. When I had to go do it I thought it was a drag. I mean, every week I had to go recite my sins.

(Sometimes it was a pretty long list.) The penance the priest gave me was never too bad, though—some prayers and stuff. I did feel better after I had done all of that, but maybe I was just glad I was through with it for another week.

My grandpa was a good man. He attended services, made confession, and lived a good life. Now the church tells me I can't pray him out of purgatory. That seems pretty cruel to me. But then they say that there isn't any purgatory. What they haven't told me is Where Is Grandpa?

My parents and their friends have a lot to say about the pope. I do agree that the pope has done some pretty rotten stuff. Everybody knew when he backed the emperor against our prince that he was just doing it for the money. Dad says he just wanted all the taxes we paid. Well, that's over now!

I can see how the pope was wrong, too, about indulgences. You've got to admit, it was a convenient idea, though. I could do whatever I wanted, if I had enough money, and just buy my way out of purgatory. Hmmm. I think Grandpa bought a few of those. That's a shame 'cause I bet they did him no good when he got there to find there was no purgatory.

Who knows? Grandpa was a Catholic when he died. How would that work? We changed our minds about so much that we believe. It's hard to know what's really the truth.

TIMELINE OVERVIEW

In the midst of World History...

1517 The Reformation begins.

1518 Forks are first used at a banquet in Venice.

1519 Magellan sets out to sail around the world.

1520 Europe: Chocolate is introduced.

1528 The first manual of surgery is written by Paracelsus, a physician.

1533 Henry VIII marries Anne Boleyn and is excommunicated by the pope.

1536 Anne Boleyn is executed and Henry VIII marries Jane Seymour.

Christian History unfolds...

1517 Martin Luther posts his ninety-five theses—Lutherans.

1523 Zwingli leads Swiss Reformation.

1525 Anabaptist movement begins.

1528 Capuchins founded.

1532 Germany: The Peace of Nuremberg allows some Protestants to practice their religion freely.

France: Calvin starts the Protestant movement.

1534 Henry VIII is declared head of the Church in England by the Act of Supremacy—Anglicans.

Spain: Ignatius Loyola founds the Society of Jesus, also known as Jesuits.

Continued

TIMELINE OVERVIEW (CONTINUED)

In the midst of World History...

Christian History unfolds...

1535 Sir Thomas More is executed for refusing to take the oath agreeing to the Act of Supremacy.

1536 Calvin and the *Institutes of Christian Religion*—Calvinism

England: The dissolution of the monasteries starts. The money from selling monastic lands is used to help pay for wars with France.

1540 Pope approves the Jesuits—Counter-Reformation and political tool.

1543 Copernicus, astronomer and priest, states on his deathbed that the Earth moves around the sun.

North America: Oil is found in Texas by the Spaniard Luis de Moscoso.

1545 Council of Trent and the Catholic Counter-Reformation

1547 French becomes the official language of France rather than Latin.

1549 Cranmer and *Book of Common Prayer*—Anglicans

Japan: The Christian missionary St. Francis Xavier arrives.

1550 North America: The Spanish bring the first beef cattle to North America.

1555 Mary I leads England to return to Roman Catholicism. Protestants are persecuted and about 300, including Cranmer, are burned at the stake.

Violins as we know them today began to appear.

1558 Mary I is succeeded by Elizabeth I. Catholic legislation in England is repealed.

1559 John Knox in Scotland—Presbyterians

1560 England: The first Puritans appear. Many are Protestants who left England to escape persecution under Mary.

1561 England: English sea captain John Hawkins starts England's involvement in the slave trade when he takes 300 African slaves from a ship bound for Brazil.

1563 English soldiers catch the plague while in France and bring it back to England. It kills over 20,000 in London alone.

1563 England: The Thirty-nine Articles combining Protestant beliefs with Roman Catholic organization and stating that the ruling monarch is the head of the church are adopted.

Russia: Ivan the Terrible conquers part of Livonia

1565 England: Sir John Hawkins introduces sweet potatoes and possibly tobacco.

1566 Pope Pius V —Reformer

Netherlands: Religious riots break out between Catholics and the followers of John Calvin.

1572 St. Bartholomew's Day Massacre: Over 20,000 Huguenots are killed—French Protestants.

1587 Mary, Queen of Scots, is beheaded.

1602 Hungary: Counter-Reformation gathers force. Protestants in Bohemia and Hungary are persecuted.

1604 James I bans Jesuits from England.

1605 Shakespeare writes *King Lear*.

1608 Netherlands: Hans Lippershey invents the telescope. The first checks are used for monetary transactions.

1608-10 Anglican Splinter groups.
1. Pilgrims—Purify Anglicanism through reform.
2. Separatists—Leave Anglicanism.

1611 Publication of King James Bible.

1620 Pilgrims sign Mayflower Compact.

1621 Pilgrims celebrate the first Thanksgiving Day.

1626 Italy: Physician Santorio Santorio measures the temperature of the human body for the first time with a thermometer.

1629 Construction begins on the Taj Mahal in India in honor of the wife of Shah Jahan (finished in 1650).

1631 The multiplication sign "x" is first used.

1634 Germany: The first passion play (life of Christ through the Last Supper to the death on the cross) is performed to mark the end of the plague.

1636 France: Tea appears for the first time in Paris.

1638 Japan: The Shimabara uprising. For several months 40,000 Christians held out against the Shogun's army. The Christians were slaughtered. In the aftermath, the few surviving Christians practiced their religion in secret.

1646 The Westminister Confession of Faith

1648 George Fox founds the Society of Friends, called Quakers after 1650.

THE STORY OF THE TIMES

The world of the Middle Ages was a changing world for sure. The Roman Catholic Church had survived the fall of the Roman Empire, the rise and fall of barbarian invaders, and the rise of European and British nations. Somehow this Christian empire had survived the almost unstoppable progress of Muslim expansion as well as the almost continual conflict between rulers and popes over issues of power. Simply put, the governments of the day wanted to control the church, and the church wanted to control the governments. When a balance could be found, there was great prosperity and peace. When one side or the other pushed too far or too hard, there was conflict and social upheaval.

The church had faced its foes and survived. In fact, in the late Middle Ages, the church had prospered and become very rich. In that environment, the conflict between church and state was about more than power. It was also about money. With the arrival of the Renaissance and exploration of the New World, the church grew even richer and more opulent. Rome once again became the showplace of an empire: the empire of the Roman Catholic Church.

THE PLAGUE

At the beginning of the sixteenth century, however, all was not well in Christendom. Europe was periodically besieged by the bubonic plague, the Black Death. The plague had reached Europe from the East in 1348. By 1350 it had killed as much as half the population. This drastic reduction of labor had given the peasants a much greater freedom. There had even been labor uprisings in France (1358) and England (1378) that were slowly dismantling the strict feudal system of the earlier centuries. As we saw earlier, there had been a sharp development in the middle class at these times, too. By the end of the Middle Ages, social change was a reality as the feudal system slowly lost its grip.

Social change was not in the forefront of the people's minds so much as the threat of the Ottoman Turks. These Muslim invaders had already captured the "unconquerable" city of Constantinople and had designs on conquering much more of Europe. The sixteenth century was thus a century of anxiety over the unpredictable return of the Black Death, and out-and-out worry over the coming invasion of the Turks.

THE "ENEMY" WITHIN

The church seemed prepared to take on the current threats from the outside. Where they seemed less prepared was their ability to take on the enemies within. There was change bubbling under the surface in the church. Some of it had already reached the surface. Men like Wycliffe and Hus had already stated good cases against existing church policy. Wycliffe was condemned for heresy posthumously (ouch), and Hus was executed. In 1498, on the eve of the sixteenth century, an Italian preacher and reformer named Savonarola was executed for his activities and beliefs. He was a Dominican who rose to power in Florence by preaching the need for both political and church reform. As a leader he instituted tax reform and transformed Florence from a corrupt, pleasure-seeking place into a virtual monastery. He also preached against and denounced Pope Alexander VI and the corrupt papal court. Alexander struck

 THE MORE THINGS CHANGE...
(Death, Taxes, and Other Immutables)

Everyone knows what minimum wage is, but have you ever heard of a maximum wage law? England passed such a law in the 1340s. The Black Death had left England with a labor shortage. There simply weren't enough people to bring in all the crops. This led to many workers asking for, and receiving, more than they customarily had gotten for their services. The king forbade this but to no avail. Landowners who paid more than the maximum wage were fined, and, eventually, taxes were raised on wages to keep the peasants poor. This led to a brief rebellion by the peasants in 1381 during which many noblemen, including the royal treasurer (the head of the medieval IRS), were beheaded. Ah, the good old days.

SINNERS AND SAINTS
THE DOMINICANS

The Dominican order, or the Order of Friars, as it is also called, was founded by the Spanish religious leader St. Dominic in 1216 by permission of Pope Honorius for one express purpose—preaching against heresy. From the early days of the Order, Dominicans became revered teachers of theology, teaching in many famous universities. Well-known Dominicans include Albertus Magnus and St. Thomas Aquinas. So much for the saints...the Spanish Inquisition brought to light a notorious Dominican. The Inquisition, a religious court that tried suspected heretics, was created in 1231 under the Dominican friar Tomas de Torquemada (1420–1498). Under Torquemada the Inquisition became a personal and political vendetta.

The marriage of Ferdinand and Isabella (the same monarchs who sponsored Columbus's voyages) had united the kingdoms of Castile and Aragon. This, along with Ferdinand's military acquisition of other territories, created the kingdom we now know as Spain. However, the young country was still more of a loose amalgamation of states and suffered a political disunity that Isabella's confessor, Torquemada, thought he could stabilize. His plan? Drive all the non-Catholics out of Spain. Torquemada went to work for the Inquisition and, shortly thereafter, was named the first Inquisitor General of Spain. By means of political pressure, torture, and *thousands* of public executions, he drove *hundreds of thousands* of Jews and Muslims from their homes.

Eventually, the atrocities of the Inquisition subsided and were even condemned by the Catholic Church. Today, the Dominicans are once more well known as teachers and preachers and boast a membership exceeding 120,000 persons.

back by excommunicating Savonarola and threatening Florence with an interdict. (An interdict is a censure that bars a person or an area from participating in the sacraments and from receiving a Christian burial. In effect it's a mass excommunication.) This threat frightened the people of Florence, who turned against Savonarola, leading to his execution.

In 1516, another church insider, Erasmus, created a controversy in the church by publishing a new Latin translation of the New Testament based on the original Greek. Erasmus, an ordained priest, was a true humanist and had a great admiration for the Greek language and culture. In the preface to this translation, however, he called for the Bible to be published into the common languages of Europe, an opinion very similar to that of Wycliffe. Erasmus was not a reformer, however, and remained a faithful Roman Catholic throughout his life.

There was plenty of pressure within the church to reform, though. Almost everyone was aware of the church's excesses and questionable policy. Unfortunately, most of those excesses and policies had become part of the very fabric of the church and her traditions. In spite of this, popular opinion was not to break away from the church. The church had been reformed from within before, and it could be again. At least that's the way most people looked at it.

A CHANGE IS COMING

Martin Luther did not plan his life to be a reformer. By 1505, he had finished his master's examination and was set to begin his study of law. A few months later, however, he changed course and entered an Augustinian monastery in Erfurt. In 1507, he was ordained as a priest and was assigned to the University of Wittenberg in 1508. It could have seemed that his life would take on the calm pattern of a priest working in an academic setting teaching moral theology. Then came Luther's trip to Rome in 1510.

Luther was German and the son of a copper miner. He was the product of a German culture that was unique in the Europe of that time period. Technically, the ruler of Germany was the

Holy Roman Emperor. Since 1276, that power had lain with the Hapsburg dynasty, which continued to rule until the empire's dissolution in 1806. Germany was not a united nation in the same sense as France, England, or Spain. As a result, the typical German did not feel the same connection with the grandeur of a monarchy that, for instance, a Frenchman would have felt.

On his mission to Rome, Luther was shocked by the spiritual laxity he saw in high ecclesiastical places. According to historical records, in Rome he would have been surrounded by a world where excess was the rule. He would have seen more wealth accumulated and displayed at the Vatican than he could have imagined. He certainly could have seen church officials participating in such immoral activities as extramarital sex, gambling, gluttony, and drunkenness. Rome was a corrupt city where anything a person desired was available for a price. Even the Italian writer Machiavelli wrote that the nearer one got to Rome, the more corruption he found.

Whatever Luther saw in Rome, when he returned to Wittenberg he was deeply upset. He developed a great spiritual anxiety about his own salvation. Importantly, he turned to the Bible for an answer to his questions. In his study of the scriptures in 1513, he found a loving God who gave sinful humans the free gift of salvation, received by faith alone, and not by works. It was a theological breakthrough. If Luther's view of salvation was correct, he could come to no other conclusion: The Roman Catholic Church was going about church the wrong way.

NINETY-FIVE THESES

On October 31, 1517, Martin Luther chose to post an academic paper, called a disputation, written about indulgences, a mainstay of the Catholic Church. It was not an uncommon thing for a professor of biblical studies at the University of Wittenberg to post this kind of thing. In fact, his disputation, called *Ninety-five Theses*, was written with the moderate tone that academic papers still demand. The truth of what he wrote, though, was not moderate. Furthermore, the response to his *Ninety-five Theses* was anything but moderate. Within weeks, the news of what this monk/professor had written had spread all over Europe. The monk in Wittenberg, in spite of himself, had become famous (or infamous depending on the point of view). Luther's proposal was to examine the theology of indulgences in the light of the abuses that had grown up through the years. In other words, he questioned the status quo.

INDULGENCES

An indulgence was usually issued on a piece of paper signed by the pope (or forged). This piece of paper did not forgive sins as some mistakenly believed. Medieval Christianity taught that salvation came through being forgiven and blessed by a priest. Thus, the medieval Catholic Christian was not really afraid of hell. He had no intention of dying without the blessing of a priest. He was afraid of purgatory, however.

In the cosmology of the Middle Ages, heaven and hell were final destinations, and purgatory was a stop along the way. Purgatory was the place where even Christians were punished for every sin they had committed. The church taught that a Christian must be cleansed of all sin before he could reach heaven. Purgatory was the place where the Christian was cleansed.

In its original sense, the indulgence was a way for a sincerely penitent Christian to be released from a penance placed upon him by a priest. In theory, the indulgence "commuted" the penance. In practice, however, the indulgence was seen as the way to avoid doing penance altogether if one had the money. Further, most Christians (including the poet Dante) believed that an indulgence could shorten the time of suffering required in purgatory. In other words, just as an indulgence could relieve someone of earthly penance, it could also relieve someone of penance in purgatory. That was a very attractive package, and through the years, the church had capitalized on people's desire to save themselves the trouble of penance or the suffering of purgatory.

LUTHER'S PROBLEM WITH INDULGENCES

Luther's problem was actually not with the ideal concept of

indulgences. His argument was with the additions and perversions that had crept into the practice of indulgences in his day. He saw no scriptural authority for the buying and selling of an indulgence. He recognized that the indulgence had become a "hot" product for the church. Indulgences created great cash flow! The practice of indulgences also encouraged people to sin. Other than having to spend a little extra money, there was no "down side" to sin. It's human nature to find the money for favorite pastimes, sinful or otherwise. In Luther's day, that equaled out to finding the money for forgiveness.

Just as important to Luther was the fact that the indulgence took the focus of a Christian's life away from Christ and God's forgiveness. Forgiveness was not the product of Christ's life, death, and resurrection but rather it was a financial transaction. Although it seems amazing to us now, this was exactly the point that irritated the church and caused Luther his future problems. As we

QUOTABLES

"Here I stand. I can do no other."
Martin Luther,
Diet of Worms, 1521

have seen, the popes of the Middle Ages claimed much more authority as the years passed. The pope had become the head of an empire, and as such, his decrees became law. The pope had assumed authority over the secular rulers of the time. He was not always able to actually order a monarch to do something (although that was not infrequent in Italy and France.) Instead, he used the power of his "good will" to act as either a powerful ally or a powerful opponent of a ruler. By the Renaissance, the popes had become masters of leverage.

EXCOMMUNICATION

The ultimate leverage was the idea of excommunication. Up until the Middle Ages, excommunication usually meant that a person or group was excluded from the Christian group to which they belonged and was not allowed back in. In the Middle Ages, excommunication became a powerful tool in the fight against heresy. Excommunication meant that a person was turned out of the church and, as a result, could not participate in the sacraments. Without participation in the sacrament of penance, the excommunicated person was condemned to hell. With that power, the authority for salvation lay not in the authority of God and scripture but under the control of the church. Through excommunication, the church held the power of heaven and hell over any church member.

So, when Luther challenged the authority of the church to control salvation through the selling of indulgences, he was challenging the authority of the church itself. The power of the medieval church was *based* on the authority to control salvation. Without that authority, the secular/political power of the church would be greatly reduced. In other words, without that authority, the medieval empire of the Roman Catholic Church was in real trouble.

That is one reason the news of Luther's *Ninety-five Theses* spread so quickly. Friends of the church establishment recognized that Luther's conclusions were a serious threat to the temporal power of the church and were upset by it. Many of those people who were also calling for church reform were excited by Luther's ideas. Still others, from both reformers and friends, were confused and disturbed by the whole issue. After all, the church had been operating this way for hundreds of years. Did a few problems justify calling into question the whole authority of the church?

 QUOTABLES

"Unless I am convinced by the testimony of the Scriptures or by clear reason (for I do not trust either in the pope or in councils alone, since it is well known that they have often erred and contradicted themselves), I am bound by the Scriptures I have quoted and my conscience is captive to the Word of God. I cannot and I will not retract anything, since it is neither safe nor right to go against conscience."
Martin Luther,
Diet of Worms, 1521

LUTHER HAS TO ANSWER

Luther posted his disputations the last day of October. By December of that year, the archbishop of Mainz had complained to Rome about him. Luther's position led almost immediately to his having to answer to his own Augustinian order in 1518. He was called to answer to papal authorities in Augsburg that same year. Confronted by Cardinal Cajetan, Luther's stance became even firmer. When he was summoned to Rome afterwards, Luther fled the town. In Leipzig in 1519, Luther entered into a disputation with his fiercest intellectual opponent, Johann Eck. Although the arbitrators rendered no verdict after the debate, public opinion gave the victory to Eck. In 1520, Eck went to Rome. When he returned to Germany, he did so as papal legate with instructions to enforce a papal bull (decree or mandate) that condemned Luther as a heretic. Luther was ordered to recant the positions he assumed in the *Ninety-five Theses*. He refused. So Luther was excommunicated on January 3, 1521. In April, he was called to answer for his beliefs before Emperor Charles V at the Diet of Worms. There, in spite of pressure from the emperor, Luther again refused to recant his beliefs unless someone could refute his beliefs on scriptural grounds. That in itself was an insult to the authority of the church but was entirely consistent with Luther's stance that scripture is the only real authority. As a result, he was made an outlaw by the emperor. For his own protection, Luther was seized and taken to Wartburg Castle where he was held under the protection of Frederick of Saxony.

When Luther refused to recant his beliefs, the Reformation really began. Luther was, after all, a loyal member of the church; not only that, he was a member of a religious order. As a scholar it was his nature to consider ideas, even new ones. That tradition went all the way back to the second and third centuries as Tertullian and Origen presented their views of Christianity. There was even a long tradition of church dissenters, some of whom had lost their lives for their ideas. But in Luther's case, his refusal to recant came at exactly the right time and started a firestorm. He stood up not only to the pope but also to the

Holy Roman Emperor. That inspired people all over Europe, and a new age began.

THE REFORMATION IN SHORT

Over the next twenty years or so, the spark that Luther ignited burst into flames over much of Europe. The ensuing religious revolution had three main areas of influence, each with its own leaders and area of protest.

SET THE STAGE! THE DIET OF WORMS

In the medieval Catholic Church, a "diet" was a legislative assembly or conference. When an important issue arose, a diet would be called to discuss important issues or settle disputes. The diet that was held to discuss Luther's plight was held in the German town of Worms, thus, the Diet of Worms. When the council had established their position on the issue, they listed it as an edict, in this case, the Edict of Worms.

The followers of Luther dominated in Germany and Scandinavia.

The followers of the Swiss reformer Zwingli and the Frenchman John Calvin were found primarily in Switzerland, France, Holland, and Scotland.

The Church of England developed in a wholly different way, but became a powerful force of the Reformation.

The Reformation was not a united movement under one leader. It was more like a movement whose time had come in the hearts of many people. There were sharp disagreements among the protesting sects. There was much on which they could agree, however.

THE BROAD VIEW

It can be easy to become myopic when looking at the period of the Reformation. Keep in mind that a lot was happening in the world besides the upheaval of the church and the creation of the Protestant branch of Christianity.

The 1520s were not a time of peace. In 1519, the Holy Roman Emperor Maximilian I had died, and Spain's Carlos I was elected emperor as Charles V. The election was controversial from the very beginning. There were accusations that a powerful family of Augsburg merchants, the Fuggers, and some other Augsburg merchants fixed the election by bribing some electors. Even in Spain, the election provoked controversy when the *communeros*, a group of cities led by Toledo's Juan Lopez de Padilla, took exception to the king's leaving the country and the siphoning off of Spanish men and money for the empire. At the Battle of Villalar, Charles V defeated the communeros and eliminated all resistance to his rule. However, since the French had supported the insurgents, a war broke out between France and Spain that would last eight years. In spite of this, Spain's power and influence grew day by day because of the nation's efforts in Central and South America. In 1519, Cortez launched his attack on the Aztecs led by Montezuma and conquered them.

In 1525, Spanish and German forces defeated France's François I and his Swiss mercenaries at the Battle of Pavia. This battle marked the end of the supremacy of armored knights, largely because of the invention of the gun. The gun had changed the way battles were fought, and the knight had became an anachronism. Six thousand Frenchmen were killed in this battle, and François was taken to Madrid as a prisoner.

In Scandinavia, Denmark's Christian II invaded Sweden with a large army of French, German, and Scottish mercenaries. Previously, he had persuaded Pope Leo X to excommunicate Swedish king Sten Sture the Younger and place Sweden under an interdict. Although Christian II defeated Sture at the Battle of Bogesund in January, the war went on for months because the king's widow rallied the peasantry to fight the Danish invaders. However, by November the peasants had been defeated, and Christian was crowned hereditary king of Sweden at Stockholm's cathedral. In the aftermath, two of Sweden's leading bishops were convicted of heresy and violence against the church. At midnight November 8, they were beheaded in the public square at Stockholm. The Danish rule over Sweden was brief, however, and by 1523, King Christian II was deposed by the Danish nobility.

THE OTTOMANS

In southern Europe, Belgrade fell to the Ottoman sultan Suleiman in 1521, and the sultan's forces begin making raids into Hungary. By the next year, the Ottomans attacked Rhodes, where they fought against the Knights of St. John who had ruled the island since 1306. After a six-month siege, the sultan's forces defeated the knights and captured the island. In 1526, the Hungarian king Louis II was killed by the Turks at the battle of Mohács. In 1529, the Ottoman Empire reached the height of its power when the sultan's armies completed their conquest of Algeria. Then, on September 3, Suleiman I arrived at Budapest with 250,000 troops and three hundred cannons. He took the city in only six days. Afterward, the sultan marched against Vienna. His main army arrived there on September 27. Vienna was poorly defended with only 20,000 men and 22,000 cavalry, but the Turks had become overextended and poorly supplied. Thousands of them died of cold and hunger, and when an infantry charge on October 14 failed, Suleiman's army was forced to return to Constantinople,

In January 1526, France's François I signed the Treaty of Madrid, having been a prisoner for nearly a year of the emperor Charles V. Once he was released, however, he claimed the terms of the treaty had extorted and that the treaty was therefore invalid. He formed an alliance with the Ottoman sultan Suleiman the Magnificent against Charles. He was also joined in 1527 by England's Henry VIII through the Treaty of Westminster. Soon afterward, François began new attacks against the emperor Charles V. After a series of bloody conflicts,

SET THE STAGE!

Suleiman's people didn't call him "the Magnificent." They called him Suleiman the Lawgiver.

particularly in Italy, the Peace of Cambrai was signed on August 5, 1529. The treaty settled the conflict between France and the emperor Charles V. The two leaders were not even present. Louise of Savoy signed on behalf of François I, who gave up all French claims in Italy, Flanders, and Artois. Margaret of Austria signed on behalf of her nephew Charles V, who renounced any claims to Burgundy. Henry VIII acceded to the treaty August 27, ending any conflict between the empire and the English.

MEANWHILE...IN SWITZERLAND

In our time, Switzerland is more renowned for its natural beauty and high-tech industry than for being a hotbed for change. It was not always that way, however. During the Renaissance, Zürich and its canton (a small territorial division of a country, especially in Switzerland) became influenced by the humanism movement. In the 1520s, the time and place were perfect for a radical change to occur.

Ulrich Zwingli was born on January 1, 1484, in Wildhaus, Sankt Gallen, in the northeastern part of Switzerland. He was educated at the universities of Vienna and Basel, and in 1506 he was ordained as a priest. He was assigned to a parish in the town of Glarus. At that time, Glarus was a well-known center for recruiting mercenary soldiers. On two occasions Zwingli was called upon to act as a chaplain for these mercenaries fighting on foreign soil. These experiences led him to denounce the mercenary system that was an important part of the Swiss economy. It is often forgotten that the renowned Swiss policy of neutrality had its roots in the country's mercenary industry. It was far easier to sell mercenaries if their home country had no stake in the conflict. So, in retaliation for his denunciation of mercenaries, certain town officials decided to make his position at Glarus uncomfortable and ineffective. As a result, in 1516, Zwingli accepted an appointment at Einsiedeln, southeast of Zürich.

ZWINGLI'S CRISIS OF FAITH

From 1516 through 1518, Zwingli served as a priest in Einsiedeln. It was during his ministry there that Zwingli began to have doubts about certain church practices. Unlike Luther, whose changes had been rapid, Zwingli's dispute with these church practices was a slow, intellectual process. In 1516, he read a Latin translation of the Greek New Testament published by the Dutch humanist Desiderius Erasmus. Later, he transcribed the translation into notebooks and memorized it verbatim. As a result of his study of scripture, Zwingli charged in sermons that the doctrine of the church had strayed too far from the Bible. Zwingli focused particularly on what he considered the exaggerated role of relics and saints, on the promises of miraculous cures, and on the abuses in the practice of indulgences. His beliefs made him famous, and on January 1, 1519, he was appointed vicar at the great cathedral in Zürich.

The beginning of the Reformation in Switzerland dates from the lectures Zwingli delivered on the New Testament there in 1519. He quickly attracted large audiences to the cathedral by expounding the original Greek and Hebrew scriptures chapter by chapter and book by book, beginning with the Gospel of Matthew. These oral translations of the original scriptures broke sharply with church tradition that was based on the Vulgate and the church fathers. In these sermons, Zwingli proclaimed the scriptures to have sole authority, the same issue that caused Martin Luther so much trouble to the north. Then, in 1519, one of Zwingli's followers placed a printing press at his disposal. Soon the reformer's message had become widespread. That same year Zwingli read the writings of his contemporary Martin Luther for the first time. He was encouraged by the conviction of Luther's stand against the church and emperor. So, in 1520, Zwingli persuaded the Zürich council to forbid all religious teachings without foundation in the scriptures.

ZWINGLI AND THE POPE

Zwingli's actions angered the pope, Adrian VI, who first forbade the vicar from preaching any more and then called upon the council of Zürich to condemn him as a heretic. Zwingli appeared before the council in 1523 to defend himself. Zwingli presented his doctrines in

 **SET THE STAGE!**

Zwingli wanted to bring about a "Renaissance of Christendom" and put the control of the church in the hands of the people, not the hierarchy.

sixty-seven theses. Instead of renouncing his position, Zwingli attacked the church's position of the worship of saints, the sacrament of the Eucharist, and the required celibacy of the priesthood. Instead of condemning the renegade priest, on January 29, 1523, the council decided to withdraw the Zürich canton from under the jurisdiction of the bishop of Constance. By taking these steps, the council officially adopted the Reformation. In 1524, Zwingli married Anna Reinhard, a widow with whom he had lived openly. Thus began his life as a married clergyman.

Having broken away from the church, Zürich became a theocracy ruled by Zwingli and a Christian magistrate. The city underwent tremendous changes, including the conversion of monasteries into hospitals, the removal of religious images, and the elimination of Mass and confession. The Mass became a simple service with an emphasis on preaching. Zwingli also carried his message to cantons other than Zürich. Six of them became aligned with his reform movement. However, the remaining five, known as the Forest Cantons, remained Catholic. There was a great deal of antagonism between these two groups, great enough, in fact, to threaten the Swiss Federation.

THE END OF THE SWISS REFORMATION
In 1529, the hostility between the reformer and Catholic cantons turned into civil war. Though he had publicly opposed the mercenary system, Zwingli went to war with his reformers. On October 10, 1531, at Kappel am Albis, Zwingli was wounded while acting as chaplain and standard-bearer for the reformer forces. He was later executed by the victorious troops of the Forest Cantons. His death effectively ended the Reformation in Switzerland, and even today the country is half Catholic, half Protestant.

THE ANABAPTISTS
Both Luther and Zwingli had political allies. Luther was protected from arrest and punishment by the German elector Frederick the Wise. In addition, there were a number of other German princes who supported Luther because of their own desire for

THE MORE THINGS CHANGE...

(Death, Taxes, and Other Immutables)

National flags came into use during the 1700s in Europe and North America, but since the days of the ancient Egyptians in the third century B.C., flags have played an important historical role. The original uses of flags seem to have been to let generals know where their troops were positioned on the field of battle and to indicate which way the wind blew so that archers could more accurately position themselves and aim their arrows. During the Middle Ages, nobles flew personal banners, whose size and shape denoted the rank of the person represented, as rallying points for their troops. Knights had square flags with streamers called *Schwenkels*. When a knight received promotion to knight-banneret, the next status level up, the streamer was removed and the resulting square flag was known as a *banner*. As nations began to stabilize, personal flags began to give way to national flags, which represented the identity of the whole country. Crosses displayed on many European flags have their roots in the crusades. Likewise, the eagle of Saladin (symbol of an important Arab ruler who fought the crusaders) appears on the national flags of many Arab nations. At many times throughout history, troops have been so demoralized by the capture of their flag that they have surrendered. Conversely, Francis Scott Key, while a prisoner aboard a British ship during the War of 1812, was so inspired by the sight of the American flag flying high through the night of a battle that he wrote "The Star Spangled Banner," our national anthem.

more political freedom than they had under the Holy Roman Emperor and the pope. Zwingli had the support of the council of Zürich as a buffer between himself and punishment.

There were reformers in Zwingli's movement, however, who felt that simply replacing Rome with Zürich was not enough. They wanted the church to reform very quickly back to the ideals of the churches of the first century. Instead of church hierarchies and political systems, they wanted the church to become self-governing, ruled only by the Holy Spirit. The issue that brought this dissenting group into sharp conflict with the main group of Zwingli's followers was baptism.

Zwingli's church had continued the practice of infant baptism. The dissenting group pointed to the scripture and proclaimed that adult baptism was more scriptural; therefore, they wanted adult baptism to become the church practice. On January 21, 1525, however, the Zürich council commanded them to stop their arguments over the issue of baptism. The dissenting group saw this as just another example of the interference of the state in religious matters, so that very night they assembled in a nearby village and baptized each other. It was not long before their enemies were deriding them as "rebaptizers," or Anabaptists. The derisive name stuck.

WHAT THE ANABAPTISTS WANTED

For the Anabaptists, church reform was simply not enough. They wanted to return the church to the same level of simplicity and purity they saw in the early church described in the scriptures. Instead of a political institution, which the church had steadily become over its history since A.D. 312, the Anabaptists wanted a family of faith created by God. They were staunch advocates of the separation of church and state because they saw the church as something totally separate from society, even a "Christian" society. The real enemy in their eyes was any institution which influenced the conscience of a believer. In their value system, neither a political nor a religious organization had the right to determine a person's beliefs.

As a result, they were opposed not only to political/religious institutions such as the Roman Catholic Church and Zwingli's Swiss Reformers, they were also opposed to church hierarchies, as well. For the Anabaptists, the church consisted of voluntary congregations of converts (those who had undergone believer's baptism). You were not born an Anabaptist, you became one. Additionally, they became the first people to practice democracy in the congregation. They could do this because they believed that God spoke not only through bishops and councils (much less through papal decrees) but also through the individual congregations. This was a revolutionary idea at a time when in most of the world the pope was the sole authority on religious matters.

MEANWHILE...BACK IN ITALY

Even while groups such as the Lutherans and the Anabaptists were changing outside the Catholic Church, the Catholic Church itself was changing. Even as the role of the monastery-bound orders declined in power, other orders were founded to respond to the changing times. In 1528, the Italian monk Matteo da Bascio founded a branch of the Franciscans at Montefalco in Umbria. They were called the Capuchins because of the cowl (*cappuccio*) they wore as a headdress.

The Franciscans, or Order of Friars Minor, were founded in 1208 by St. Francis of Assisi and approved by Pope Innocent III in 1209. St. Francis and twelve disciples obtained the use of the little chapel of Santa Maria degli Angeli from the Benedictine abbey on Mount Subasio. With this as their base they began, in imitation of Christ, a life of itinerant preaching and voluntary poverty.

As time passed, the order grew. The only order of equal power was the Dominicans. The Franciscans, however, became plagued by disunity, and in 1517, Pope Leo X divided the order into two bodies: the Conventuals, who were allowed to own property as a group like other monastic orders, and the Observants, who sought to follow the Franciscans' teachings as closely as possible.

The Capuchins were founded out of the Observants. The order required them to observe literally the Rule of St. Francis. In a time of excess on behalf of the church and even many of the monastic orders, the Capuchins were an attempt to move back to the ideals that Assisi had preached. The friars of the order were to be celibate, to own nothing, and to work tirelessly as preachers and missionaries. In some ways, this new order can be viewed as a small attempt toward the reformation of the Roman Catholic Church. Historically, the monastic orders had been the element of the church that called the church to reform. In that light, the Capuchins were an attempt to move backward in time and recapture an idealism for Christian values that had been largely forgotten. In 1538 an order of Capuchin nuns, properly a branch of the Poor Clare order, was founded in Naples.

SINNERS AND SAINTS
ST. BRIDGET

There are two Roman Catholic saints with the name Bridget. The one with which we shall at this point concern ourselves is a patron saint of Ireland, lived from about A.D. 451 to 523, and was also called St. Bride. As legend has it, Bridget was a very beautiful and talented woman. Because she sought to devote her life solely to worship and spiritual pursuits, she prayed that she would become ugly so as not to be distracted by the attentions of would-be suitors. Her request was granted, and she lived out her days as an unattractive, albeit pious, nun under a big oak tree.

BACK TO LUTHER

When we last saw Martin Luther, he was in hiding at Wartburg Castle under the protection of Frederick of Saxony. It was during this period that Luther's career as a writer really took shape. He devoted his energies to translating the New Testament into German so that anyone could read it. This work was a natural extension of his belief that scripture is the ultimate authority. If that was true, then Luther felt that every person should have access to the scripture in a form he could understand. For the next twenty-five years, Luther wrote in German so that Christians could clearly understand his beliefs and see his side in the conflicts with the Catholic Church. He published an account of each of his conflicts with Rome so the people could judge the arguments for themselves. By doing so, he gave the ordinary Christian a place in the future of the church. Church doctrine was no longer just the property of the church hierarchy. It was also the property of any believer to accept or reject based on its scriptural merits. Luther's followers increased at an amazing rate.

In 1529, friends of Martin Luther and Ulrich Zwingli became concerned over doctrinal and political differences that had developed between the two reform leaders. They arranged a meeting between them at Marburg an der Lahn in west central Germany. At this meeting (known since then as the Marburg Colloquy), Luther and Zwingli clashed over the question of the Lord's Supper. Zwingli saw the Eucharist as a spiritual reception of the Lord's body. Luther saw it as something more concrete, and the two men could not reconcile their differences.

Also in 1529, at the Diet of Speyer, Emperor Charles V attempted to stop the movement Luther had created. Some of the German princes stood up in protest his actions, and the reform movement found a new name: Protestant. This was a defining moment in the reform movement. From this point on, the movement which had intended to reform the Catholic Church from within became separated from the church. It became known as the Protestant Reformation.

BREAKING NEWS

GERMAN COUNCIL SAYS SOME PROTESTANTS CAN WORSHIP FREELY!

Dateline: 1532
Nuremberg, Germany

A council declared today that Protestants can exercise their faith freely. This decision is not seen as permanent, however. Another council will be called within a year to reconsider the question.

A REFORMATION BY ANY OTHER NAME...
The label change between "reformers" and "Protestants" was an important one. The church had always had reformers. Some had even gone so far as to declare ideas that the church declared heretical. Many had been excommunicated. Almost all of them had tried to work their reforms within the framework of the church. The Protestant movement went further. There

were grave risks to be taken. The church still had the force of an earthly empire. Every decision could legally be judged in unkind ecclesiastical courts. There was no turning back. The Protestant movement was literally a revolution that sought to throw off the political and theological bounds of the Catholic Church and create something new. Martin Luther had a certain level of refuge in Germany. Temporarily Zwingli had the support of several Swiss cantons. The next wave of reform came from a Frenchman.

JOHN CALVIN

John Calvin was born in Noyon, France, on July 10, 1509. With a desire to become a priest, Calvin studied for the priesthood at the Collège de la Marche and the Collège de Montaigue. Calvin's father encouraged him to pursue a profession in the law instead of theology, and so the obedient son also attended the universities at Orléans and Bourges. It was in that study that Calvin began to appreciate humanist thinking and to be attracted to the reform movement. His first major publication was a commentary on Seneca's *De Clementia* in 1532. The work showed his great potential as a humanist scholar. Around that time, the young Calvin became friends with the new rector of the University of Paris, Nicholas Cop. In 1535, Cop came out publicly in support of Martin Luther, and he and his friend John Calvin had to flee Paris. It was also about this time that Calvin underwent a personal religious experience that affected him deeply.

For the next two years, Calvin was on the run. His association with Cop, as well as his emerging reformist beliefs, made it necessary for Calvin to avoid church authorities. During that time, he studied, wrote, and formulated from the Bible and Christian tradition the primary principles of his theology. In 1536, he published the first edition of his *Institutes of the Christian Religion*. This work sought to systematize Protestant thinking, and it almost immediately thrust Calvin into the forefront of Protestantism as a thinker and spokesman.

CALVIN FINDS GENEVA

During the same year, Calvin visited Geneva on his way to Strasbourg. While he was there, Guillaume Farel asked him to assist in the city's Reformation movement. Calvin accepted the offer and stayed in Geneva for the next two years. Then, in 1538, Farel fell out of favor in Geneva and both men were asked to leave. Calvin completed his interrupted journey to Strasbourg and worked there until September 1541. While he lived in Strasbourg, Calvin married a widow named Idelette de Bure. During their married life, the couple had one child who died in infancy. It was also during his time in Strasbourg (1539) that Calvin published the first of his many commentaries on books of the Bible, his *Commentary on Romans*.

In 1541, a group of Genevans asked Calvin to return and lead them again in reforming the church. Calvin took on that task and the task of improving the life of the city's citizens through better government. In many ways, he was the father of the city's constitution. He drafted the basic laws and ordinances that were adapted into a constitution for Geneva that governed both secular and sacred matters. Calvin also supported the development of a good public school system. The centerpiece of that system was the Geneva Academy for the very best students. That academy, begun in 1559, eventually became a full university.

Calvin was never to find a truly safe place. Geneva was under constant threat of Catholic armies seeking to destroy the city as a Protestant stronghold. Life was harsh there. People who dissented against the government or religious doctrine were often expelled from the city. There was even one man who was put to death as a heretic. Mostly, however, Calvin worked to improve life in the city. As a man who suffered with chronic bad health, existence in Geneva was often a hardship. However, his work there left a huge legacy of sermons and commentaries. He contracted a fever in 1558 which seriously weakened his already feeble health. He died on May 27, 1564, and was buried in an unmarked grave.

CALVIN'S THEOLOGY

Calvin was a man who loved organization. He showed a gift for applying organization to such matters as municipal management, but his real genius was in the systematization of the new Protestant theology. Whereas Luther in some ways reacted to the world around him, participating in disputes and debates as a means of presenting his beliefs, Calvin took a more methodical approach.

According to Calvin, the Bible was simply *the* authority. It was the authority not only on spiritual matters but also on the nature of all human institutions. Thus, his statements on doctrine began and ended in scripture. That is not to say that he did not frequently cite the church fathers and earlier thinkers. As we have seen, Augustine was an important influence on both Martin Luther and John Calvin. However, Calvin believed that a little speculation on divine questions went a long way, and he tried to tie all issues back to the Bible.

Calvin's masterwork was *Institutes of the Christian Religion*, which he revised at least five times between 1536 and 1559. In this work, Calvin tried to explain biblical theology in a sensible way, following the articles of the Apostles' Creed. The four books in the 1559 edition focus on the articles "Father," "Son," "Holy Spirit," and "Church."

FATHER

God created the world and made it good. Since the fall, however, man has tried to use his own powers to comprehend God. This seldom works toward any benefit. Fallen mankind simply cannot reach an understanding of God on its own that would allow for a full spiritual communion with God. Through the grace available through Jesus Christ as described in the Bible, God solved this problem and allowed mankind to see God clearly.

SON

Each person inherits the sin of Adam and Eve and is therefore worthy only of destruction. But Jesus Christ calls the elect into eternal life with God (the elect are believed by some to be those people selected by divine will for salvation). Christ invites the chosen into new life. He intercedes for them, and He reigns at God's right hand. In his writing, Calvin emphasized how the new Protestant doctrine was consistent with the orthodoxy of such statements of belief as the Nicene Creed.

SPIRIT

God's Holy Spirit, the third Person of the Trinity, gives power to the believer in four ways. He gives power to the reading of scripture so the reader can gain understanding. He gives power and vitality to the devotional life of believers. He is a powerful force in the Christian's growth in Christ, also called sanctification. The Holy Spirit also allows the Christian to have faith that through God's resurrection of the dead, He will bring the saved into His presence.

CHURCH

Through His grace, God also gives the world His church and the sacraments. The church and the two sacraments of baptism and the Eucharist were given for the edification of the elect and the good of the world. How can one know the real church? It can be recognized by the preaching and hearing of God's Word and the proper administration of the sacraments. Officers and leaders in the church should be those individuals who try to follow in Christian discipleship. Their authority cannot depend on their own righteousness, however.

PROTESTANT THEOLOGY

The theology which was revolutionary to the Catholic Church in the 1500s was nothing new. In fact, it was the boileddown theology of the church *before* the Middle Ages: It was scripture without the well-developed church hierarchy and tradition to assist or complicate it. The great reformers looked at this "pre-empire" church and saw three great principles that they wanted to return to.

GOD'S AUTHORITY IN THE WORD

The Protestant theologians believed that God spoke to His people. He instructed them, inspired them, and even convicted their hearts. They believed He did so through the Bible. As we have seen, the Bible was the sole authority over doctrine. It could only be so because it continued to speak to believers through the words that were spoken to the prophets and to the apostles. The Word was alive, not simply a text. It was the source for truth and could always be trusted.

It would be unfair to say that the Roman Catholic Church did not accept the authority of scripture. It did. However, it also placed *tradition* alongside scripture as pathways to the truth. The *tradition* was expressed in the decrees of popes and councils and was seen as the only legitimate interpretation of the Bible.

This *tradition* also included such church issues as music, architecture, and art. In that regard, the followers of Calvin's theology rejected these outward traditions much more than did the Lutherans. The Protestants agreed on rejecting many other elements of the Catholic faith which they did not think had a scriptural basis. They rejected the authority of the pope, the salvation benefit of good works, indulgences, the necessity of mediation by the Virgin Mary, the doctrine of transubstantiation, the doctrine of purgatory and prayer for the dead, private confession of sin to a priest, celibacy of the clergy, and the use of Latin. They also rejected all the sacraments which they believed had not been instituted by Christ. That eliminated all the sacraments but baptism and the Eucharist.

GRACE

Martin Luther's theology would change the world. His influence was felt by every reformer around him or after him. His theology was complex and was developed and described over many years, but all of it sprang from a few simple realizations. As a monk, Luther had been searching for God's pardon and peace. What he found instead was a new worldview and a new approach to communion with God.

In the monastery, Luther had seen and lived a life of devotion and study. He had obeyed his order and carried out his duties. Despite his efforts, he felt no closer to God at all. He recognized that mysticism was merely an attempt for man to climb his way up to God, an insurmountable task in Luther's mind. The academic theology he had studied and was supposed to teach was merely speculation about God, not the certain truths which could bring the peace for which he was seeking.

Luther recognized that all of these approaches had a fatal flaw. Each of them was based on a belief in man's ability to get close enough to God for Him to accept us. Luther realized that it was not a matter of God being far away from us and man having to strive to get nearer. Instead, the opposite was true. Because man was fallen and sinful, he was not on the long path to God. God had made the trip in the form of Jesus. God had come all the way to us through Christ.

This in itself was not a discovery of a new truth; it was the old gospel of grace which had become buried in church doctrine and practice. Where Luther differed was the means by which that grace comes to the believer. For Luther, the mechanism that brought grace to the believer was faith. Through faith the

 SET THE STAGE!

The Reformation had a profound effect on music of the day. Up to this time, almost all religious music was sung in Latin. Martin Luther and his followers understood the importance that music can play in a healthy spiritual life and encouraged more singing in church. They also stressed the importance of hymns sung in the native languages of worshipers as a means for facilitating a more personal involvement for churchgoers. This led to the creation of a new kind of music, called the *chorale*, which started in Luther's home country of Germany and was, in its original form, sung in German. Similarly, the liturgical musical forms of *service* and *anthem* were developed by the Church of England as the need arose for worship music in English. The Calvinists believed that only Scripture should be sung in church, and so they set many of the Psalms in French to music.

believer came into direct relation with Christ, who was the all-sufficient source of grace. That grace is made available by the power of the Holy Spirit expressed through the Word of God. This approach was in sharp contrast with the practice of the church. Church doctrine had placed levels of mediation and activity between the believer and grace. To the Protestants, however, these levels were obstacles. Since grace was available to each believer directly by faith, there was no need for the Virgin to mediate on his behalf; there was no need for the clergy to serve as priests; there was no need for the departed saints to serve as intercessors.

For the Roman Catholic, works were placed alongside God's grace as factors in salvation. A person could be justified, made acceptable to God, through good works and God's grace working along parallel lines. The Protestant did not disagree or disapprove of good works. However, the Protestant saw them as the product of justification, not a condition of it.

THE PRIESTHOOD OF BELIEVERS
In the Catholic Church, the priest acted as a mediator between the believer and God. The Protestants argued that there was no evidence in scripture that a Christian *needed* a priestly mediator. Every person could be his or her own priest. Thus, there was no longer a need to separate believers into the spiritual and lay camps. There was only one justification and that by grace through faith. Thus, there was only one status of all believers before God. Along these lines, the Protestants argued that within God's plan for His people, individuals were called to different tasks, teacher or farmer, preacher or merchant. Whatever the calling, it was the believer's responsibility to serve God through his situation.

HENRY VIII AND THE CHURCH OF ENGLAND
The stories of Luther, Zwingli, and Calvin can inspire us even if we disagree with their theology. The story of the birth of the Church of England does not inspire much admiration. It is crucial, however, not only to the history of Christianity but to the history of Europe, as well. Instead of the story beginning with a renowned theologian, it begins with a young prince.

HENRY VIII

King Henry VII of England had played politics on a big scale. He had ascended the throne as the victor in the War of the Roses. To win he had even used the help of the French, who were usually the dreaded enemy of the English. His eldest son, Arthur, died in 1502, leaving young Henry the heir to the throne at barely eleven years old. As the second son, his education to that point had not been aimed at the throne but at service in the church, the Roman Catholic Church, that is. But, after Arthur's death, Henry VII found himself with young Henry as heir and Arthur's widow hanging around. If she had not been Catherine of Aragon, it would not have been a big deal. But Arthur's marriage to the daughter of Queen Isabella of Spain had been quite a coup for Henry VII. He could not afford to injure relations with the Spanish Empire. So Henry VII made arrangements to marry Catherine to his younger son. Catherine was five years older than the young prince.

The king requested a special papal dispensation so that the widow could marry her brother-in-law. The negotiations went slowly, and near the end, Queen Isabella got impatient. As a result, she received a brief of the dispensation first, and then later she received the papal dispensation itself. These two documents were to cause trouble later. Though the young prince officially protested the marriage, some nine weeks after his father's death in 1509, he carried out the marriage contract.

Under his leadership, but especially the leadership of Wolsey in the council chamber, England truly became a European power. In 1512, he joined with Pope Julius II, Ferdinand of Spain, and the Venetians to form the "Holy League." This alliance was put together to drive the king of France and other foreign influences out of Italy. Though there were no glittering successes, Henry was on good terms with the pope, who awarded him the golden rose in 1510. In 1514, the new pope, Leo X, bestowed on him the honorific cap and sword.

As soon as the "league" broke up, Henry formed an alliance with the king of France. This alliance held great power on the continent. In 1515, Henry's advisor, Wolsey, was made a cardinal, and he came to influence the young king more and more.

However, in 1519, he was against the secret negotiations over Henry's efforts to become the Holy Roman Emperor. Both Henry and the king of France were outdone, many say outspent, by Charles V of Spain, who was elected to the post.

HENRY: DEFENDER OF THE FAITH

With that in place, Henry spent the next few years in the complicated struggle that erupted between France and the Holy Roman Empire. He also worked on his theology. In 1521, he published an attack against Luther, *Assertio Septem Sacramentorum*. In this work the king vindicates the church's dogmatic teaching concerning the sacraments and the celebration of the Mass. Henry also insists upon the supremacy of the papacy. Pope Leo X was so pleased that he conferred upon the king the title of "Defender of the Faith." So far, Henry had not shown much potential as a Reformer.

Henry's marriage with Catherine had produced a child, Mary. But, his problems with the church started in 1527 when he fell in love with Anne Boleyn. His being married put him in a terrible position. He felt that divorce was the only answer. In those days, despite the church's official policy against divorces, the pope had certainly been known to issue some if there was some good reason, and the divorce might work to the advantage of the church. Henry's case was a flop on both accounts. Henry had it privately rumored that there were some doubts concerning his daughter Mary's legitimacy. When that effort went nowhere, Henry turned to the lawyer's approach.

Since there were two, possibly contradictory, documents establishing Henry's right to marry his sister-in-law, Henry's people argued that the Julius II bull of dispensation had been obtained through false pretenses, and that the marriage was *never* legal. Henry might have even gotten his way with this one except for a few entanglements. The Holy Roman Emperor had tremendous sway over the pope in those days, and there was no love between Charles V and Henry VIII. Charles V was totally opposed to the divorce for personal reasons, in addition to his religious convictions against it. The single biggest reason was that Catherine was his aunt, his mother's sister. By divorcing Catherine, Henry VIII would be heaping shame at the feet of the emperor's family. He simply could not allow the pope to go along with Henry's charade, and the pope did not. In July 1529, the pope refused the appeal of the English king's envoys.

The refusal was the downfall of Wolsey and the occasion that propelled Thomas Cranmer and Thomas Cromwell into leadership. It was Cranmer who recommended in the fall of 1529 that his king should consult the leading thinkers and theologians of the day on the question of his marriage to Catherine. Henry loved the idea and soon the "investigation" was underway. Of course, the results turned out as planned, and the answers were presented to Parliament. As Parliament debated on what to do, Thomas Cromwell was making his influence felt. It was his idea that Henry should simply throw off the papal supremacy and declare himself the head of his own religion. To do so, they first had to discredit the church. Starting in 1529, the king's advisors began to discredit church leaders. One of the first victims was Henry's former advisor, Cardinal Wolsey.

HENRY GETS HIS WAY

In 1530, Parliament passed an edict which forbade the payment of a yearly tax to Rome and solicited the king to solve his difficulties with the pope. This was, of course, a barely veiled threat to withhold the money indefinitely unless the divorce was granted. By the summer of 1532, the king's chancellor, Sir Thomas More, resigned since he could no longer do what the king asked him. By August 1532, Henry had appointed Cranmer as his archbishop of Canterbury, and he had complete control over the church in England. On April 15, 1533, Cranmer was consecrated, and, on May 23, he declared Henry's marriage to Catherine invalid. On May 28, he declared the marriage with (the very pregnant) Anne Boleyn valid. On June 1, she was crowned queen, and on September 7 she gave birth to a daughter, the future Queen Elizabeth.

If Henry acted quickly that summer, Pope Clement did, as well. On July 11, 1533, the pope issued a bull of excommunication against Henry. Over the course of the next year, the breach between the Roman Church and England was completed. An Act of Succession was passed, which placed the succession of the English throne with Anne Boleyn's children. The Act required an oath be sworn to uphold it. Thomas More simply would not sign the oath and was imprisoned in the Tower of London. He was executed in 1535. There were other martyrs, but most clergy were willing, under the threat of death, to declare that "the bishop of Rome hath no greater jurisdiction conferred upon him by God than any other foreign bishop."

In November 1534, the Parliament went one step further and issued the Act of Supremacy, which declared the king the "Supreme Head of the Church of England." Thomas Cromwell was rewarded for his help in the matter by being named the vicar general to rule the church in the king's name. He began a "reign of terror" against the Catholic establishment that still existed. Monasteries were looted and their treasures seized. Properties owned by the church were either seized by the king or given to the wealthy nobility to keep them appeased.

HENRY AND HIS CHURCH

Though Henry used the emotional energy of the church reformers whenever it was beneficial, he remained a product of the old Catholic sacramental system. In 1539, the Statute of the Six Articles enforced a doctrine that was almost entirely Catholic. The Statute punished nonconformance with such religious beliefs as transubstantiation (the bread and wine actually become Christ's body), confession to a priest, and the celibacy of the clergy. The king was no reformer of doctrine. In fact, he oppressed through inquisition-type practices any nonconformance with the very traditional doctrine he wanted for his church. There were many executions. For example, on July 30, 1540, there were six executions. Three of the victims were Reformers executed for heretical doctrine. The other three were Catholics who were hanged and quartered for denying the king's supremacy. Such was the beginning of the Church of England.

MEANWHILE...OUTSIDE THE PALACE

As we have seen, the Church of England did not grow out of a revolutionary new doctrine. Nor did it develop as a ground swell of reform or as a public decision to establish a Protestant state as in Geneva or Zürich. It came about because of the machinations of a king who happened to run afoul of the Catholic hierarchy. Most historians agree that prior to Henry's actions, England was a remarkably orthodox place. There were a few Lollards (those who followed the teachings of John Wycliffe) still around, but these were in no way a threat to the orthodox Church in England. Luther was known but had few followers there. Part of the reason that Henry VIII was even considered as the Holy Roman Emperor was that he was seen to run a very orthodox, nonreformist country.

As we have also seen, Henry's Church of England was, for all intents and purposes, the Roman Church without the pope or a monastic system. There must have been incredible confusion among the people. There was certainly fear, much of it justified.

MEANWHILE...WITH THE ROMAN CATHOLICS

Since the fourteenth century, there had been a growing demand in the church for reform. Efforts to reform it, however, had been by quarrels within the church, particularly the Great Schism. As we have seen, the result was that the church became home to many ills such as simony, worldliness, corruption among the higher clergy, ignorance in the priesthood, and general spiritual apathy. It was not until 1534, when Paul III became pope and St. Ignatius of Loyola founded the Jesuits, that major reform began.

Pope Paul recognized the desperate need for a reassessment of the church and called an ecumenical council to consider it. After much negotiation with the French king and the Holy Roman Emperor, Trent in northern Italy was determined to be the site. The topic of the council was monumental: The church had to respond to the split in the church and try to renew the Roman Church by reforming it.

SINNERS AND SAINTS
IGNATIUS LOYOLA (1491–1556)

Ignatius Loyola was a Basque soldier who converted in 1521 while recovering from a serious wound. He began to study religion and to seek the truth as Luther had. But whereas Luther found truth by rejecting the traditions of the medieval church, Loyola found it in the strict observance of Christianity in the medieval tradition. He wrote an account of his spiritual pilgrimage and published it as *The Spiritual Exercises*. In 1534, in Paris, he and five others took vows of poverty and chastity as the founding members of a new religious order, the Society of Jesus (the Jesuits). The six were ordained in 1537. In 1538, they were received by the pope, and in 1540, Loyola won papal approval for his new religious order. In 1541, he was elected general of the order, a post he held until his death.

THE COUNCIL OF TRENT

The council met in three main sessions: 1545–1547, 1551–1552, and 1562–1563. These sessions were three different gatherings with varied attendance. The first was the smallest. It opened with only four archbishops, twenty bishops, four generals of monastic orders, and a few theologians. The second was larger with the largest number of attendants being fifty-nine. The final session was by far the largest. The meetings of that session had as many as 255 participants.

This third session was also the most productive. The participants reexamined many areas of Catholic doctrine, especially those that had come under fire from the Protestants. The council reaffirmed medieval orthodoxy in areas such as transubstantiation, justification through faith *and* works, the celibacy of the clergy, and the seven sacraments. The doctrine of purgatory and the doctrine of the indulgence were both declared right and proper. However, the church job of indulgence-seller was abolished, and the abuses of the indulgence system were condemned. In addition, the authority of the pope was confirmed, and his power was actually increased by giving him the right to enforce the decrees of the council and by requiring church officials to promise obedience to the pope. In the end, the reforms triggered by the council touched all aspects of religious life and set the pattern of modern Catholicism.

THE JESUITS

The Jesuits became the council's reformers in the field. Loyola's order was quite unusual. It had no special uniform; it required no special penance or fasts; it required no choral recitation of a daily liturgy. It did require years of training (as many as fifteen years was common) and obedience, especially to the pope. The Jesuit was to develop a strong inner life based on meditation and on Loyola's *Spiritual Exercises*.

An important weapon of their Counter-Reformation efforts was education. The Jesuits founded schools and performed extensive missionary work. The schools helped to keep children in the orthodox faith. They also provided the church with well-educated, orthodox leaders.

The Jesuits were not founded to fight Protestantism, but as the Reformation gained strength in the sixteenth and seventeenth centuries, it became a priority. With their close ties to the papacy, the Jesuits were a natural choice when a pope tried to "cement" relations with a country leaning toward Protestantism. They were an effective force both in reforming the Catholic Church and in spreading the word of traditional Catholic doctrine.

MEANWHILE...BACK TO ENGLAND

Even though many of his enemies may have felt differently, even Henry VIII had to die sometime. His rule over his people was powerful, and though he had officially pulled England away from the Catholic Church, his personal doctrine and the doctrine of his church were very much orthodox Catholicism. After his death, his young son, Edward VI, assumed the throne, and England truly entered the Protestant Reformation.

The man who would bring England into the Protestant Reformation was Henry's archbishop of Canterbury, Thomas Cranmer. Cranmer was one of the architects of the king's divorce, and he had been well rewarded. However, the archbishop had become familiar with Luther's writings and influenced by them. There was not much he could change about the Anglican Church as long as Henry lived, however. When Edward VI became king, Cranmer became one of his regents. He seized that opportunity to bring England into the Reformation.

 DID YOU KNOW?

The first 22 popes were later made saints. Number 23, Novatian, was not canonized. The next 14 popes after Novatian were sainted.

In all, nearly 80 of the 264 popes recognized by the Catholic Church have been sainted. The last pope canonized was St. Pius V, who reigned in the sixteenth century.

With the help of a scholar named Nicholas Ridley and a preacher named Hugh Latimer, Cranmer moved forward to transform the Anglican Church into a Protestant entity. He removed images from churches and allowed the clergy to marry. His policies encouraged Calvinist scholars such as Martin Bucer and Peter Martyr to come to Oxford and Cambridge to teach. All of these reforms went to the issues in conflict with the Catholic Church, but the real issue in question for Cranmer was the worship service. The Mass was still said in Latin yet was neither Catholic nor Protestant.

So Cranmer headed a committee to develop a new liturgy that would be comfortable to both the Catholic and the Protestant. The resulting work, the *Book of Common Prayer*, was a compromise. The liturgy used stately ritual like the Catholic Mass, but certain elements were removed that would offend Protestants. In 1549, Parliament passed a law, the Act of Uniformity, that made the use of this liturgy the law.

As time passed, the Protestant Reformation became even more of a force in England, and by 1552 the first edition of the *Book of Common Prayer* was considered too Catholic. It was

SINNERS AND SAINTS

WILLIAM TYNDALE

William Tyndale had a great idea: the Word of God in the language that people actually spoke. He saw it as a way to enable people to come to faith. Tyndale didn't realize that in order to translate the Bible into English he would have to flee his own country and send it back in as contraband.

That's what happened, though. Eventually Tyndale was imprisoned and then killed because of his translation work—and the power it may have cost the church leadership.

replaced that year with a second, more Protestant edition.

ENGLAND...A MICROCOSM?

While English history is a prominent factor in the Reformation, that certainly does not imply that things of great importance were not happening elsewhere. After all, this was still the age of discovery and early colonization. There were several main powers in Europe: France, Spain, the empire of the Holy Roman Emperor, and England. The Holy Roman Emperor was trapped between the orthodoxy of the pope on one side and the Lutheranism of German princes on the other. The Spanish were immersed in their own race for power and wealth. Their empire was the largest in the world and was growing daily. South America was divided between the Spanish and the Portuguese. The era would bring other countries to greater power. Explorers from the Netherlands and various states in Italy were increasing their circles of power. The church reached as far as Japan when, in 1549, the missionary St. Francis Xavier arrived there.

England was still growing in power and influence. Henry VIII had taken advantage of his father's successes, and soon England would have another powerful ruler who would even take on the Spanish—Elizabeth I. Before her reign, however, England went through a very difficult period that illustrates the types of issues occurring throughout Europe at that time.

BLOODY MARY

In 1553, the short reign of England's Edward VI came to an end when the young king died of tuberculosis. He was only fifteen years old when he died at Greenwich on July 6. His death threw the issue of succession into a mess. He was succeeded by his Catholic half sister Mary, who was then thirty-seven years old and the daughter of Henry and his first wife, Catherine of Aragon. For political purposes, a treaty of marriage was arranged between Mary and Spain's Philip, who was the son of the Holy Roman Emperor Charles V. Under the terms of the treaty, Philip was to be given the title of King of England but was to have no hand in the government and have no right to succeed Mary. With her familial connections made back to the Holy Roman Emperor, Mary began a plan to restore the Catholic faith to England.

She was assisted in this effort by Cardinal Pole. Pole was a Catholic humanist who was sympathetic to certain Protestant beliefs, such as justification by faith. As cardinal archbishop of Canterbury, he was charged with the task of restoring a faith that had been discredited for many years under Henry VIII and Edward VI. He would probably have had much more success without the interference of the queen. She wanted the Protestant movement stopped in England, and in her bigotry and intolerance, she did not care what methods were used.

In 1555, she began a persecution of Protestants. With the support of the Catholic Church and her ties to the orthodox Catholic Spanish monarchy, she felt confident to turn the tables on the Protestants who had sought to destroy the Catholic Church in England. Mary carried out her own reign of terror. Under her direction, about three hundred Protestants, including the archbishop of Canterbury Thomas Cranmer, were executed. For this persecution she came to be known as *Bloody Mary*. In the end she probably caused much damage to the Catholic cause in England by creating intense hostility toward her on behalf of the English people. Her effort to reconvert England was not just terror and reprisals, however. She also caused legislation to be enacted that sought to reinstate the Catholic Church.

Even those efforts were reason for hostility from her people. In the end, she was a hateful queen who was hated by her people.

ELIZABETH I

Elizabeth I was crowned November 17, 1558. Mary Tudor had died at age forty-two and was succeeded by her half sister Elizabeth, who was now twenty-five. Mary had been the daughter of a rejected Catholic wife; Elizabeth was the child of Anne Boleyn, who had been the cause of the king's divorce. Though Elizabeth's mother had been subsequently executed in 1536, Elizabeth had become a Protestant sympathizer.

Elizabeth permanently reestablished Protestantism in England during her reign. She was a woman of incredible bravery. Reestablishing the Anglican faith in England meant political troubles with the two other European powers. Both France and Spain had taken a hard line against Protestantism. Elizabeth's approach was not conciliatory to her two royal counterparts.

Elizabeth was wise in her approach, however. She worked slowly to replace Catholic Church officials with Protestants. She renewed the use of the *Book of Common Prayer*. She took the title "supreme governor" of the church, not "head" of the Church of England. She maintained an ecclesiastical hierarchy and a liturgy in the Anglican Church, a move that angered many Calvinists who were coming to England as refugees from Switzerland. Her real threat came from the Catholics, however. They saw that she was building great power in England, and many Catholics intrigued and plotted against the queen. They were doing so on orders of the pope, who had instructed Catholics to oppose Elizabeth. The conflict between the Protestants and Catholics and the conflict between England and its European peers both mixed together in a terrible mess. Somehow, however, Queen Elizabeth was able to reign long and well under those circumstances and establish a powerful European state that was truly Protestant.

JOHN KNOX AND SCOTLAND

The sixteenth century was terrible for Scotland. Its nobles led the country into confusion with their friendships and alliances with both England and France. Scotland was also in the middle of the action in the conflict between Protestant and Catholic.

Lutheranism had come to Scotland early. By 1528, a Lutheran preacher named Patrick Hamilton had been burned at the stake there. Another Protestant leader, George Wishart, was executed in 1548. His execution had been ordered by the Catholic Cardinal Beaton. After Wishart's death, a group of Protestant rebels responded by killing the cardinal. When French forces were sent in to seize the rebels, they captured John Knox, who had been a Wishart supporter. As a result, Knox spent nineteen months as a galley slave. After he was released, he moved to Protestant England, where he stayed until Mary I came to the throne. Then, like many English Protestants, Knox fled to Europe, ending up in Geneva, where he became one of John Calvin's most attentive disciples.

While he was away, Scotland became even more Catholic with the marriage of Mary, Queen of Scots (not Bloody Mary), to the heir of the French (and very Catholic) throne. Along with many of his countrymen, Knox was afraid of what would happen to Scotland under Catholic French control. He returned to his home country in 1559 and helped lead a literal Protestant revolution against Mary. The Protestant forces won, and in 1560 the parliament passed a Calvinistic profession of faith written by Knox and others. The Parliament stated that the pope had no authority in Scotland and that the Mass was forbidden.

To replace the Catholic order of the country, Knox and others composed the *Book of Discipline*, which set up an entire Presbyterian church government. It also set out the plan for an entire educational system, including universities. To guide the Presbyterian worship in the absence of Catholic liturgy, Knox wrote the *Book of Common Order*, which owes a debt to the teachings of John Calvin.

MEANWHILE...BACK IN ENGLAND

Though the Church of England had been operating independently of Rome since its creation by Henry VIII in 1534 (except
for the rule of Mary I), its episcopal basis was not established
until the adoption of the *Thirty-nine Articles* in 1563. The articles
are not officially acknowledged as a binding creed or confession
of faith, but they do record the doctrinal foundations on which
Anglican tradition grew.

The *Thirty-nine Articles* was the product of the Convocation
of Canterbury of the Church of England. Parliament gave them
the status as statutory law in 1571. It was the final product in a
process that aimed at providing a doctrinal uniformity to the
Church doctrine. The process had proceeded through the *Ten
Articles* of 1536, the *Bishops' Book* of 1537, the *Six Articles* in
1539, the *King's Book* in 1543, and the *Forty-two Articles* in 1553.
Thomas Cranmer, archbishop of Canterbury under Henry VIII
and Edward VI, was the primary author of the *Forty-two Articles*.
These were revised by Matthew Parker, who was archbishop
under Elizabeth I.

The doctrine that appeared in the *Thirty-nine Articles* was
mostly Protestant; however, the church service was still liturgical. This liturgy was reminiscent of the liturgy established by the
Council of Trent by the Catholic Church. Further, the church was
set up to have a hierarchy similar to that of the Roman Catholic
Church with the exception that the monarch of England is
named as the head of the church, not a religious leader.

Many Christians in England were simply not happy with
the adoption of the *Thirty-nine Articles*. Some felt that the doctrine was *too* Protestant and that too much of the Catholic influence of the church had been lost. Others felt that the church
had sold out as a Protestant body, and that some changes
would have to be made. The influence of these people would be
felt throughout Europe and into the New World.

A LITTLE TOUR OF GERMANY

In Germany, Luther's challenge to the church had made him
a hero. The powerful landowners of Germany, even if they

were not religious, did not want to pay tax to Rome. The Reformation "took off" in Germany. Following Luther's death, the Holy Roman Emperor decided to make war against the Protestants in Germany. The reformers realized this and organized the Schmalkald League, a kind of defensive alliance. War broke out in 1547, and the emperor was successful. However, the Protestant Maurice of Saxony fought back well. The Treaty of Passau ended the conflict and made the recognition of Protestantism official.

A LITTLE TOUR OF SWITZERLAND
The Reformation in Switzerland had heard of Martin Luther, but it was an independent effort. Zwingli and Calvin worked to create Christian societies in Zürich and Geneva, respectively. After their deaths, Zwingli and Calvin were replaced by Bullinger and Beza, respectively. These men pushed the Reformation forward and exported their Reformation to France, Holland, England, and Germany.

A LITTLE TOUR OF THE NETHERLANDS
In the Netherlands, the Reformation was originally inspired by Luther. There were martyrs for Lutheranism as early as 1523 in the Netherlands. As time passed, the Reformation there became more and more influenced by Calvinism.

Either way, the Netherlands was a terrible place to be a Protestant at that time. The Netherlands was ruled by Spain, which remained orthodox and committed to its Catholic traditions. It is said that the Spanish duke of Alva was responsible for the persecution and deaths of over 100,000 Christians between 1567 and 1573. However, the reform movement continued in its strong desire to have independence from Spain. In 1584, the northern Netherlands formed a federation under William the Silent trying to free themselves from under the thumb of the Roman church and the Spanish crown. After a long struggle they were successful.

A LITTLE TOUR OF FRANCE

The Reformation was different in France. In Germany and Switzerland, when the message of the Reformation had been preached, it had taken hold. France was different in that the people offered little support for the movement. Without the ground swell of support, the early reformers were simply executed. Nevertheless, Calvinism did catch on slowly. By 1555, there was a Calvinist congregation in Paris. Seventy-two churches were represented at a synod of French Calvinist churches in 1559. By the early 1660s, there were as many as two thousand churches with 400,000 members. These Protestants became known as Huguenots.

There had been fighting between the Huguenots and Catholics in 1562 that erupted in a massacre of Huguenots at Vassy. The Huguenots fought back, however, and the conflict settled into a protracted struggle.

In 1572, there was hope that the two sides of the battle in France, Calvinist versus Catholic, could be reconciled to each other. After all, there was a royal wedding in the works. The groom, Henry of Navarre, came from a strong Protestant family. The bride was a solid Catholic. She was Marguerite of Valois, sister of King Charles IX and daughter of the powerful Catholic woman Catherine de Medici.

A MASSACRE OF PROTESTANTS

As Catherine planned Marguerite's wedding, some historians believe she also planned the assassination of the Huguenot leader, Gaspard de Coligny. While Catherine's role is disagreed upon by many, supposedly her son (the king and brother of the bride) commented to Marguerite, "Why don't you just kill all the Huguenots in France, so that there will be none left to hate me." However it happened, on August 24, 1572, St. Bartholomew's day, Coligny was murdered in his room, and mobs were formed to hunt down other Huguenots in Paris.

The Huguenots were easy to find since they were mostly prosperous business people in the city. Soon what had started as a small attack turned into a bloodbath. The lower class, fueled by resentment for the middle class, turned against their fellow citizens and started murdering Huguenots. Even children were killed in the melee. Hundreds of people were killed, their bodies piling up in the streets. Others were just pushed into the Seine, denying them the opportunity for a decent burial.

 SET THE STAGE!

According to Henri Estienne, the name "Huguenot" is from the practice of the French Protestants of meeting at night near the gate of King Hugo.

The violence that started in Paris spilled over into the countryside. Catherine was finally able to stop the violence in Paris by having the king issue a statement that there was no purge of Huguenots going on, that the people killed had been part of a huge conspiracy. Despite orders from the king to the provincial governors, the killing went wild throughout the country.

There was a particularly terrible incident in Lyons. There, the Huguenots were literally herded into a monastery for their own protection. When the monastery became too crowded, they were moved into a prison. Despite these precautions, a mob stormed the prison and killed all those inside. Throughout the country these kinds of incidents became commonplace.

Some estimate that as many as 100,000 Huguenots were killed in this uprising. Amazingly, however, the spirit of the Huguenots was not broken by it, and they somehow survived. Between 1572 and 1589, there were five more civil wars between the Roman Catholics and the Huguenots in France. After the last of these wars, the groom at the wedding mentioned above, Henry of Navarre, became king. As he had done before, he held his own Protestantism in check for political reasons. He did try to help the Protestants a little with the Edict of Nantes.

EDICT OF NANTES

The Edict of Nantes gave the Huguenots a certain amount of religious freedom in France. They were given political control in certain parts of the country. However, the Roman Catholic religion was still the official religion of the state, and the Catholics controlled the vast majority of the country. The Edict did not settle the conflict between Protestants and Catholics in France. It did create an uneasy truce. That truce was finally revoked by King Louis XIV in 1685. Interestingly, the Jesuits were largely responsible for its revocation. Their tactic worked: Thousands of people reconverted to Catholicism. Fear was a strong motivator.

Thousands more Huguenots fled France to Germany, Geneva, England, and America. Since the Huguenots were largely middle-class, skilled people, some historians say that this exodus was large enough to impact the French economy. Regardless, the persecution of the French Protestants was a dark spot in the history of the Reformation but a bright one for the spread of Protestantism throughout the New World.

MEANWHILE...BACK ACROSS THE ENGLISH CHANNEL

The reign of Elizabeth was one of the most amazing eras in history. England blossomed as a true world power by taking advantage of an idea as old as Alfred the Great. Elizabeth built on the policies of her grandfather (Henry VII) and father (Henry VIII) and built the English navy into a truly formidable force. To that point, the English at sea were better known as pirates attacking Spanish shipping in the West Indies. Even noblemen such as Sir Francis Drake had sunk a Spanish frigate or two. An attack on a Spanish ship was technically an act of war, but in reality, the attacks were mostly piratical. That, of course, was fine with Queen Elizabeth, but it did provide her with little plausible deniability.

By 1588, the tensions between Spain and England had grown so great that King Philip II of Spain launched a great fleet for the purpose of invading England. The Spanish Armada was commanded by the Duque de Medina-Sidonia and consisted of 130 ships and a force of thirty thousand sailors and soldiers. The Armada's mission was troubled from the start. It was delayed by storms and finally set sail from Lisbon in May 1588. The English fleet, commanded by Charles Howard, sailed from Plymouth and confronted the Armada. It was able to inflict some long-range damage on the Armada, but the experienced Spanish sailors

SINNERS AND SAINTS
LOUIS XIV

The reign of Louis XIV lasted seventy-two years, longer than any monarch in modern European history. Born in 1638, Louis officially became king at the age of four when his father died, and though his mother ruled on his behalf for a time, he took full control of the office in his early teens. Bent on returning France to her previous glory, Louis entered into four major wars during his tenure, and though he won back many formerly French territories, he created enemies all over Europe in doing so. He also found ways to make enemies within his own country: Louis was a staunch Catholic and made Cardinal Mazarin (who was his godfather) chief minister of France. Mazarin's unpopular policies led to an uprising among the nobles which took several years to quash. Additionally, the reign of Louis XIV was marked by vicious persecution of the Huguenots (French Protestants). For nearly a century, the Edict of Nantes had provided Huguenots freedom of religion, but Louis revoked the Edict in 1685 and made things so hard on Protestants that thousands, including many important businessmen and craftsmen, fled France for fear of their lives. Lavish living was a hallmark of the French king. He built an ornate palace the size of a city and housed all of France's nobility there (so he could keep an eye on them, no doubt). Even his nicknames ran to excess: He usually referred to himself as the "Sun King," but other monikers included "God-given," "Louis the Great," and "The Grand Monarch." He also allegedly said *"L'etet, c'est moi,"* which translates as "I *am* the State." Louis *did* have a better side, however, and was well known as a patron of art and music. (Does anyone remember Nero?)

did not break their formation. If they had, they could have been picked to pieces. The Armada anchored off Calais. The Spanish commander had intended to pick up Alessandro Farnese's army in Flanders and take it to England for the attack. But on August 7, the English set ships on fire and sent them into the Spanish anchorage to scatter the Armada. Then they attacked the fleeing ships at close range. The Armada escaped to the north and was forced to sail around Scotland and Ireland before returning to Spain. They had lost half of their ships in the failed mission.

England came out of the conflict as a major sea power. This laid the groundwork for England's vast colonial empire, beginning, of course, with North America.

JAMES I

Elizabeth died in 1603, after an amazing forty-five-year reign. Her reign ended the 118 years of the Tudor family on the throne of England. She was succeeded by the son of the former Scottish queen, Mary Queen of Scots. James VI of Scotland was crowned James I of England in 1603. He began the reign of the Stuart family over England.

One of his first accomplishments was making peace with Spain in 1604. With that conflict out of the way, he concentrated on the colonization of America. He also concentrated on the religious situation in the country. In January 1604, he presided over a conference at the palace at Hampton Court. The conference included both Anglicans and Puritans (a reformist branch of the Anglicans). The conference issued a proclamation that enforced the Act of Uniformity and banished Jesuits and seminary priests. The Jesuits were seen as a disruptive tool of the Catholic Church, which created conflict for Protestants wherever they went.

KING JAMES BIBLE

The conference also commissioned nearly 450 scholars to retranslate the Old and New Testaments. The scholars were to work to create the best English translation they could. The king's concern with the existing Bibles was that he had seen notes scribbled in the margins of many Bibles that questioned the divine right of a

THE MORE THINGS CHANGE. . .
(Death, Taxes, and Other Immutables)

In the early 1600s, King James I of Britain became one of the first antitobacco activists, publishing a pamphlet on the dangers of smoking.

king to rule. He planned that *his* translation would have no such scribbling.

The translation that resulted from these scholars' work was the King James Version published in 1611. The translation was a work of exceptional poetic beauty and variety. It became, and still is, a standard beside which Bible translations are measured.

THE PURITANS

Not everyone was happy with the Anglican Church. Under Elizabeth's rule the church remained much as it had under her father's. Cranmer's *Thirty-nine Articles* in 1563 had defined Anglicanism, but for some the church had not gone far enough to throw off its Catholic roots. During Elizabeth's reign there developed a group that desired the church to be more reformed, more like John Calvin's church in Geneva. The members of this group worked to purify the Anglican Church of its Catholic practices and were therefore called "Puritans."

Under Elizabeth, the Puritans wanted mainly to eliminate some of the ceremonies that were held over from the Catholic Church, such as use of the cross at baptism and kneeling at communion. Many of the Puritans wanted to do away with bishops and have the church run by elders and synods. Though the Puritans had strong support in Parliament in the early years of Elizabeth's

DID YOU KNOW?

In 1675, Dr. Robert Wilde made a bequest to Cambridgeshire, England's All Saints Parish Church of St. Ives. The bequest provided for six Bibles to be awarded annually to one of a dozen children, the winner being the one with the best dice throws *upon the church altar*. The yearly gamble continues to this day.

reign, the queen would not allow any tampering with the church. When James I ascended the throne, he was equally against the Puritans' changes.

SEPARATISTS AND CONGREGATIONALISTS

As a result, many Puritans felt frustrated within the church. In the second half of the sixteenth century, some of these Puritans broke away and formed an-other group, the Separatists. This group was led by Robert Brown and Robert Harrison. Brown was the pastor, and Harrison acted as the teacher of the church. They withdrew completely from the Anglican church and in time became the English Independent or Congregationalist movement.

 **SET THE STAGE!**

Although many people came to America for religious freedom, that didn't always mean they were interested in tolerating the beliefs of oth-ers. In 1647, Massachusetts passed a law which barred Roman Catholic priests from entering areas controlled by the Puritans.

Because of religious per-secution from the Anglicans, many of these Separatists left England altogether and moved to the Netherlands. The Dutch were more tolerant of reli-gious nonconformity. Eventually, some of the Separatists living in the Netherlands emigrated to New England as the Pilgrims.

THE PILGRIMS

On November 11, 1620, the *Mayflower* out of Southampton arrived off Cape Cod with 102 Pilgrims aboard. Two of their number were babies who were born on the sixty-six-day trip. These Pilgrims had emigrated to the Netherlands in 1608, but had decided in 1617 to seek a new home in order to preserve their English identity. They had obtained a patent from the London Company to settle in America.

Upon arriving in the New World, the colonists discovered that Cape Cod was outside the jurisdiction of their license, and so they chose Plymouth instead. Before they disembarked, they signed the Mayflower Compact. This agreement established a form of government based on the will of the colonists rather than on that of the Crown. By their signing of the document, a new type of society was created in America. The Pilgrims were opening a new era with their religious independence and their democratic approach.

WE NEED A TRIP TO...GERMANY

Germany was not a calm place during the Reformation. There was a strong current of conflict between the Holy Roman Emperor and the reform-minded Germans. The other factor at play was the comparative disunity of the country. Whereas the French, Spanish, and English kings had more or less subdued the nobility, the German nobility was never really subservient. For many of them, the Reformation was an excuse for political rebellion. During the second half of the sixteenth century, there was a great increase in tension in Germany. Then, in 1618, the Jesuit-educated Ferdinand II became emperor and king of Bohemia. Religious tensions came to a head as anti-Protestant violence broke out in Bohemia. The Bohemian nobles appealed to Ferdinand for protection but none was offered. As a consequence, they rose in a revolt against the king and emperor. The war began as a conflict between the Calvinists and the Catholics. Though Lutheranism had been legalized in 1555, Calvinism had not, a point that was constant trouble for the Calvinist nobles.

The 1618 revolt began when the Calvinist nobles declared that Ferdinand II was deposed. They then named the ruler of the Palatinate, one of the major German states, as the new emperor. When the ruler of the Palatinate accepted the crown, the fighting began. What began as a war between Calvinists and Catholics eventually involved the Lutherans, Danes, Swedes, and even the French. The conflict dragged on sporadically for thirty years. Finally, between 1643 and 1648, a treaty was hammered out in the German province of Westphalia. That treaty was known as the Peace of Westphalia.

The thirty years of war had destroyed Germany. Only one province, Brandenburg, escaped major destruction. Much German culture was destroyed, and the economy was shattered.

Mercenary troops from Bohemia, Denmark, France, Spain, Sweden, and the German states themselves had destroyed roughly eighteen thousand villages, fifteen hundred towns, and two thousand castles. It would take decades for the country to recover. The Peace of Westphalia signaled the end of religious wars in Europe.

MEANWHILE...BACK IN ENGLAND

The Peace of Westphalia did not mark the end of civil wars in Europe with religious causes, however. Under the reigns of James I and Charles I, there was rising discontentment with the Anglican church. The Puritans pushed constantly for a more Calvinist Church while the king pushed for more and more power to the episcopal system (the hierarchy by which the power of the church lay with the bishops, not the local churches). The argument was a harbinger of things to come for the next 150 years.

A strong episcopal system was easily controlled by the king. He could simply have "his" people in key positions and the church would be no threat to his authority. If the church reformed along Calvinist lines, a form of democracy would take over. In lieu of bishops, there would be elders and synods. The king's authority over the church would be severely reduced, and as kings had known for centuries (all the way back to Constantine in the Christian church), the leader who does not control the church is controlled by it.

To complicate the matter, both James and Charles had strong familial roots in Scotland, which was strongly Calvinist. Both kings tried to make the Scots conform to the Anglican religion, and the results were terrible. Charles also had terrible problems with Parliament. In 1640 he called for a Parliament, (which was fully within the power of the king) and when it was elected, it strongly opposed him. In that same year he called for the election of another Parliament. This Parliament was largely Puritan, and the king began to have real trouble with it. In 1642, the civil war began as Charles I sent his Cavaliers against the Puritan parliament at York. Early in 1643, this parliament completely abolished the episcopal system. To design and implement something in its

THE MORE THINGS CHANGE...

(Death, Taxes, and Other Immutables)

Hair has played a pivotal role in how people are perceived throughout history. Mary's act of drying Christ's feet with her hair is seen as a purposeful sign of her conversion. Samson's long hair was a symbol of the strength God granted him.

Many nations cut the hair of prisoners or army recruits. Aztec authorities sheared the locks of sorcerers to take away their magic powers prior to execution. Fijian chiefs believed haircuts weakened them. Their rather extreme remedy to this problem was to cook and eat other people to gain strength before getting a haircut.

In the English civil war (1642–1651), short hair was seen by some as a sign of rebellion and intolerance and long hair as a sign of vanity and a bourgeoisie view. The war pitted the long-tressed royal army of Charles I against Oliver Cromwell's close-cropped Puritan parliamentary forces (whom the Royalists simply called "roundheads"). Cromwell prevailed and, as a result, most men in the Western world have had short hair since that time.

Today some Christian monks shave all or part of the head to signify humbling themselves before God in penitence. Orthodox Jews do just the opposite, growing long curls on the sides of their heads as a sign of faith in God.

Recent "hair statements" have included the "duck tail" hairdo of the 1950s, the long, straight hair of the '60s, the "Afro" and "Mohawk" styles of the '70s, the shaved heads, "corn rows," and "fades" of the '80s, and the revival of Rastafarian "dreadlocks" in the '90s.

place, Parliament summoned an assembly at Westminster Abbey. One hundred and twenty-one ministers attended, as well as thirty lay people. There were even representatives from the Scots.

WESTMINSTER CONFESSION

As the civil war raged and the king's forces went from one defeat to another, this assembly ironed out the plan for an English Calvinist church. In 1646, the same year the Charles I surrendered to the victorious Puritans, the assembly issued the *Westminster Confession*. This document is a classic of Calvinist thought. Among its ideas, the *Confession* taught on four of the main subjects of the Calvinist faith. First, it declared the Bible as the sole authority in Christian belief: The scripture could be fully trusted because its writing was "inspired from God."

Second, the *Confession* included an explanation of the doctrine of predestination. In simple terms it said, "Some men and angels are predestined unto everlasting life, and others are foreordained to everlasting death." This entire concept was absent from the *Thirty-nine Articles* which had governed the church for many years.

Third, the *Confession* emphasized that God was connected with His people through a covenant relationship. Further, the document explained that salvation comes about as a kind of balance between God's sovereignty and man's responsibility.

Fourth, the *Confession* defined the proper rule of the church by elders rather than priests and bishops. The episcopal system, which had actually been around since the first few centuries of the church, was to be dismantled.

The *Confession* also established that, in the Church of England, transubstantiation was not to be believed, and that the believer is bound to the observance of the Sabbath. The Sabbath was described as a day strictly devoted to worship.

THE SOCIETY OF FRIENDS

Opposition to the Anglican Church did not come solely from the Puritans and Separatists. Many sects and denominations arose out of even small differences with the church. The diversity was logical in a way. The Protestants taught that the sole authority for doctrine was scripture. It quickly became a problem then to decide *whose* interpretation of scripture was the authority. The Puritans had disagreed with the Anglicans over many items, but they both agreed that there was a need for a clergy.

George Fox disagreed. He found nothing uplifting in the formal denominations that were dominating the Protestant arena. He felt that even these Protestant churches were too tied in to the state, and that the result was really not much better than a state religion. His disagreement led Fox on a spiritual mission.

He turned to friends and to other believers, but no one could help him find the spiritual answer he was seeking. Then one day he heard a voice say, "There is one, even Jesus Christ, who can speak to thy condition." The experience changed Fox, who dedicated his life to following the "Inner Light" that he believed was in all men. The clergy was not necessary because all people have the capacity of communing with God. By following the "Light" God had given them, believers could find redemption.

Fox called his followers The Friends. The rules for this new group were simple but strict. The members could not swear oaths; they had to dress simply and eat little. Notably, they opposed warfare and would not participate in it. Even with these restrictions, The Friends grew quickly due to Fox's preaching. The meetings were held in homes, and both the nobility and common people worshiped together.

The movement created controversy because it was certainly unconventional and probably threatening to some of the "normal" churchgoers. Finally, Fox was arrested and forced to present himself before a judge to answer charges. In the court, Fox warned the judge that he should "tremble at the Word of God." The judge replied, "You are the tremblers, the quakers."

The name stuck, and The Friends survived. Cromwell had personal admiration for the honesty of the group, but he did not extend toleration to it. However, despite his persecution the group survived and grew.

THE RESTORATION

Charles I was beheaded January 30, 1649, at Whitehall. His son of eighteen was proclaimed Charles II at Edinburgh, in parts of Ireland, and in the Channel Islands. In reality, England became a republic headed by the Lord Protector Oliver Cromwell, whose Commonwealth ruled until 1660. During that time, the Calvinist ideals promoted in the *Westminster Confession* would be a cornerstone of the Commonwealth's religious policy.

Puritan leadership of England was short-lived, though. In 1658, when Oliver Cromwell died, no other strong leader asserted himself enough to take the reigns of the powerful Cromwell. His son Richard took his father's position as Lord Protector of

England, but he could not hold the Commonwealth together. Scotland, however, held on to the religious practices of the *Confession.*

 DID YOU KNOW?

In 1651, King Charles II of England and Colonel William Carlos avoided capture by Cromwell's Parliamentary forces by sleeping the night in a large oak tree.

On May 8, 1660, after eleven years of exile, the son of the late Charles I was proclaimed king. The twenty-nine-year-old prince had spent most of his life on the Continent. He landed at Dover on May 26 and arrived at Whitehall on May 29. After the reign of the Puritans, his return was met with almost universal hope in England. He would bring a renaissance of a sort to England and would reign until 1685 as Charles II.

In the time of the Commonwealth, the times had changed. There was a new wind blowing, influenced by thinkers from all over Europe. There was a new optimism in the air that contrasted with the serious religion of the Puritans.

ULTIMATE IMPACT OF AND ON CHRISTIANITY

If the Middle Ages were the long childhood of the church, the era of the Reformation was its adolescence. These were times of turmoil. The church that had reigned supreme for nearly a thousand years became the center of a controversy so great that it actually drew the religious boundaries we have today—four hundred years later. It is impossible to adequately describe the impact of the Reformation because its impact is being felt just as much today as it was when Luther first started a revolution of faith.

MARTIN LUTHER

At the turn of the millennium, a number of news organizations selected a Man of the Millennium. In several of these Martin Luther won "hands down." He won because he initiated, whether intentional or not, the changes that led to the Christian world we live in today. The Christian world today is incredibly diverse.

There is an amazing diversity of sects, faiths, and denominations that make up the church. Luther opened that door by insisting that there *was* an alternative to the orthodoxy of the Roman Catholic Church of his day. If we accept that basic premise, we are led to the conclusion that there might be other alternatives that are just as appropriate as Luther's, or Calvin's, or Zwingli's, or George Fox's, or Thomas Cranmer's, or even Oliver Cromwell's. When Luther opened that possibility, he opened the floodgates. We are still living in the flood with no signs of its cresting.

Theologically, it was Luther and Calvin's insistence on the authority of scripture that allowed this diversity. Without the authority of a universal church hierarchy to interpret scripture, each individual is free to interpret in his own way. Great theologians or church leaders are often our guides; however, even Luther and Calvin would agree that the truth of scripture is realized in the heart and mind of a person studying the scripture and being led by the Holy Spirit. Even in the act of corporate worship, *that* is a personal act. The long-term effect of that approach is that it has become the responsibility of the individual to find the church which interprets the scripture in a way that most resembles his own. This was a fear of the Roman Catholic Church, and it has come to pass. Even today, the large denominations struggle on a regular basis with doctrinal changes. They are called upon to interpret scripture in light of the era and place in which they live. So the diversity which Luther initiated is still growing.

JOHN CALVIN

Although Calvin rejected the "imperial" papacy and placed the church in the hands of local leaders, he also promoted the idea of the Christian society. Both he and the Swiss reformers took the approach that religious freedom could mean the opportunity to establish an exclusively Protestant society. The modern age is still struggling with this issue. Modern issues in the United States, such as prayer in school, all reflect back to the ever-evolving relationship between church and state. The Protestant "experiments" in Zürich and Geneva continued the

Roman Catholic precedent of secular and church law being intermingled. As we watch the continuing battles in the U.S. and other countries over the use of religious (or antireligious) beliefs to design secular legal policy, we should remember that we are still in the process of defining the relationship between church and state.

THE CATHOLIC CHURCH

We should also remember that the Reformation did not signal the end of the Roman Catholic Church. In fact, the result of the Council of Trent was a stronger church that was recommitted to the idea of the spread of the Christian faith. The dominance of the Roman Catholic religion in areas colonized during this era is a part of that legacy. Through the legacy of the Jesuits, the Catholic Church took even more strides toward being a true giant in providing education throughout the world.

EDUCATION

The importance of education is also a legacy of this era. The importance of learning that started its growth during the Renaissance continued through the Reformation. The church leaders were not just educated in monasteries or cathedrals. They were the products of great universities in France, England, and Germany. These universities not only provided knowledge, they taught the students how to search for the truth themselves. The search took the thinkers of this era in a whole new direction. After several thousand years of being dominated by emperors and kings, Western culture began turning back to the power of the individual. Before it expressed itself as a threat to the governments of the day, this spirit of individual determination threw off the power of an imperial pope. The Reformation, fueled by the Renaissance and by a weariness with absolute authority, began the process of changing the world into a place where kings and emperors would be hard to find.

CHAPTER SEVEN

The Enlightenment
(a.d. 1648 to a.d. 1789)

👁 UNDERSTANDING THE TIMES

While the enlightenment was a time of scholarship and discovery, being a college student in the 1700s was confusing. Consider this scenario...

Being a college student at the beginning of the 1700s was truly confusing. He had been raised in the church. His parents were good Anglicans and didn't have much patience with Presbyterians or Independents. He wasn't so sure what he believed anymore. He read a lot these days, but there were so many different opinions he stayed confused. One writer said that man was basically good, but the world corrupted him. Another said that man was basically bad and that society rescued him from destroying himself. His father said that all men sin and need forgiveness from God. But how did that happen?

The Catholics said that you had to do good works, but nobody else said so. The Protestants said you had to be "justified by faith" but could not agree on what baptism had to do with it. In some churches they sang psalms, in others they sang hymns. In some they did not sing at all.

TIMELINE OVERVIEW

In the midst of World History...	Christian History unfolds...
1650 England: First coffee house opens in Oxford.	**1600s** Rationalism spreads.
1653 France: Mailboxes and postage stamps are first used in Paris.	
1657 France: First stockings and fountain pens are made in Paris.	
1658 England: John Milton begins writing *Paradise Lost* (finished in 1663, published in 1667).	
1665 England: Worst attack of plague since the Black Death in the fifteenth century. Kills more than 60,000 people in London alone.	
1666 The Great Fire of London begins in a baker's shop, rages for four days, destroys 87 churches and 13,000 homes. It is stopped by blowing up buildings in its path.	**1670** England: Charles II of England and Louis XIV of France sign the secret Treaty of Dover in which Charles agrees to restore Roman Catholicism to England in return for an annual pension.
The first Cheddar cheese is made.	
Stradivari begins to make violins.	**1675** Philip Jacob Spener and Pietism
	1678 John Bunyan publishes *The Pilgrim's Progress*.
	1689 The Toleration Act grants freedom of worship to dissenters in England.
1703 Construction begins on Buckingham Palace in London.	**1707** Isaac Watts publishes *Hymns and Spiritual Songs*.
1709 The first piano is made by Cristofori.	
1714 Fahrenheit invents the mercury thermometer and a new scale of degrees for measuring temperature.	**1713** Vietnam: In a war against Christianity, French missionaries are driven out of Tongking.
1716 The agricultural revolution is on the rise.	
	1729 Jonathan Swift's *A Modest Proposal*
	1734 Alexander Pope's *Essay on Man*
1742 The first playhouse opens in New York.	**1735** Jonathan Edwards and the Great Awakening
1753 North America: Benjamin Franklin and William Hunter are chosen to run the postal service in America.	**1738** John Wesley converted.
1754 North America: Start of the French and Indian War	
1766 North America: The Mason-Dixon line is established.	
Benjamin Franklin invents bifocals.	
1770 France: First porcelain lifelike false teeth.	
The first public restaurant is opened in Paris.	**1773** First Unitarian Church established in London

Dean Swift said that man was not worth loving; Pascal said that man gets to God through his heart; the Bible says, "Love thy neighbor."

In all this confusion, though, he felt hope. His reading told him that one thing was possible above all else: change. The debates raged around him and in his own mind. He didn't know where things were going, but he knew they were going somewhere.

THE STORY OF THE TIMES

The reformers of the Reformation stepped right out into deep and uncharted waters. They were willing to question the doctrines of the Roman Catholic Church, many of which had not been seriously challenged in nearly a thousand years. Their efforts were not done out of spite, though much of Martin Luther's writing was in direct response to his adversarial relationship with the church.

The abuses that the reformers pointed out were serious: simony, corruption in the clergy, papal abuse of authority, and the indulgence system. Even the faithful among the Roman Catholic Church were aware of these problems. The Council of Trent and the efforts of the Jesuits were two efforts to correct what the church saw as internal problems.

The Reformation moved quickly from abuses, however, to a totally different way to look at Christianity. It was not a new way. Most of the reformers took their cues from the earliest churches, the churches founded by the apostles and disciples. The reformers' theology was not new theology; it was based on scripture without the ornamentation and tradition that engulfed the Catholic doctrine. In a move that was to hold consequences for the next five hundred years (at least), the reformers took the authority for Christian truth out of the sole hands of the clergy and placed it in the hands of the believer. The believer was to be guided in the attainment of truth by the Holy Spirit. The priesthood was of less importance because each believer could interpret the scripture for himself, and because salvation was the product of faith, not the participation of sacraments. Good works were the product of salvation, not its cause.

To some extent, these revolutionary ideas were the product of the Renaissance. The Renaissance had refocused many theologians on a more humanistic approach. Even, perhaps especially, the Roman Catholic Church had embraced this humanism. Many of the great works of art of the Renaissance were commissioned by the church and were concerned with biblical themes. Still others were commissioned by humanist Christians and dealt with classical Greek deities. For the Renaissance man, there was little difference between the two. Both approaches presented man and his relationship with God, a relationship that the Renaissance changed drastically and that precipitated the end of the Middle Ages.

WHAT COULD BE NEXT?

It is not terribly difficult, with the benefit of hindsight, to see that the Reformation was taking the world in a whole new direction.

That new direction had to do with the successful overthrow of an imperial church. That new direction had to do with a faith-based religion rather than a works-based religion. That new direction had to do with the right to challenge commonly held knowledge based on one's own beliefs rather than those of the institution in authority.

What came next was the Enlightenment. It is interesting that we still use this term for the period of the seventeenth and eighteenth centuries. The term is one of the few that we hold to, although it offers us a value judgment on the era. We have cast aside the term "Dark Ages" to describe the terrible years of the early Middle Ages. We cast that term aside because it failed to recognize the accomplishments and culture of the barbarians of the age. We hold on to the Enlightenment, however.

THE ENLIGHTENMENT

The Enlightenment was a philosophical movement that emphasized the use of reason to seek after and analyze beliefs of all kinds, ranging from pure mathematics to moral philosophy. Unlike the Renaissance, which began in Italy and slowly spread northward, the Enlightenment began in the North. France, England, Germany, and Holland (the Netherlands) were centers of Enlightenment thinking. There were also many contributions made to Enlightenment thinking from Switzerland.

Perhaps it has already appeared to you that the centers of the Enlightenment were, with the possible exception of France, the hotbeds of the Reformation. That was of course no accident. There were several ways the Reformation actually led to the rise of the Enlightenment.

THE TRANSITION

The Reformation had taught that authority did not emanate from an earthly institution. It came from the spiritually guided study of scripture. It was not a difficult leap for some philosophers to identify that spiritual guide as *reason*. The idea of *reason* has its roots all the way back in Greek philosophy. For the Greeks, *logos,* or reason, was the unifying and creative force that causes all things to be as they are. Even John, the writer of the fourth Gospel, recognized the relationship between God/Jesus/the Word and *logos* in the first chapter of that Gospel. He used that Greek principle to personify Jesus' role in the universe. Since then, almost every theologian had been forced to wrestle with the battle between reason and faith as the sources of understanding.

The thinkers of the Enlightenment were to fight this battle, as well. However, for the first time, that conflict would be fought without the overriding institution of the church which said, "It does not matter which way you believe a person reaches understanding, the church says..." These thinkers might study Augustine or Aquinas, but not as the authorities on the subject. The Reformation had taught that each man can discern the truth, and the thinkers of the Enlightenment took that to heart.

Finally, the Reformation had taught that an institution as monolithic and powerful as the Roman Catholic Church could be wrong. For the Protestant Christians who came afterward, the implication of that simple fact was enormous. If the church was wrong all those years, what could man rely on? There were plenty of answers for that in the Enlightenment. Before we go further into the era, we should examine what a few of its leading thinkers had to say. The first answer we come to is that there is nothing reliable at all.

RENÉ DESCARTES

Descartes was a French philosopher, mathematician, and scientist. He is often called the "father of modern philosophy." His primary interest was mathematics, and he founded the study of analytic geometry. His primary philosophical works were *Discourse on Method* (1637) and *Meditations* (1641). He established his principle of basing metaphysical certainties on a mathematical basis rather than on the scholastic method used for centuries.

René Descartes is most famous for his statement "I think, therefore I am." Well, that is almost what he said. In the context of his philosophy, Descartes asserts that we must doubt everything, that there is no proof of anything. The world of certainty, which the doctrine of the Catholic Church had maintained for so many centuries, was a thing of the past. In its place, Descartes found only uncertainty. It was in that uncertainty, however, that he found something he could trust: Only one thing cannot be doubted and that is doubt itself. His famous line could read, "I doubt, therefore I am because I know uncertainty is real." From this certainty, Descartes expanded what he could know, step by step, to admit the existence of God (as the first cause). From there he could expand to "accept" the reality of the physical world.

BARUCH SPINOZA

Spinoza was a Dutch philosopher who was also a member of Amsterdam's Sephardic Jewish community. He was educated in the medieval tradition but also read the works of Descartes. He was excommunicated from the Jewish community in 1656 for heretical thinking, and afterwards changed his first name to Benedict. The only work he published during his lifetime was *A Treatise on Religious and Political Philosophy*. After his death, his controversial *Tractatus Theologico-Politicus* (1670) was published. It shows that the Bible, if properly understood, gives no support to the intolerance of religious authorities or to their interference in political or secular affairs.

Spinoza shared with Descartes a mathematical view of the universe. Like Descartes, he believed that truth, like geometry, followed from first principles and was therefore accessible to the mind that used logic and reason. Unlike Descartes, who separated the world of ideas from the reality of the physical world, Spinoza saw the two worlds as different aspects of the same *thing*. He called that *thing* both Nature and God. To Spinoza, God was Nature taken at its fullest. The philosopher was condemned for this theory. His ideas were considered to be *pantheistic* and heretical.

SPINOZA AND FREE WILL

Spinoza was also controversial in his opinion of free will. He did not believe that free will actually existed. Instead, he proposed that man acts out of his own idea of self-preservation. A person who acts out of understanding is powerful or good. That understanding, however, is not necessarily the product of the church or even the scripture. It is, instead, the product of being guided by one's own nature. If one acts out of ignorance of his own self, evil is the result.

As you can easily see, in Spinoza's universe, morality is totally separated from mere obedience to laws or commandments. This was a radical departure even from the opinions of the radical theologians of the Reformation. It is, however, a logical extension of their belief in man's ability to discern truth for himself with the benefit of scripture and the Holy Spirit. In Spinoza's worldview, however, scripture was replaced by understanding of self, and the Holy Spirit was replaced by reason. His philosophy was not godless, however. For Spinoza, the ultimate attainment of understanding was the "intellectual love of God."

SET THE STAGE!

Pantheism is a system of belief that identifies the universe with God. Some proponents of pantheism see God as the center, as the only thing in the universe that is truly permanent and divine. For them, the universe is merely a finite and temporal emanation from God. Others regard nature as a great, inclusive entity that encompasses all things.

With Spinoza we take a step into a new type of thinker. He was a true philosopher who was seeking the truth and was willing to look in new places and in new ways. Descartes had been much the same; however, his conclusions hit much closer to the mark of Christian doctrine than did those of Spinoza. For the first time in the Christian era, philosophers began to truly question the "givens" that Christianity had rested on for so long.

JOHN LOCKE

John Locke was an English philosopher who is primarily remembered for his work in the fields of human understanding and political theory. He was a widely influential writer and thinker in both fields. His work on how humans understand is still basic to the study of that field some three hundred years later. His political theories were to become the handbook for the political change of the eighteenth century. Both of Locke's most important works, *Essay Concerning Human Understanding* and *Two Treatises on Civil Government,* were published in 1690.

John Locke could not accept the premise that there are ideas that are simply innate to humans. Rationalists of his day were claiming that there was a set of innate ideas in a person that was passed down to him by virtue of his birth. (From a twenty-first century viewpoint, what they were proposing was not entirely different from the non-behaviorist psychologists of the nineteenth and twentieth centuries. Nor is it entirely unrelated to the current study of human genetics.) For Locke, however, the implications that these ideas existed were not consistent with what he observed. Locke's observations of human beings, on the other hand, led him to be called the "father of British empiricism."

 DID YOU KNOW?

Empiricism is a philosophical doctrine which claims that all knowledge is derived from experience. That experience can be of the mind or of the senses.

For the theologian, empiricism was a minefield. For hundreds of years, the church had described man as made of clay with the "breath of life" in him. God had made man in His own image and brought him to life with His breath. Didn't that mean that there was a little piece of God in everyone? Even if you describe God simply as a rational force, *logos,* then that logos would indwell each person. In a nutshell, that was the Neoplatonist, rationalist position.

Locke disagreed.

For Locke, each person was born with a "tabula rasa," a blank slate. Nothing is written onto that slate until you have your first experiences. Then, in a pattern of increasing complexity, those experiences are overwritten but not erased. What we become as a human being is the sum total of all that scribbling. We can become, based on our experience and not God's law or our sin, either good or evil.

WHERE IS THE TRUTH?

This theory and belief led Locke to devote much of his energy to understanding how humans experience their lives. Locke's theory was that there are both primary and secondary qualities of things. The primary qualities (solid or liquid, 2 or 40, for example) affect our senses in a mechanical way (i.e., we can tell the difference between ice and water), so we can trust them to reflect reality faithfully. The secondary qualities (the ball is blue, the rose smells delightful) create a direct impact on the senses and cannot be trusted. For Locke, science was the examination of the primary qualities. It could be trusted for the reason that it was based on qualities that were themselves trustworthy. This empirical approach has been the dominant approach of British philosophy since Locke. Most empiricists have stipulated that there are certain truths that just seem to exist, especially principles of logic and mathematics.

POLITICS?

For many of us, it is a long stretch from empiricism to political theory. For Locke, they were intimately related. He theorized that since the "tabula rasa" was truly blank, there was no inherited unhappiness or sin to ruin human life. Thus, the natural state of man was to be happy, reasonable, and tolerant. As such, it was each person's right to pursue "life, health, liberty, and possessions." (That sounds familiar!) In order to live in a society, people establish a social contract that forms a state governed by natural law—and that natural law guarantees those rights. It was a nice package of political philosophy, nice enough to serve as one of the philosophical cornerstones of the United States.

IMPLICATIONS FROM LOCKE

John Locke was one of those thinkers who came along and changed the world. His empiricism still influences scientific thought. His political theories are still being tested in the political system of the United States. Theologically, Locke took us in a new direction. While Descartes may have founded his philosophy on doubt, he still found the divine as the "first cause." Locke turned our search for the divine in a different direction and taught us how to find empirical truth.

GOTTFRIED WILHELM, BARON VON LEIBNITZ

Leibnitz was a German philosopher, mathematician, and diplomat. Leibnitz was a brilliant mathematician who invented calculus independently of Sir Isaac Newton. His primary philosophical works were *Theodicy* (1710) and *Monadology* (1714). His major work, however, was *New Essays on Human Understanding*, a study of John Locke's *Essay Concerning Human Understanding*. The treatise was written in 1704, but because of Locke's death, it was not published until 1765.

Leibnitz, like others of his time, was not just a great philosopher, he was a great mathematician and scholar. With mathematics as his starting point, like many of his fellow thinkers, Leibnitz was willing to even take on the composition of the universe as a suitable subject. As early as 1711, he challenged the idea that the universe just "sprang" into existence from nothing, even with God's hand in it. His study of science made it hard for him to believe the theological explanation of how the universe came about, so he attempted to reconcile the truths of natural science with the idea of divine will. This argument led him to the conclusion that all living matter is not composed of dead atoms but, instead, of living "monads." In his understanding of the world, these living entities are the basic building blocks of the entire universe.

Leibnitz is also known for a position he took on the moral nature of the universe. His philosophical writings present the idea that since the world is the product of an infallible divine plan, then we are living in "the best of all possible worlds." Though the idea is brilliantly presented in his works, Leibnitz was severely satirized by his fellow rationalist Voltaire in his work *Candide*.

On first glance, Leibnitz's position that this is the "best of all possible worlds" seems ludicrous based either on our observations of the world (the modern approach) or on the authority of scripture (the Reformation approach). For centuries the world had been viewed as corrupted by the sin of Adam and Eve. Their sin not only condemned man to separation from the blessed state he enjoyed in the Garden of Eden, it corrupted the world so that disease, famine, war, and natural disasters were the rule, not the exception. The scripture supported this position, and so did man's observation of the "fallen" world around him. Leibnitz contended, however, that because the world conformed to God's plan, a plan born in reason and goodness, the world was indeed good. Its appearance of "fallenness" could be due to our inability to comprehend the plan.

Though this theory was condemned by many, it was adopted by many, as well. Once again, we see that the thinkers of the Enlightenment were willing to follow their guiding light of reason wherever it led them, even if sometimes their conclusions did not seem logical at all.

WORLDVIEWS

The difference in the worldviews of Martin Luther and John Locke is incredible even though the English philosopher was born less than eighty years after Luther's death. They lived in different worlds, however. The seventeenth century was dominated by the rise of even more powerful monarchs in France and England. It was a time when the twin authorities of church and state became more and more restrictive just as an emerging middle class began clamoring for power. Protestants and Catholics denounced each other as followers of Satan, and people could be imprisoned for attending the wrong church. All publications were subject to prior censorship by both the church and state to ensure that no "dangerous" or "heretical" ideas were being propagated.

The middle class consisted more and more of merchants. Its members began to hold middle-class values such as the idea that their earnings were the result of their hard work, unlike that of the aristocracy whose wealth was property based. This idea, among many others, promoted a spirit of individualism. Much of this individualism found a home in the Reformation.

However, it was not long before the Protestants were turning away from their traditional adversaries, the Catholics, and were attacking each other. It is not surprising, then, that a feeling of skepticism began to be a part of the religious scene. If each church knows the truth, but the truths are all different, how can anyone know what is the truth? The churches responded in their traditional ways, each different from the other, and so skepticism became easy.

Individualism also led people to want to change the world in which they lived. There were two main obstacles to that change: the church and the state. In this context, the church could be the Roman Catholic Church as in France, but it could just as easily be the Church of England or the Lutheran Church in Germany. Each of these institutions was a monolith that, in spite of its revolutionary origins, quickly became an opponent of outside ideas, and as we have already seen, there were lots of ideas being proposed in the seventeenth and eighteenth centuries.

THE "REAL" HISTORY

In fact, most of the history of the Age of Enlightenment is a tale of ideas. There was certainly a lot of history going on. Not much of it is different from that of any other period. There were, however, two areas which deserve some attention.

The first was the continued expansion of Europe's major empires throughout the world. Spain, France, and England had major land holdings in North America alone. South America was dominated by Spain and Portugal. By the middle 1700s, there had been a war between the French and English over possessions in North America. By the late 1700s, there had even been a revolution of the English colonies against the home country. By 1789, there was a new country in America founded on the ideas of John Locke.

For much of this time (1643–1715) France was ruled by one man, Louis XIV, who brought a magnificence to that country that was unparalleled. As we will see in our discussion of Voltaire and Rousseau, France was a fertile place for thinkers in spite of the tremendous power of the Catholic Church there. The magnificence of France under Louis XIV, Louis XV, and Louis XVI came at a tremendous cost, however. Poverty in the lower class and relentless taxation of the middle classes led to revolution in 1789. Though the French Revolution turned out much differently than the American, they both emanated philosophically from the thinkers of the Enlightenment. The French colonial holdings were huge. In America alone, their territory encompassed much of the land west of the Mississippi, with the exception of the land held in the west by Spain.

 DID YOU KNOW?

When Louis XIV was king of France, his palace at Versailles was home to some five thousand people. There were only two toilets in the palace. Imagine the line in the morning.

WARS, WARS, AND MORE WARS

The second area that needs a mention is the seemingly endless cycle of wars that dominated all the European countries. In the five years 1700–1705 alone, these conflicts were being fought:

The ***Great Northern War*** involved Russia, Poland, and Denmark as they allied against Sweden to break the Swedes' supremacy in the Baltic. By 1702, the war had settled onto mainly Polish soil as King Charles XII of Sweden invaded that country.

The ***War of the Spanish Succession*** began in 1701. In a complicated political mess, Philip of Anjou gained recognition as the king of Spain, and the Holy Roman Emperor Leopold I moved to take over Spain's possessions in Holland and Italy. To escalate the matter, England and Holland, who were both afraid that Louis XIV of France would join with Spain, formed a Grand Alliance with the emperor. In 1703, the war further escalated when the Grand Alliance declared war on France.

England fought German forces in 1702 at Kaiserswerth on the Rhine in June, Venlo on the Meuse in September, and Liège on October 29.

In a war between competing German states, Bavaria invaded Tyrol in 1703.

In 1704, the English captured Gibraltar from the Spanish and held it for centuries.

This five-year period illustrates the level of conflict that was present between the European powers during the Enlightenment. In light of these struggles, it is easy to see how Leibnitz and Locke's optimism seemed out of place. It is obvious that these thinkers were idealists who could close their eyes and cover their ears just a little bit as they theorized.

DAVID HUME

In such a chaotic world, it was hard for the institutions of the church and the monarchy to maintain the faith of the people. In Scotland, one man took Descartes's skepticism to a whole new level.

David Hume was a Scottish philosopher and historian. As a follower of John Locke, Hume pushed empiricism to the logical extreme. He was a skeptic who, like Locke, wrote major works on human nature and politics: *A Treatise of Human Nature* (1739–1740), *Political Discourses* (1752). He also wrote on religion: *The Natural History of Religion* (1755), and history: *History of England* (1754–1762).

For David Hume, Locke had been a little easy on the truth. Though Hume followed Locke's empirical philosophy, he felt that his mentor had been a little generous in assigning the truth to certain levels of experience. For Hume, the answer was a radical skepticism that questioned even the possibility of knowing something with certainty. He recharacterized the impressions that certain experiences had on the mind. He found, in contrast with Locke, that all that exists in the mind is the series of impressions the world gives us. Whenever we think we see cause-and-effect emerge from these sensations, it is just because we have had two impressions that coincide in some way. As he wrote in *Treatise on Human Nature*, "If a rock is dropped, it is not reason that tells us the rock will fall but rather custom and experience. Truths, like mathematical axioms, are true by definition, but to believe that any observed effect follows any cause by force of reason is folly."

VOLTAIRE

To many people, Voltaire's works epitomize the Enlightenment. He opposed dogma and tyranny but did not advocate revolting against them. His volume of work was immense and his influence enormous. His most famous and influential works were *Candide* (1759) and the *Philosophical Dictionary* (1764). It is this work that best exposes Voltaire's political and religious points of view and biases. He was unjustly imprisoned twice and banished to England in 1726–1729. It was during that time that Voltaire was influenced by the liberalism of the English.

When he returned to France, he lived in the area of Lorraine. In 1749, he went to live at the royal court in Prussia, but left four years later to move to Geneva. He was given a hero's welcome upon his return to Paris in 1778, and it appears as if it was too much for him: He died soon afterwards.

Voltaire once wrote, "If God did not exist, it would be necessary to invent him." Such was the worldly viewpoint of this great writer. Voltaire considered himself a thoroughly reasonable man. He used satire and wit to point out the flaws of his society, and in his fellow philosophers, as well. He was truly an enemy of tyranny, and yet he lived among the high society of Europe that had the most potential for it. Of course, to attack the aristocracy could be fatal. The church was a much easier target.

Voltaire hated dogma. For him, dogma was the true opponent of change. While Voltaire had none of the optimism of Locke, he did believe that change was possible. Whereas Locke placed the responsibility to change society in the hands of common individuals, Voltaire was too much of a snob for that. Instead, he believed that it was possible for intelligent, well-educated people to exercise their reason over their world and thus improve it.

Dogma was an obstacle to that process, and so Voltaire opposed it. The Reformation had made conflicts over dogma commonplace, if still not legal or accepted. Voltaire spent much of his writing undermining the dogmatic fundamentals of Christian belief such as the divine inspiration of the Bible, the incarnation of God as Jesus Christ, and the damnation of unbelievers. Despite his attacks on Christian beliefs, Voltaire was incredibly popular. In some ways, he spoke the nagging doubts of his contemporaries, and spoke them with humor. He turned their discomfort into something less troubling by defusing it.

He was not so kind to Leibnitz, however. His belief in the possibility of progress was in sharp conflict with Leibnitz's faith that this is the "best of all possible worlds." *Candide* provided an exposure of so many ways that, in Voltaire's opinion, this is not the best the world can be.

JEAN-JACQUES ROUSSEAU

Rousseau was a Swiss-French philosopher who was one of the main figures of the French Enlightenment and perhaps the most influential on the Romanticism which developed in the nineteenth century. His influence was felt for a very long time in the fields of political theory and education. His most famous proposal was the "natural man" theory, which asserts that men are basically good and equal in their natural state. This theory is developed to a great extent in his works *Discourse on the Inequalities of Men* (1754) and *Social Contract* (1762). His educational theories are expounded in his novel *Émile* (1762).

Starting in the 1760s, Rousseau suffered with mental illness (persecution mania) and lived in seclusion.

Rousseau was born in Geneva, home of Calvinism, but was certainly no Calvinist. For sixteen hundred years, the Roman Church had taught the necessity of salvation. The Reformation had confirmed this belief for the Protestant churches. Man must be saved because he inherited Adam's sin. It is the task of the church to provide the opportunity of salvation from that sinful state.

Rousseau said "hogwash" to that whole argument. In Rousseau's mind, man was born in a "natural" state of innocence. He was not in need of salvation because he was not corrupt. As man then lived, he was corrupted by such economic forces as property ownership, agriculture, science, and commerce. His life was manipulated by bad government and by dogmatic religion.

To Rousseau, the way to limit the effects of this corruption would be to refine these earthly institutions into their highest form. Since monarchy can easily lead to tyranny, something like the self-rule of a democracy would be better. Rousseau was no anarchist. He believed that men entered into a social contract among themselves, establishing governments and educational systems to correct the inequalities brought about by the rise of civilization.

Rousseau's theory about the "natural man" could not have come at a better time than the age of exploration and colonization. The explorers and colonists were encountering native peoples on every continent. Often these people were captured and brought back for display in the courts of Europe. It was this theory that prompted the idea of the "noble savage," a man who had

SET THE STAGE!
VOLTAIRE VS. ROUSSEAU

Voltaire: Aristocrats can use their minds and education to solve society's problems.

Rousseau: Aristocrats are part of society's problems because they betray important traditional values.

Voltaire: Equality is impossible.

Rousseau: Equality is natural; inequality makes a good "social contract" impossible.

Voltaire: The intellect is supreme.

Rousseau: The emotions are part of our natural self and should not be ignored.

not been corrupted by society's corrupting influence. Although this theory was periodically discarded, it continues to resurface, usually in novels or movies. Writers such as Edgar Rice Burroughs have explored the idea in numerous books. Writers such as William Golding in *The Lord of the Flies* have questioned or discounted it. Regardless, the influence of Rousseau's theories on the natural man and the social contract is still felt today.

SO WE KNOW WHAT THEY THINK, WHAT DO THEY BELIEVE?

Though there are many more thinkers of the Age of the Enlightenment than these seven, these men do provide a good introduction to the ideas and approaches that were prevalent during the Age of Enlightenment. What did they have in common? Varying levels of skepticism. Their theories are complex and based on reason. (Even Rousseau was not anti-intellectual; he simply wanted the emotions to get their credit for their part in human experience.) They were also all, to one extent or another, iconoclastic about the Christian faith. When they applied the principles of rationality to the individual doctrines of the church, for them, the doctrines did not hold up to the scrutiny. For example, the virgin birth of Jesus did not conform to the rules of the universe; therefore, reason forced the rationalist to be skeptical.

DEISM

There is no real doubt that God exists among the philosophies of these men; the only issue is God's nature. Almost all the philosophers of the Enlightenment were *deists*. In the strictest definition, a deist was a person who believed, based solely on reason, that God created the universe and then abandoned it. God maintained no control over life, exerted no influence on nature good or bad, and gave no supernatural revelation to man to aid his understanding. There were many people who rejected the traditional

 SET THE STAGE!

DEIST GOD VS. CHRISTIAN GOD
Deist: God created the universe then left it to run on its own.

Christian: God created the universe and is active in the lives of His people.

Deist: God does not exercise any control over His creation.

Christian: God has repeatedly exercised control over His creation. God's will for His creation is to be involved with His people and the world in which they live.

Deist: God does not reveal His plan or purpose to man. Man must use reason to discern as much as he can.

Christian: God's plan is revealed to man through the Holy scripture under the guidance of the Holy Spirit.

churches, both Catholic and Protestant, in lieu of deism. Deism presented them with none of the inconsistencies that a rationalist saw in traditional doctrine. It allowed them the comfort of

SINNERS AND SAINTS
THOMAS JEFFERSON

You probably know that Thomas Jefferson was our third president. You might know that he was also the author of the Declaration of Independence. These two things alone would have assured him a place in history, but in his time he was famous for a number of other important achievements that, when viewed in the light of his more well-known accomplishments, lend a richer hue to our picture of this founding father.

Jefferson was one of our country's leading architects: He drew the plans for the University of Virginia (which he founded) and Virginia's capitol building. The beautiful estate of Monticello, which Jefferson designed as his own residence, is one of the most famous and revered examples of architecture from the period.

An ardent student of science and philosophy, Jefferson was at one time president of the American Philosophical Society, an early American organization dedicated to intellectual and scientific research. Among his own inventions were a better plow, a decoding device, a lap desk, an improvement of an early copying machine, and the dumb waiter.

In addition to the famous Declaration of Independence, Jefferson authored some of the first written vocabularies of Native American languages and a Manual of Parliamentary practice. He also is responsible for the ten-based currency system used by the United States.

believing the universe is a place, despite appearances to the contrary, where reason rules. Deism denied the opportunity of God's intervention in the world, but also denied His interference in it.

Deism was a tremendously powerful force and continues to be in the institutions created during the Enlightenment. Following the lead of their guiding light, John Locke, most of the leaders of the American Revolution—Jefferson, Washington, Franklin, and Paine—were deists. The God who endowed rights in the Declaration of Independence was the same one that Rousseau worshiped, not the one venerated in the Protestant or Catholic churches of the time. That traditional Christian God was the one who endowed kings with "divine right" to rule. To the deists, the God of the church was not the god of a revolution but a God who opposed it.

BLAISE PASCAL

Not everyone who wrote philosophy in the Age of Enlightenment was convinced that Reason was the true path to understanding. One of the best counterexamples of that approach was a French theologian named Blaise Pascal. Pascal was a brilliant mathematician whose work in the area of calculus and probability would have brought him fame if he had never written a word of philosophy. His works as a scientist led to the invention of the hydraulic press.

Pascal was a groundbreaker in both those areas, but he was a true maverick in the area of philosophy. As a young man he had been influenced by a group of radical Christians called the Jansenists. The members of this group were followers of a Dutch Roman Catholic theologian and bishop, Cornelius Jansen (1585–1638). Jansen's work *Augustinus,* which was published posthumously, initiated a reform movement in the Roman Catholic Church that sought to return Christians to the holy Christian life described by St. Augustine. Jansen's doctrine was radical. He promoted a form of predestination even more radical than Calvin's; he denied the existence of free will and claimed that human nature is incapable of good.

The Jansenists caused great controversy within the Catholic Church, as you might imagine. Their beliefs were attacked by papal bulls in 1705 and 1713, and the group itself was declared heretical by the Roman Catholic Church.

Pascal had heard of their beliefs, and they attracted him. His work *Provincial Letters* was a defense of the Jansenists. In 1654, Pascal entered the Jansenist monastery at Port-Royal near Paris as the result of some kind of deep religious experience. The remainder of his life was centered on religious writings.

SINNERS AND SAINTS
PASCAL

Pascal was a mathematical prodigy who founded the theory of probability and contributed to the development of differential calculus. He was also a scientist and religious philosopher. Pascal's most known works were  *Provincial Letters* (1656) and the posthumously published *Pensées* (1670). The latter work proclaimed the necessity of mystic faith in understanding the universe. As such, it was out of step with the Age of Enlightenment but anticipated the Romantic era to follow.

WHAT PASCAL BELIEVED

The best way to examine Pascal's religious beliefs is through his work *Pensées*. This book essentially consists of the philosopher's thoughts and beliefs published after his death. These writings reveal a man who has taken his own spiritual journey and followed a different path than his peers. His basic point of view concerning the role of the emotions or the intellect in the search for God was summed up in this passage from *Pensées:* "It is the heart which perceives God and not the reason. That is what faith is: God perceived by the heart, not by the reason."

This belief is in total contrast with the rationalists of the era who scoffed at the unreliability of the emotions. To them, the emotions were a "necessary evil" part of human beings that gets in the way of our being truly rational beings. Pascal did not discount the importance of thinking in our human endeavors. As he wrote (again in *Pensées*), "Man is obviously made for thinking. Therein lies all his dignity and his merit; and his whole duty is to think as he ought." In this view, however, thinking is not the path to enlightenment, just a part of our walk as people.

The same could be said for science. Pascal was a brilliant scientist, but laid no faith in science as the hope of the world as did some philosophers of his era. To Pascal, science was inferior to the study of morality. Again he wrote, "Knowledge of physical science will not console me for ignorance of morality in time of affliction, but knowledge of morality will always console me for ignorance of physical science."

 SET THE STAGE!

The stoic philosophy, founded by Zeno about 308 B.C., taught that human beings should be free from passion and should calmly accept all occurrences in their lives as the unavoidable result of divine will or of the natural order.

In contrast with the essentially stoic rationalists, Pascal believed in the richness of a life full of emotion, open to experiences on all (including mystical) levels. Like John Locke, he recognized the role of the senses in experience, but unlike Locke, he saw faith as the "editor" of our distrustful senses, not reason. He wrote, "Faith certainly tells us what the senses do not, but not the contrary of what they see; it is above, not against them."

THE FAITHFUL

It is very important to point out that faith was certainly not dead in the Enlightenment. There were faithful Christians going about their daily lives of obedience and worship as there had been for seventeen or so centuries. For the first time in a very long time, however, there was a competitor on the scene for the religiously minded. For all of the Middle Ages and even the Reformation, the Christian tradition was really not challenged. There were hundreds of conflicts within the church and many with pagans or heretics and even other religions, such as Islam and Zoroastrianism. None of these challenged the essential fabric of the society as Christian, however. In its own way, the deism of the Enlightenment did create a real threat. It created it because so many of the finest minds "jumped ship" from the church and pursued religious satisfaction elsewhere. As we have seen earlier, the church tried to oppose the more radical movements of the Enlightenment mostly without success. The powerful monarchies of the era embraced some of the rationalist ideas because they challenged the authority of their biggest rival, the church. In the end, however, the kings regretted that decision because the followers of thinkers like Locke brought political revolution to the doors of the palace.

Meanwhile, both Catholic and Protestant Christians continued in their lives. Some Christians even tried to reform their churches and make them conform more to a scriptural model. One of these was Philip Jacob Spener.

 DID YOU KNOW?

The first law regarding religious toleration in the British Empire was passed in Maryland in 1649. The law, which promised freedom of religion to all Christians, was soon repealed.

FINALLY, BACK TO GERMANY

Philip Jacob Spener (1635–1705) was not happy with the state of the Lutheran Church. After studying theology at the University of Strasbourg, Spener was well educated in the biblical languages, church doctrine, and history he would need to be a good clergyman. But Spener recognized that something was missing. The enthusiasm of the Lutheran Church had "cooled off" greatly since its early days and seemed much more concerned with the correct doctrine than matters of faith.

Spener recognized that scholarship was crucial, but he felt that it should be refocused on personal experience, not issues of importance but with no relevance. In 1666, he became a member of the senior clergy in Frankfort. Almost immediately he began preaching some new ideas. In his sermons, he taught the need for personal devotion over correct dogma.

For Spener, the problems in the church had to do with "too

much head" and "not enough heart." He was willing to try new things, so in 1670 he set up devotional meetings for prayer, Bible study, and sharing of Christian experience. These devotional meetings would not be held in the church but in someone's home. This idea was so radical in its day that many people found it threatening. However, these meetings, called *Collegia pietatis,* quickly became very popular and multiplied. They became part of an entire movement called Pietism, which had begun in the early sixteenth century in the Dutch Reformed Church. That movement stressed the importance of the new birth of the Christian, emphasized personal faith, and placed great value on the warmth of the Christian experience.

SET THE STAGE!
THE DUTCH REFORMED CHURCH

As the Reformation had spread throughout Europe, a number of different denominations had developed. The Dutch Reformed Church grew in the sixteenth century from the Calvinist branch of the Reformation. In 1571, a synod at Emden adopted a Presbyterian (nonepiscopal) organization and designed its liturgy. Its primary doctrine was presented in the *Belgic Confession of Faith* (1561) and the *Heidelberg Catechism* (1563).

SPENER ON CHURCH LEADERSHIP

In another radical move, Spener recommended that lay people, not just clergy, play important roles. Though the pastor was important, the other church members were responsible to some extent for the nurturing of their own and each other's faith. Thus, the clergy had a very different role in the churches that adopted Pietism. He had to know his Bible and theology but also needed to know how to deal with his church members. He must be willing to walk a path of spiritual devotion so he could lead his congregation in one. Even a clergyman's preaching had to change, Spener thought. A sermon should not just be a lecture; it should also apply scripture to life and inspire the listeners.

Needless to say, Spener's teachings caused a great deal of

controversy. He was forced to leave Frankfort and move to Dresden. Later, in 1654, while living in the friendlier atmosphere of Berlin, Spener and August Franke formed the University of Halle. Under Franke's leadership, the university became a center for evangelism.

Pietism restored the life to the Lutheran Church and to Germany itself. After the destruction of the Thirty Years' War (1618–1648), Pietism helped to bring back a vitality in the life of the German people. It brought a new energy into their spiritual life, encouraged close relations between Christians, and even rekindled the writing of hymns and spiritual songs which Luther had begun but which had languished since his death. In contrast with the stoicism of the secular philosophers and the cold scholasticism of the Lutheran Church of the time, Pietism brought emotion into worship and created partnerships in its followers' spiritual journeys. The legacy of Spener and the movement he popularized are still felt today. Through their missionary efforts, the message of Pietism was spread throughout the world, and it had a profound influence on how common folk viewed the church, especially in America.

JOHN BUNYAN AND THE COMMON FOLK

Thomas Aquinas was brilliant. Martin Luther changed the world. René Descartes made skepticism a part of our mind frame for four hundred years, so far! However, none of the writings of these three men had as much impact on the common Christian as a book by an uneducated son of a tinker.

John Bunyan was born in the town of Elston in Bedfordshire. He grew up as the son of a tinker who traveled this area in the south-central part of England pushing a cart and repairing people's metal pots. John received a grammar school education, but like most boys of his social class, he planned to follow in his father's career footsteps. He fought in the English civil war (presumably on the side of the Puritans), and married at nineteen.

In 1651, he attended a meeting at the Independent Church in Bedford, the county seat. The preacher was passionate about the scripture and piqued an interest in John. On his own, he began to pore over the Bible, looking for answers for the conflicts in his life. Finally, salvation came to John Bunyan. He had solved his conflicts with the assurance of grace.

Soon he had joined that congregation at Bedford and began to preach there. Before long he found he had some problems. Though King Charles II had promised religious freedom, in reality, the Anglican Church was the only accepted church. The Independent churches were "too radical," and as an Independent preacher, Bunyan went to jail for his preaching. He remained there until the Declaration of Indulgence was issued in 1672 which extended leniency to non-Anglicans.

After his release, Bunyan went back to the church in Bedford and began to preach again. This time he even received a license to do it. By 1675, the Independents were a religious force in the area, and "Bishop" Bunyan was back in jail. This time while in prison he began his most famous work, *The Pilgrim's Progress*. The book was published in 1678.

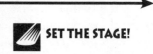 **SET THE STAGE!**

The Pilgrim's Progress gives the English language a number of great phrases such as "Hanging is too good for him." It also gives the enduring image of Vanity Fair. The image has its roots in the book of Ecclesiastes 1:2, "Vanity, vanity... all is vanity." Bunyan's image is a fair where everyone is involved in utterly worthless activity, useless idle amusement, and frivolity with no meaning and no substance.

This work presents an allegory of salvation as Pilgrim walks from the City of Destruction to the Celestial City. It portrays that journey in a way that has touched readers for over three hundred years. Drawing from his own experience on that journey and from the Bible, Bunyan was able to create a portrait of salvation with which almost anyone could identify. To Bunyan's mostly Puritan audience, the book was a treat. The Puritans had been denied access to Shakespeare and most of the great literature of the previous ages. In many circles, *The Pilgrim's Progress* was second only to the Bible in how many people read and owned a copy.

MUSIC AND THE CHURCH

Music of one kind or another had been part of Christian worship since the early days of the church. With the Reformation, music's role in worship was redefined by Martin Luther. Luther loved music and composed hymns to be sung as part of the worship liturgy. Many of these hymns, such as "A Mighty Fortress Is Our God!" and "Away in a Manger," are among the favorites of churchgoers even today.

Unfortunately, as part of the general loss of energy the Lutheran Church suffered at Luther's death, the output of great liturgical music dropped sharply. Then, in 1685, two men were born less than a hundred miles apart in Germany who would provide the world some of its greatest musical masterpieces.

JOHANN SEBASTIAN BACH

Bach was born in Eisenach, Germany, into an already musical family. He studied music from his father and brother, and in 1703 he became a violinist in the Weimar Royal Chamber Orchestra. He did not remain in this position long before he left to take a position as a church organist in Arnstadt, where he remained for four years. He married a cousin, Maria Barbara Bach, who was an accomplished singer. They had seven children before Maria died in 1720. Bach was remarried in 1721 to Anna Magdalena Wülken. In all, he had twenty children before he died in 1750.

To support his family, Bach worked tirelessly as a church organist in Mühlhausen (1707–1708) and Weimar (1708–1717) before he became the musical director for Prince Leopold at Cöthen in 1717. In 1723, he accepted a post as cantor and music director of St. Thomas Church in Leipzig. It was a very respected position, and Bach held it until his death.

Bach was a true musician. He not only played as the church organist, he also composed cantatas and other service music and even taught music. In addition to a huge number of secular works, Bach wrote hundreds of sacred pieces and well over two hundred cantatas. It was during his years in Leipzig that he wrote *St. John Passion*, the Mass in B Minor, and well over two hundred cantatas.

It would be easy to separate Bach from his era, but it would be a mistake. Just as the scientists of his day were developing theories about the very nature of the stuff of life, Bach developed the principles of polyphony to an amazing degree. His work has passion, but it was a passion that was under the restraint of strict musical rules, mostly of his own invention. His music reflected a mathematical precision of composition and conveyed an image of the world fully under the control of God. In Bach's music there was a great faith in a reasonable universe created and maintained by a reasonable God.

SINNERS AND SAINTS
BACH

Johann Sebastian Bach was one of the most prolific and greatest composers in Western music. He wrote more than two hundred cantatas, the *Saint Matthew Passion* (1729), the Mass in B minor (1733–1738), orchestral works such as the six *Brandenburg Concertos,* and a huge number of works for organ, harpsichord, other solo instruments, and chamber orchestras.

If this belief sounds familiar, it is because it reflects the doctrine of a devout Lutheran. Even Bach's secular compositions contained dedications such as "in Praise of the Almighty's Will." He considered music as an integral part of church worship and applied his life to producing beautiful music for that purpose. It is interesting that in his day Bach was not known as a great composer, but instead as a virtuoso on the organ. It would be the nineteenth century before another composer, Felix Mendelssohn, would rediscover and popularize Bach's compositions all over the world. Bach's music was written for the church but has transcended its original use. Even his sacred works are performed simply for their beauty and precision.

GEORGE FREDERICK HANDEL

George Frederick Handel was a master of baroque composition. He composed in nearly every genre of his era, including opera, oratorios, cantatas, suites, and concertos. In our modern era he is best known as the composer of the oratorio *Messiah*. However, he wrote an additional thirty-one oratorios, including *Acis and Galatea* (1720), *Esther* (1732), *Saul* (1739), and *Judas Maccabeus* (1747). He also wrote forty-six operas and over one hundred cantatas.

At one time or another almost everyone has heard the "Hallelujah Chorus" from Handel's *Messiah*. It is one of the landmark works of sacred music. It was written by a man who very easily could have opted for a life outside of the field of music.

Handel was born in the town of Halle. That town may sound familiar to you. It was the site of the University of Halle founded by August Franke and Philip Jacob Spener. Handel grew up in a Pietist home, the son of a barber-surgeon. His father did not want his son to pursue music and forbade him to study it. Legend has it, however, that young Handel would sneak into the attic at night to practice the clavichord. (Legend has never explained how or why the clavichord got *into* the attic, but that's another story.) Instead, Handel's father wanted him to become a lawyer, but eventually he had to give in and allow his son to study with the local organist. However, when the court in Berlin offered to further young George's musical education, his father refused.

 SET THE STAGE!

Polyphonic music was created by the harmonic interweaving of several independent melodic lines. These independent "melodies" interact in very specific ways through the use of a technique called *counterpoint*. In short, the rules of counterpoint are the framework which the composer can use to connect the simultaneous melodies.

The father could not win in the end, however, and after one year of studying law George gave up his studies to become a violinist in a court orchestra. He also began to write operas in Italian. The first of them, *Almira*, was performed in Hamburg on January 8,1705. Handel was only twenty years old.

Soon afterwards, Handel moved to Italy, which was the place to go if you wanted to learn to write operas. In 1712, he moved to England and continued to write music. In 1717, he wrote *Water Music* for King George I. He continued to live in England until 1741, and during that time wrote over forty operas. Unlike his religious work, Handel's operas usually reflected the Enlightenment's interest in classical subjects such as Julius Caesar and Atalanta.

As early as 1732 he began to write oratorios. An oratorio is a musical composition for voices and orchestra which tells a story. It is different from an opera in that there are no costumes or scenery, and there is no dramatic action. *Esther* was first performed in 1732, and *Saul* was first performed in 1739. The first performance of his oratorio *Messiah* was in Dublin in 1742.

Musically, Handel walked between the two worlds of secular and sacred music with ease. Though we know him today on the basis of his most famous oratorio, we cannot separate that one piece out from his long, successful career. For example, his anthem "Zadok, the Priest" (1727) has been used at all British coronations since that of George II. Handel recognized that by using the tools of the opera he could create great oratorios that glorified God. He was raised a Pietist, and in some ways his father's lessons stuck with him. For Handel, faith was more than just words; it was the product of the heart. His music reflects that belief.

ISAAC WATTS

These days, you are not likely to hear an Isaac Watts composition on the same radio station that would play one by Bach or Handel. That is not to say that his influence has not been as great.

As a composer, Watts started with a problem. Whereas the

German Lutheran Church embraced music (with organists like Bach, who wouldn't?), the Anglican Church held conservatively to the "no hymns" policy. The Anglicans had the *Book of Common Prayer*, but its liturgy did not include music. Since 1562, congregations had been allowed to use a collection of metrical psalms. In 1696, Nahum Tate and Nicholas Brady had provided a new version of the psalms that was more "singable," but there were still no hymns.

As early as 1623, George Wither had tried to create a hymnbook, but his efforts went nowhere.

The Anglicans were just not going to budge. But the Anglicans were not the only church in town. The Baptists had no problems with hymns and neither did the Independents. (Remember that the Independents were a group that broke away from the Anglicans in the second half of the sixteenth century. The American Pilgrims were members of this denomination.)

 SET THE STAGE!

King George II of England (whose coronation included Handel's anthem "Zadok, the Priest") was a colorful figure. Not only was he the last British monarch to lead his troops on the battlefield, but he also was something of a pioneer in the field of entertainment. During George's reign, tickets were sold by which an audience could watch the king and his family eat dinner. Had they had public access cable TV or digital cameras at the time, there probably would have been a channel or Website devoted to it.

In fact, Independent preacher Isaac Watts decided his congregation *needed* some hymns. The problem with the psalms was that they had much to say about faith, but they did not show clearly any of the Christian teachings Watts thought were important. He thought that congregations should be able to sing about things like Christ's birth, His crucifixion, and His resurrection. He thought there should be songs about the church itself and about the Holy Spirit.

So Watts began to write them, and he kept writing, and he kept writing. In fact, he incredibly wrote over six hundred hymns. In 1707, he published *Hymns and Spiritual Songs*. In 1719, he published *Psalms of David Imitated in the Language of the New Testament*. In this work, Watts used psalms as his "jumping-off" point. The hymn "Jesus Shall Reign Where'er the Sun" is based on Psalm 72, and "Joy to the World" is based on Psalm 98.

Many of Watts's hymns are part of the common church music of today. His influence on other hymn writers has been immense. That influence was restricted to non-Anglican churches, however, until 1861 when the first Anglican hymnbook appeared. Although they had rejected the idea of hymns for so many years, when *Hymns Ancient and Modern* did appear, you can be sure that some of Isaac Watts's hymns were included.

FROM MUSIC TO LITERATURE

Any look at the Age of Enlightenment would not be complete without at least a brief look at its literature. It was an age of great literature, poetry, and drama. There were incredibly vibrant literary and dramatic scenes in many of the cities of Europe. The London theater was particularly active and impressive. Playwrights such as John Dryden brought the stage back to life with tragedies and comedies. The theater seats were full of people seeking entertainment.

It had not been so during the rule of the Puritans. Under the leadership of Cromwell, the Parliament had actually outlawed the theater, so they had no choice but to close. The Puritan era had been a brilliant time for other writing, however. The real star of that time was John Milton, an English poet and essayist. He is most known for his epic poem *Paradise Lost*, but he also wrote powerful prose works such as *Areopagitica* (1644), which argues against censorship. He wrote poetic drama and twenty-three sonnets, which are considered among the finest ever written in the English language. Milton was one of the greatest poets and prose writers who ever lived. He was a devout Puritan who supported the Presbyterian struggle to reform the Church of England with pamphlets attacking the episcopal form of church. Gradually, Milton became disillusioned with the Presbyterians and attracted to the Independents. In 1649, he wrote *The Tenure of Kings and Magistrates,* which supported the Independents who had imprisoned Charles I. It argued that a king's subjects may depose him and even put him to death if he is unworthy of their loyalty. That argument was the politically correct thing to say at the time, and he was given a Latin secretaryship in Cromwell's Commonwealth government.

He retired after the restoration of Charles II and wrote *Paradise Lost*, which he finished in 1667. This epic is the work of an artist who was a product of the Renaissance, the Reformation, and the Puritan revolution in England. It captured and refined the Greek and Latin epics of Homer and Virgil, yet it had the humanism of the Renaissance. The purpose was not to cry for God's forgiveness, but instead to "justify the ways of God to men." It was also the product of a Puritan who had been a part of the revolution that was Cromwell's Commonwealth and had seen it collapse. His theology is complex. For example, it is Satan, not Christ, who is the most dynamic, interesting character. It is not a work of doctrine, however; it is a masterpiece of poetry.

 DID YOU KNOW?

The late sixteenth and early seventeenth centuries witnessed the birth, in many ways, of modern theatrical drama. In 1576, James Burbage built England's first noted public theater, called (appropriately enough) The Theatre. In 1599, Shakespeare opened the Globe Theatre. Among the principal actors (and shareholders) of the Globe was Burbage's son Richard, who was the first person to play Hamlet, Othello, and King Lear.

JOHN DRYDEN

After the Restoration, there was great poetry and drama from men like John Dryden (1631–1700). Dryden wrote hundreds of works, including great plays such as *All for Love* (1678). He wrote long narrative poems such as *Absolem and Achitophel* (1681), which tells the story of two of King David's sons. In 1678, he published a poem entitled "Religio Laici" (or "A Layman's Faith"). In this

SINNERS AND SAINTS
WILLIAM SHAKESPEARE

Against the backdrop of the Reformation, a son was born to a glovemaker in the town of Stratford-on-Avon. He would grow up to be the most well-known author of all time. William Shakespeare (1564–1616) had firsthand experience in some of the political and religious rifts of the times. He was born just six years after the end of Queen Mary's bloody reign over England, during which time the queen forcibly reinstated Catholicism as the state religion and executed many Protestants. He entertained Queen Elizabeth, the last of the Tudor monarchs, and enjoyed the patronage of James I, first of the Stuart line to sit upon England's throne and a staunch Protestant. The Shakespeare family were all members of the Church of England, and his mother's family, the Ardens, were primarily Roman Catholics. These tensions seem to reflect in some of the underlying themes of Shakespeare's writing. A very common theme in many of his works is the way in which foolish pride, greed, and miscommunication can cause catastrophe and split nations, families, or lovers asunder. Shakespeare also did much to chronicle the history of England by writing plays about (then) recent monarchs and the Wars of the Roses between the royal houses of Lancaster and York. Folk themes and superstitions of the times also play a part in Shakespeare's work: ghosts, witches, and magicians, believed to be real by many people of the time, all appear in his plays. Aside from the depth of his talent, one thing that set Shakespeare apart from other writers of the time was that he often acted parts in his own plays. Many critics of the times attacked this practice,

Continued

SINNERS AND SAINTS (CONTINUED)

being of the opinion that a common actor could not be a great playwright. Nonetheless, Shakespeare was the most popular playwright of his own time, and history seems to have borne him out in matters of critical distinction. During the same time in which the modern world's best-known writer plied his trade in England, the *King James Bible*, perhaps the best-known book of all time and certainly one of the most beautiful translations ever undertaken, was being written by a team of nearly 450 scholars under the direction of England's King James I. Just four years after Shakespeare's death, a group of the conservative Puritan religious movement headed toward the shores of America aboard the *Mayflower*.

poem, Dryden took special aim at some enemies of the church. In particular he attacked Deism. From Dryden's viewpoint, reason is fine as far as it goes, but reason alone cannot be the basis for religion. As Dryden shows in the poem, there are things that reason simply cannot do. Further, Dryden asserts that the end result of relying on reason for your faith is that you become your own God. As he writes, "Thus man by his own strength to heaven would soar, / and would not be obliged to God for more."

Dryden was not alone in his skepticism about the predominant philosophical ideas of his day (which is ironic because skepticism *was* a central idea). A leader in the beliefs of his time was Jonathan Swift. Swift was an Irish-born English writer and poet. His most famous work is the satire *Gulliver's Travels*, published in 1726.

JONATHAN SWIFT

Jonathan Swift was born in Ireland of English parents. He studied at Trinity College in Dublin then joined the household of Sir William Temple as a secretary. Temple had a fine library, and Swift used it well. At one point during his time with Sir William, Swift left for a time and served as an Anglican parish priest in northern Ireland. In 1704, he published his first two satires, *A Tale of a Tub* and *The Battle of the Books. A Tale of a Tub* was written in reaction to a new "style" of preaching that had entered both the Anglican and Puritan churches. Preachers adopting this style were "witty," using elaborate metaphors and developing elaborate arguments.

But the actual target of the satire is the corruption of the church and learning. He presents an allegory for the history of the Christian church. In the allegory there are three brothers: Peter (the Roman Catholic Church), Martin (moderate Protestants like Lutherans and Anglicans), and Jack (Calvinism and other radical reformers). As Swift narrates the story, these brothers were supposed to get along, but they fall out with one another. Peter kicks the other two out the door.

From there, the story turns allegorically to the Reformation. The three brothers have coats. Martin tries to restore his coat to its original condition but notices that it has some stains that cannot be removed without damaging the coat. He cleans his coat the best he can but leaves the stains he cannot get out. When Jack notices the stains on his coat, he flies into a rage and rips it to pieces. However, the end result is that from a distance Peter's and Jack's coats look identical. Martin, the moderate, is hated by both other brothers.

 DID YOU KNOW?

William Shakespeare might not have become a world-renowned poet had it not been for the bubonic plague. Between 1592 and 1594, many theatres were closed due to repeated outbreaks. Accordingly, the market for new plays slowed down considerably. It was at this time that the already well-known playwright began writing the poems that would double his fame as time went on.

The words *eventful, assassination, bump,* and *lonely* are all believed to have been invented by Shakespeare. Additionally, he is credited with originating the phrases *catch cold, fair play, disgraceful conduct,* and *foregone conclusion.*

SWIFT AND THE CHURCH

The satire of the work makes it clear that Swift sides with none of the brothers, though he feels that Martin's moderate path is the best. His area of concern is not which church is best but, instead, the dangers of extremism. Jack (Calvin) is not condemned for his beliefs, but he is a target of the satire for his frenzied state. Swift's position seems to be (and this is always dangerous with Swift) that the truest faith is the one that is present in the "trenches" of actual church service. As we said earlier, Swift had served as an Anglican parish priest in Ireland and knew that whatever importance theological arguments might have among scholars, it was the Christian that mattered, not the doctrine.

This theme also underlies Swift's *A Modest Proposal*, published in 1729. At this point in his life, Swift was serving as dean of St. Patrick's Cathedral in Dublin. He had aspired to be a bishop, but his own opinions had probably prevented his advancement that high. While living in Ireland, he developed strong feelings about the English and the Irish. *A Modest Proposal* presents a terribly ironic solution to the problem of starvation in Ireland. Swift proposes that Irish children be sold as food. In his argument, the narrator presents, in great detail, the economic and social benefit of the scheme and even provides recipes.

 SET THE STAGE!

Entertainment took many forms in the England of the late 1500s. The plays of Shakespeare competed for public attention with public executions by hanging or beheading, and harpsichord and madrigal music vied with such grisly sports as bullbaiting and bearbaiting, in which bulls or bears, respectively, were tied to poles and set upon by hungry dogs (does that remind you a bit of the gladatorial games of the Roman Empire?). Also at the time, a new form of music called *opera* was just starting to make a splash.

The work is a masterpiece of irony. Swift targets the English for their treatment of the Irish and the Irish for their submission to the English. Importantly, however, he is also attacking the rationalists who applied cold logic to religious or human affairs. The argument is a wonderful example of reason and logic. It is also hideous and terribly wrong; its reasonableness is just the disguise of its error.

SWIFT AND REASON

Swift recognizes, then, that Reason (capital R) is far too fickle to be a god. It can be manipulated and is itself subject to interpretation. In his books, however, he presents little alternative except basic human decency. He rejects humanism completely since he does not find man worthy of praise. In fact, he finds mankind beyond contempt. As he says, however, in a letter to his colleague and fellow poet Alexander Pope, "Principally I hate and detest that animal called man; although I heartily love John, Peter, Thomas, and so forth." If religion is to be correct, Swift would contend, it must serve these individual people in spite of the fact that in this fallen world the effort is bound to fail.

Looking through Swift's eyes helps us understand the position of the Anglican Church. It is easy here in the twenty-first century to perceive the Anglican Church of that era as cold and doctrinal. After all, there was dissatisfaction within the Anglicans that led to denominations such as the Independents. Swift reminds us, however, that there were people in the church, on the local level, who were trying to do the right thing. They were trying to hold to the doctrine they believed against the pressures of the more radical Protestants, against their own Puritan reformers, and against the English political reality of being a state church. As Swift himself pointed out, "I never saw, heard, nor read, that the clergy were beloved in any nation where Christianity was the religion of the country. Nothing can render them popular, but some degree of persecution."

When Swift wrote to his friend Alexander Pope, he was writing to a man with as much a gift at irony and satire as himself. Unlike Swift, Pope was a true citizen of London and relished the witty society of the city. His friends (and enemies) were the leading lights of philosophy, literature, and drama. Much of his writing was done in direct response to his peers' writing; much of his satire was directed at his social enemies. He was then an example of a truly social man. Unlike so many other writers and philosophers of his time, Pope, like Voltaire, enjoyed the society in which he lived.

SINNERS AND SAINTS
ALEXANDER POPE (1688–1744)

Alexander Pope was the greatest poet of his age. He was a master of poetic form and the great poetic satirist. Pope suffered from physical disabilities but nonetheless was a leading social figure as well as a literary giant in his own time. Though he was largely self-taught, by the age of seventeen he was regarded as a prodigy. He wrote all types of poetry, including pastoral poetry: *Pastorals* (1709) and *Windsor Forest* (1713), a mock-heroic: *Rape of the Lock* (1714), literary criticism: *Essay on Criticism* (1711), translations of epics: *Iliad* (1720) and *Odyssey* (1725–26), an edition of Shakespeare (1725), other satires and his famous *Essay on Man* (1734).

His pleasure did not get in the way of his critical eye, however. His writing is almost always directed at the foibles and folly of man (a kind of Jerry Seinfeld of the early modern world). Like Swift he found much to criticize, but if anything, his pen was sharper. He would not only attack the issue of ignorance, for example; he would attack a particular person who had acted ignorantly. His famous poem *The Rape of the Lock* is such an attack. Pope found much in his world to criticize and even more at which to laugh.

ESSAY ON MAN

There were at least two subjects about which Pope was really serious. The first was poetry itself. His *Essay on Criticism* was not just a work about literary criticism; it also presented the relationship between poetry and the universe. In the *Essay on Man,* Pope turned directly to the subject of the philosophies and religion that swirled around him in one of the great cities of the Enlightenment.

Pope's position was strongly influenced by the philosophy of Thomas Hobbes. Hobbes was an English political philosopher whose most prominent work was *Leviathan,* published in 1651. Hobbes was tremendously influential in his theories of social and political development. Philosophically, Hobbes was the direct opposite of John Locke. Whereas Locke believed in a state of innocence that preceded experience, Hobbes believed that man's original state was fundamentally selfish and therefore corrupt. To Hobbes as well as Pope the concept of Nature is crucial. As we saw earlier in this chapter when we read about Spinoza, in the Enlightenment, Nature could be used to describe the entire created universe as it reflected God's reasonable perfection. That is precisely how Pope used the term. As he wrote in *Essay on Man,* "The state of nature was the reign of God." For Pope, corrupt man was born into perfect Nature. Instead of conforming to Nature's perfection, man tried his own path. However, by bonding together with his fellow man as society, man was able to overcome his imperfections and live as he should. Or at least, that is what Pope thought he ought to do. As is evident from Pope's satire, mankind did not follow the theory well.

The *Essay on Man* was designed to sort through the misinformation and bad belief that were keeping man from following his right path. If man could conform to what Nature (and Reason) teach, he could have the life that was meant for him. But here Pope took a different tack. In a twist that reminds us a little of Milton in *Paradise Lost,* Pope writes, "The proper study of mankind is Man." He is saying that the way for man to correct himself is not to look at perfection but to look at himself with his own eyes open.

There is a theological lesson there that is relevant both backward in time to the Reformation and forward in time to the religious revival which came at the conclusion of the Enlightenment. The Reformation had taught that there was a process of perfection at work in the world. Old ways, doctrines, and beliefs could be discarded if they were incorrect. Pope is saying that the process of perfection is a return to where we should have been in the first place except for our selfish nature. Nature itself is perfect. (In theological terms, God's creation was perfect.) Man should be striving to reach that perfect state, as well. That perfection is not only personal, it is also social and political. It is the responsibility of a good person to be personally charitable (to work against man's basic selfishness), and if he is given the chance, he must rule with integrity.

THE ENLIGHTENMENT AND A NEW AGE ALTOGETHER

As we have seen, the Enlightenment was an age of skepticism, an age of disagreement, and a time of ideas. It was a time of great literature as writers tried to reconcile theory with reality, and religion with philosophy. The Anglican Church in England and the Lutheran Church in Germany were tremendously influenced by the new ideas that rose up and the skepticism that eroded the traditional faith. The Roman Catholic Church, especially in France, found itself at odds with the greatest minds of the age, including Voltaire and Galileo Galilei, who was imprisoned by the Inquisition in 1633 for saying that the sun forms the center of the universe.

The enthusiasm and energy which the Reformation had triggered was dwindling in the face of political opposition to more social change; it was dwindling because many of the best and brightest minds had gone elsewhere philosophically; and it was dwindling because the revolutionary institutions of the Reformation had become the new establishment. What was needed was a revival of that energy.

JONATHAN EDWARDS AND THE GREAT AWAKENING

The Pilgrims who had landed in America in 1620 had been full of determination and religious zeal. Their Separatist beliefs had forced them out of England to Holland and from Holland across the dangerous Atlantic to America. In 1630, ten years later, a great wave of Puritans followed their lead and came to Massachusetts to form a Christian commonwealth. These Puritans were different from the original colonists. Whereas the Pilgrims were Separatists, the Puritans wanted to establish a new society that would serve as an example for the Puritans still living in England.

 SET THE STAGE!

Oftentimes in British colonial America, followers of the same religious group would all settle in the same area. Sometimes a denomination became so heavily concentrated in a particular colony that it controlled the political bodies in that colony and became the established church, the official state religion of a particular colony. This led to some colonies actually levying taxes to support the established churches and denying religious freedom to other denominations. Tensions caused by these abuses of power helped set the stage for the reform movement known as The Great Awakening.

It was a noble ambition, but in time the religious fervor cooled as it did in Europe. In the Massachusetts colony, there were opportunities for money and influence that would not have been possible at home, and the Puritans became more concerned with the things of the world and less concerned with their religious mission.

There were many who recognized this spiritual malaise and felt that they should return to the mission of becoming a Christian commonwealth. One man who chose to do something about it was an energetic young preacher named Jonathan Edwards.

Jonathan Edwards was born in Connecticut, New England, the son of a pastor.

He was a precocious child who was fluent in Latin, Greek, and Hebrew at thirteen and entered the Collegiate School of Connecticut (later Yale University) that same year. As a student there he showed great talent as a student of philosophy. He graduated at the head of his class in 1720 and served as a Presbyterian minister in New York City before accepting a position as a senior tutor at Yale in 1724. In 1727, Edwards had a strong religious experience and became the pastor of the Congregational Church of Northampton, Massachusetts, that same year. He served as a pastor at that church and even as a missionary to the Indians until 1758, when he became the president of the College of New Jersey at Princeton. He died of smallpox soon thereafter.

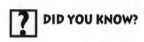

? **DID YOU KNOW?**

A Massachusetts law passed in 1675 required the locking of church doors during services. The purpose of the law was to prevent worshipers from leaving in the middle of lengthy sermons.

SCHOOLING

Though he was the son of a pastor, Edwards had put his life on an academic track. His brilliance in school had opened doors back at Yale where he had attended. In 1727, however, he had a personal religious experience which he described in his *Personal Narrative* in 1739. This experience led him to give up his academic post and take on the job of pastoring a Congregational church.

He became a minister at the Congregational Church of Northampton with his grandfather, Solomon Stoddard. Stoddard himself had been a successful leader of revivals in his sixty years as a minister. During his career, he had seen five "harvests" when there had been dramatic increases in church attendance and a renewed Christian spirit in the community. Edwards joined him at his church in 1727 and served with him until 1729 when Stoddard died. When Edwards took over the church, he

SET THE STAGE!

We sometimes assume Western technology moves fastest, but that's not always true. At the time of Jonathan Edward's death due to smallpox, people in Turkey were already being inoculated with a weak form of smallpox to prevent dying from it later. Called ingrafting, the procedure was performed by placing smallpox pus (eeew!) from a weak strain of the disease *directly into the patient's veins*. After a weeklong incubation period, the patient got sick for a week and was thereafter resistant to the disease. Lady Mary Wortley Montagu chronicled this in a letter to England in 1717 in which she doubted that the procedure would catch on in her home country since the doctors there stood to make more money by treating the more prolonged, if often fatal, form of the disease. Fortunately, the technique of inoculation (without the pus these days, thanks very much) eventually caught on.

found his congregation not at all "revived." In the early 1730s, Edwards prayed that he could lead his church into a "harvest" and that God's Spirit would come revitalize the Christian community. In 1734, he began a revival, preaching on the basic premise of Protestantism— justification by faith. By the end of that year he could see a change. As he put it, "The Spirit of God began extraordinarily to set in."

His message was Calvinist. Though he believed that only the elect would be saved, he also believed that the preacher had a responsibility to preach as if everyone could be saved. He should preach as if his entire congregation were elect. Taking that approach as his baseline, Edwards concentrated on the idea of repentance. His sermons presented the absolute "terribleness" of sin and the absolute necessity of turning away from it. His most famous sermon, "Sinners in the Hands of an Angry God," delivered in 1741, is a masterpiece, though not typical of Edwards. The sermon presents the peril of the sinner who will not repent. He uses the vivid image of the sinner as a spider being held over a flame. At any moment He can drop the sinner into certain death. As Edwards wrote in this sermon, "There is nothing that keeps wicked men at any one moment out of hell, but the mere pleasure of God." In Edwards's worldview, man deserves nothing but torment and eternal punishment, and God's wrath burns against sinful man. This sermon is frightening; its view of God is menacing. Though Edwards would sometimes use this emotional approach, it was not his usual fare. His normal sermon was much less emotional in content and approach. However, "Sinners" shows Edwards's ability to use emotion to motivate his congregation.

For several years Edwards's preaching drew larger and larger crowds to church, and more and more converts. By the time the Awakening reached its peak, Northampton had become a religious center of revival. News of this revival spread all over the colonies, and similar revivals happened elsewhere. The news even traveled back to England where it served as a source of encouragement for ministers wishing to start a revival in their communities.

 DID YOU KNOW?

The first college commencement on American soil was held in 1642 at Harvard. The graduating class that year was a whopping nine people.

The Bronx, New York, got its name after Jonas Bronck, a seventeenth-century man whose farm was north of Manhattan. The Broncks' place became the Broncks' and then simply the Bronx.

SUCCESS BRINGS CONTROVERSY

Edwards's success in Massachusetts did not go unnoticed by other ministers in America, even by those who opposed his theology. In 1741, his "Sinners in the Hands of an Angry God" was published in pamphlet form. In 1743, Charles Chauncy, who pastored the Congregationalist church in Boston, challenged the emotional revivalism of Edwards in a pamphlet "Seasonable Thoughts on the State of Religion in New England." Chauncy's position was one of theological liberalism. As the years went on, Chauncy became one of Edwards's biggest detractors. In the end, New England moved away from Edwards's Calvinism and toward a more liberal theological position. Nevertheless, Jonathan Edwards's Awakening was to have a major impact on efforts to revive the church in America and Europe.

OTHER "REVIVORS"
Jonathan Edwards was not the first minister in America to take on the task of revival. As early as the 1720s, Theodore Jacobus Frelinghuysen had started a revival in the Raritan Valley in New Jersey. Frelinghuysen was a Dutch Reformed minister from a Pietist background in Germany. He was a passionate preacher who had great success but who earned the disapproval of the church officials in Amsterdam. These officials still controlled the American congregations of that denomination.

Also in New Jersey, Gilbert Tenant was encouraged by Freylinghuysen's success and led a revival to the Presbyterian denomination. But the greatest of the itinerant revivalists was George Whitefield (pronounced whit-field). Whitefield arrived from England in 1740 for his second American visit and set off on a six-week tour. This tour led to the most widespread awakening that America had yet experienced. Soon after he started, his crowds were too large to be held in churches, so Whitefield started preaching in the open air. Before he left the Boston stop on his tour, he preached a farewell sermon to approximately twenty thousand people.

These men, and others, rekindled a religious spirit in the American colonies. Meanwhile, preachers such as Whitefield had started a similar awakening in England. Whitefield had friends there who were about to start a new movement. They were the Wesley brothers.

TRANSATLANTIC REVIVALISM
The spirit of revivalism was not just an American phenomenon. While it had strong roots in the non-Anglican churches in England, there were two Anglican brothers who had an amazing impact on the whole idea of revival. They were John and Charles Wesley. These brothers were born in the rectory of the church at Epworth in Lincolnshire. They grew up to be English preachers,

evangelists, hymn writers, and the founders of Methodism. Their father was a staunch Anglican clergyman, but their grandparents had been nonconformists. Their mother, Susanna Wesley, was a strong woman who had a great influence on her sons.

John was born in 1703 and Charles four years later. The young men showed both talent and intellectual capacity. In 1726, Charles entered Oxford University just as his older brother was finishing his study there and moving on to be a fellow at Lincoln College. John had prepared to be a clergyman (he was ordained in 1728), and he returned to Lincolnshire to serve as his father's curate. He returned to Oxford in 1729 to find that his brother had organized a group of fellow Christians into the Holy Club. This group included Charles, John Hervey, and George Whitefield. This Holy Club had strict rules. The members met at first on Sunday evenings for strict observance of sacrament. Then it met every evening to read the classics and the Greek New Testament. Wednesdays and Fridays were fast days for the boys, and they actually were boys. Charles was twenty-two, but both Whitefield and Hervey were only fifteen. It was Charles who guided George Whitefield in the devotional reading that led to Whitefield's conversion.

Not long after John's return, the older brother took over leadership of the group. John imposed an even more methodical approach to the group's spiritual work. The group was very methodical and very organized in how they met and what they studied. They were of course the victims of jeering and undergraduate taunting. The members were called Enthusiasts, Bible Moths, and Sacramentarians, but the tag that stuck to them was Methodists.

In April of 1735, the brothers lost their father to death. In October, the brothers left for Georgia with two other Methodists and a party of Moravians. The trip was on behalf of a missionary group, The Society for the Propagation of the Gospel. Their ship, *Simmonds,* encountered storms in the Atlantic, and John, despite his convictions, found his fear stronger than his faith. The trip was not a success. Charles returned to England in 1736 because his health was failing in Georgia, and in 1738 John returned. Upon his return to England he founded a society that met for the first time on May 1.

The brothers were changed by their trip, and they had been very influenced by the Moravians, including Peter Böhler. During one week in May 1738, both brothers had a deep religious experience. John's experience occurred on May 24, and it changed him forever. John was at a Moravian meeting in Aldersgate Street when a passage from Martin Luther's *Preface to Romans* was being read. The experience convicted him in three ways. First, Wesley felt that it was a true, *personal* conversion. The result of the conversion was a total conviction that Christ had died for him. The death and resurrection of Christ was not an act with the *general*

SINNERS AND SAINTS
THE MORAVIANS

The Moravians were (and are) an evangelical Christian group. They originated in Bohemia among some of John Hus's followers, who broke with Rome in 1467. They were severely persecuted but survived. They had a renewal after 1722 on the Saxon estate of Graf von Zinzendorf. In America the sect founded Bethlehem, Pennsylvania, in 1740. That city remains the center of the Moravians in the United States. The Moravians take scripture as the authority over faith and morals. They have a simple liturgy and a modified episcopal organization.

effect of forgiveness. Instead, Christ's death was for individual sinners. Since Christ was willing to die for each of us, Wesley believed that we must therefore trust in Christ alone for our salvation.

TRAVELING EVANGELISTS

After these experiences, the two brothers felt that the people must hear this message of salvation no matter what. The parish church was fine for some things, but the Wesleys believed their message had to be spread to all people. They felt called to travel from place to place bringing the message to the people. Whenever it was possible, they preached in churches, but before long they were encountering opposition that drove them into the markets or onto the town common area. In many ways being forced out of the churches helped give impetus to their revival. Often the churches were known more for their lack of spirit than their presence. Also, the "High Church" was becoming more and more the church of the upper class. By being forced into the markets and onto the commons, the Wesleys were able to reach the working lower class.

The brothers worked tirelessly. In 1749, Charles married Sarah Gwynne and made his home in Bristol. There he supervised the society that met at New Room. In 1771, he moved to London. He was one of the most gifted and prolific hymn writers ever. He wrote over seven thousand hymns

 DID YOU KNOW?

As a hymn writer, Augustus Toplady was a contemporary of Charles Wesley. Toplady's hymn "Rock of Ages" (written in 1775) was composed on the back of a playing card, a six of diamonds.

and poems. He almost single-handedly popularized the hymn as a part of the worship experience. Hymn singing became an integral part of evangelical worship and was one of the powerful factors in the success of the revival which the Wesley brothers started. In addition to his development of church organization, John Wesley left us his *Journal* for posterity. This work records the travels of the man who rode 250,000 miles on horseback to spread the gospel.

THE METHODIST SOCIETY

The Wesley brothers' success led to a problem—how could they take care of the needs of the people they converted? Their answer was the Methodist society. The brothers would take down the names and addresses of their converts, and these would be shared with other converts. The result was a Christian community taking care of each other's spiritual needs. Methodism began, then, not as a denomination or even a sect. John Wesley had no intention of breaking away from the Anglican Church. He assumed that the members of the Methodist societies would attend services in an Anglican Church and take sacraments there.

The parent society of Methodism was in London. As early as 1739 John had bought a deserted gun factory outside London for his prayer meetings. This location was to become the central hub of Methodism until 1778 when the City Road Chapel opened. From that hub, the Methodist societies grew nationwide. In 1743, John drew up a common set of rules for all the societies. In 1744, the first conference was held within Methodism to determine the best way to carry "on the work of God" throughout England. The solution was a series of circuits or "preachers' rounds." The circuits were under the supervision of an assistant who, if need be, could step in and take the place of one of the parish ministers. The assistants reported to Wesley himself.

With this organization, Methodism became firmly established in all areas of Britain except Scotland (which remained firmly Presbyterian). Starting in 1760, the Methodist movement arrived in America in the person of an Irish Methodist named Robert Strawbridge who settled in Maryland and started evangelizing there. However, the person given the credit for establishing American Methodism was Francis Asbury. He answered the call to come to America in 1771 and remained in the colonies throughout the Revolutionary War. In 1784, John Wesley appointed him and Thomas Coke as superintendents for the Methodist Church in America. Later, a conference voted Coke and Asbury bishops and renamed the church in America the Methodist Episcopal Church.

Also in 1784, Wesley had prepared a legal Deed of Declaration that ensured that on his death his authority would pass to the Methodist Conference, which was composed of one hundred members of the Methodist societies. In 1787, the Toleration Act enabled the church to license its own "preaching places." In 1795, Methodism seceded from the Anglican Church and became its own entity, ready to evangelize the world.

Methodism was in many ways a step into a new era. The stoic days of the Enlightenment were quickly fading as the eighteenth century came to a close. There would soon be a recognition in philosophy, literature, theology, and art that Reason was no God after all. The revolutions in America and France, which had been justified by rationalists' arguments, created whole new societies in France and the New World. The revolutions may have had good, rational justifications, but they

DID YOU KNOW?

The colony of Maryland was founded, in part, as a haven for Catholics seeking religious freedom.

were acts of passion. As writers, artists, and philosophers realized, emotion and passion can be pathways to truth as well. This was no surprise to the revivalists. They had discovered a zeal for their faith in the conversion of the heart.

ULTIMATE IMPACT OF AND ON CHRISTIANITY

Some Christian writers have written that Descartes's moment of doubt was one of the darkest days in the history of the church. They feel that his doubt set off a chain reaction that led to our modern skepticism, cynicism, and lack of faith.

They could very well be right.

They could also trace a little further back and see that Descartes's doubt was inevitable. His doubt was simply the long-term effect of the shattering of certainty that was the Reformation. The church, rightly or wrongly, had held the world's philosophical certainty in its hands for a thousand years. The Reformation put it in the hands of ordinary men. It gave each man the right to study the scripture in a search for truth.

It was no coincidence that some who made that search came up with uncertainty. It is true that the uncertainty of our time is a product of the Enlightenment. We can trace the history of doubt from Descartes's *Cogito, ergo sum* in his time to Heisenberg's uncertainty principle in our own. (In layman's terms, Heisenberg said that anything that we observe is influenced by our position and by our attempts to observe it. We can never know, then, with certainty what is real because we can never see it.) In the Enlightenment, doubt fostered lack of religious faith. The thinkers of the Enlightenment looked for things they could rely upon, and they latched on Reason. When writers pointed out the possible failings of Reason, the doubt came creeping in again.

THE CHURCH'S RESPONSE
The church in the Enlightenment either had no defense against the prevailing thought of the age or did not exercise it well. The Roman Catholic Church simply opposed any thoughts that differed from its views of the world. For that church, change was still the enemy. The Protestant churches did little better, if at all. The Anglicans and Lutherans lapsed into tedium. We do not read of great spiritual leaders in this era, though certainly there were some. They were overshadowed by the age's best minds who either left the church or wrestled with the church throughout their lives. In some ways, then, it is the Enlightenment that places secularism as a real opponent of the church. Is that not a huge challenge for us today? Do the best and brightest go into the work of the church as they did in the Middle Ages? Is the allure of secular philosophy or even scientific endeavor greater than a life's work in theology? These are questions that we are forced to think about.

In the United States, we are challenged almost every day in our newspapers to think about the political impact of John Locke. The hottest social issues of our time, including abortion, the death penalty, prayer in school, all rest on Constitutional arguments. Locke's influence was immeasurable on the framers of our Constitution, as was their belief in Deism. In that way, the United States, as a nation, is really a product of the Enlightenment.

But as a people we are much more. Our government may have been formed out of rationalistic ideals, but our original citizens were the products of religious dissension. It is easy to see that our culture was shaped by our ancestors being outsiders, people who did not like the status quo and separated from it. Our country may reflect the democratic ideals of Locke, but it also reflects the Puritan ideals of Jonathan Edwards. We may not be a Puritan country (perhaps after the original colonies we never were!), but religious conservatism has left a serious imprint on our national psyche.

The Age of Enlightenment, with its beginning of revival, was very brief, but it changed the world. It ushered in a belief in science that led to the Industrial Revolution. It confronted the new institutions of the Reformation with Deism, rationalism, skepticism, and doubt. It also confronted them with a new energy of revival. Methodism confronted the world with a missionary spirit, but it was certainly not unique in that regard. The Presbyterians, the Independents, the Baptists, the Pietists, and scores of smaller movements also dispersed throughout the world spreading their version of the gospel.

POLITICS

In politics, the Enlightenment set the stage for the French and American Revolutions. The English already had their revolution out of the way (the execution of Charles I and the establishment of the Commonwealth in 1649). The Reformation had shown that overthrow of a massive power was possible, and the Enlightenment provided the philosophical basis for the right to overthrow an unjust ruler. In religion, as well as politics, a new age was being born in which the people held greater power than they had in centuries. We in the twenty-first century are the beneficiaries of that change. Though monarchies and even an emperor lay in the future for Europe, power would rest more and more in the hands of the governed. We can thank the Enlightenment for that.

We can thank the revival of the eighteenth century for re-energizing the church into a vital cog in society. Many denominations are evangelical today because of their awakening in the seventeenth and eighteenth centuries. This revival took religion out of the pews where a stalled Reformation had placed it, and put it in the workplace, the town square, and in the home. The concept of the Christian life most people hold today dates from these early evangelists. The prevailing emphasis on personal faith has its roots in Luther's writings to be sure, but it comes to us through the preaching of eighteenth-century evangelists, especially John Wesley. We should not forget, either, that almost all of our Christian musical heritage has its roots from the tireless work of Isaac Watts and Charles Wesley, who made hymn singing an act of worship on a par with hearing a sermon. From John Wesley and Jonathan Edwards, we have inherited the idea that though not all people are elect, the preacher should preach as if they were. This is a core issue to evangelism and missionary work.

The Age of Enlightenment was much more than merely a pause between the upheaval of the Reformation and the development of the modern state. It was the source of much of what we believe about our political and social lives and how we educate our children. It was the age in which the Protestant churches grew up and started taking their messages throughout the world. It was the age that created numbing doubt and started the slow climb toward the modern world of today.

CHAPTER EIGHT

revolutions and revivals
(a.d. 1789 to a.d. 1900)

👁 UNDERSTANDING THE TIMES

Living in the nineteenth century must have felt like everything was up for grabs. New ways of thinking. New ways of working. New ways of manufacturing. New ways of governing. New ways of theologizing. New ways of writing.

Industrialization changed the way most things were done. Romanticism changed the way most things were thought about. Liberal theology and historical criticism changed many tools of the faith.

The American Revolution birthed a new nation, a soon-to-be world power. The French Revolution left France changed forever. The Industrial Revolution, spawned in Britain, sped up and streamlined manufacturing in a way that affected worldwide economy.

Faith communities became more distinct. Denominations organized. The wild West was won. Missions ran like wildfire.

FROM ONE REVOLUTION TO ANOTHER

The *World Book Encyclopedia* states, "People who work to replace an old system with a new one are called revolutionaries." According to that definition, history is full of revolutionaries. The nineteenth century was overflowing with them.

The Renaissance revolutionized the way people expressed themselves. The Reformation revolutionized the way people believed. The Enlightenment revolutionized the way society thought. The nineteenth century revolutionized the way individuals experienced life and faith.

The revolutions of the nineteenth century actually began toward the end of the eighteenth century, maybe as early as the American Revolution. During the Reformation, church leaders and lay leaders had been brave enough to say to the church government, "No. We won't do it this way anymore." At the end of the eighteenth century, people found the courage to say that to their own governments. In this way America came into its own. Inspired by that, Frenchmen took their stand.

FAITH REVOLUTIONS

The birth of the church happened in Jerusalem. It was in Palestine that Jesus did His work. Faith spread out from there in semiconcentric circles. First Paul and the early church leaders spread the word all around the Mediterranean and into Europe. Then Christianity spread throughout Europe by the nature of Christian governments and the powerful Catholic Church.

But as Christianity spread, the outer edges seem to be where the life was kept. As the church of the Holy Roman Empire grew stale, the lands that they had evangelized took up the flame. As the circle spread out through Europe and on into America, missionary zeal and revival fervor led the way. Often the newest generation of converts became the missionaries back to the nations that led to their conversion. That tendency remains even today.

Certainly in the nineteenth century Christianity weakened. Some even say it died in Europe. It wasn't just the intellectualism of the Enlightenment that did it. It was the secularization of the masses. It was the increasing belief and worldview that we can define ourselves without God as one of the reference points.

THE STORY OF THE TIMES

THE AMERICAN REVOLUTION

While the tension had been building for years between the United Kingdom and its American colonies, the actual American Revolution began in 1775 with a military conflict that lasted for eight years. During that eight-year conflict, the American leadership signed the Declaration of Independence. The conflict ended in 1783 when the United Kingdom signed the Treaty of Paris, recognizing the independence that the colonies had declared for themselves officially in 1776. Soon after, the American government organized into the three branches that it still functions in today.

In the aftermath of the war, the American government, the United Kingdom, and the French government were left in severe debt. The thirteen colonies recovered largely through taxation (with representation). The United

TIMELINE OVERVIEW

In the midst of World History...

Christian History unfolds...

1776 North America: The Declaration of Independence

c. 1780 The Industrial Revolution begins in Britain.

1789 The French Revolution begins.

U.S.: The U.S. Constitution is established.

1793 William Carey's mission to India

1798 Wordsworth and Coleridge impact Romantic poetry.

1799 Egypt: The Rosetta Stone is discovered.

1811 Disciples of Christ founded.

1812 American Board of Commissioners for Foreign Missions sends Adoniram and Ann Judson to India.

1816 AME Church founded by Richard Allen

1830 First American missionaries reach Hawaii.

1830 U.S.: Charles G. Finney begins to hold revivals in urban areas—organizes revivals in a modern way.

1833 Britain: Oxford Movement is established to reform the Anglican Church.

1852 David Livingstone begins his work in Africa.

1858 Transatlantic cable is laid.

1859 Britain: Charles Darwin publishes *On the Origin of Species*, explaining his theory of evolution.

1854 Hudson Taylor extends missions in China.

1854 Charles Haddon Spurgeon begins his ministry.

1861 North America: The Civil War begins (ends in 1865).

1869 The Suez Canal opens, joining the Mediterranean and Red Seas.

1865 Salvation Army founded by William Booth

U.S.: The first transcontinental railroad is completed.

1869 Pope Pius IX calls the First Vatican Council.

Russia: Tolstoy completes *War and Peace*.

1873 U.S.: First commercial typewriters are manufactured.

1873 Dwight L. Moody begins as a traveling evangelist.

Kingdom recovered through taxes and (ironically enough) their increased trade with the very colonies they had just fought to keep hold of. France nearly went bankrupt because of the aid they offered to the colonies during the Revolutionary War. The financial straits that France experienced laid the groundwork for the French Revolution.

THE FRENCH REVOLUTION

The cry of the French Revolution was "Liberty, Equality, and Fraternity." The revolution, inspired in part by the American Revolution, began in 1789 with the storming of the Bastille, a fort and former prison that had become a symbol of oppression among the French people.

The Bastille was a fortress built in 1370. It later became a prison in which the king could imprison anyone who displeased him. By the time the workers of France stormed the Bastille, there were only a few prisoners held there. The charge was not meant to free the prisoners, but rather to take the gunpowder housed there to provide artillery for the conflict. The day after the event, the people began to tear the structure down.

The Revolution officially lasted until Napoleon Bonaparte took over the government in 1799. During the Revolution, both the king,

 DID YOU KNOW?

George III of England (1738–1820) was king during the American Revolution. What most people *don't* know is that he was prone to bouts of insanity. During one of these, he got out of his coach and shook hands with a tree, having mistaken the majestic oak for the King of Prussia. Maybe *that's* how he got all those crazy ideas about taxing the Americans.

We all know of George Washington's military exploits as a U.S. general during the Revolutionary War, but few people stop to ask where he got the experience to be such a fine commander. He got it, of course, by working his way up to colonel in the British army before there was a U.S.

The first major bill passed by Congress was a tax bill. I bet you could have guessed that.

Louis XVI, and his wife, Marie Antoinette, were executed by guillotine in what was called the "Reign of Terror."

The French Revolution did not result in a democratic government. It did result in a government that had a new inkling of an understanding about the power of the populace.

THE U.S. CONSTITUTION

The same year that the Paris workers stormed the Bastille, the United States leadership signed the Constitution. Religious freedom was such an important issue in the colonies. Because of this, the first amendment of the Constitution addressed the relationship between religion and government.

Amendment 1: Freedom of religion, speech, and the press; rights of assembly and petition

Congress shall make no law respecting an establishment of religion, or prohibiting the free exercise thereof; or abridging the freedom of speech, or of the press; or the right of the people peaceably to assemble, and to petition the government for a redress of grievances.

Considering the history of religious oppression that brought many of the forefathers to America, it's understandable that the Constitution would provide some protection against religious persecution. Today this amendment has been interpreted into what is commonly called "the separation of church and state."

From the days of Constantine, the church, for all its mistakes, had great influence on government decisions and

 IMAGINE THAT!

The American Revolution and the French Revolution are both celebrated in July—July 4 and 14, respectively.

Both countries celebrate with parades, music, and parties. The French failed to celebrate their independence day from 1939–1945 due to the occupation of France by the Germans.

policies. In fact, during some of the eras since Constantine, the church controlled the government. Through the Constitution, America set as law that the church was to be a voluntary organization, separate from the government. This was an intentional limit on too much control by government. In setting this limit, though, the church gave up some of its corporate influence in political arenas.

LIBERALISM IN GOVERNMENT
The word "liberalism" applies to the nineteenth century on several levels. First of all, it applies to government.

Today we have many conceptions of liberalism. If you are talking to someone who considers himself conservative, most of those conceptions are not positive. The root of the word liberalism is the same as that of liberty. Liberalism in nineteenth-century politics was a voice for the middle class: voting rights, representative legislature, freedom to earn without government intervention. Liberalism was a movement for freedom.

 SET THE STAGE! PREAMBLE TO THE CONSTITUTION
We the people of the United States, in order to form a more perfect Union, establish justice, insure domestic tranquility, provide for the common defense, promote the general welfare, and secure the blessings of liberty to ourselves and our posterity, do ordain and establish this Constitution for the United States of America.

LIBERALISM IN THEOLOGY
The nineteenth century was also marked by liberalism in theology. The Enlightenment had been an opening of the public mind. It was an age of Reason. During the nineteenth century, those critical skills were turned upon the very nature of faith and of the Bible. Scholars, inside and outside of the circle of faith, began to demand that the same tactics for establishing the veracity and historicity of any ancient manuscripts be applied to the Bible. This was called "historical criticism."

To many this criticism seemed to be doubt, even sin. To many today it still does. The Bible was subjected to great scrutiny by theologians and scholars alike. Harry Emerson Fosdick, pastor of Riverside Church, held that the central aim of liberal theology was to make it possible for a man "to be both an intelligent modern and a serious Christian." His perspective was similar to that of Clement of the third century, who worked to make his faith palatable to the educated people of his day.

Protestant liberalism finds some of its origins in the same questions the church asked itself from the beginning: How do we show our world the relevance of faith? How do we speak their language?

The problems were not simply with the methods of literary criticism. The problems were the same faced in the Enlightenment. Would Reason rule or would faith rule? Using critical methods to understand the tools of our faith is one thing. Using critical methods to determine our faith or even in place of it is something different.

 QUOTABLES

H. Richard Niebuhr (theologian) described the watered-down faith that he believed nineteenth-century liberalism spawned in this way: "A God without wrath brought men without sin into a kingdom without judgment through the ministrations of a Christ without a cross."

Instead of starting from scripture as the absolute rule, liberalism focused on modern thought and Christian experience, neither of which is made up of absolute truth.

MISSIONS

Early in the nineteenth century, Protestant Christianity scarcely existed outside Europe and America. There were traces in India and the East Indies (because of the Dutch). Africa was a dark mystery. Even though the Christian faith was in a state of decay in Europe, the nineteenth century was a huge era of expansion for Christianity through missions. Not since the fifth century was there such an expansion, and even that was not proportionately as large as the news that was spread through the missions and revivals of the 1800s.

WILLIAM CAREY

In regard to missions, William Carey was a mover and a shaker. In fact, he is called the "Father of Modern Missions." After spending most of his life as an English cobbler, Carey traveled to India in 1793. He built a life and ministry there, and by doing so he introduced the world to a new way of thinking about missions.

Previous to Carey's influence, missions was seen as a message taken to individuals. Carey, on the other hand, had a vision for whole countries. It was not the forced national conversions of the past. Rather, it was the idea that instead of carrying a missionary's own culture to another world, the missionary should carry just the message and let the message infiltrate that culture in its present form. In Carey's way of thinking you wouldn't go to India and teach the people American Protestant Christianity (for instance) and stay as the leader. Instead you would go, understand the Indian way of life, share with them the news of the gospel, give them the scriptures in their own language, train leaders from their own people, and then let them follow the Holy Spirit as they walk out their faith.

Carey worked with Andrew Fuller and together they did missions just that way. Carey also formed the Baptist Missionary Society, supervised six complete translations of the Bible, and published his own works, including *An Enquiry into the Obligation of Christians to Use Means for the Conversion of the Heathen* (1792).

 QUOTABLES

"Never had any other set of ideas, religious or secular, been propagated over so wide an area by so many professional agents maintained by the unconstrained donation of so many millions of individuals."
Kenneth Scott Latourette, historian, on missions in the 1800s

MISSIONS AND MERCHANDISING

In Carey's most famous written work, he made a great point to the Christian culture of his day. He addressed five obstacles that most complained stood in the way of missions to "heathens":

- The distance to be traveled
- The barbarism to be faced
- The danger of the travel and, sometimes, the experience itself
- The difficulty of raising financial support for the endeavor
- The language difference

After categorizing the difficulties, Carey made an undeniable observation: These obstacles had not stopped merchandising from expanding. Why should it stop Christianity? So he looked at what a trading company would do and encouraged missions to do the same thing. He created an organization of volunteers called the Baptist Missionary Society and carried on. He studied Hindu (learning his market). He lived in Serampore (going to the marketplace). He impacted the Indian culture and the rest of the world with his well thought-out philosophy of carrying the message of Christ.

VOLUNTEERISM
Carey's mission society highlights a trend of the nineteenth century: voluntary societies. Volunteer organizations were a tremendous influence in the nineteenth century. They focused on a task rather than theological similarities. Because of this they...

- Enabled interdenominational interaction,
- Caused people to explore forms of organization different from the traditional church, and
- Influenced the power structure of the church by empowering lay leaders.

Thus far along the historical path, the connections and associations that Christianity had formed were focused on worship practices and theological premises. In the nineteenth century, with the beginnings of organizations that we now think of as "parachurch," there was a whole different way of thinking. The London Missionary Society, founded in 1795, left behind denominationalism altogether in its zeal for evangelism. In fact, it referred to denominationalism as bigotry. The ironic thing about this is that the original Catholic Church of the second and third centuries came from a similar perspective. Then the reformers, in an effort to correct the mistakes of the church, formed branches of the faith. With the volunteer organizations came a move back toward a joint faith.

In the U.S.A., missions organizations were forming as they were in Britain. In 1810, the American Board of Commissioners for Foreign Missions was established at Congregational Andover Theological Seminary. The group was led by Samuel J. Mills and spawned such missionaries as Adoniram Judson.

By the end of the nineteenth century, almost every Christian body around the world had a plan and an organization for evangelizing at least a target group of the world.

THE INDUSTRIAL REVOLUTION

Not only was the nineteenth century a time of a missions revolution, it was the time of an Industrial Revolution, as well. While both of those revolutions spread throughout the world, their epicenter was Great Britain. In the late 1700s, London was the world center of finance. It was then and there that the Industrial

SINNERS AND SAINTS
ADONIRAM JUDSON

Adoniram Judson was a Baptist clergyman in the early nineteenth century. He graduated from Andover Seminary (Congregationalist) and was instrumental in founding the American Board of Commissioners for Foreign Missions. While Judson eventually parted ways with the Congregationalist denomination, he spent his life working as a missionary in Burma. He wrote a Burmese grammar and eventually completed a translation of the Burmese Bible. He also compiled an English-Burmese dictionary.

Revolution began, but by the early 1800s it had spread throughout western Europe and into the northeastern United States.

Two hallmarks of the Industrial Revolution were power-driven machines and organized factories. Both of these factors increased the rate of production and the burnout of the workers. Looking back from a more modern view, it is not difficult to underestimate the resounding changes in society because of the Industrial Revolution. We are so accustomed to assembly lines and power tools and mass production. Keep in mind, though, that the changes of this time didn't just affect the way things were made and services were performed. They affected the way people lived.

Previous to this point in history, most people made their income through agriculture or through handwork. There was *some* organization among workers called *guilds*. With the advent of industry, all that changed. People needed to be near cities to find work. And since work depended more on the efficiency of machines than the skills of the people who ran them, the employee became a much less valued commodity. By the end of the nineteenth century, many of the abuses of workers had been corrected or at least regulated, but industry raised a lot of questions in regard to how much should be expected of workers.

 SET THE STAGE!

In 1779, an armed mob of some eight thousand people destroyed factory machines in England. The angry rabble, mostly textile workers, believed that the machines were taking jobs away from workers. Sound familiar? The movement behind the incident, and others like it, was called Luddism and died out after increased production and lower costs, due mostly to the machines, led to wage increases for most workers.

The Industrial Revolution changed life and business in positive and negative ways. No matter which you focus on, it changed the world forever.

THE PROTESTANTS: A REVIEW

Since the Reformation, the body of Christ has appeared in more forms than at any time previously. By the nineteenth century, the Protestant branch of the Christian faith had followed this kind of course:

1500s: The first groups that broke away from the Catholic Church retained many of the basic beliefs and worship practices they were familiar with. These groups included the Lutherans (followers of Luther's teachings), the Reformed or Presbyterians (followers of Zwingli and Calvin), and the Anglicans or Episcopalians.

1500–1600s: Since the first wave of Protestant groups retained many Catholic practices, the next wave of reformers snubbed them as if they were not reformers at all. This next wave of Protestant groups adopted much different forms of worship. These groups included the Anabaptists, Quakers, Separatists, and Shakers.

SET THE STAGE!

The 1800s, era of the Industrial Revolution, were witness to some of the worst pollution the world has ever seen. The industrialized part of England was referred to as the "Black Country," a desolate, barren area where plants were dead or dying and the land was blackened "as far as the eye could reach" from coal smoke with a high sulphur content. This period prompted some of the first environmentalists to action.

1500–1600s: The free church movements included the Congregational and Baptist denominations. By the end of the nineteenth century, the Baptist denomination was the largest in the United States.

1700s: The Methodists were marked by personal devotion and a commitment to morality. They were sometimes called Wesleyan because they grew from the followers of the teaching of John Wesley.

1800–1900s: The more conservative and enthusiastic branches of Methodism gave birth to the Holiness Movement, including the Nazarenes. In the early 1900s, the Holiness Movement, in turn, inspired a movement called Pentecostalism.

Pentecostalism has become one of the most rapidly growing forms of Protestantism. The Pentecostals worship in an enthusiastic style that is most often described as charismatic.

LOW CHURCH AND HIGH CHURCH

The Protestant denominations of the nineteenth and twentieth centuries can be categorized according to their polity (government) and their theology (beliefs), and by their worship practices. Most worship practices are described as either "High Church" or "Low Church."

When a church is described as "High Church," it usually means that symbolism and ritual will play an integral part in their service. They will more likely recite previously written prayers and follow a more strict order of service.

In a "Low Church" service, the message is still the focus, but the methods are much more up for grabs. The services can be less predictable and sometimes less organized.

Both styles of worship can be given to ritual because by nature humans default to what they are comfortable and familiar with. But the priorities at the start of planning the services are different, even though they work toward similar ends.

 SET THE STAGE!

When referring to style in worship, the word "liturgy" comes up a lot. Mostly we talk about the liturgies of more High Church styles of worship, rituals that are repeated formally. The most familiar liturgies would probably be the Eucharist or Communion. The truth is that even the churches that walk away from formal worship styles develop their own kind of liturgy, just more of an informal brand.

ROMANTICISM

Romanticism played a large role in the cultural development of the nineteenth century.

Romanticism is a style. This style can be found in a lot of different places: art, music, writing, etc. Romanticism is an emphasis on passion and emotion and the supernatural rather than reason and rationalism. It is freedom of expression. It is flavored with spontaneity rather than control.

The Enlightenment had been a time of rationalism. It had, in some ways, all but squeezed the breath out of any connection with God and celebration of His creation. While the liberalism of the nineteenth century built on the rationalism of the eighteenth, Romanticism went a different way. It was the arts taking that deep breath right back in, trying something new, trying it a new way, letting the classical way of doing things fade and some new methods take hold.

While most historians identify the Romantic period as being from the late 1700s to the mid-1800s, it was not so cut-and-dried as that. Romantics have been around in every century. But this was definitely a period when not only industry was "bustin' loose," the arts were, as well.

ROMANTICISM IN LITERATURE

One of the biggest Romantic accomplishments in literature was the Gothic novel. The plot of a Gothic novel typically included mysterious and supernatural events, and most of them were intended to give the reader the "heebie-jeebies." Most of the stories took place in gloomy, medieval places with secret tunnels and high towers.

While the earliest Gothic novels were written in the late eighteenth century, elements of the style carried into the nineteenth century in works such as *Frankenstein* (Shelley) and *Wuthering Heights* (Brontë). American writers such as Nathaniel Hawthorne and Edgar Allan Poe were influenced by the Gothic style. Eventually, though, love won out over terror, and the hot novels of the day became more about romantic love.

ROMANTICISM IN POETRY

When historians refer to Romanticism in nineteenth-century poetry, they never fail to mention William Wordsworth. The works of Wordsworth and his associate, Samuel Taylor Coleridge, are regarded as the beginning of the English Romantic Movement.

Wordsworth believed that poems should be accessible to the reader both in the language they use and in the stories they tell. He claimed that poetry should be "emotion recollected in tranquility."

Wordsworth and Coleridge both still hold influence even in the poetry of this century.

GOVERNMENTAL CHANGES

The end of the French Revolution was marked by Napoleon's rule. He led France through many military conquests but died as an exile. It was in 1815 that Napoleon's empire collapsed. That collapse signaled the end of an era. While monarchies still existed (and do until this day), the totalitarian monarchies of the previous centuries were an element of history. People and societies had stepped forward claiming their right not only to individual belief but to self-government. As the people quickly moved closer and closer to the individualism of the modern world, whole cultures did the same thing.

THE CLAPHAM SECT

In England, just before the turn of the nineteenth century, two religious sects were making a difference. One was the Clapham Sect (also called the Clapham Friends) led by William Wilberforce. The Clapham Sect spawned such organizations as the Church

 DID YOU KNOW?

By the 1800s, Shakespeare's work had gained such admiration that many snobbish, self-styled "experts" began to doubt that William Shakespeare, a *mere* actor and the humble son of a glovemaker, could have ever written such great works of literature. They proposed several candidates whom they thought more likely to be the "real" Shakespeare, almost all of whom were, of course, noblemen. It's a strange but true historical fact that makes many modern scholars shake their heads in laughing disbelief, but drama enthusiasts of the nineteenth century held such a high regard for the Bard of Avon that *they began to doubt he really existed.*

Missionary Society, the British and Foreign Bible Society, the Society for Bettering the Condition of the Poor, the Society for the Reformation of Prison Discipline, and many more. While the societies met for Bible study and prayer, they were also integrally involved in the affairs of their day.

 SINNERS AND SAINTS
CHARLES HADDON SPURGEON

Around the time that the Clapham Friends were fighting slavery, Charles Haddon Spurgeon was becoming one of the greatest British preachers of the nineteenth century. He began preaching around 1850 in the Baptist denomination, first in Cambridge, then in London. A six-thousand-seat auditorium, The Metropolitan Tabernacle, was built for his large audiences.

SLAVERY

The Clapham Friends influenced their community in many ways, but none so great as in the fight against slavery. As a member of Parliament, Wilberforce fought the British slave trade with every opportunity.

Britain's slave trade had begun with Sir John Hawkins in 1562. By 1770, there were around 100,000 slaves a year exported from West Africa by British slave traders. Wilberforce began his fight against the slave trade in 1789. By 1807, slave trade was made illegal. By 1833, the slaves in the British Empire were freed. Wilberforce died four days after this emancipation.

The Clapham Friends provided a great example of a religious organization bringing about national change after the separation of church and state. They still serve as an instance of Christians who become involved in government and patiently but effectively enforce change.

THE OXFORD MOVEMENT

While the Clapham sect submerged themselves in popular culture to effect change, the Oxford Movement stepped apart from society to make their reforms. The Oxford Movement was begun by three men:

- John Keble
- John Henry Newman
- Edward Pusey

These three men turned their sense of indignation with British society and government into a movement. They started simply by writing a series of tracts called *Tracts for the Times*. The men, in fact, became so associated with these tracts that the group came to be known as "Tractarians."

The Tractarians held up the early church as a model for reform in the Church of England. They shunned the name Protestant and claimed the name catholic (lowercase c), but only as the original church used it to mean the universal church. The members of the Oxford Movement set about to return to the most traditional forms of worship rather than reforming into a new way of doing church.

Many Tractarians converted back into the Roman Catholic Church. Others stayed in the Church of England but maintained many of the rich rituals of the Catholic Church. Mostly the Oxford Movement served to highlight the unique position of the church as a power separate from the government but powerful nonetheless. The Tractarians influenced greatly the Episcopal denomination in the Americas.

HOW THE WEST WAS WON

After the Revolutionary War, the United States began to grow westward. Pioneers of the American wilderness carried not only their dreams for land and freedom, but also the message of the gospel. From 1792 to 1821, nine new states were added to the first thirteen. By the middle of the nineteenth century, half of Americans lived west of the Appalachians.

More striking than the statistics of America's growth is this: In 1776, when the Declaration of Independence was signed, only 5 to10 percent of Americans were church members. While many groups came to the continent to escape religious persecution, obviously more came to start a new life.

One of the key players to change that was Lyman Beecher, an American clergyman. He preached a sermon called "A Plea for the West" describing the opportunities opening up in the American wilderness. He was a huge influence on the vision of a Christian America. The strength of his vision affected all of American Protestantism.

THE FIRST CAMP MEETING

About the time that Lyman Beecher was preaching about evangelizing the Wild West, James McGready was doing it. McGready held the first of what is now referred to as a camp meeting. It was held in Gasper River, Kentucky, in the summer of 1800. The meeting lasted for several days and included pioneers from as many as one hundred miles away.

McGready did something new for his time. It's an idea that has been expanded and adjusted but to this day remains in some form. Eventually camp meetings moved inside but followed the same format with the likes of Charles Finney, Dwight Moody, and eventually Billy Graham.

CHARLES FINNEY

Around 1830, Charles G. Finney was one of the first to move the camp meeting to urban settings. He began to hold "revival meetings" in urban areas. Finney was a lawyer before he was a preacher. His preaching was organized and reasonable. He ended his sermons by calling people to an "anxious bench" similar to the altars that many traditional congregations still use as a place of repentance and commitment.

Finney did even more than preach the gospel. He also dealt with contemporary social issues of his day such as slavery and temperance.

DAVID LIVINGSTONE AND AFRICA

At the same time that slavery was rising to the forefront as a

SINNERS AND SAINTS
ANTISLAVERY REFORMERS

Theodore Weld studied under the great preacher Charles Finney. Since Finney was a staunch opponent to slavery, it is not surprising that his protégé Weld wrote works such as *The Bible Against Slavery* (1837) and *Slavery As It Is*.

Harriet Beecher Stowe (daughter of Lyman Beecher) read *Slavery As It Is* over and over again. It became a major influence and impetus on her famous work *Uncle Tom's Cabin*.

key issue in both America and Britain, one missionary went right to the heart of things. David Livingstone began his work in Africa in the middle of the century. His first ten years were typical missions work. Then he started to travel across the continent. He became more of an "Indiana Jones" explorer type than the stereotypical missionary would have been. It was through his travels and then his descriptions of his travels

QUOTABLES

"I place no value on anything I have or may possess, except in relation to the kingdom of Christ."

David Livingstone, missionary to Africa

that Africa finally became a place the world knew about rather just a dark void in awareness and understanding.

Livingstone called the slave trade of central Africa the "open sore of the world." He fought the atrocity by training the Africans in commerce and in Christianity. His hope, of course, was that if he could help the people find a legitimate way to create income, they wouldn't fall so quickly into the fast money of slave trade.

ITALIAN UNITY

While Protestantism was blossoming in Britain and America, Catholicism was going through its own transition. Until the middle of the nineteenth century, Italy had been a loose confederation of states that shared the same boot-shaped peninsula. In the middle was a group of territories called the Papal States that were governed by the pope.

A movement hit midcentury which was called *risorgimento*, or "rebirth." This was a move to unify the whole boot with no foreign powers left in control. This movement was not unusual. Nationalism (a governmental form of individualism) was on the rise all over. This movement affected the power of the Catholic Church, however.

THE PAPAL STATES

The Papal States ran northeast from Rome across the peninsula. They were ruled by the pope, not just spiritually but politically, as well. In 1848, Pope Pius IX gave the Papal States a constitution which allowed the people of those states some power of choice. Shortly afterward, though, he renounced those rights and became once again absolute ruler. In this age of revolutions and rights, the people wouldn't stand for it. In 1870, Rome came under attack, and the pope took refuge in the Vatican. A year later the king, Victor Emmanuel, took up residence in Rome against the wishes of the pope.

 DID YOU KNOW?

Vatican City, the sovereign nation within the city of Rome and the official seat of power for the Catholic Church, occupies one-sixth of a square mile and is home to some one thousand people, making it the world's both smallest and least populous country.

This signaled a significant change. In the past, the pope had been able to strong-arm kings of many different nations with threats of excommunication. The king's residence marked the end of that power. The pope had no control over what the king did. For one thousand years, the Papal States had been a form of government, but no more. The pope tried several tactics, including compelling the Catholic population to refuse to take part in government. That, of course, was cutting off his nose to spite his face and left him with even less power. In fact, the pope didn't officially give up until 1929 when, in Mussolini's Lateran Treaty, the pope renounced all claims to the former Papal States and received full sovereignty only in the Vatican.

THE INFALLIBILITY OF THE POPE

The late 1800s were a time of testing the pope's authority in a variety of ways. In 1854, Pius IX declared as dogma the belief that Mary had been conceived without original sin. This wasn't news to the Catholic Church. It had been a stated position for years. But the pope made it official dogma without any committee consent. It was "ex cathedra," or "from the chair." This marked an increased sense of power on the pope's part.

Then, it was in 1870 that the First Vatican Council announced an official position on the infallibility of the pope. Infallibility didn't really carry the weight of "he doesn't have the ability to make a mistake." Rather, it was an expression of sovereignty regarding spiritual and church matters (it was more like "Whatever he says, goes"). During this time there were hymns addressed to the pope rather than God. Pius IX was even called "the vice-God of humanity." It's interesting to note that as the pope was losing power and authority outside the church, he was gaining control inside the church.

NINETEENTH-CENTURY COMMUNICATION

The nineteenth century was a quickly changing world in terms of communication.

As early as the 700s, books could be mass-produced, but only through a cumbersome process called "block printing." Then moveable type was invented, first in China in the 1000s, then by the Europeans in the 1400s. By the 1600s, print media was in heavy use for sales, record keeping, and news.

In the 1700s books, magazines, and newspapers were available for entertainment as well as information in many parts of the world. Late in the 1700s, Claude Chappe developed a visual telegraph that was basically a succession of towers between some large French cities. An operator controlled jointed arms on the roof of the towers to spell out messages. The next tower then relayed that message on (which is better than a string and tin can, but a lot bigger to manage).

In the 1800s, photography was developed, as well as the telegraph and telephone. The first real high-speed communication was the electric telegraph. Around 1830, Samuel Morse developed the Morse Code and a telegraph with a stable current. By the 1860s, most major cities were linked by telegraph lines. Around that time the first transatlantic cable was laid. For the first time in history, a message could be sent almost instantaneously between continents. Telephone use followed within decades. That means in less than one hundred years the world went from letters carried across the ocean on ships taking weeks and longer for delivery to the first instant messaging. It was a far cry from AOL, but it was still impressive.

 SET THE STAGE!

During the rule of Pope Pius IX, the U.S. president was the vaguely remembered Buchanan. Buchanan's presidency was overshadowed in many people's memories because the next president after Buchanan was Abraham Lincoln. Buchanan's term (1857–1861) was not, however, without a few noteworthy points. During his term of office, several states seceded from the Union in a tense prelude to the Civil War, the Pony Express flourished for eighteen months (and in that short time gained a permanent place in the mythos of the American West), telegrams crossed the sea on the first transatlantic cable (Buchanan received one from Queen Victoria of England), and the new song "Jingle Bells" became an instant favorite. Buchanan is also remembered as the only U.S. president who never married.

THEORIES ON ORIGINS

It was in the nineteenth century that the theory of evolution rose to the forefront. Charles Darwin's work *On the Origin of Species* remains the most famous writing on evolution. Darwin's work was based in part on an earlier work, though: *Principles of Geology* by Sir Charles Lyell, published in the early 1830s.

The theory of evolution typified the conflict between nineteenth century Christianity and science. It was and is a daunting conflict. When science seemed to contradict the Bible, the question was begged: Which should a person trust?

 DID YOU KNOW?

You've probably seen a zillion Westerns in which the Pony Express plays a role, but the innovative equine postal delivery system was suspended permanently on October 24, 1861, after just eighteen months of operation. The new technology of the telegraph was faster, cheaper, and didn't leave the same kind of mess behind.

Rarely in this conflict does there seem to be room to "wait and see." Often when science has seemed to conflict with the Bible, eventually the two come more into a parallel kind of agreement. The theory of evolution, though, was volatile to the utmost. It seemed to cut God out of the picture entirely regarding creation.

To add the theories of evolution to the theological liberalism of the nineteenth-century was to throw gasoline on a bonfire. The fire continues even to this day.

SLAVERY IN AMERICA

By 1830, there were about two million slaves in America. From 1800 to 1830, the antislavery movement was stronger in the South than in the North. Gradually, that pattern switched. Slaves became an important part of the economy of the South. Also, some saw the mention of slaves in the Bible as approval of the practice in theory.

In America, Charles Finney took on the role against slavery that Wilberforce of the Clapham Friends had in Britain. Finney was less successful, though. By 1861, the issue was incendiary enough that some states were willing to leave the Union over it. The Civil War broke out.

After the war, the role of the Christian subculture changed in both the North and the South. The South was battered and recovering. In the North, the conservative Christian element began to focus on the belief that the world would get worse and worse until Jesus returned. Unintentionally, this resulted in a decline in interest in social issues. If the world was going to get worse and worse anyway, it would have seemed that the best tactic was to convert as many as possible and let the world decline. Increasingly after this time American churches began to concentrate on Bible study and personal holiness as opposed to social issues.

DWIGHT L. MOODY

One of the preachers who rose to the forefront after the Civil War was Dwight L. Moody. Moody began as a traveling evangelist and urban revivalist. He was a good example of the trend of focusing on personal conversion and preparation for the coming of Christ.

Though men like Moody rose up in America during the nineteenth century, the chasm between the church and popular culture was widening. The different concerns of those who considered themselves "secular" from those that considered themselves "religious" grew more distinct.

A NEW KIND OF ARMY

Though the churches of the late nineteenth century in America may have become more introspective, the parachurch organizations in America, as well as in Britain, maintained concern for the social issues of the day. In 1865, the Salvation Army was founded in Britain by William Booth. Booth started as a street preacher evangelist. By 1888, he had established one thousand British Salvation Army Corps and had dispatched more to other continents.

THE ULTIMATE IMPACT OF AND ON CHRISTIANITY

If the Reformation began the adolescence of the body of Christ, the nineteenth century must have equaled the raging mid- to late-adolescent years. It seemed that everything was up in the air, including a core identity.

INDUSTRY
The Industrial Revolution cannot be underestimated. Before that time people were more tied to the land and, thus, the elements. There was a kind of faith essential to the success of crops. There was a tie to the Creator because the tie to nature was so much tighter. But with the advent of the factory, work and success seemed to rely on nothing more than the invention of power and the ingenuity of mankind. That was a shift that reverberated throughout societies.

CRITICAL THINKING
The liberalism of the nineteenth century was damaging to the church. Certainly God is big enough for our questions, but we can bring those questions to Him in faith. Both the skepticism of the critics and the rage and fear of the conservative denominations resulted in a kind of turning inside out effect for churches and other Christian communities.

MISSIONS
Missions was definitely a hallmark of the nineteenth century. Even with the theological disagreements and the ever-changing perspective as the world became "modern," there seems to have been agreement that the message needed to go out.

QUESTIONS FOR THE CHURCH
In the nineteenth century the same questions that had arisen in each era of the church somehow remained unanswered. The tension between message and method was still a puzzle as each denomination swung its own direction in regard to how

to integrate and influence the world yet stay true to the heart of Christianity. Leaving the nineteenth century, the dividing lines were drawn between those who chose to bear witness by separating from the world and those who chose to bear witness by their involvement in the messes the world continued to create.

CHAPTER NINE

THE twentieth century

 UNDERSTANDING THE TIMES

The twentieth century is just past. So much happened. In terms of evangelism we've virtually reached to the end of the earth, at least we're close enough to shine our flashlights in the dark corners. Technology is zooming. The world is a global community. Even where national oppression still exists, it is increasingly exposed.

The twentieth century was an age of increasing technology. By 1900, electric power had replaced steam and coal. It was a century that moved from nationalism to individualism. It was an age of pluralism and often confusion.

The church of the twentieth century moved ahead, sometimes bigger and bigger, sometimes smaller and smaller. The questions remained the same. Did the answers change?

By the time the twentieth century rolled around, Christianity could be seen in the world in three different forms.

The Catholic Church was still the foremost branch of the Christian tradition and still a large influence in most of the world.

The Eastern Orthodox Church descending from the Byzantine Empire still held its sway in the Near East.

The Protestant Movement was prominent in Britain and in the Americas.

TRENDS

Walking away from a century can be like walking away from a painting. When you are standing right in front of the painting, you see each small touch of the brush. The broad brush strokes become clearer with distance.

We still stand almost in the face of the twentieth century, but these may be the broad strokes that become clearer with time:

A worldwide tendency away from colonization. At its start, the twentieth century saw lands previously unknown divvied up between world powers. Africa, for instance, was divided into colonies of several European jurisdictions. The missionary expansion of the nineteenth century may have even encouraged colonization in an effort to reach their target people groups.

The consequences of advanced technology. The advances of the nineteenth century created some wear. The environment of the twentieth century had dirtier air and fewer trees. The rivers weren't as clean and the ozone wasn't as protected. The weapons of war were deadlier and more accessible. This led to an uprising of environmental groups.

A move back toward older traditions and customs. As countries and people claimed their independence, they also claimed their heritage. This caused the church to face some of the age-old questions about dividing out the core of Christianity from the customs of a culture.

Pluralism. The twentieth century was replete with varieties of beliefs and religions. There were plenty of points of view to go around. It was an age similar to that of the Romans in that whenever the Romans conquered a country, they incorporated the religious beliefs of that culture. Since the twentieth century was an age of increased tolerance across the board, faith in many cases became an amalgamation of modern culture.

TIMELINE OVERVIEW

In the midst of World History...

1914 The Panama Canal opens to shipping.
      World War I begins (to 1918).
1916 U.S.: The first birth control clinic is opened in Brooklyn.

1920 U.S. Women are given the right to vote.

1923 Germany: Hitler writes *Mein Kampf* (My Struggle).
1926 Britain: A. A. Milne publishes *Winnie the Pooh*.
1927 U.S.: First "talkie" movie, *The Jazz Singer*
1929 The Great Depression begins.
      The first Academy Awards are given.
1928 Britain: Alexander Fleming discovers penicillin.
1931 Canada becomes an independent nation.
1933 U.S.: Prohibition ends. Roosevelt promises the "New Deal."
1939 World War II begins.
      Sigmund Freud dies.
1938 U.S.: Orson Welles directs a radio production of H.G. Wells's novel *War of the Worlds*, about an invasion from Mars; listeners panic because it is so realistic.
1940 Charlie Chaplin receives a death threat from Hitler after the release of his film *The Great Dictator*.
1945 The first electronic computer is built at the University of Pennsylvania.
1946 U.S.: Benjamin Spock publishes *The Commonsense Book of Baby and Child Care*.

1949 South Africa: Government adopts apartheid as an official policy.

1956 U.S.: Elvis Presley and Rock 'n' Roll rise to popularity.

1961 Germany: The Berlin Wall is built.

1964 The Vietnam War
1967 Middle East: Six-Day War between Israel and Arab states
1969 U.S.: Apollo 11 lands on the moon.
1972 China improves relations with the West.
1980 U.S.: AIDS first recognized.
      The beginning of the Silicon Revolution (computers).

1989 Germany: The Berlin Wall comes down.

Christian History unfolds...

1906 Pentecostalism begins.
1910 Fundamentalist movement begins.
1913 Albert Schweitzer carries the gospel to French Equatorial Africa.

1919 Karl Barth and Neo-Orthodoxy

1921 Age of electronic ministries starts with the first Christian radio broadcast.

1930 India: Gandhi leads the Salt March against the British.

1942 C. S. Lewis publishes *The Screwtape Letters*.

1948 World Council of Churches is formed.
      Mother Teresa begins her ministry in Calcutta.
1949 Billy Graham holds Los Angeles crusade.

1960 Charismatic movement begins.

1962 Pope John XXIII calls Vatican II.
1963 Social revolution of the '60s

THE STORY OF THE TIMES

PENTECOSTALISM

At the turn of the twentieth century, the Pentecostal Movement was birthed. The Holiness Movement of the 1800s was similar, but Pentecostalism took its own shape and form through two distinct events. The first influence came from a man named Charles Parham, a preacher who is believed to have originated the Pentecostal-style revival. Even more influential was the work of Joseph Seymour, who in 1906 led the people of Azusa Street Mission into an experience with the Spirit that spawned denominations such as the Church of God (Cleveland, Tenn.), the Assemblies of God, the Church of God in Christ, and the Pentecostal Holiness Church.

FUNDAMENTALISM

Another movement that gained a kind of launching pad at the beginning of the twentieth century was fundamentalism. At its root, fundamentalism is just what it says, a movement back to the fundamentals of faith. While there have been church leaders throughout history who have called the church back to the basics, this movement is dated according to a series of twelve books that began to be published in 1910. Three million copies were distributed to church leaders all over the world with the express intent of calling the church back to a more conservative viewpoint regarding scripture and holiness. The books were called *The Fundamentals*.

Fundamentalism was a direct reaction to the biblical criticism and liberal theology of the nineteenth century. It is still a strong Separatist movement today.

THE EDINBURGH MISSIONS CONFERENCE

While *The Fundamentals* were being published in America, another significant Protestant event was happening in Scotland, the Edinburgh Missions Conference. This was the beginning of the twentieth-century ecumenical movement. It was an interdenominational event focused on spreading the gospel.

There was an interesting mix at the conference. The conference discussed the world, but only Protestants attended and 80 percent of attendees were from Britain and North America. Only eighteen of the twelve hundred attendees were from beyond Europe and North America. Nevertheless, the conference kicked off at least a step beyond the denominationalism of the nineteenth century.

SHIFTS IN NATIONAL POWERS

The twentieth century saw multiple shifts in national powers around the globe. It was as if, on a national level, everyone was figuring out who the biggest bully on the playground was. In other words, who could push whom and get away with it?

You can trace the hand of nationalism in the early twentieth century by the wars fought.

1912 The Balkan Wars involved the countries in the southeast corner of Europe and the beginning of the end of the Ottoman Empire. The Balkan states started claiming their independence from Greece as early as 1829. This continued on until 1912 when the first of the two wars we now call the Balkan Wars broke out. The conflicts were finished by 1913, and the land was redistributed.

1914–1918 World War I was the first time the whole playground broke out into a fight. This war involved more countries and was more destructive than any previous

 SET THE STAGE!

In 1900, 49.9 percent of all Christians lived in Europe; by 1985, only 27.2 did.

In 1900, 81.1 percent of all Christians were white; by the year 2000, only around 40 percent.

In 1900, there were, at most, a handful of Christians who were experiencing special gifts of the Spirit similar to those recorded in the New Testament. By the end of the century, more than a quarter of the confessing Christians could be identified as Pentecostal or charismatic.

In 1900, there were about 520 million people worldwide affiliated with Christian churches. Of those, about 135 million were Protestant (including Anglican), 115 million were Orthodox, and 265 million were Roman Catholic.

war. The technology available to both sides brought the conflicts to a new level. While the war started with an assassination, it involved much more than that. And of course as with any war, it came down to a power struggle. This one was between the Central Powers (Austria-Hungary and Germany) and the Allies (originally France, the United Kingdom, and Russia backing Serbia). In the end, the Central Powers surrendered, but both sides lost much.

1939–1945 World War II began when Germany invaded Poland. Within a year, the United Kingdom was the only European country still standing against Hitler and his voracious German army.

 SET THE STAGE!

In 1943, the Air Corps of the U.S. Army gathered 30 million bats to equip with small explosives and release over enemy cities where they would start countless small fires. Though they were never used intentionally, some were once accidentally released and destroyed an aircraft hangar and a general's car.

World War II was even more destructive than the First World War. Many historians claim that the war happened because of unresolved issues from WWI. Again there was an alliance involving Germany. The Axis began as an alliance between Germany, Japan, and Italy. The Allies included the U.S., the U.K., China, and the Soviet Union. In the end, the Allies overpowered the Axis. Germany and Japan, the two left standing, surrendered in 1945.

There were more wars in the twentieth century, but these two were the farthest reaching. They changed the shape of borders and alliances and set up the globe for the rest of the century.

INDEPENDENCE

It wasn't just wars that brought independence to nations of the world in the 1900s. Colonies such as Algeria, Kenya, and Vietnam fought with weapons for their freedom. Other nations fought with diplomacy to stand on their own. In 1931, Canada requested and finally received her independence from the British Empire. By the end of the century, only the U.S., the U.K., and France held a few island colonies, but most of those islands made the choice to remain colonies.

Other freedoms came in the form of international relations. One of the highlights of the century was the destruction of the Berlin Wall in 1989 and the subsequent unification of East and West Germany. Another highlight was China opening relations with the West in 1972. All these factors were a part of the global community leaving their doors open a little later at night.

MISSIONS

The missions fervor from the nineteenth century carried over into the twentieth. Some great leaders stepped up to affect the world for the cause of Christ. One such man was Albert Schweitzer. Schweitzer was a clergyman, doctor, philosopher, musician, and writer. He was committed to serving mankind. In 1952, he won the Nobel Peace Prize, and in 1955 the Order of Merit was awarded him by the queen of England.

 QUOTABLES

"Resistance to tyrants is obedience to God."
Thomas Jefferson,
writer and inventor,
author of the Declaration
of Independence

Schweitzer is a good example of the kind of missions that grew in the last century, combining both social action and the news of the gospel. More and more, missions have involved both. Missionaries have come out of every point along the theological spectrum, from conservative to liberal.

And missions have continued to take on different shades of color. For instance, with the influx of immigrants into the United States, a missionary can reach as many foreign people groups without leaving the country as he can hopping a plane. The world continues to become smaller in this way. Early in the twentieth century, physical factors such as the Panama Canal opening to shipping connected the world in a new way. Later in the century, the advent of personal computers and cybercommunication did the same thing in a virtual-world kind of way. The ends of the earth have come rushing back to the middle in many ways during the past century.

THEOLOGY

One of the most famous theologians of the twentieth century was Karl Barth (1886–1968), a Swiss minister in the Swiss Reformed Church. It was the tragedy of World War I that caused Barth to rethink his liberal viewpoint. He took a firm stand against the legacy left by the liberal theologians of the nineteenth century. He became convinced that God is "wholly other" than mankind, that man's reason cannot reach a God who is beyond understanding. Barth's most famous work is *Church Dogmatics,* in which he presents a new traditional church dogma including God, Creation, and Jesus Christ.

 DID YOU KNOW?

Teddy Roosevelt (after whom the Teddy Bear was named) visited Panama in 1906 while the Panama Canal was under construction. When he did so, he was the first U.S. president to travel in a foreign country while in office.

Deitrich Bonhoeffer was a German theologian that was also affected by a world war. Bonhoeffer bucked against Hitler's Germany. In fact, he left Germany to avoid serving under Hitler, but returned convinced that he must take a stand. Bonhoeffer's theology was not traditionally conservative, but his writings from prison affected many twentieth-century Christians.

In America, Reinhold and Richard Niebuhr were theological influences. The brothers were both theologians and both wrote and taught in the area of ethics. They encouraged twentieth-century Christians to stand firm in their desire to affect their culture. Reinhold, in particular, wrote that while there may not be the possibility of an ideal world, that is no reason not to continue to better the world that does exist.

RISE OF WOMEN

Women of the twentieth century became more and more visible. It was not until 1920 that women were given the right to vote. Even earlier than that (1916), the first birth control clinic gave them the option to abort. Women's issues were on the rise throughout the century, and many important milestones were gained.

A large price was extracted, as well. Throughout history women have carried a heavy and most often thankless load. In the twentieth century, as their opportunities were expanded, their load became even greater.

MEDIA

The twentieth century had never known a time not affected by media. The influence of media (movies, magazines, TV, radio) has only become stronger with the years. By the end of the first quarter of this century, "talkies" were introduced in the U.S. Since then, motion pictures have become the art form of the century. Used in everything from war propaganda to Saturday matinees to elementary education, motion pictures have been an important part of the modern landscape. In 1938, radio listeners experienced a full-fledged panic at the radio production of H. G. Wells's novel *War of the Worlds* (about an invasion from Mars). It's been said that in 1940, Charlie Chaplin received a death threat from Hitler after the release of his film *The Great Dictator*. Doesn't that beautifully address the irony of the power of the media? A world power is concerned about a possible jab made through a movie?

Since that time, the media in all its written and recorded forms has increased in its influence in the world.

BIBLE TRANSLATION

Bible translation became a large part of the missionary work of the twentieth century. It's certainly understandable why that would happen. As the world was becoming smaller and smaller, people groups with their own dialects and languages were becoming more visible. Also, mission efforts were more and more committed to letting Christianity grow within each culture. How could that happen if that culture didn't have the scriptures in its own language?

In 1934, Wycliffe Bible Translators was founded as an organization committed to putting an indigenous Bible in the hands of each people group. The organization was named for the great reformer John Wycliffe, who created the first English translation of the Bible (which was considered illegal at that time—a bootleg Bible).

To this day, Wycliffe Bible Translators uses every available technology to accomplish their challenge. Their centers include computer technical support, and some of the Wycliffe missionaries are computer programmers who repair hardware and create software to enable translation to occur for tribes that do not even have a recorded grammar or alphabet.

SILICON REVOLUTION

No discussion of the twentieth century would be complete without mention of the computer. By the end of the century, more than one-third of American households had a computer, and the count was on the rise.

Automatic counting machines (which were rudimentary forms of computers) can be traced back as far as the 1600s. Blaise Pascal, a French theologian, philosopher, and mathematician, was the first known to invent one of these automatic calculators. In the 1670s, a mathematician improved Pascal's design and in the process created the binary numeration system (the backbone of present-day computing).

By the 1800s (still no electricity, mind you), punch-card kinds of computer machines were used, first for weaving looms, then for a census. These worked a little like voting booths you may have used where you use a metal stylus to punch through your vote, which is then recorded electronically.

A man named Hollerith was responsible for the punch-card census recorder. Hollerith continued to perfect his tabulation machines, eventually incorporating into a business called CTR. In 1924, that business changed its name to International Business Machines, or, as it's more commonly called, IBM.

ELECTRONIC COMPUTERS

Starting in 1939, electronic computers began to be created by mathematician types at universities and research sites. At the University of Pennsylvania in 1945, a computer called ENIAC was produced. It was a general purpose computer with the ability to store memory.

In 1951, a more advanced computer called UNIVAC became the first commercially successful computer. It was used in the 1951 American census (coming full-circle, you might notice).

With the invention of the transistor, computers became smaller and smaller and thus more accessible to more people. With the invention of the silicon integrated circuits (early sixties), the memory contained in computers became larger and larger. By the late 1960s, many large American businesses relied on computers. It was during this decade that the American government started developing a network system for computer installations. It was called ARPANet and connected university and military computers.

By the seventies, Macintosh and Microsoft were up and running, and personal computers were on their way to changing the way the world worked. By the eighties, ARPANet had become the Internet. By the nineties, the World Wide Web had been established and computers were then changing the way the world interacted.

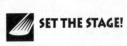

SET THE STAGE!

Benjamin Franklin, U.S. statesman and signer of the Constitution, was also, among other things, a scientist and inventor. His inventions include the lightning rod and bifocal glasses. His improved woodstove put out twice as much heat while using one-quarter the fuel required by traditional models. He was also the first scientist to chart the course of the Gulf Stream and to do preliminary research on electric currents, without which the computer revolution could never have happened.

ECUMENISM

As the world became more and more connected in general, the church was working toward the same kind of thing. There were many moves toward Christian unity among the church in the twentieth century. The term "ecumenical" (universal or worldwide) was a calling card. The "Ecumenical Movement" was an attempt to join together Christians of all denominations. Many conservative groups chafed against the idea. Wouldn't that require a watering down of faith, they wondered?

It's interesting to note that the early church started out with the term "catholic," which means "universal," with the full intent of creating one church that would fill the world with the message and love of Christ. But doctrinal distinctives were so great by the time the term "ecumenical" was tried that it seemed to hold some threat to the truth rather than being a facilitator of it.

The first significant attempt toward unity among Protestants was the Evangelical Alliance in England in 1846. In time, the Alliance formed branches throughout Europe, but by the turn of the century the enthusiasm had waned.

In 1908, the Federal Council of Churches was formed by thirty-one American denominations. It had a reputation for liberal theology and was eventually absorbed into the National Council of Churches of Christ.

More powerful yet was the World Council of Churches formed in Amsterdam in 1948. This council was a product of several conferences tracing back to Edinburgh in 1910. Out of the missionary conference came the Conference on Faith and Order and the Conference on Life and Work. Those conferences then issued a call for the World Council of Churches. That call was issued before the days of Hitler and World War II, and it was not answered until after the war.

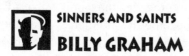

SINNERS AND SAINTS
BILLY GRAHAM

Billy Graham started his career with a mission organization called "Youth for Christ." He worked in both England and the United States. In 1949, he led a large crusade in Los Angeles that set a pattern for his life. The crusade was a success in terms of wide-scale evangelism. Billy Graham spent his life leading crusade after crusade. He has become a twentieth-century icon of accountability and evangelism.

AFRICA

While the 1800s presented Africa as a dark and mysterious continent, by the mid-1900s it was anything but dark in terms of Christianity. By 1975, most of the Western colonization of Africa had ended and over forty African countries had joined the United Nations. Africa continues to push the questions of how much evangelicals can let the Christian faith penetrate and become indigenous to a new culture rather than force them into a cultural mold. Africa has also pushed missionaries on the question of whether spiritual needs can or should be met apart from physical needs in the preaching of the gospel of Christ.

ASIA

Christianity has had plenty of competition in Asia. Between the Communists, the Hindus, and the Muslims, there are many there who live their whole lives without the message of the gospel. In fact, until the last twenty years of the century, there were no known organized Christian churches in Communist China and North Korea. While Christianity has maintained a presence in India, it has been under the careful eye of the Indian authorities.

LATIN AMERICA

The Roman Catholic Church has been the official church in Latin America since colonization there. Yet, as recently as 1914, the Catholic Church as well as the Protestant considered the number of Christians in Latin America at 17 percent or lower. By the end of the twentieth century, though, Latin America proved to be a fertile field for evangelism, particularly for the Pentecostal movement. There are now Pentecostal churches in Latin America that seat in excess of twenty thousand attendees.

VATICAN II

In the Catholic branch of the Christian church, Vatican II was a significant sign of change. The Catholic Church, even more so than the conservative evangelicals of North America, retreated to familiar traditions in the face of the threat of unfamiliar modernity. By the middle of the twentieth century, Pope John XXIII was already calling the Catholic Church to open up to the modern world. In 1962, he did it officially through Vatican II.

Many of the gatherings in the early church were called to face off one heresy or the other. Vatican I held elements of that staunch boundary setting. Vatican II was different, though. It was meant to be for and not against. It was meant to be a proactive step into the world to influence and pastor, not a fence to separate from it.

SINNERS AND SAINTS
MOTHER TERESA

Mother Teresa, a short, slight Catholic nun, received the Nobel Peace Prize in 1979. Teresa was born in Macedonia as Agnes. She joined a religious order and was sent to India. In 1948, she was given permission to go and work among the people. That same year she became an Indian citizen. She was called a "Saint of the Gutters." She was a beautiful example of a Christian following Christ's example of servanthood.

THE U. S. A.

During the second half of the twentieth century, American pop culture has been one of experiential revolution and self-focus. The sixties were a social revolution. The seventies were an age when the religious became separated from the spiritual to the point that many saw the Christian culture as a culture completely outside of the church. During the eighties and nineties, churches came to be evaluated not according to the service a member could give but the service a church could provide.

Also during the last half of the century many of the traditional givens were altered. Divorce was made more accessible, abortion was legalized, censorship was halted, alternative lifestyles were accepted. Things that for centuries were acknowledged, but still wagged at, were suddenly on street corners expecting fully to be heard. Conservative America responded. In 1979, the Moral Majority was formed. In 1989, it was the Christian Coalition. Conservative Christians struggled in the twentieth century with the same questions that first-century Christians struggled with. At what point do we stand against cultural change, and at what point do we work within it? Different Christians fall at all points on the spectrum in answering that question, as with any other.

 SET THE STAGE!

When George Washington served as America's first president, the entire U.S. population (4 million people) was about half the number of people who live in present-day New York City. In those days, our country's border stopped at the Mississippi River. When Washington took office, there were eleven U.S. states. When he left office, the total had jumped to a whopping sixteen. When Washington traveled from New York City to Philadelphia, a distance of ninety miles, the trip took three days. Present-day New Yorkers can make the trip in an hour and a half, although many maintain that, during rush hour, it still feels like three days.

THE ULTIMATE IMPACT OF AND ON CHRISTIANITY

The twentieth century for the church has been somewhat like the game Fruit Basket Turnover. Society changed so drastically that it was impossible to make rules quickly, enough to keep up with it. Who the church was to be in the world was changing. Why? Because the world was constantly changing.

In the world wars, Christian churches were present on both sides. Rather than the church leading the crusade, the church had to decide how to react to the crusade.

The church definitely had an impact on the world in the twentieth century. Through missionary work and the fervor of the Pentecostal movement, Christianity spread significantly south of the equator.

The church was definitely impacted by the twentieth century. In trying to answer the question "In what ways have we become irrelevant to our culture when we know our message is not irrelevant?" churches have begun to experiment with different structures of ministry. Many Western churches are targeting their audiences in much the same way retailers do. Perhaps a better way to describe it is that churches are treating their own culture as a mission field and adapting their methods to that culture.

The twentieth century has served to give the church a taste of the kinds of changes that will surely increase. In this way it has prepared the church for the future.

Epilogue

The church is a living, breathing, growing organism. In some ways, it has Jesus as its heart and from Him flows its life-giving blood. The history of the church is like the account of a life from infancy on. It is not a tale of unbroken progress or failure but a story of how God came to earth and adopted a family that is still growing and growing up. The history of the church is like the collection of family stories that our ancestors preserved by passing them on to us. It is the story of our *real* family, founded by God the Father and His Son, Jesus Christ. The church is our inheritance as God's children. We should love our brothers and sisters. We should take the love our family has and share it with the world.

THE QUESTION IS...

Now what?

Now that we've walked this path as a body of believers through persecutions and national power,

Now that we've divided into more branches than we can count,

Now that we've examined and evaluated the Bible from every possible angle,

Now that we've second-guessed our tactics and strategies,

Now that we've spread the Word and continue to do so,

Now that we live in a world where news is practically instantaneous,

Now that we live in a world where right and wrong are situational at best from the perspective of most,

Now that we have watched our culture evolve to the point that we don't recognize it all the time,

Now that we have seen how power affects us,

Now that we have stood up for our rights of independence and changed the strategies for influencing government,

Now that we are left with the same mission, but a different world in which to carry it out,

Now what?

How will we be as wise as serpents and as harmless as doves?

How will we influence government?

How will we effectively use media?

How will we learn from the mistakes of the past so we can serve God better in the present and future?

How will we explain our faith with our minds and hearts as well as our spirits?

How will we worship God in His mystery and complexity and yet trust Him with our everyday needs?

How will we serve God together with Christians who differ greatly from us in practice?

How will we live as a body in unity and yet stay true to the calling we each have experienced in Christ?

How will we love each other as Jesus has commanded us to do and yet remain pure in terms of our doctrine?

This next leg of history is ours to make. It is the responsibility and privilege given us to be a part of the legacy of Christ in the world He came to redeem. It starts in our hearts and souls, then moves to the community of faith that we join with as a part of

Christ's body, then takes us into a world that is our mission field and our gift from God.

Now what?

Who knows what we can make of the next chapter?

sources

And I Quote, Ashton, Applewhite, William R. Evans III, Andrew Frothingham (St. Martin's Press, 1992).

Anecdotes from History, Grant Uden (Barnes and Noble, Inc., 1968).

Atlas of the Christian Church, Henry Chadwick and G. R. Evans (Equinox Ltd., 1987).

Bartlett's Familiar Quotations, John Bartlett (Little, Brown and Company, 1882).

Brewer's Dictionary of Phrase and Fable, Ivor H. Evans (Harper & Row, 1959).

Children's Atlas of World History (The), Neil DeMarco (Peter Bedrick Books, 1997).

Christians as the Romans Saw Them (The), Robert L. Wilken (Yale University Press, 1984).

Church History in Plain Language, Bruce Shelley (Word Publishing, 1982).

Church History, An Essential Guide, Justo Gonzalez (Abingdon Press, 1996).

Condemned to Repeat It, Wick Allison, Jeremy Adams, Gavin Hambly (Viking Press, 1998).

Disease and History, Frederick F. Cartwright (Thomas Y. Crowell Company, 1972).

Foxe's Book of Martyrs, John Foxe (Whitaker House, 1981).

Great Mysteries of the Past, Reader's Digest Books, 1991.

Hinge Factor (The), Erik Durschmied (Arcade Publishing, 1999).

History of Christianity (A), Owen Chadwick (St. Martin's Press, 1995).

History's Last Stand, Gerard & Patricia Del Re (Avon Books, 1993).

How We Got Our Denominations, Stanley I. Stuber (1965).

Introduction to the History of Christianity, edited by Tim Dowley (First Fortress Press, 1995).

Jumbo's Hide, Elvis's Ride, and the Tooth of Buddha, Harvey Rachlin (Henry Holt and Company, 2000).

Kingfisher Illustrated History of the World (The), Kingfisher Books, 1992.

Lucy's Bones, Sacred Stones, and Einstein's Brain, Harvey Rachlin (Henry Holt and Company, 1996).

Mammoth Book of Eye-Witness History (The), Jon E. Lewis (Carroll & Graf Publishers, Inc., 1998).

Milton's Teeth & Ovid's Umbrella, Michael Olmert (Simon & Schuster, 1996).

On This Day, Carl D. Windsor, Ph.D. (Thomas Nelson Publishers, 1989).

Oxford Illustrated History of Christianity (The), edited by John McManners (Guild Publishing, 1990).

Quotations for Public Speakers, Robert G. Torricelli, ed. (Rutgers University Press, 2001).

Rise of Christianity (The), Don Nardo, ed. (Greenhaven Press, 1999).

Short History of Christianity (A), Martin Marty, (Fortress Press, 1987).

Story of Christianity (The), Michael Collines, Matthew A. Price (DK Publishing, Inc.,1999).

Story of Christianity (The), Tim Dowley (Lion Publishing, 1981).

Turning Points, Mark Noll (Baker Book House, 2000).

Unsolved Mysteries of History, Paul Aron (John Wiley & Sons, Inc., 2000).

What They Don't Teach You About History, Tim Wood and Ian Dicks (Dorset Press, 1992).

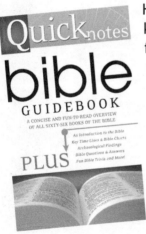